Progress toward Liberalization of the Postal and Delivery Sector

Topics in Regulatory Economics and Policy Series

Michael A. Crew, Editor
Center for Research in Regulated Industries
Graduate School of Management, Rutgers University
Newark, New Jersey, U.S.A.

Previously published books in the series:

Cherry, B.A.:
The Crisis in Telecommunications Carrier Liability: Historical Regulatory Flaws and Recommended Reform
Loomis, D.G. and Taylor, L. D.:
The Future of the Telecommunications Industry: Forecasting and Demand Analysis
Alleman, J. and Noam, E.:
The New Investment Theory of Real Options and its Implications for Telecommunications Economics
Crew, M. and Kleindorfer, P. R:
Current Directions in Postal Reform
Faruqui, A. and Eakin, K.
Pricing in Competitive Electricity Markets
Lehman, D. E. and Weisman, D. L.
The Telecommunications Act of 1996: The "Costs" of Managed Competition
Crew, Michael A.
Expanding Competition in Regulated Industries
Crew, M. A. and Kleindorfer, P. R.:
Future Directions in Postal Reform
Loomis, D.G. and Taylor, L.D.
Forecasting the Internet: Understanding the Explosive Growth of Data
Crew, M. A. and Schuh, J. C.
Markets, Pricing, and Deregulation of Utilities
Crew, M.A. and Kleindorfer, P.R.
Postal and Delivery Services: Pricing, Productivity, Regulation and Strategy
Faruqui, A. and Eakin, K.
Electricity Pricing in Transition
Lehr, W. H. and Pupillo, L. M.
Cyber Policy and Economics in an Internet Age
Crew, M. A. and Kleindorfer, P. R.
Postal and Delivery Services: Delivering on Competition
Grace, M. F., Klein, R. W., Kleindorfer, P. R., and Murray, M. R.
Catastrophe Insurance: Consumer Demand, Markets and Regulation
Crew, M. A. and Kleindorfer, P. R.
Competitive Transformation of the Postal and Delivery Sector
Crew, M. A. and Spiegel, M.
Obtaining the Best from Regulation and Competition
Crew, M. A. and Kleindorfer, P. R.
Regulatory and Economic Challenges in the Postal and Delivery Sector

Progress toward Liberalization of the Postal and Delivery Sector

edited by

Michael A. Crew
Center for Research in Regulated Industries
Rutgers Business School
Rutgers University
Newark, New Jersey, U.S.A.

and

Paul R. Kleindorfer
Risk Management and Decision Processes Center
The Wharton School
University of Pennsylvania
Philadelphia, Pennsylvania, U.S.A.

Springer

Library of Congress Control Number: 2005934307

ISBN:10: 0-387-29743-X
ISBN-13: 978-0387-29743-9
e-ISBN-10: 0-387-29744-8
e-ISBN-13: 978-0387-29744-6

Printed on acid-free paper.

Printed in the United States of America.

9 8 7 6 5 4 3 2 1

springeronline.com

CONTENTS

Liberalization and Quality of Service

Pricing Issues

Demand Studies

Legal and Regulatory Issues

Postal Reform in Japan

CONTRIBUTORS

Xavier Ambrosini, Competition and Strategic Diagnostic Expert, La Poste

Bernard Amerlynck, Freelance Postal Expert, EXPOST Consulting

Tom Balogh, Postal Services Commission

François Boldron, La Poste

Lawrence G. Buc, President, SLS Consulting, Inc.

Robert H. Cohen, Former Director, Rates Analysis & Planning, U.S. Postal Rate Commission

Michael A. Crew, CRRI Scholar and Director – Center for Research and Regulated Industries, Rutgers Business School, Rutgers University

Helmuth Cremer, Professor of Economics, GREMAQ and IDEI, University of Toulouse

Gonzales d'Alcantara, Professor in Economics, University of Antwerp

Paul W.J. de Bijl, Research Coordinator, Tilburg Law and Economics Center, Tilburg University

Philippe De Donder, Professor of Economics, GREMAQ and IDEI, University of Toulouse

Elena Diakova, Manager, Strategy Projects, Pitney Bowes

Roisin Doherty, Policy Manager, Postwatch

Paul Dudley, Head of Regulatory Economic Analysis, Royal Mail Group

Richard Eccles, Partner, Bird & Bird

Cátia Felisberto, Research Associate and PhD candidate, École Polytechnique Fédérale de Lausanne (EPFL)

Fabio Filpo, Associate, O'Connor and Company – European Lawyers

Alessandra Fratini, Partner, O'Connor and Company – European Lawyers

Beat Friedli, Head of Corporate Development, Swiss Post

Stefano Gori, Head of Economic Research, Strategic Planning, Poste Italiane

Martin Grossmann, Researcher, University of Zurich

John Haldi, President, Haldi Associates, Inc.

Sofia Beatriz Henriques, Economist, Strategic Development, CTT Correios de Portugal S.A.

Roger Hill, Business Strategy Modeller, Royal Mail Group

George Houpis, Director, Frontier Economics

Luis Jimenez, Senior Vice President and Chief Strategy Officer, Pitney Bowes

Siôn Jones, Divisional Director, London Economics

Per Jonsson, Postal Adviser, Swedish Post and Telecom Agency

Charles Kenny, Senior Economist, The World Bank

Paul R. Kleindorfer, Anheuser–Busch Professor of Management Science and Economics, Wharton School, University of Pennsylvania

Daniel Krähenbühl, Economist, Corporate Development, Swiss Post

Pauline Kuipers, Partner, Bird & Bird

Almudena Lara, Frontier Economics

Pierre Larouche, Professor of Competition Law, Faculty of Law, and Vice-Director, Tilburg Law and Economics Center, Tilburg University

Ian Leigh, Managing Director, Postwatch

Joy M. Leong, Partner, Sidley Austin Brown & Wood LLP

David M. Levy, Partner, Sidley Austin Brown & Wood LLP

Shoji Maruyama, Senior Manager, Japan Post

Richard Moriarty, Director – Competition and Regulation, Postal Services Commission

William J. Olson, Principal, Olson Law Offices

Emiliano Piccinin, Economist, Strategic Planning, Poste Italiane

Alberto Alves Pimenta, Director, Strategic Development, CTT Correios de Portugal S.A.

Michael K. Plunkett, Manager – Pricing Strategy, United States Postal Service

Amelia Porges, Counsel, Sidley Austin Brown & Wood LLP

Matthew Robinson, Postal Rate and Classification Specialist, U.S. Postal Rate Commission

Richard Robinson, Senior Business Modeller, Royal Mail Group

Frank Rodriguez, Head of Economics, Royal Mail Group

Simona Romito, Manager, Strategic Planning, Poste Italiane

Bernard Roy, Manager of European and National Regulation Division, La Poste

Ricardo Jorge Moreira Goulão Santos, Economist, Strategic Development CTT Correios de Portugal S.A.

Gennaro Scarfiglieri, Head of Core Business Strategic Marketing, Strategic Planning, Poste Italiane

Sten Selander, Director – Postal Affairs, Swedish Post and Telecom Agency

Paul Smith, Economic Advisor, Postal Services Commission

Gregory Swinand, Senior Consultant and Division Director, Regulatory Division, London Economics

Chrystal Szeto, Strategy Analyst, Pitney Bowes

Urs Trinkner, Economist, Swiss Post and University of Zurich

Eric van Damme, Professor of Economics, CentER, and Director, Tilburg Law and Economics Center, Tilburg University.

John D. Waller, Director, Rates Analysis & Planning, U.S. Postal Rate Commission

Mark Williams, Manager, Frontier Economics

Spyros S. Xenakis, Economist, U.S. Postal Rate Commission

SPONSORS

Pitney Bowes
Royal Mail
Deutsche Post World Net
United States Postal Service
Canada Post Corporation
FedEx
La Poste
La Poste / De Post
R.R. Donnelley & Sons Company
UPS
Swiss Post
CTT Correios de Portugal S.A.
IBM Business Consulting Services
Postcomm – The Postal Services Commission
Siemens AG
United States Postal Rate Commission
Posten AB
Finland Post Corporation
Canadian Union of Postal Workers
Anacom
An Post
A.T. Kearney GmbH
Poste Italiane
Postwatch
TPG Post
Haldi Associates
Sidley Austin Brown and Wood LLP
Frontier Economics
Bird & Bird
Envelope Manufacturers Association
London Economics
National Association of Letter Carriers
New Zealand Post
Oxera
Venable LLP
Association for Postal Commerce

PREFACE AND ACKNOWLEDGEMENTS

This book arises out of the Thirteenth Conference on Postal and Delivery Economics held in Antwerp, Belgium, June 1-4, 2005. Leading practitioners, postal administrations, and the courier industry, as well as a number of regulators, academic economists, mailers, consultants, technology suppliers, and lawyers came together to examine some of the major policy and regulatory issues facing the industry. Issues addressed included the universal service obligation, regulation, liberalization, competition, access, worksharing, demand, cost, service quality, and postal reform.

The conference and the book follow our earlier conferences. In 1990, the first Conference on Postal and Delivery Economics (CPDE) was held at Coton House, Rugby, England, July 22-25, 1990, in honor of the one hundred and fiftieth anniversary of the Penny Post and the contributions of Sir Rowland Hill. The ensuing book, *Competition and Innovation in Postal Services*, was published by Kluwer Academic Publishers in 1991. In 1992 2nd CPDE was held at Village PTT, La Londe les Maures, France, on March 18-21, 1992. This conference resulted in *Regulation and the Nature of Postal and Delivery Services,* published by Kluwer Academic Publisher in 1993. Both conferences were recognized by the European Express Organization with the Hermes Award 1992 at its annual award dinner in Munich on June 22, 1992. The first workshop, The Workshop on Postal and Delivery Economics, was held June 23-26, 1993 in Daun, Germany. In 1994 the 3rd CPDE was held in Stockholm, Sweden, May 18-21,1994, and a workshop, in Hakone, Japan, June 1-4, 1994 combined to produce the volume *Commercialization of Postal and Delivery Services,* published by Kluwer Academic Publisher in 1995. A workshop was held in Naantali, Finland, June 7-10, 1995. The 4th CPDE was held in Monterey, California, May 22-25, 1996, and resulted in the book *Managing Change in The Postal and Delivery Industries,* published by Kluwer Academic Publisher in 1996. The next book, *Emerging Competition in Postal and Delivery Services* was a direct result of the 5th and 6th CPDEs; the former was held in Helsingor, Denmark, June 11-14, 1997; and the latter held in Montreux, Switzerland, June 17-20, 1998. The 7th CPDE was held in Sintra, Portugal, June 23-26, 1999, which resulted in the book *Current Directions in Postal Reform,* published by Kluwer Academic Publishers in 2000. The 8th CPDE, was held in Vancouver, Canada, June 7-10, 2000, resulting in the book *Future Directions in Postal Reform*, published by Kluwer Academic Publishers in 2001. The 9th CPDE was held in Sorrento, Italy, June 6-9, 2001, and the book *Postal and Delivery Services: Pricing, Productivity, Regulation and Strategy*, was published by Kluwer Academic Publishers in 2001. The 10th CPDE was held in Potsdam, Germany, June 5-8, 2002, and the resulting book, *Postal and Delivery Services: Pricing, Delivering on Competition,* was published by Kluwer Academic Publishers in 2002. The 11th CPDE was held in Toledo, Spain, June 4-7, 2003, and the resulting book, *Competitive Tranformation of the Postal and Delivery Sector*, was published by Kluwer Academic Publishers in 2004. The 12th CPDE was held in Cork, Ireland, June 2-5, 2003, and the resulting book, *Regulatory and Economic Challenges in the Postal and Delivery Sector*, was published by Kluwer Academic Publishers in 2005.

The 2005 conference was made possible by the support of the following organizations: Pitney Bowes; Royal Mail; Deutsche Post World Net; United States Postal Service; Canada Post Corporation; FedEx; La Poste; La Poste / De Post; R.R. Donnelley & Sons Company; UPS; Swiss Post; CTT Correios de Portugal S.A.; IBM Business Consulting Services; Postcomm – The Postal Services Commission; Siemens AG; United States Postal Rate Commission; Posten AB ; Finland Post Corporation; Canadian Union of Postal Workers; Anacom; An Post; A.T. Kearney GmbH; Poste Italiane; Postwatch; TPG Post; Haldi Associates; Sidley Austin Brown and Wood LLP; Frontier Economics; Bird & Bird; Envelope Manufactures Association; London Economics; National Association of Letter Carriers; New Zealand Post; Oxera; Venable LLP; and Association for Postal Commerce .

We would like to thank sponsors not only for financial support, but also for their advice and encouragement, and for serving on the organizing committee. In particular, we would like to thank Anthony Alverno, Elizabeth Amend, Gary Battaglia, Maynard Benjamin, Geoff Bickerton, Philip Burns, Ralph Carter, Jeff Colvin, Robert Curry, Gonzales d'Alcantara, Bernard Damiens, Gene Del Polito, Richard Eccles, Charles Fattore, Stephen Ferguson, Beat Friedli, Stefano Gori, John Haldi, Greg Harford, Jan Bart Henry, Jason Hergert, George Houpis, Helen Jenkins, Luis Jimenez, Daniel Krähenbühl, Ian Leigh, Joy Leong, David M. Levy, Walter Maschke, Richard Moriarty, Pedro Duarte Neves, Heikki Nikali, George Omas, Wolfgang Pickave, Alberto Pimenta, Leon Pintsov, Wolfgang Pordzik, Frank Rodriguez, Bernard Roy, Jim Sauber, Michael Shinay, Paul Smith, David Spence, Gregory Swinand, David Treworgy, Urs Trinkner, Mark van der Horst, Anton van der Lande, Lars Vesterlund, Ian Volner, Sture Wallander, John Waller, and Ingo Willems.

The host country plays an important role in these conferences. This year's conference, the *Thirteenth Conference on Postal and Delivery Economics*, benefited greatly from the efforts of our host PO, La Poste / De Post. Their representatives Gonzales d'Alcantara and Bernard Damiens were gracious hosts.

We would like to thank our distinguished dinner speakers, Johnny Thijs, James C. Miller III, and Matthias Krause. In the tradition of these conferences we very much enjoyed the speech by Johnny Thijs, Chief Executive Officer of La Poste / De Post. His keynote speech at the Conference provided an outlook on the future of postal and delivery networks from the unique perspective of La Poste / De Post. James C. Miller III, Chairman of the Board of Governors – United States Postal Service presented an interesting discussion of postal reform in the United States. Matthias Krause gamely stood in for Stefan Keh, President of Postal Automation Division – Siemens AG, who was unable to be present because of illness. Matthias provided commentary on the role of a leading technology provider in the future of the mail.

It gives us great pleasure to thank Pitney Bowes for their generous lead contribution to fund the endowment of a chair in regulatory economics at CRRI, Rutgers Business School. We would especially like to thank Michael Critelli and Luis Jimenez for their interest in the program and for their part in making this gift possible.

Finally, we would like to thank Andrew Mearman, Senior Lecturer in Economics, the University of the West of England and Jeremy T. Guenter. Andrew provided editorial assistance. We are especially appreciative of the efforts of Jeremy T. Guenter, Assistant Director of the Center for Research in Regulated Industries, in making this book possible. We would like to thank him not only as editors but also on behalf of the authors to whom he provided considerable assistance. He continues to develop a research tool available to all through the CRRI web site providing access to the many references used in this and other postal books in the series as well as regulatory economics more generally. The database now has over 9000 entries, updated continuously. Visit us on the web at http://crri.rutgers.edu.

The usual disclaimers are applicable. In particular, the views expressed reflect the views of the authors and not necessarily those of the sponsors.

Michael A. Crew
Paul R. Kleindorfer

Universal Service Obligation

Chapter 1

The Welfare Effects of Entry and Strategies for Maintaining the USO in the Postal Sector*

Michael A. Crew and Paul R. Kleindorfer
Rutgers University and University of Pennsylvania

1. INTRODUCTION

The debate on entry policies in the postal sector has centered on how to continue to provide Universal Service without undermining the financial viability of the incumbent Postal Operator (PO). The debate continues as the European Commission conducts a prospective study, as required by the Postal Service Directive, to assess the impact on universal service of complete liberalization in 2009 for each member state. However, several member states have already entered a very clear path leading to full liberalization ahead of this date.[1] This presents a potentially serious problem in that unless the Universal Service Obligation (USO) is eliminated, POs will still have to satisfy the USO without the traditional reserved area. In addition, incumbent POs will face continuing challenges in setting the terms of access offered to entrants. Pricing and contracting will become much more competitive, and access policies will have to take into account

* The authors wish to acknowledge the support of Royal Mail Group in the preparation of this paper. The views expressed are solely those of the authors and may not reflect those of Royal Mail Group. We thank Frank Rodriguez for valuable comments on an earlier version of this paper, as well as our discussants Robert Campbell and Sture Wallander at the Conference. We also acknowledge with thanks the assistance of Scott Campion in programming the model underlying the results of section 4 of this paper.

1 Sweden and Finland no longer have protection of their markets by means of a reserved area. Other countries, notably, Germany, the Netherlands and the United Kingdom, also face the loss of their reserved areas and full liberalization ahead of the rest of the EU.

increasingly important competitive concerns with the revenue required to maintain the USO. Finding a workable solution to these problems is critical since if inappropriate policy choices are made, the changes that are then ushered in could be extremely costly to undo.

In the next section, we review the background to the problem. In particular, we review the nature of the USO and the impact of liberalization on funding the USO. We argue that full liberalization provides small potential welfare gains relative to the risks it entails.[2] Section 3 discusses the options that might be pursued to allow POs to remain viable under full liberalization. These include increased commercial freedom, changes in regulation and relaxing the scope of the USO. Section 4 then provides some illustrative simulations to explore these issues and options. We conclude in section 5 with some implications of our analysis.

2. BACKGROUND AND STATEMENT OF THE PROBLEM

Liberalization of postal markets has been taking place sporadically over the last decade and in Europe, at least, the policy has developed momentum and will not easily be abandoned. This policy is driven by a number of forces including the desire by business to get lower priced service and the desire of competitors to enter postal markets. Competition has long been considered by economists as a force that increases efficiency or welfare by driving prices to costs and by driving costs down. It is this virtuous cycle of cost and price reductions and increased demand that make it attractive. Unfortunately, under full liberalization, this virtuous cycle in the postal sector is likely to be a vicious cycle of higher costs through loss of scale economies, and consequent financial losses.[3]

---

2 At the Cork Conference, when making his discussant comments, John Panzar stimulated our thinking on this point by expressing his opinion that there were unlikely to be any significant benefits from entry in this industry.

3 While experience in other industries is not conclusive, it may be instructive to note that even with technological change and demand growth on their side financial viability has continued to plague telecommunications under competition. Given the absence of these advantages in the postal sector, it is hard to see how competition would be more effective in the postal sector. Of course, competition could have considerable benefits if structured properly (see below), and the dangers of ultimate bankruptcy of the postal operator are more pronounced in some circumstances than others. Our point here is that the circumstances that seem best suited for reaping the benefits of competition are also those (with steep route profitability profiles, per Crew and Kleindorfer, 2001) that have the largest risk of driving the PO to insolvency under unrestricted entry. We explore this point more fully below.

Currently competition in the letter market varies considerably, from Sweden and New Zealand where there is open competition, to the United States where there is no competition in letter delivery but significant competition upstream. The centerpiece of the debate on postal policies and strategies remains the USO. The USO is the obligation to deliver letters and parcels ubiquitously and, in the case of letters, at a uniform price. In addition, there is an obligation to provide some uniformity in service quality. While outlying areas get lower quality service, the consensus is that delivery standards should not be drastically different across areas. In the eyes of the public and governments around the world, the USO has remained a necessary foundation for postal policy for a number of reasons, including its transparency, its low transactions costs and its ability to provide a simple method of consumer protection through the easily recognizable single-piece uniform price.

To satisfy the USO, POs have typically been granted a reserved area, a weight or price limit below which, they are the only legal providers. Absent the obligation of the uniform price and some service uniformity, the ubiquity requirement could be satisfied without a reserved area. The question then is whether the USO can survive without a reserved area. Crew and Kleindorfer (2000, 2001) have argued that the traditional USO is unlikely to be feasible absent a reserved area or some other stable method of funding the USO. The presence of the two forces of technological change and liberalization policies promoting competitive entry puts the traditional USO at risk for two reasons. First, technological competition has provided substitutes for and reduced demand for letter mail. This results in an increase in a PO's unit costs as it loses some of the benefit of scale economics because of the lower output. Meanwhile, the fixed costs of the USO will continue. Second, changes that eliminate the POs' reserved area take away the means of funding the USO.

These twin changes will require changes not only in the way POs operate but may require further changes in the legal framework to assure the continuing ability of POs to fund their USO. Specifically, it seems unlikely that the lettermail USO can be supported without a reserved area, unless service standards are relaxed dramatically. Absent a reserved area, entrants would price below the incumbent in the low cost markets. The incumbent would raise its (uniform) prices making a larger market more attractive to the entrants. The process may result in a graveyard spiral of increasing prices and continuing losses. In view of the limited options for new revenue from, notably, parcels and other mail services (see Crew and Kleindorfer, 2002, 2004), if POs are to remain financially viable, then other sources of funding have to be found to support the USO. We rule out tax/subsidy schemes as infeasible for reasons argued elsewhere (Crew and Kleindorfer 2000). So if liberalization is to continue to the point at which there is no longer a reserved area, we will clearly need other approaches to funding the USO.

There continues to be a strong desire on the part of the public and consequently government in retaining the USO in essentially its current form. There is also a clear commitment by policy makers in the EU and elsewhere to promote liberalization. However, the joint objectives of achieving full liberalization of postal markets and maintaining the USO in its current form demonstrate a lack of understanding and natural propensity of policy makers to address mutually inconsistent but separately desirable alternatives sequentially rather than confront the inherent tradeoffs that would arise from addressing them simultaneously. The issue of funding the USO that would arise under full liberalization illustrates just this type of behavior. Solutions to the problem are likely to be complex.

3. STRATEGIES FOR MAINTAINING THE USO UNDER ENTRY

When faced with a continuing USO and the loss of its reserved area, POs have a number of options. The feasible options consist generally of a combination of greater commercial freedom with the increased commercial operations and competition implied by this, and a reduction in the scope of the USO. We now consider these options in detail and note some of their interdependencies.

Greater commercial orientation can take a number of forms, resulting in increased cost control, more flexible pricing and the ability to adjust the product line with reduced regulatory oversight. POs can lower their costs by becoming more efficient in both their production processes and in the design of their networks. On the face of it, this is not in the least controversial. POs, the government and consumers would all be very positively inclined toward this objective. The problem is that it is easier said than done. The labor force would not react well to increased efficiency if it meant lower pay or loss of jobs. Regulators, by putting pressure on a PO, may argue that they are performing the same role as the competitive market, namely, driving down costs. The problem is that regulators, unlike a competitive market, which by its very nature cannot be influenced by the individual participants, are influenced by the participants and by government. Therefore, the likelihood of regulators mimicking the competitive market is extremely unlikely, especially since regulators lack the information to enable them to set prices at competitive levels. Thus, the idea that POs can fund their USO by becoming more efficient at the behest of regulators is not promising. Similarly, if strong competition is introduced rather than regulation, costs may be reduced, but without sufficient surplus resulting to cover the USO.

If, along with the competition the PO loses some of the scale economies, the welfare benefits are reduced further.

Increased commercial freedom might also encompass increasing the PO's product lines and allowing them to compete by price much more aggressively. In principle, there is nothing in most countries to prevent a PO from increasing the scope of its product lines under current regulatory policies. However, attempts to do so are typically accompanied by significant delays and regulatory transactions costs, thus discouraging or eliminating the possibility of flexible changes in product line to meet changing customer needs and competitive conditions. Increased commercial freedom means that such regulatory hurdles would be minimized or eliminated.

Merely increasing its product lines may not benefit a PO. This is particularly true where the increase in the product line is induced by regulators, such as in the case of mandatory downstream access. In requiring access, regulators have cited fairness to competitors, opening up the market and providing additional opportunities for profit.[4] Our research has shown that access does, indeed, provide an opportunity for POs to earn additional revenues, but they may not be sufficient to fund the USO under free entry. This is especially true if access is mandated and its price strictly regulated without regard to the impact such access could have on the ability of the PO to support its USO.

Adding product lines freely and the ability to price more aggressively without requiring regulatory approval are major examples of increased commercial freedom. Crew and Kleindorfer (2002, 2004) have shown that both strategies offer ways in which POs can generate additional net revenues and provide a critical combination if financial viability is to be achieved. If POs do not apply these strategies effectively, they are unlikely to be able to survive, but applying them effectively does not guarantee survival where POs retain a significant USO.

Pricing flexibility is a key strategy for POs under liberalization. In the face of entry, failure to compete on price effectively guarantees a graveyard spiral as POs lose more and more of the profitable business. Pricing flexibility requires POs to change their approach to pricing. What previously worked well might be a recipe for greater losses under free entry. This is true in the case of upstream discounts, for example, presort or barcode discounts, which have been highly successful for some POs, notably USPS. However, the efficiency consequences of upstream discounts depend in important ways on whether or not the PO has a monopoly on local

---

4 The British regulator, Postcomm, has argued that providing access would be a means to making Royal Mail profitable.

delivery (as is the case with USPS). In particular, applying existing approaches mechanically may cause serious problems under liberalization.

Commercial freedom could extend to direct and perhaps strong competition on the part of POs. Instead of blandly sitting back while cream-skimming entrants capture market share, POs need the freedom to compete head on. It would not just be a matter of offering attractive access prices but lowering prices including end-to-end prices to retain business in the face of entry. This kind of commercial freedom and pricing flexibility would require regulatory policies that did not require regulatory approval for price changes. The majority of a PO's products would be deemed competitive and not subject to regulatory approval if the PO decided that it needed to change its prices to remain competitive.

Reducing the burden of the USO *prima facie* appears to be a highly effective way of enabling as PO to survive when facing entry. The general idea is that if the uniformity constraint of the USO is relaxed, then the PO is likely to remain viable under a broader set of demand, cost and entry scenarios than it could under more stringent uniformity constraints. However, it is difficult to see how the uniform price can be eliminated for single-piece mail, which since the inauguration of the Penny Post in 1840 has been the hallmark of modern postal service. The economic benefits of the uniform price are primarily felt in the transactions cost savings of single-piece mailers. The effect of a uniform price is also to put a ceiling on the prices that can be charged to small customers, including those in the highest cost zones. Even for large customers, format pricing is driving pricing more in the direction of uniformity.

Relaxing service quality standards has been discussed as a way of partially mitigating the cost of very high-end routes, thereby significantly decreasing the USO burden and the reserved area required to support this burden. For example, Haldi and Merewitz (1997) and Cohen, Ferguson, Waller and Xenakis (2000) discuss the benefits of decreasing the USO burden under entry by making significant changes in the service standards, with high cost areas receiving significantly lower service standards (e.g., three-days a week delivery instead of five or six). The logic of the approach relies on decreasing the cost of high-cost routes and the required subsidy for these, under uniform pricing, from low-cost routes. The primary reduction in cost is likely to arise from reducing the fixed costs of daily delivery. Relaxing service quality standards in this or other ways, however, may undermine the value of the USO itself, as it is typically understood to embody ubiquity and some uniformity in service quality. Reductions in quality would likely be concentrated on remote high cost areas resulting in significant differences in quality between high and low cost areas. Whether the extent of the differences in quality would be acceptable is an unexplored area. Not only customers in the high cost areas might find the service standards unacceptable but also large customers might find low service quality in the high cost areas to be unacceptable. Thus, quality reductions provide no guarantee that the bottom line will be greater. They reduce demand as well as variable costs. However, if they fail to reduce fixed costs, the benefits are limited unless the variable cost reduction greatly exceeds the loss in revenue from demand erosion. Furthermore, reducing service standards may cause not only a reduction in demand but also a reduction in cost of serving these areas by entrants. The latter may make some regions attractive that were previously not attractive to entrants.

To illustrate some of the potential outcomes, and the complexity of navigating these, we explore now some scenarios using an extension of the simulation model originally developed in Crew and Kleindorfer (2005). The model is focused on the factors that would alleviate or exacerbate the effects of entry on overall welfare and on the financial sustainability of the PO facing a USO, where the structure of USO-related costs can be changed through the pricing and service quality strategies discussed above.

4. ILLUSTRATIVE POLICY OPTIONS IN A SIMULATION-MODEL-BASED FRAMEWORK

In this section, we will examine some of the consequences of liberalization with illustrative results derived from a simulation model. The model is described in a Technical Appendix[5] and is an extension of our earlier model, Crew and Kleindorfer (2005). The purpose of the simulations is to throw light on the effects of liberalization on a PO with a continuing USO. These can include serious threats to the PO's financial viability, which could be sufficiently severe to give rise to a graveyard spiral as noted above. The analysis makes it possible to examine the directions that entry policy might take, including a comparison of the approaches to entry being considered by various countries. TPG, for example, is opposed to mandating access, while Postcomm, the UK regulator, and Royal Mail are putting in place comprehensive mandatory access offerings. In the US, extensive upstream access (worksharing) arrangements have been employed for many years. In addition, USPS provides downstream access although it is not universal, unlike worksharing. As a further element of pricing flexibility, not considered here, downstream access might be treated (and priced)

[5] Available on the CRRI website at http://crri.rutgers.edu/pub/appendix2005.pdf.

differently for direct customers of the PO than for (customers served by) entrants.[6]

4.1 Model Structure

There are several approaches to representing the nature of competitive interaction between the incumbent PO and entrants. The model here assumes that entrants form a competitive fringe,[7] which is a reasonable representation when there are many actual or potential licensed entrants. There are two mail products, residential mail and business mail where class of mail is identified by the originator. Residential mail is assumed completely non-contestable in that the entrant does not enter that market. Business customers, on the other hand, are served by both the PO and entrants.

The fundamental dynamic of entry is captured by allowing entrants to price completely flexibly while the PO is required to maintain a uniform price (for single-piece letters) for the PO. The PO provides not only end-to-end service for its customers but also can provide access services, whereby mail collected and presorted by entrants can be turned over to the PO for delivery, with the delivery or access charge depending on the ultimate destination of the mail (i.e., access charges may differ according to delivery zone). We are interested in modeling the portion of the total mail demand captured by entrants, especially in the low-cost, high-margin delivery zones, and the consequences of this under various policy options for the ability of the PO to support its USO.

---

6 Note that the European Union Postal Directive specifies that direct customers of the PO may not be treated differently than competitors in respect to access or other services(other than through cost-based differences that might arise from volume discounts, etc.), although it should be noted that downstream access itself is not mandated in the EU Postal Directive. According to Article 12 of the Directive, "whenever universal service providers apply special tariffs, for example for services for businesses, bulk mailers or consolidators of mail from different customers, they shall apply the principles of transparency and non-discrimination with regard both to the tariffs and the associated conditions. The tariffs shall take into account the avoided costs, as compared to the standard service covering the complete range of features offered for the clearance, transport, sorting and delivery of individual postal items and, together with the associated conditions, shall apply equally both as between different third parties and as between third parties and universal service providers supplying equivalent services. Any such tariffs shall also be available to private customers who post under similar conditions." For a survey of recent developments in the EU, see WIK (2004).

7 A competitive fringe is a simpler alternative to a Cournot or Bertrand approach as all members of the fringe take price as given. See De Donder et al. (2002) for a discussion of alternative models of competition.

For business mail, the demands for the PO's mail and the entrants demand are not only functions of each other's prices but also incorporate "loyalty", a term we borrow from the marketing literature. The idea of "brand loyalty" or "switching costs" captures the effect of a consumer's cost of switching to another supplier, and incorporates both elements of familiarity and knowledge of purchasing arrangements as well as relationship-specific investments by customers in working with a particular supplier. In the literature on the graveyard spiral, the effects of loyalty were incorporated by d'Alcantara and Amerlynck (2004), and their notion of loyalty is essentially what is used here. Namely, loyalty (to the incumbent) is represented as the level of price discount that must be offered by entrants to compete on an even footing with the incumbent. Such loyalty effects will depend on the customer segment, and on the delivery zone of mail arising from this segment. The technical representation of loyalty in the demand equations has the same effect as the perceived quality of the incumbent's service relative to entrants (a matter discussed further below).

Loyalty is an important concept for a PO as it is sometimes argued that the USO, because of the ubiquity obligation, confers visibility and enhances the PO's brand name. This may mean that the PO may be able to charge a somewhat higher price than an entrant without suffering significant demand erosion, and the loyalty variable is intended to capture such effects. Over time, such advantages are likely to diminish, especially in the case of business customers, and loyalty parameters could be adjusted accordingly.

The cost structure of entrants and the incumbent are likely to be different. The incumbent is expected to have higher costs because of the USO and these are incorporated through higher fixed costs. In addition, the incumbent may have labor agreements that result in higher costs. Putting this together, it seems likely that the incumbent will have a cost advantage in the high cost routes because of ubiquity and the entrant on the low cost routes because of his ability to employ lower priced labor. To allow for zonal cost differences, our model has 10 zones, with the highest cost zone being 10 and the lowest 1. Similarly, the parameter values for loyalty are set to imply no loyalty (to either the incumbent or entrants) in the low cost zones, growing to a loyalty discount of over 20% for the incumbent in high-cost areas.

Base case cost parameters are given in Table 1[8]. In particular, we assume per unit upstream costs (collection, consolidation and presortation costs) are identical for both entrants and incumbents in the base case (denoted C_{IU} and C_{EU} in Table 2 below). We assume (as in Crew and Kleindorfer (2002)) that there is a cost associated with entrants' turning over mail to the incumbent (e.g., receiving and billing costs) of C_a per unit. Delivery costs (assumed

[8] Details can be found in the Technical Appendix to this paper, available http://crri.rutgers.edu/pub/appendix2005.pdf.

constant per unit) for the incumbent ($C_{ID}(k)$) and entrants ($C_{ED}(k)$) rise as the zone increases from 1 to 10, where the entrants have advantages in the low-cost zones and the incumbent has advantages in the high-cost zones.

4.2 The Effect of Reducing the Burden of the USO

There are a number of ways of reducing the burden of the USO. One approach is to reduce reliability. That is, service to high cost areas might become less reliable. Instead of being delivered in say 2 days with a probability of 95 percent, mail would be delivered in 2 days at probability of, say, 60 percent. This might correspond to providing lower priority in mail processing operations to mail destined for high cost areas, treating it, in effect, similar to Second Class Mail in two-tier systems. We do not examine this. Instead, we examine an approach frequently proposed, namely reducing the frequency of delivery to high cost areas. Instead of six deliveries per week, such areas would get, say, three deliveries per week. To model the effects of this in our simulation model, we assume that delivery costs are reduced in the five highest cost areas relative to the Base Case, thus reducing the cost of the USO, leaving the delivery costs in the five lowest cost areas the same. This reduction in the quality of service is likely to have an adverse impact on demand. To reflect this, we assume that the impact of service quality reduction is to increase the perceived price of the service (by a pre-specified amount), thus reducing demand relative to the *status quo* in these areas as a result of the reduction in the quality of the service. Naturally, cost savings for a PO have an unambiguously beneficial effect on financial viability. Moreover, to the extent that the zones have costs in excess of the uniform price, demand reductions would also have a beneficial financial effect in that less money would be lost because of the lower volume.

The specific cases we modeled allow the PO to relax the USO service quality in higher cost zones (those with indices greater than a specified zone k*). We report here only one case in which service quality for the USO was relaxed in zones 6 through 10, for both the incumbent PO (I) and entrants (E), with assumed consequences as follows: 1) fixed costs of the incumbent PO are reduced by 20% (overall); 2) variable costs for both I and E are reduced by 20%; 3) the required mark-up for entrants in zones 6-10 is discounted from 40% to 32% (a reduction of 20%), reflecting the lower fixed costs under the relaxed service quality standard; 4) demand reductions occur corresponding to an effective price increase of 20% (these lead at the base case breakeven analysis for I to average volumetric demand reductions in these zones of about 5%). These four assumptions illustrate more generally the set of cost and demand impacts that would have to be estimated to assess the consequences of service quality reduction.

Table 1: Base Case Values for Cost Parameters
"20% Red" Refers to a Service Quality Reduction in Zones 6-10

Upstream Cost for I (C_{IU})	10
Upstream Cost for E (C_{EU})	10
Adaptation Cost (C_a)	2
USO Fixed Cost (F)	100,000

Zone k	$C_{ID}(k)$ Base Case	$C_{ED}(k)$ Base Case	$C_{ID}(k)$ 20% Red (k = 6-10)	$C_{ED}(k)$ 20% Red (k = 6-10)
k=1	12	10	12	10
k=2	14	12	14	12
k=3	16	16	16	16
k=4	18	20	18	20
k=5	21	25	21	25
k=6	24	30	19.2	24
k=7	30	40	24	32
k=8	45	55	36	44
k=9	60	70	48	56
k=10	75	90	60	72

4.3 Pricing of End-to-End and Access Services and the Role of Commercial Freedom

Pricing decisions for end-to-end services and for access services provided by the PO to entrants are made within the framework of these demand and cost structures. Three pricing approaches are used for access and worksharing discounts. Avoided Cost (ACE), Approximate Delivery-Zone Access Prices (DAP) with Limited Information and Approximate Delivery-Zone Access Prices with Full Information (DAPFI). The first two are recognized in the literature and ACE is employed by many POs as their basic framework for pricing access and worksharing discounts. ACE is a close approximation to DAP as indicated by Crew and Kleindorfer (2002).

ACE is defined in the usual manner and is sometimes referred to as the (top down) efficient component pricing rule (ECPR). It is the single-piece price less the value of the cost savings of the incumbent as a result of the entrant performing upstream work (typically collection, bar-coding and presortation). One problem with ACE is that it assumes implicitly that the top down price is close to economic cost. Given that, the single piece uniform price is too high in the low cost areas and too low in the high cost areas, ACE is going to perpetuate these inefficiencies. Take the case of a high cost area costing 50 cents a letter, but the uniform price is 30 cents and the presort discount 10 cents. To charge an access price of 30 minus 10, namely, 20 cents would exacerbate the funding problem. The correct (DAP) price would be 40 cents but the entrant would not pay this, as the single piece price is 30 cents. Thus, an access price of 40 cents for a high cost zone would lead the entrant to use the PO to carry all of the letters of its customers to that zone at the single-piece rate of 30 cents. Accordingly, DAP takes the cost of delivery in the area concerned and deducts any presort discount as long as the resulting access price is 30 cents or less. Otherwise, the access price is the single piece price of 30 cents. It is based, in effect, on the value of the work still required when the letter enters the mail stream, but truncated by the single-piece rate, which is always available to entrants under the USO.

DAPFI is an extension of DAP in the sense that it assumes perfect knowledge by I of the costs of the competitive fringe. Thus, it takes entrants' costs into account and adjusts access prices accordingly. DAPFI enables the PO to compete more effectively and therefore provide more funding for the USO. As perfect information about entrants' costs is not available, DAPFI cannot be employed in practice, but it should be noted that DAPFI represents an upper limit on the benefits from commercial freedom related to access pricing. In addition, it indicates that there may be some potential benefit to an incumbent in making an estimate of entrants' costs and a PO with the requisite commercial freedom would likely use this information for pricing and depart from simple DAP.

The model implies considerable commercial freedom for the PO in all three cases. The PO is assumed to set prices for end-to-end service and for access to break even, and is not subjected to a price cap as faced by many POs.[9] The access pricing regimes allow varying degrees of commercial freedom in the pricing of access. ACE allows the least based as it is on the avoided cost rule. DAP allows the PO more freedom and DAPFI as it is able to charge any rate it deems appropriate within the constraints of the upper limit resulting from the single-piece price.

In addition to the pricing flexibility embodied in the access prices, we also assume further pricing flexibility in some scenarios that allows the PO to cut prices in the low-cost areas for business customers. In the results reported here, we assumed the following price discounts in zones 1-3: Discount in zone 1 = 30%, Discount in zone 2 = 20%, Discount in zone 3 = 10%. With an eye on Table 1, this means that when pricing flexibility was allowed, the effective single-piece price for end-to-end service and for ACE

---

9 The impact of a price cap is clearly going to make a PO's financial viability after liberalization more tenuous if it is set low initially and the regulator is slow to allow increases.

access pricing (similar results for DAP and DAPFI access pricing hold, based on the PO's price for end-to-end service to that zone) for business customers in these zones is as follows:

Table 2: End-to-end (E2E) and ACE Access Price for Incumbent PO for Base Case and for Scenarios in which Pricing Flexibility in Low-Cost Zones is Permitted

Scenario	Zone 1	Zone 2	Zone 3	Zones 4 - 10
Base Case E2E Price	P_I	P_I	P_I	P_I
ACE Access Price for Base Case	$P_I - C_{IU} + C_a$	$P_I - C_{IU} + C_a$	$P_I - C_{IU} + C_a$	$P_I - C_{IU} + C_a$
E2E Price under Pricing Flexibility	$0.7*P_I$	$0.8*P_I$	$0.9*P_I$	P_I
ACE Access Price under Pricing Flexibility	$0.7*P_I - C_{IU} + C_a$	$0.8*P_I - C_{IU} + C_a$	$0.9*P_I - C_{IU} + C_a$	$P_I - C_{IU} + C_a$

As access prices are derived from the uniform single-piece rate, possibly discounted in low cost zones, according to one of the three access pricing policies employed, we need only determine whether there is a uniform price that will allow the PO to break even, given the assumed access pricing regime and any pricing flexibility allowed. A search process accomplishes this. Absent a feasible uniform price, a graveyard spiral results.

4.4 Illustrative Results

We report here a few of the illustrative results from our simulations. We capture these in five cases, as shown in Tables 3-7 below.

Our Base Case assumes that entrants can bypass I and engage in end-to-end delivery. It also assumes no pricing flexibility for I in low-cost areas and no service quality reductions in high-cost areas. The Base Case shown in Table 3 shows the expected result that the more commercial freedom is given for access pricing (moving from ACE to DAP to DAPFI), the lower the single-piece price and the higher the welfare (relative welfare effects are not large here; survival and avoiding the GYS is the main issue). We see that the fraction of revenue at breakeven prices accounted for by fixed costs is about 40% for ACE and DAP pricing, roughly in line with the value of this ratio in many POs. We also note that the single-piece price and the volume-weighted entrant's price across zones decreases slightly in moving from ACE to DAP to DAPFI. This reflects the increased efficiency of DAP and DAPFI over ACE in reducing subsidies for access to high-cost zones.

We report also the volume-weighted incumbent price, but this is identical to the single-piece price since no pricing flexibility is allowed in the base case.

For the Base Case, the percentage of total revenues for I and E that are accounted for by worksharing is rather small. Customers use either I's end-to-end services or E's end-to-end services, when bypass is allowed. The only mail that is workshared (consolidated by E and given to I to deliver) is for the high-cost zones serviced by E for its customers.

Table 3: Base Case
Bypass Allowed; No Pricing Flexibility
Standard USO with No Service Quality Reductions
Entrants' Markup = 40%; Access Pricing Methods as Shown

Access Pricing Method	ACE	DAP	DAPFI
Single-Piece Price	63.96	63.65	60.75
Incumbent's Fixed Costs (F)	100,000	100,000	100,000
Weighted Incumbent Price WPI	63.96	63.65	60.75
Weighted Entrants' Price WPE	40.32	40.31	40.18
F/(Incumbent's Revenue)	0.4021	0.4006	0.3388
Incumbent's Market Share	51.61%	51.81%	61.89%
Percentage Workshared	1.91%	1.91%	1.93%
Total Welfare	1,254,157	1,254,530	1,266,607
Fixed Cost (F) at which Graveyard Spiral is Induced	133,000	133,500	142,500

Now let us consider the Base Case where Bypass is not allowed. In this case entrants must tender all mail they collect to I for final delivery. Given the reduced scope of their activity, we reduce the Entrants' markup to recover fixed costs in this case to 10%. We see the results in Table 4. Comparing these results to those of Table 3, we see that the single-piece price and all other prices for I and E are considerably lower and welfare is higher than when bypass is allowed. Notably, the fixed cost at which the GYS is induced is much higher when bypass is not permitted.

The weighted entrants price (WPE) in this case is higher than the case where Bypass is allowed, as WPE is derived from the access price for E plus E's upstream collection and consolidation costs C_{EU}. Since $C_{EU} = C_{IU}$ in the Base Case, this means (e.g., for ACE access pricing) that

$$\begin{aligned} WPE &= (1 + M_E)*[P_A(k) + C_{EU}] \\ &= (1 + M_E)*[P_I - C_{IU} + C_a + C_{EU}] = (1 + M_E)*[P_I + C_a] \end{aligned}$$

where M_E = entrants markup over cost (to recover their fixed costs), assumed in this case to be 10%. Even if the entrants' markup were 0%, we see from this that (under the assumption that $C_{EU} = C_{IU}$) the WPE would exceed P_I by

C_a in the case of ACE access pricing and by more than this in the case of DAP or DAPFI access pricing.

Table 4
Bypass Not Allowed; No Pricing Flexibility
Standard USO with No Service Quality Reductions
Entrants' Markup = 10%; Access Pricing Methods as Shown

Access Pricing Method	ACE	DAP	DAPFI
Single-Piece Price	43.6	43.2	43.2
Incumbent's Fixed Costs (F)	100000	100000	100000
Weighted Incumbent Price WPI	43.6	43.2	43.2
Weighted Entrants' Price WPE	50.1	50.6	50.6
F/(Incumbent's Revenue)	0.248	0.248	0.248
Incumbent's Market Share	88.84%	89.08%	89.08%
Percentage Workshared	38.44%	38.46%	38.46%
Total Welfare	1,324,628	1,324,988	1,324,988
Fixed Cost (F) at which Graveyard Spiral is Induced	>300,000	>300,000	>300,000

Table 5
Bypass Allowed; Pricing Flexibility
Standard USO with No Service Quality Reductions
Entrants' Markup = 10%; Access Pricing Methods as Shown

Access Pricing Method	ACE	DAP	DAPFI
Single-Piece Price	64.1	63.8	61.1
Incumbent's Fixed Costs (F)	100,000	100,000	100,000
Weighted Incumbent Price WPI	60.4	60.2	57.6
Weighted Entrants' Price WPE	41.1	41.1	41.0
F/(Incumbent's Revenue)	0.389	0.388	0.330
Incumbent's Market Share	53.80%	53.99%	64.18%
Percentage Workshared	1.93%	1.93%	1.95%
Total Welfare	1,265,710	1,266,007	1,277,489
Fixed Cost (F) at which Graveyard Spiral is Induced	136,169	136,169	145,772

Table 5 shows the consequences of allowing pricing flexibility (see Table 2). As expected, pricing flexibility allows the USO to be supported at a higher level of fixed costs and welfare is higher at the base case level of fixed costs (F = 100,000). The uniform price actually increases under pricing flexibility, while the weighted price decreases slightly. This reflects the fact that pricing flexibility discounts the price to business customers in the low-cost areas, where the discount is taken off the uniform price. As a result, for a given level of fixed costs, the overall level of the uniform price must be increased (slightly) to maintain breakeven operations.

Table 6 shows the additional impact of allowing pricing flexibility (see Table 2) in addition to prohibiting bypass by entrants. The results are similar to Table 4, except now there is a difference for weighted Incumbent price (WPI) from the results of Table 4, with WPI being lower as a result of the allowed pricing flexibility (even though the single-piece price is increased somewhat relative to Table 4). Welfare is increased relative to Table 4 since price in the high-demand, low-cost areas is closer to marginal cost.

Table 6
Bypass Not Allowed; Pricing Flexibility Allowed (See Table 2)
Standard USO with No Service Quality Reductions
Entrants' Markup = 10%; Access Pricing Methods as Shown

Access Pricing Method	ACE	DAP	DAPFI
Single-Piece Price	46.83	46.46	46.46
Incumbent's Fixed Costs (F)	100,000	100,000	100,000
Weighted Incumbent Price WPI	43.24	42.94	42.94
Weighted Entrants' Price WPE	48.70	49.02	49.02
F/(Incumbent's Revenue)	0.250	0.249	0.249
Incumbent's Market Share	88.69%	88.91%	88.91%
Percentage Workshared	38.17%	38.19%	38.19%
Total Welfare	1,329,600	1,329,875	1,329,875
Fixed Cost (F) at which Graveyard Spiral is Induced	>300,000	>300,000	>300,000

Tables 7-8 show the consequences of service quality reductions and pricing flexibility when bypass is allowed. Comparing these results with the base case in Table 3, we see some increase in welfare and increases as well in the survival level of USO fixed costs that can be supported under these regimes. While the welfare increases are not as substantial as under the case of prohibiting bypass, they are nonetheless significant, and indicate the potential of commercial freedom and redesign of the scope of the USO to contribute to the sustainability and efficiency of the PO under entry.

Table 7
Bypass Allowed; No Pricing Flexibility
Relaxed USO with Service Quality Reductions in Zones 6-10
Entrants' Markup = 40% in Zones 1-5, 32% in Zones 6-10
Access Pricing Methods as Shown

Access Pricing Method	ACE	DAP	DAPFI
Single-Piece Price	55.6	55.3	53.6
Incumbent's Fixed Costs (F)	80,000	80,000	80,000
Weighted Incumbent Price WPI	55.6	55.3	53.6
Weighted Entrants' Price WPE	39.3	39.3	39.2
F/(Incumbent's Revenue)	0.326	0.325	0.286
Incumbent's Market Share	54.78%	55.01%	62.92%
Percentage Workshared	4.19%	4.19%	4.22%
Total Welfare	1,293,130	1,293,366	1,301,431
Fixed Cost (F) at which Graveyard Spiral is Induced	157,000	157,000	166,000

Table 8
Bypass Allowed; Pricing Flexibility Allowed (see Table 2)
Relaxed USO with Service Quality Reductions in Zones 6-10
Entrants' Markup = 40% in Zones 1-5, 32% in Zones 6-10
Access Pricing Methods as Shown

Access Pricing Method	ACE	DAP	DAPFI
Single-Piece Price	56.33	56.06	54.49
Incumbent's Fixed Costs (F)	80,000	80,000	80,000
Weighted Incumbent Price WPI	52.77	52.53	51.02
Weighted Entrants' Price WPE	40.10	40.10	40.06
F/(Incumbent's Revenue)	0.316	0.315	0.278
Incumbent's Market Share	57.00%	57.22%	65.24%
Percentage Workshared	4.24%	4.25%	4.27%
Total Welfare	1,302,521	1,302,684	1,310,403
Fixed Cost (F) at which Graveyard Spiral is Induced	160,700	160,700	172,000

5. SUMMARY AND CONCLUSIONS

First, we note the complexity of the interaction between demand, pricing, cost structures and the effects of liberalization. In addition, we see that several factors could determine whether a graveyard spiral would occur. The fixed costs of the USO clearly have a direct and major impact on viability of the PO. In addition, (comparing, e.g. Table 3 with Tables 4-5) the welfare consequences of full liberalization are small, while the risks of a graveyard spiral (see the final rows in these tables) are significantly greater than under the case where entry is restricted to upstream access/worksharing only. Thirdly, access pricing policies can have effects on both efficiency as well as survivability in the face of a significant USO, though commercial freedom in the form of pricing flexibility will be required to take advantage of these improvements. Finally, while commercial freedom can increase a PO's viability, it is only one of the factors affecting viability, and has only a small effect in improving the PO's viability for the scenarios considered here. Further improvements in the financial viability of the PO arise from reducing the burden of the USO (compare, e.g., Tables 3 and 6 or 7), but these may also lead to only small welfare gains because they simultaneously erode demand. As to full liberalization, comparing Tables 3 and 4, its welfare impact is negative for these examples, because the entrants cherry pick the low-cost mail, leading to significant increases in the single-piece price to maintain breakeven operations. Thus, while our results suggest that under full liberalization, pricing flexibility and a significantly relaxed USO increase financial viability, the impact of liberalization on overall welfare could well be negative (as it is for these examples). We are mindful, of course, that liberalization could spur dynamic efficiency, product innovation and other benefits of competition, but we should be careful before attributing too much from these sources. If the PO is not sustainable as a result of entry, the resulting loss in the scope of the USO could imply much higher welfare losses than the transitory gains from competition.

These results point to a number of policy implications that will need careful consideration in the continuing USO debate:

The scope of liberalization, including commercial freedoms permitted for the PO, has to be matched with the scope of the USO. Opening the gates to full liberalization without providing any additional commercial freedom to the PO and while maintaining the scope of the USO can lead to a graveyard spiral, depending on cost and demand characteristics.

The focus of liberalization (on upstream or downstream operations) is at least as important as its scope. Liberalization of upstream operations is occurring in many countries, and clearly contributes to welfare through the benefits of upstream competition. However, as we have seen, allowing end-to-end competition, i.e. bypass, can have negative welfare consequences,[10]

[10] Note that, for the cases analyzed in our simulation study, prohibiting bypass yielded greater welfare than any of the cases that allowed bypass.

primarily because it erodes scale and scope economies by the PO and weakens considerably the PO's ability to sustain the fixed costs of the USO.

Liberalization has its own dynamic, and once launched it may no longer be controllable by regulators. Thus, while the above policy implications suggest a careful balancing of the scope of the USO and of liberalization, it is not clear to what extent regulators can control matters once full liberalization is launched.

Who controls the pace and nature of the balance between the scope of the USO and liberalization is central. This could be either left primarily in the hands of the PO, to determine on the basis of market conditions and its cost structure, how to reduce the scope of the USO. Alternatively, it could be the continuing responsibility of regulators to define the USO and to provide the means of remaining financially viable to the PO.

All of this raises the broader question of whether the USO has had its day. As the current process moves towards liberalization, market forces will naturally take over. These impersonal forces do not mix well with notions of uniformity of price and quality, nor of equity or affordability. Rather as full liberalization takes hold, we can expect willingness-to-pay, cost, profitability and segment-specific drivers of service to rule the day. For the reasons discussed and analysed in this paper, the process may lead to negligible gains in efficiency. Unfortunately, it may also lead to public disillusionment with the results if the USO is undermined and the re-distribution of the surplus generated in the sector only serves to enrich a few cream skimmers.

REFERENCES

Campbell, J.I., A.K. Dieke, A. Niederprüm and S. Schölermann. 2004. "Main Developments in the European Postal Sector." WIK Consult, Bad Honnef, Germany, July.

Cohen, R.H., W.W. Ferguson, J.D. Waller, and S.S. Xenakis. 2000. "Universal Service without a Monopoly." In *Current Directions in Postal Reform*, edited by M.A. Crew and P.R. Kleindorfer. Boston: Kluwer Academic Publishers

Crew, M.A., and P.R. Kleindorfer. 2000. "Liberalization and the Universal Service Obligation in Postal Service." In *Current Directions in Postal Reform*, edited by M.A. Crew and P.R. Kleindorfer. Boston: Kluwer Academic Publishers

Crew, M.A., and P.R. Kleindorfer. 2001. "Whither the USO under Competitive Entry: A Microstructure Approach." In *Future Directions in Postal Reform*, edited by M.A. Crew and P.R. Kleindorfer. Boston: Kluwer Academic Publishers.

Crew, M.A., and P.R. Kleindorfer. 2002. "Balancing Access and the Universal Service Obligation." In *Postal and Delivery Services: Delivering on Competition*, edited by M.A. Crew and P.R. Kleindorfer. Boston: Kluwer Academic Publishers.

Crew, M.A., and P.R. Kleindorfer. 2004. "Access and the USO for Letters and Parcels." In *Competitive Transformation of the Postal and Delivery Sector*, edited by M.A. Crew and P.R. Kleindorfer. Boston: Kluwer Academic Publishers.

Crew, M.A., and P.R. Kleindorfer. 2005. "Competition, Universal Service and the Graveyard Spiral." In *Regulatory and Economic Challenges in the Postal and Delivery Sector,* edited by M.A. Crew and P.R. Kleindorfer, Boston: Kluwer Academic Publishers.

d'Alcantara, G. and B. Amerlynck. 2004. "Financial Viability of the Universal Postal Service Provider Under Uniform and Cost-Related Tariffs." In *Competitive Transformation of The Postal and Delivery Sector*, edited by M.A. Crew and P.R. Kleindorfer. Boston: Kluwer Academic Publishers.

De Donder, P., H. Cremer, and F. Rodriguez. 2002. "Funding the Universal Service Obligation under Liberalization." In *Postal and Delivery Services: Pricing, Productivity, Regulation and Strategy*, edited by M.A. Crew and P.R. Kleindorfer. Boston: Kluwer Academic Publishers.

Haldi, J., and L. Merewitz. 1997. "Cost and Returns from Delivery to Sparsely Settled Rural Areas." In *Managing Change in the Postal and Delivery Industries*, edited by M.A. Crew and P.R. Kleindorfer. Boston: Kluwer Academic Publishers.

Chapter 2

Universal Service Obligations in the Postal Sector

*Economic Learnings from Cross-Country Comparisons**

Xavier Ambrosini, François Boldron, and Bernard Roy
La Poste

1. INTRODUCTION

The 2nd European Postal Directive requires an assessment of the scope and sustainability of the universal service obligation (USO) under full market opening. The requirements for each of these, the scope of the USO and the market opening, as well as the incumbent's sustainability under alternative scenarios may well differ across countries as a number of previous contributions to the postal debate have pointed out.[1] Universal service is a set of measures aiming to grant permanently all users in all points of a territory a sufficient level of service. These obligations take the

---

* The view expressed in this paper are those of authors and do not necessarily reflects the views of La Poste. We would like to thank all the correspondents that answered our questionnaire and provided fruitful discussions: Margaret Arblaster, Australian Competition and Consumer Commission; Gerard Power, Canada Post Corporation; Gunnar de Gier Thornfeldt, Road Safety and Transport Agency; Pekka Leskinen, Finland Post Group; Marcella Mooren, DPAG; Peter Quander, RegTP; John Hearn, ComReg; Stephen Ferguson, An Post; Stefano Gori, Poste Italiane; Shoji Maruyama, Japan Post; Jeannette van der Hooft, TNT; Greg Harford, New Zealand Post; Kristin Bergum, Posten Norge; Ricardo Goulão Santos, CTT - Correios de Portugal, Rajko Jerenec, Agencija za pošto in elektronske komunikacije; Beatriz Galván Santiago, Correo y Telégrafos; Mathias Henricson, PTS; Sture Wallander, Posten AB; Daniel Krähenbühl, Swiss Post; Denise Bagge, Postcomm; Frank Rodriguez, Royal Mail; John D Waller, Postal Rate Commission.

1 See Crew and Kleindorfer (2005), Cohen et al. (2004), Bernard et al. (2002), and Gallet and Toledano (1997).

form of constraints, and apply to a range of products or services. They involve quality, in the broad sense, and price controls. The existence of obligations means that, in their absence, the market may not provide a sufficient level of service, or whole scope of products, or at least not at an affordable price level for all users. The loss of degree of freedom created by the existence of constraints creates an opportunity cost.

According to Cremer et al (2000), the cost of the USO is the difference between the profits the universal service provider could obtain if the obligations were not imposed and the actual profit realized under USO. This approach is similar to Panzar's (2001) loss of potential profits, and Choné et al.'s (2002) competitive neutrality.

Calculating when the incumbent faces a break-even rule, or when the profits are bound, is clearly problematic. This is why in the 'potential profits' approach, in a regulated monopoly situation, the question of the (net) cost of universal service is irrelevant.

In a competitive environment, the calculation of the cost of universal service is crucial, for evaluating the competitive handicaps of the incumbent, and for finding the appropriate mechanisms for its financing (e.g., compensation funds or state subsidies.).

As most postal operators in the world enjoy a protected monopoly for financing their USO, cost projection in a liberalized environment may be misleading. The losses due to liberalization must not be confused with the cost of USO.

Nicolas Curien, at the postal conference organized by the Institut D'Economie Industrielle (2001),[2] has drawn a very clear picture (see Figure 1) that summarizes well the different methods proposed to derive the cost of USO.

Figure 1: Cost of USO and Cost of Liberalization.

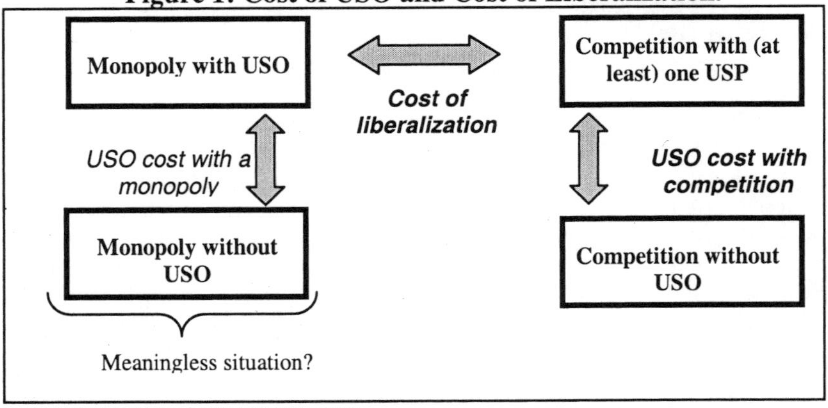

[2] Second Conference on "Competition and Universal Service in the Postal Sector", December 2001, Toulouse, France.

Currently, there is no consensus over how to cost universal service in the postal sector. Although the "profit differential" approach is often considered in literature, the cost of universal service could be the direct loss (revenue minus cost) occurred by the services. In this case, the question of cost allocation must be solved, i.e., incremental costs or fully-distributed costs. This paper will not deal with any costing method, but instead with the first step, which is the definition of universal service constraints. This question will be examined using a survey instrument distributed to 19 postal operators. As expected, our survey findings show significant differences across countries in the current scope of the USO.

2. UNIVERSAL SERVICE OBLIGATIONS: A CROSS COUNTRY COMPARISON

The overview is broken up into three axes: First, the scope of products under USO; second, the quality, in its multiple aspects, such as accessibility, number of deliveries, and door deliveries; and thirdly, the way the price constraints are set on the universal service products, e.g., through uniform pricing, price caps, and break-even rules). The countries are then ranked according to the strength of the constraint in "absolute value."

It is important to note that consideration of how difficult it is to satisfy the criteria is not taken into account. Indeed, the satisfaction of the same constraint in different countries can be more or less costly according to geographical aspects, the degree of competition, the number of items per capita, etc. This question is outside the purview of this paper.

2.1 The Variations of the Scope of Products Subject to Universal Service Constraints.

Quite surprisingly, the detailed list of products in the field of universal service is not always precisely defined. In Europe, the scope is first of all defined by directive 1997, which uses categories of product and a weight limit (0-2 kg for mail and 0-10/20kg for packets). It also includes particular services, namely registered mail and declared value services. Some countries, such as France, have a publicly-available detailed list of all universal service products. In the United Kingdom, Postcomm, the regulator, recently published such a list. In the Netherlands, the list can be considered *de facto*, as the non-USO products are defined. In Ireland, the regulator also publishes a list. In these latter three countries, regulators underline the importance of adaptability of universal service to the needs of users.

Therefore, they regularly evolve the content of the list, as well as the related constraints.

Concerning the scope *stricto sensu*, the items concerned are quite homogeneous: mail less than 2kg, including all kinds of bulk/direct mail; international mail; newspapers; registered letters; and a portion of the parcels. Nevertheless, our inquiries reveal some quite large differences: from a single piece at a retail outlet to the whole scope of products. This remains true even in the subset of European countries to which the European directive applies.[3]

The Netherlands excludes a part of bulk mail (direct mail) from universal service. The Dutch regulator believes that, under complete liberalization, universal service should be limited to single-piece items. However, as long as competition is undeveloped, all mail weighing less than 50g must be included in the ambit of universal service. The Netherlands case is an exception: as a general matter, direct mail is a universal product for the large majority of countries, even those in non-European directive countries. There are discussions in Finland to exclude 2nd class mail from the scope of universal service. The delivery of periodicals is already outside the scope. In the United Kingdom, Postcomm has differentiated single and bulk products in its analysis. Only one category of bulk mail would fall into the universal service scope, under the assumption that large mailers do not need the protection of universal service.

Important to note is that the scope of universal service can be extended or varied over time. In some countries, governments have included in their definition of universal service some products that one would expect to be outside of the scope. For instance, *poste restante* in the UK, cash on delivery in Germany, special rates for Northern Food Delivery (by air) in Canada, the revenues issued from the rent of post office boxes in the Netherlands are unusual extensions.

Additionally, the consideration of the relative size of the scope of universal service with relation to what the universal service provider offers on the whole is important. Indeed, differences exist in the cost of universal service constraints and its compensation between countries that have the same scope but different relative size. For instance, some operators provide financial services, while others do not. All the operators provide products outside the scope of the universal service (e.g., express services in Japan, unaddressed mail in France). However, the USA is one exception: all USPS products are included in the scope of the universal service.

---

3 Also, although there are significant differences in the "universal service parcels," lack of information on this lead us to not develop the topic.

To summarize, countries fall under three categories (see Table 1): those with a reduced scope, those with a large one, and the particular case of the USPS.

Table 1: Ranking according to the scope (number of products) of the universal service

Reduced scope	Large scope	All the products
New Zealand (NZ), Netherlands (NL), Finland (FI), United Kingdom (UK).	Australia (AT), Canada (CA), Switzerland (CH), Germany (DE), Denmark (DK), France (FR), Ireland (IE), Italy (IT), Japan (JP), Norway (NO), Portugal (PT), Slovenia (SI), Spain (SP), Sweden (SW).	United States (US).

We will now analyze the constraints upon quality, in a broad sense, imposed on the universal service scope of products.

2.2 Different Levels of Quality Requirement

Quality is at the core of universal service. In this paper, quality must be understood in a broad sense, involving many aspects: the frequency of delivery and collection, the existence of transit time objectives, door deliveries, the accessibility of the retail outlets or the mailboxes, the treatment of complaints, the responsibility over lost or damaged items, and delayed mail. The quality directly impacts the cost function. The universal service grants quality levels upon the scope of items, reducing the degree of freedom universal service providers have, since they would be tempted to reduce quality levels in an unconstrained situation. Indeed, if only price was regulated, monopoly rents would easily be extracted this way.

We now look at the aspects of quality for which we believe impact the cost function the most. It is important to note that the quality should be understood here as the universal service requirements concerning quality, *not* as the level of quality actually provided by the universal service provider.

2.2.1 Delivery and Collection

The number of deliveries per week has a direct impact on the fixed cost of delivery,[4] and its reduction can allow significant cost savings. Directive 1997 imposes in Europe a minimum of 5 deliveries and collections per week. Generally, this obligation was transposed from the directive to the national laws according to existing practice. Consequently, several countries required delivery 6 days a week for the universal service provider. Some countries requested the European Commission to make exceptions, notably the United

[4] See Roy (1999).

Kingdom, where geographical areas that are too isolated[5] are not subject to this obligation.

Table 2: Ranking according to the number of deliveries

No constraint	5 per week	6 per week with exceptions	6 per week
US	CA, IT, PT, SI, SW	AT, NZ, NO, JP	CH, ES, FR, NL, DE, DK, UK, IE, FI

Table 3: Ranking according to the number of collections

No constraint	5 per week	6 per week
AT, JP, NZ, US	CA, IT, PT, SI, SW	CH, DE, DK, ES, FI, FR, IE, NL, NO, UK.

The number of collections and deliveries per week concerns the processing of mail and not directly the supply. Surprisingly, this aspect is rarely linked to the transit times imposed on universal service products. Indeed, imposing a constraint upon industrial organization makes sense only if it is compatible with the characteristics of the products sold. In this case, such a constraint makes sense only with Day+1 objective. This leads us to the time transit dimension of the quality.

2.2.2 Transit Times

The domestic mail of universal service is generally subject to a time transit control (as can be seen in Table 4). Only the United Kingdom and Portugal have set up a complex system to regulate the transit time of universal service items.

Table 4: USO transit time objectives

Australia	No objectives fixed by USO (However, the regulation does fix such objectives).
Canada	Obligations exist, but details were not available.
Denmark	93% D+1 for priority mail, 93% of D+3 for economic mail.
Finland	95% of D+1 for 1st class mail.
France	85% of D+1 and 95% of D+2 for priority mail.
Germany	Letters mailed: at least 80% of D+1 and 95% of D+2.
Ireland	94% of D+1.
Italy	87% of D+1 for priority mail, 93% of D+3 for economic mail.
Japan	Ordinary mail is delivered within 3 days after posting by customers.
Netherlands	95% of D+1 (items of correspondence weighing up to 100g).
New Zealand	No such objectives.
Norway	85% of D+1 for priority letters and at least 97% of D+3, 85% of D+4 for non-priority letters, and at least 97% of D+6.
Portugal	Priority Mail: 94% of D+1.
Slovenia	At least 95% of D+1, and at least 99.5% of D+2 (but not for direct mail).
Spain	Obligations exist, but details were not available.
Sweden	At least 85% of D+1 for the domestic priority items and 97% of D+3.
Switzerland	Obligations exist, but details were not available.
United Kingdom	Obligations (and penalties in case of failure) exist, but details were not available.
United States	No such objectives.[6]

5 Isles not linked by regular sea lines or not inhabited in a permanent way.

The United Kingdom is the only country to apply different quality of service objectives to single pieces (1st and 2nd Class) and bulk mail (the *Mailsort* range). In the Netherlands, priority, single-piece and bulk mail are subject to the same quality of service objective (95%). Nevertheless, by transmitting the yearly results to the Dutch regulator, TNT must differentiate between mail deposited in the general public points of contact and mail beyond 100g deposited in sorting center.

2.2.3 Delivery to the Door

There are also often different requirements concerning delivery to the door. In the USA, this is not an obligation. Instead, the use of cluster boxes is common in rural areas. As we showed in Bernard et al. (2002), this partially explains relatively higher unit costs in the French rural areas compared to the ones in the USA rural areas.

In Slovenia, the universal service provider (USP) is bound to deliver to the door. But if users have housing units or business premises located outside a concentrated settlement, and are simultaneously more than 200 meters from the postal route, items can be delivered to attached boxes.

In Sweden, delivery is traditionally provided to the door on each floor, which implies that the postman must climb the stairs. It is not strictly a constraint of universal service; nevertheless, in practice, this modality of delivery was kept. By contrast, all the packets, even those subject to universal service constraints, are delivered to the post office.

Generally, delivery location is very important. Delivery to each floor in buildings, to mailboxes located in a hallway, to the border of a property, or the border to the nearest public way or to the home, all have a large impact on delivery costs. This is particularly the case in rural areas.

2.2.4 Accessibility

The universal service obligation of geographical accessibility envisaged by European Directive 1997 was applied, by country, according to the distance between the users and "points of access" (i.e., post offices and mailboxes) or by the presence of a retail point in a geographical zone (defined by its area or by the local administrative unit).

In Germany, the accessibility constraint requires at least 12,000 retail points, of which are 5,000 post offices, which must be company-owned and staffed. Cities of more than 2,000 citizens must have access to at least one

---

[6] Concerning the USA, the USO does not fix service standards. However, USPS has some relatively high time transit objectives. One could argue that as these standards are relatively high, there is no need to have an explicit regulation.

retail point. For cities of more than 4,000 citizens, distance between the point of contact and each citizen must be less than 2 km. And there must also be a retail point in each area of 80 km².

The fact that the network is oversized in Ireland is part of the "postal common knowledge." Nevertheless, this oversize is not qualified as universal service constraint. Accessibility for bulk mail is also treated, but in a specific way. The Irish regulator recently ruled that An Post, the Irish USP, has at least one access point per county for bulk mail.

In the Netherlands, for urban areas of more than 5,000 citizens, at least one mailbox within 500m radius and a point of contact within a 5 km radius must be available. For other areas, the requirement is at least one mailbox within a 2,500m radius. Finally, for the urban zones of more than 50,000 citizens, TNT must provide at least one point of contact per 50,000 citizens.

New Zealand Post has to maintain at least 240 full service outlets and a minimum of 880 partial service outlets, which excludes businesses that simply sell stamps.

In Japan, each municipality must have at least one post office and one letter box. Moreover, the number of post offices must be at least 24,700, while the number of mailboxes should be no less than 186,000.

In the United States, the only constraints are those of the Postal Rate Commission when the USPS chooses to close a post office.

Finally, and notably, the regulator, not the USO, defines Australia's quality requirements.

In summary, the countries are ranked according to level of universal service constraints on quality as shown in Table 5. One has to note that this ranking reflects the universal service requirements concerning quality. The ranking is not based on the level of quality actually provided by the universal service provider.

Table 5: Ranking according to the quality dimension

Almost no constraint	Low level of constraints	Intermediate	High level of constraints
AT, US	CA, ES, IT, SW	CH, DK, FR, IE, JP, NO, NZ, PT, SI.	DE, FI, NL, UK

The last element of universal service obligation deals with the degree of freedom that networks in charge of universal service have concerning their prices or pricing schemes.

2.3 The Pricing Rules for Universal Service Products

Requiring an "affordable price" is a way of preventing a monopoly from extracting rents from the consumers. In particular, the quality constraints imply a price regulation. In liberalized markets, the prices decrease by competitive pressure. Consequently, in competitive markets, price regulation is less needed. However, in the fields where the incumbent is the only provider in practice (e.g., single-piece deliveries in rural areas), prices will always tend to be high.

Listed below are several kinds of constraints over prices. Price controls are the most obvious one, covering, for example, price caps and the individual rating of products. Profit objectives create another constraint, e.g., an operator under a break-even rule faces a higher constraint than those authorized to make unlimited profits. We also look at "preferential tariffs", i.e., the practice of low tariffs for some subsets of products (e.g., newspapers) or the population (e.g., mail free of charge for the blind). Finally, we explore uniform price constraints.

2.3.1 Price Controls

The four main types of price controls, from the least constraining to the most, are:

1. *Laissez-faire*, wherein prices are only subject to competition laws and competitive pressure
2. *Ex post*, wherein controls are by regulator or government
3. *Ex ante,* wherein control by the regulator or the government takes the form of, for example, a price cap
4. Direct control, price increase subject to approval of a public authority (regulator, government…)

Of course, one country could impose a mixture of the above controls (see Table 6). For example, a product in a reserved area could be subject to tougher price controls than products offered in the liberalized markets.

Price caps can apply to the whole set of products, or to separate baskets of goods. In the United Kingdom, all the universal products are subject to a global price cap. But in Germany, while all universal service products are subjected to a price cap, three baskets differentiate services (products under monopoly conditions, products under competitive conditions and products related to access), and each basket has its own price cap. Independent of the level of the cap or its scope, the price cap in Germany is more constraining than that of the United Kingdom's.

Another particularity is in the choice of the reference index. In the Netherlands, the cap is not based on the retail price index but on the wages of the merchant area index. The postal regulator and the Ministry of Economic Affairs plan to base the price cap on the inflation index. On this subject, France also shows originality by using the price index of services.

2.3.2 Profit Objectives

The USPS faces a budget constraint (applied over time rather than every year). But most operators seek to have positive profits, or at least do not face a break-even rule. This difference has an impact on the level of prices: a budget constraint automatically reduces the degree of freedom of the universal service provider.

Table 6: Price controls in the different countries

Australia	Price cap.
Canada	Price cap for basic letters.
Denmark	Price cap for products of the reserved area, no constraint for universal service products outside the reserved area.
Finland	*Ex-post* controls
France	Global price cap for universal service products, possible split of the cap between single and bulk, price control for each product in the reserved area, notification to the regulator for the others universal service products.
Germany	Three baskets of price caps for letter mail items up to 1000 grams, other USO-products are subject to an *ex post* control (if prices are not in line with the principles of the Postal Act).
Ireland	Price control by the regulator for products in the reserved area.
Italy	Price cap for reserved products. The price cap system is applied every three years. The prices of universal non-reserved products are set "consistent" with the prices of reserved products.
Japan	Direct control for ordinary, special handling, and international mail.
Netherlands	Price increases for domestic universal services must not exceed the Dutch national wage index. Two price baskets for postal services: all domestic universal postal services and a small users' basket.
New Zealand	No controls (competition laws and market forces are seen as sufficient)
Norway	For assessing whether the tariffs are cost-based, and for detecting unlawful cross-subsidization, Norway Post keeps a product account. The regulator examines the product account.
Portugal	Price cap for products in the reserved area, *ex post* control for universal service products outside the reserved area.
Slovenia	The USP is obliged to receive price approval from the Post and Electronic Communications of the Republic of Slovenia.
Spain	Global price caps can be set (and are actually in place) by the government.
Sweden	Price cap for domestic priority mail up to 500 grams
Switzerland	Subject to the control of the federal government.
United Kingdom	Global price cap for all products where competition is not effective. Monitoring of access prices.
United States	To change rates, the USPS is required to request a recommended decision from the Postal Rate Commission.

2.3.3 Preferential Tariffs

In some countries, the universal service provider is bound by universal service constraints to deliver products without charge or at preferential/social prices:

1. Materials for the blind in many countries.
2. *Poste restante* in the UK.
3. Mail from victims in devastated areas (due to natural catastrophes) are free in Japan.
4. Special prices for specific agricultural items in Canada.
5. Newspapers benefit from special prices in Denmark and Portugal.
6. Non-profit organizations have specific tariffs in the USA.

The existence of such tariffs reinforces the constraints on prices.

2.3.4 Uniform Pricing

Although EU directive 1997 does not impose any uniform price constraint, most countries practice uniform pricing, even in the absence of a formal constraint. Here, though, we only examine regulatory constraints regardless of the practice. One difference in uniform pricing among countries is the existence of a reserved area.

Table 7: Ranking according to the existence of uniform price constraint for the reserved area

No constraints	Constraints for some products	Constraints for all the products
IE, IT	AT, US	CA, CH, DE, DK, FR, NL, NO, SI, SP, UK

Table 8: Ranking according to the existence of uniform price constraint for the products outside the reserved area

No constraints	Constraints for some products	Constraints for all the products
CA, CH, DE, FR, IE, IT, NO, NZ, PT, SP.	AT, FI, JP, SW, US	DK, NL, SI, UK

Combining the previous elements, we summarize the strength of price constraints over universal service.

Table 9: Ranking according to the strength of price constraints over universal service

Very light	Light/intermediate	Intermediate/high	Strong
NZ	CA, FI, IT, SP	AT, CH, DE, DK, FR, IE, LP, NL, NO, PT, SI, SW	USA, UK

3. A CONCEPTUAL FRAMEWORK TO ANALYZE UNIVERSAL SERVICE OBLIGATIONS AND THEIR COSTS

Following the three-dimensional analysis, the universal constraints could now be represented by a box (as shown in Figure 3 below). A high level of constraints means a lesser degree of freedom, and, therefore, a bigger box. To derive the net cost generated by universal service, we compare the situations with and without the set of USO constraints, using the Cremer et al. (2000) or Panzar (2001) approach. The question asked is: what would the incumbent's profit be without the box? The quantitative link between the size and the costs is not the purview of this paper. It is clear, though, that within a country, the bigger the box, the higher is the cost.

We nevertheless must be careful with cross-country comparisons. Although it is interesting to compare the size and shape of the boxes between different countries, as an indicator of the differences of the strength of regulation, we must bear in mind that if a country has a bigger box than another one, this does not necessarily imply higher USO costs for the former. For example, as recent postal literature broadly pointed out, the geography of the country, or the amount of traffic per addressee carried by the operator, affects directly the costs incurred by constraints. The intensity of actual competition will also have an effect on the USO costs.

To complete the analysis, we must now turn to the existence, in some cases, of other constraints, imposed by national authorities that go beyond the USO. In other words, the governments may impose additional services of general economic interest that are more binding than the USO, but which do not qualify as USO. It is therefore necessary to clearly differentiate between USO costs and those linked to other constraints.

Table 10: Examples of Non-USO obligations

	Non-USO constraints
Finland	Distribution exceptions when the addressee is physically disabled.
France	The post office network must be such that 90% of the population live less than 5 km from a post office. Newspapers benefit from special tariffs in order to promote press diversity. Electoral mail also benefits from special tariffs.
Ireland	Obligation under law to provide financial services in the retail network.
Italy	Preferential prices for periodicals.
Japan	Mergers & Acquisitions by Japan Post are restricted to a few areas that are closely related to postal activities under the ordinance.
Portugal	Several extra obligations concerning newspapers, for instance.
Sweden	Delivery in rural areas for elderly and disabled people. Material for the blind. Electoral mail. Cashier services.
Switzerland	Preferential tariffs in order to promote press variety.

Three situations are then evaluated and compared in order to compute the cost of universal service obligations (see Figure 2 below).

Figure 2: Cost of the constraints

1. No USO, and extra constraints less binding than USO would be.	***Cost of USO*** (1–2)
2. USO and no extra constraints.	***Cost of the extra constraints*** (2–3)
3. USO, and extra constraints more binding than USO	

This leads to a general framework for analyzing all constraints, represented in the following diagram.

Figure 3: The boxes of constraints

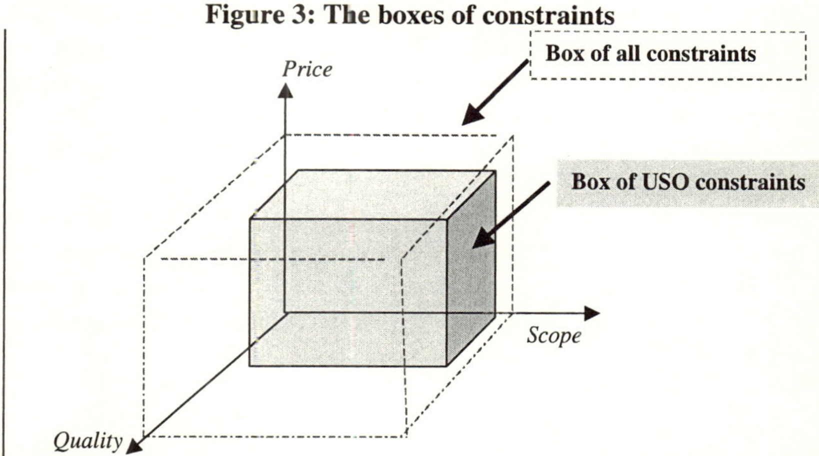

4. CONCLUSION

Most of the methods for calculating the cost of universal service have been developed in the telecommunication sector, which was liberalized in the early 1980s. But in the postal sector, where monopoly is the most common market structure in each country, there is no consensus over methodology, as its need was not obvious. The massive liberalization movement in the postal sector creates the need for USO cost evaluations

This paper analyzed the strength of universal constraints through three axes: the scope of products subject to universal service constraints, the quality of service and of course the ways prices are controlled and fixed. Given this framework, we drafted a cross comparison leading to a "constraints box," such that, the bigger the box, the more important the set of constraints is. Nevertheless, although the size of the box gives a clear idea of the strength of the constraints, another step is needed to go from the size of the box to the cost of universal service. Indeed, we have not dealt with the relative difficulty in satisfying these constraints. Clearly, for example, constraints over delivery are more or less costly to satisfy, according to geographic and demographic considerations, as well as traffic levels. Accessibility of the retail network is another example: setting the same constraint of accessibility to retail points for a highly populated country as for a very low-density country obviously has different cost implications.

Constraints outside the basket of universal service have also been emphasized. Pricing policies, for example, or constraints over retail network density, may fulfil different objectives, leading to additional costs above those borne solely with universal service constraints. In this case, to calculate USO costs, the question of the "initial" situation, the situation without USO constraints, itself will be problematic. Consequently, the debate around the precise "qualification" of constraints, within or without the scope of universal service, promises to be central.

REFERENCES

Bernard, S., R.H. Cohen, M.H. Robinson, B. Roy, J. Toledano, J.D. Waller and S.S. Xenakis. 2002. "Delivery Cost Heterogeneity and Vulnerability." In *Postal and Delivery Services: Delivering on Competition,* edited by M.A. Crew and P.R. Kleindorfer, Boston: Kluwer Academic Publishers.

Choné, P., L. Flochel and A. Perrot. 2002. "Allocation and Funding of Universal Service Obligations in a Competitive Network Market." *International Journal of Industrial Organization* 20(9): 1247-1276.

Cohen, R.H., M.H. Robinson, R. Sheehy, J.D. Waller and S.S. Xenakis. 2004. "An Empirical Analysis of the Graveyard Spiral." In *Competitive Transformation of the Postal and Delivery Sector,* edited by M.A. Crew and P.R. Kleindorfer, Boston: Kluwer Academic Publishers.

Cremer, H., A. Grimaud and J-J. Laffont. 2000. "The Cost of Universal Service in the Postal Sector." In *Current Directions in Postal Reform,* edited by M.A. Crew and P.R. Kleindorfer, Boston: Kluwer Academic Publishers.

Crew, M.A. and P.R. Kleindorfer. 2005. "Competition, Universal Service and the Graveyard Spiral." In *Regulatory and Economic Challenges in the Postal and Delivery Sector,* edited by M.A. Crew and P.R. Kleindorfer, Boston: Kluwer Academic Publishers.

Crew, M.A. and P.R. Kleindorfer. 2002. "Balancing Access and the Universal Service Obligation." In *Postal and Delivery Services: Pricing, Productivity, Regulation and Strategy,* edited by M.A. Crew, and P.R. Kleindorfer, Boston: Kluwer Academic Publishers.

De Donder, P., H. Cremer and F. Rodriguez. 2002. "Funding the Universal Service Obligation under Liberalisation." In *Postal and Delivery Services: Pricing, Productivity, Regulation and Strategy*, edited by M.A. Crew and P.R. Kleindorfer, Boston: Kluwer Academic Publishers.

Dobbs, I.A. and J. Gollay. 1995. "Costing the Universal Service Obligation: the Profitability, Distributional and Welfare Consequences of Retaining Uniform Prices." Workshop on Postal and Delivery Economics, June 7-10 in Naantali, Finland.

Elsenbast, W., F. Pieper and U. Stumpf. 1995. "Estimating the Universal Service Burden of Public Postal Operators." *WIK Diskussionsbeiträge* 150.

Gallet, C. and J. Toledano. 1997. "The Cost of Universal Postal Service in a Competitive Environment: Lessons from Telecommunications." In *Managing Changes in the Postal and Delivery Industries*, edited by M.A. Crew and P.R. Kleindorfer, Boston: Kluwer Academic Publishers.

NERA. 1998. "Costing and Financing of Universal Service Obligations in the Postal Sector in the European Union." Final Report for DG XIII, European Commission, Brussels.

Panzar, J. 2001. "Funding Universal Service Obligations: the Costs of Liberalization." In *Current Directions in Postal Reform*, edited by M.A. Crew and P.R. Kleindorfer, Boston: Kluwer Academic Publishers.

Rodriguez, F. and D. Storer. 1999. "Estimating the Cost of Universal Service Obligation in Postal Service." In *Emerging Competition in Postal and Delivery Services*, edited by M.A. Crew and P.R. Kleindorfer, Boston: Kluwer Academic Publishers.

Roy, B. 1999. "Technico-Economic Analysis of the Costs of Outside Work in Postal Delivery." In *Emerging Competition in Postal and Delivery Services*, edited by M.A. Crew, and P.R. Kleindorfer, Boston: Kluwer Academic Publishers.

Chapter 3

Profitability of the Universal Service Postal Provider Under Entry with Economies of Scale in Collection and Delivery

Gonzales d'Alcantara and Bernard Amerlynck
University of Antwerp and EXPOST Consulting

1. INTRODUCTION

We propose a model for a liberalized competitive postal market that has one Universal Service Obligation (USO) provider, the incumbent, and one entrant. In this model we take into account the existence of economies of scale in their collection and delivery activities. The study is intended to lead to conclusions about the impact of economies of scale on the postal market in various countries, as measured by mail delivery density, which is defined as the number of postal items delivered per person, per year, and according to the size of the population. We consider delivery technologies of operators in markets of different sizes, measured by both these criteria. Variable and fixed costs in the collection and delivery activities are determined by a structural cost model, which has the same form for the incumbent as for the entrant. In this latter model we will also pay attention to delivery technology parameters, which differ from country to country, such as the number of delivery points per route stop. Given a definition of the USO, assumptions about demand behavior, and the opening of the market to the entrant, the calibrated model will compute the impact of the 'cream-skimming' mechanism and the 'graveyard spiral' on volume, tariffs, market shares and the cumulative balance the entrant needs in order to finance the delivery network. In the second step, the model will also measure the effects of economies of scale on the financial requirement of the incumbent in charge of the USO, in case tariffs remain at the constant pre-competition level.

The existence of economies of scale has been recognized in the literature, e.g., Rogerson and Takis (1993), Bradley and Colvin (1995), Cazals et al. (1997), Cohen and Chu (1997), and Roy (1999). All these references show the existence and importance of economies of scale, notably in the delivery function and, to a lesser extent, in other activities in the postal value chain. Our purpose is to examine the impact of these economies of scale on the postal market in various countries. When the market opens and there are economies of scale which differ country by country, what are the long-term impacts of alternative regulatory regimes on tariffs, volumes and market shares? How do economies of scale affect the levels of the tariff differentials between both operators? What is the end result in each country when scale obviously decreases for the incumbent with the entry of the competitor? Who benefits both from increasing scale and from relatively denser delivery zones, lost by the incumbent? Which parameters are crucial for the financial requirements of the entrant, who wants to invest in a delivery network, and for the incumbent in charge of the USO, when tariffs are kept unchanged, i.e. at affordable levels?

Two types of model solutions will be examined:

1. The regulatory authorities want to achieve a liberalized postal market without giving any subsidies to finance the incumbent's USO. The incumbent and the entrant should behave as they would in a situation of competition: both operators determine their tariffs according to their unit costs, including the margins to cover their fixed costs. The incumbent, therefore, modifies the tariffs so as to keep balanced accounts.
2. If the incumbent's tariffs are required to remain equal to the costs per unit in the base period, the starting situation under monopoly, how large is the financial loss of the incumbent, the USO provider?

In this investigation, we will not take into account possible inefficiencies of the incumbent, obstacles to market access for the entrant, or transition problems that might arise in going from an inefficient and monopolistic market situation to one that is more competitive.

2. THE MODEL

The postal market is modelled with two types of customers (where the subscript j indicates a customer of type j), retail customers and business customers. The *retail customers* are afforded special attention by the regulator in regards to assuring affordability of postal rates. They are also characterized as being more loyal to the incumbent and having less elastic demand than *business customers,* who are more cost conscious. Both customers are assumed to consume a single product for simplicity: the same mix of first- and second-class mail services.

There is an *incumbent* operator, *I*, providing services upstream and downstream. This operator is the USO provider. This obligation includes delivering to the whole population of the area at least one time each of six days of the week. The tariff should be an affordable price; therefore, the tariff will be based on cost. No price cap has been instituted. The tariff should be the same for all delivery zones (tariff uniformity). The base period corresponds to a period with a reserved activity for the total volume.

In the first period, when the market is opened, there is an alternative operator: the *entrant, E*, - providing competitive services for upstream activity and also able to provide downstream activities. The downstream activity used to be the incumbent's reserved activity in the base period, but it is opened to competition in the current period. In other words, in the current period, bypass is both technologically and economically feasible for the entrant.

Total market demand is related to broad substitution possibilities for the customer among different forms of communication. Since in the base period the entrant is already providing upstream services, new opportunities to create additional mail volume when the conditions and regulations of the downstream activity are changed are not likely. In the model, what is usually called the *displacement ratio*, σ, will be assumed to be equal to 1; i.e. for a given total market demand, an increase in demand of one unit of the entrant's service necessarily leads to a decrease of one unit in the demand for the incumbent's service. To summarize, within a segment there is perfect substitution between the incumbent's and the entrant's services. No empirical evidence was found in the literature showing that the displacement ratio for the mail considered is significantly different from 1. A displacement ratio less than 1, reflecting imperfect substitution between I and E products, would naturally lead to more sustainable outcomes than the cases analyzed here.

Each country is divided into two delivery zones, the dense or *urban delivery zone*, *U*, and the non-dense or *rural delivery zone*, *R*. It is assumed that dense zones are situated in urban areas and non-dense zones in rural areas. Each of these delivery areas is characterized by a *grouping index* representing *the number of delivery points per route stop*: e.g., the average number of apartments in a building within the urban zone. It is assumed that every delivery point (apartment) is occupied by exactly one household, with a certain number of individuals per household, e.g., for the USA 2.6 people/household. For international comparisons, urban and rural zones are defined following the United Nations' Department of Economic and Social

Affairs, Population Division (2003) "Percentage population in urban area." Again, for example, for the USA, 20.9% of the people live in rural areas, corresponding to non-dense zones, so that 20.9% of the postal volume is delivered following a lower grouping index and therefore a higher delivery cost. This is true for the incumbent and for the entrant, since it depends on the urban and rural organization of the country.

Combining these elements, there are four different segments served by postal service providers: retail and business customers, where the market shares depend on customers' behavior, and following the density of delivery (rural or urban), where the market shares depend on unit cost differences.

2.1 Demand Model

As described in d'Alcantara and Amerlynck (2004), there are two steps in the demand model: the first is related to possible substitutions and complementarities of mail with respect to other communication media on the broad market. The second is related to the mail customer's behavior, given the total mail volume determined as demand. The first is a constant elasticity demand model for *total mail demand of a customer in a zone*; the second is a *market share model* for each customer, determining the substitution between postal service providers within the customers' market demand, and assuming two coefficients: one for loyalty and one for elasticity. One defines a *customer loyalty percentage* as the percentage of the incumbent's tariff that a given customer will accept to be higher than the entrant's tariff without any decrease in the demand addressed to the incumbent. Given the loyalty percentage of a customer and given total market demand of this customer, the elasticity is the percentage change of the incumbent's volume demanded by this customer and strictly replaced by the entrant's product, as a consequence of the percentage discount. Note that there is one elasticity for each customer type, *retail and business,* and for each destination, *urban and rural.* The demand model consists of two sets of equations to be solved simultaneously: a total market demand equation for each customer type and the market share equations of the two service providers for the services provided to the two types of customers in the two zones. The structure of these equations is given in an Appendix.[1]

The total market price elasticity of demand for postal services has been assumed to be -0.3. The value cannot be rejected in various econometric studies of time series estimation surveyed by Cazals and Florens (2002). At

[1] The Appendix is available from the authors or can be downloaded from the CRRI website, where the unabridged paper, with Appendix, is posted. The reader can also see d'Alcantara and Amerlynck (2004) for a discussion of the approach taken to modeling demand.

the stage of competing for the market shares, price sensitivity of retail customers is relatively lower than that of business customers. Retail customers are relatively more loyal to the incumbent's postal service. The customer loyalty parameters X_z^j are considered to be 20% for the retail customer and -10% for the business customer. The market share elasticity, η_z^j, is lower for retail customers (-0.75) than for business customers (-1.25). The values of such elasticities are smaller where there is a positive loyalty coefficient, which represents a lower tariff sensitivity The values are larger where there is a negative loyalty coefficient, representing a higher tariff sensitivity. We have taken the elasticity with zero loyalty/ disloyalty, to be minus one. Elasticities of this order of magnitude for all mail categories are in line with those found for first- and second-class mail separately in various micro-econometric demand studies, including the ones surveyed by Cazals and Florens (2002).

Figure 1: Customer behavior (market share model): the switching function

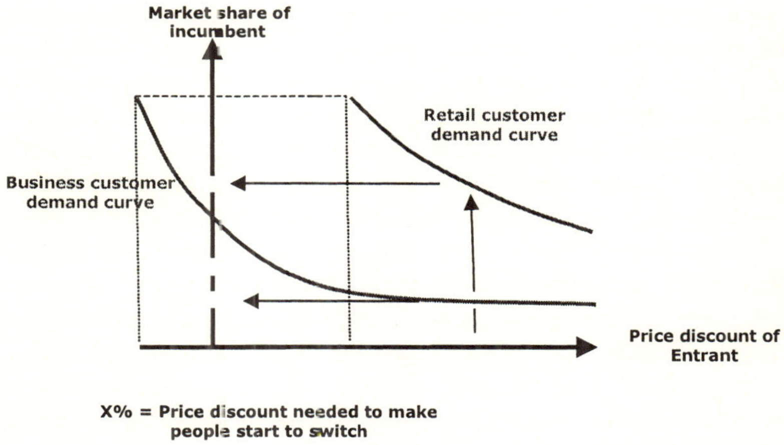

2.2 Cost Model

The detailed cost model is presented in the Appendix (see footnote 1). It is an activity-based, bottom-up cost model. Scale is defined as Mail Delivery Density and as the number of mail items distributed per person and per year. Population size is explicit in the model but is not considered to be significant as an additional size factor.

Services offered require an *upstream activity*, which includes collecting, sorting and transporting, and a *downstream activity*, comprising delivering. Our downstream model has the structure defined by Cohen and Chu (1997), including street model complements from Jasinski and Steggles (1977), and further examined by Roy (1999). Postal activity is divided into *collection*, *sorting* of the mail, *in-office delivery*, representing the sequencing of the mail into delivery routes, and *street delivery*. Street delivery is decomposed into *route travel*, *delivery access time*, and *load time*. Route travel represents walking or driving along the route without stopping at delivery points and is the main part of fixed costs associated with the delivery network. Its cost is estimated in an endogenous way by the model, which, in its first step, assumes that the operators decide their delivery networks in terms of geographical coverage. Delivery access time represents the additional time to access the delivery points. Load time represents the time to place the mail in the mail receptacle at the delivery point. Route travel has four modes: *Foot Delivery* (cost depending only on the number of hours worked by the carrier), B*icycle Delivery* (cost depending on the hours worked by the carrier and maintenance of the bicycle), *Park & Loop Delivery* (cost depending on the hours worked by the carrier and the maintenance of the car) and *Car Delivery* (cost depending on the hours worked by the carrier and of the maintenance of the car).

Each country is divided in two delivery zones, *urban*, *U*, and *rural*, *R*. Each of these delivery areas is characterized by *a grouping index*, g_z, representing *the number of delivery points per route stop*; e.g., within an urban area *z*, the average number of apartments in a building. It is assumed that every apartment (delivery point) is occupied by exactly one household. The *2003 Urban and Rural Areas* report from the United Nation's Department of Economic and Social Affairs[2] provides the population living in these two zones for each country, according to the national definition. The definition of these zones varies from country to country.

Two operators, the *incumbent*, *I*, and the *entrant*, *E*, collect, sort and deliver the mail. The entrant decides the *geographic coverage* (gc^E_z) *of its delivery network in the zone* z. The entrant's collection network is proportional to its delivery network. The entrant has the ability to hire self-employed labor. These differences will produce substantial savings in the entrant cost structure. The hourly labor cost for the incumbent has been taken as the average labor cost of the *transport, storage and communication* section (NACE code I, see Paternoster 2002). We assume a self-employed labor cost ratio of 50%.

The fact that each delivery area is characterized by different *grouping indices* representing *the number of delivery points per route stop* has a considerable impact on the unit costs of delivery. The cost ratio between rural and urban zone delivery precisely depends on this grouping index. This cost differential is the driving element in the cream-skimming mechanism. One assumes the average value of this parameter in the rural zone to be

---

2 http://www.un.org/esa/population/publications/wup2003/2003urban_rural.htm

equal to 1, as a standard. This is interpreted that in the rural zone one stop corresponds to a one-family house. The average value of this parameter in the urban zone of the USA was estimated at 2.12 in 1993 (see Appendix). For the cases reported here , the value will be fixed at 2.

The United States is the largest-scale country and will be considered as standard for the calibration. The costs of a number of other countries are derived from a set of country-related variables (some of which are interpolated to complete the data set where specific country data are missing). The variables are the following: Total population (United Nations' Department of Economic and Social Affairs, Population Division 2003), Percentage population in urban area (United Nations, 2003), Employed labor cost Nace I (Eurostat, Labour cost survey 2000), Mail delivery density (UPU 2000), Share of retail customers' mail in the market (Postal, assumed to be 50%), Delivery frequency (UPU 2000), Average household size, Percentage of foot, bicycle, Park & Loop and car delivery modes (postal), Exchange rate in purchasing power parity (1993 PPP compared to USD; for USA PPP in 2003 data compared to euro zone), Consumers price index (Eurostat), and Self-employed cost ratio (assumed to be 50%). Medium-scale countries can be compared to countries such as Norway and France. Italy and Greece are examples of small-scale countries.

Table 1: Route Characteristics

Delivery points per route	
Urban area	488
Rural area	469
Grouping index	
Urban area	2
Rural area	1
Delivery speed (km/h)	
by foot	4
by bicycle	15
by car	35
Distance between stops (m)	
by foot	20
by bicycle	100
by car	300
Delivery frequency per week	
Incumbent	6
Entrant	3
Entrant starting geographic coverage	
Urban area	10%
Rural area	0%

Our cost function is also calibrated with the USA population size and the number of mail items per person and per year as standard (=1). The statistical data about the United States Postal Service (USPS) are taken from Cohen and Chu (1997). The values for the parameters are in Table 1.

2.3 The Entrant's Behavior and Dynamic Tariff Modeling

The USO is one of the major exogenous factors of the model we have constructed. We have defined the following USO to be imposed on the incumbent by the regulator. This definition of the USO reflects the major question considered in this study, namely the impact of economies of scale on the postal market in different countries. The USO comprises six elements:

1. Daily distribution frequency (six times)
2. Constant quality ($J + 1$, $J + \mathrm{n}$ arrival percentage, which is related to frequency)
3. Distribution to all customers (retail and business, dense and non-dense zones)
4. Tariff uniformity for end-to-end and for access
5. Affordable tariffs (interpreted as keeping its present value for the retail customers)
6. Availability (interpreted to be existence)

The entrant is given the objective of being the first market player, and, therefore, to deliver as much mail as possible without endangering its competitiveness. We assume that the entrant will invest in a delivery network, as long as the resulting average cost to deliver mail is lower than the incumbent's access tariff. Between two periods, the entrant has the ability to decide whether or not to extend its delivery network. The new geographic coverage of the entrant's delivery network will be equal to the collected market share of the previous period. This justifies the financial losses made by the entrant during the first periods of entry. This amount approaches zero when investment approaches zero and the cumulative amount to be financed corresponds to the value of the capital needed to establish the business. Note that once the network has been extended, it is not possible to reduce it afterwards. The entrant does not have any USO.

The Entrant's behavior is determined by the following parameters, which can be changed in the calibration:

1. Uses self-employed labor at 50% of the national hourly wage cost
2. Distributes three times per week (different in quality level than incumbent)
3. Has same cost structure and parameters as the incumbent does
4. Has different full-cost tariffs for dense and non-dense zones
5. Invests, initially, in a delivery network with the view to distribute in the dense zones at a 10% share of the corresponding volume of the dense zone
6. Has access to the incumbent's delivery network for the residual volume, namely the volume above the bypass potential
7. Invests in own delivery network, according to yearly decision made in advance, an amount capable of delivering the excess amount collected

above the existing bypass capacity of the preceding period, but only if the resulting average delivery cost is lower than the incumbent's access tariff

Access pricing of the incumbent is set at an access-cost level, the average variable delivery cost, including fixed costs, plus a standard overhead. It would be possible to make a sensitivity analysis of the model results using a wider range of well-known access pricing methods.

The demand model is solved using the iterative method. The model iterates until finding the market equilibrium. The competitive process starts with the entry of the competing operator, and the dynamic tariff determination works as follows: The tariffs are set and fixed prior to the iterations. The demand of the previous period is the starting point. All tariffs are based on cost. The incumbent takes the total cost incurred in the previous period, without the eventual cost of entrant re-injection, and considering the total mail volume collected in the previous period. The unit cost obtained is set as the incumbent tariff of the current period. Like its end-to-end tariff, the incumbent's access tariff equals its unitary distribution cost, including the fixed costs and a general-expense margin. The incumbent satisfies tariff uniformity, both for end-to-end and for access. As the mail volume re-injected by the entrant is not predictable by the incumbent, it has been chosen to compute its end-to-end tariffs, only taking into account its end-to-end volume. The unit cost of the entrant is computed likewise but including the cost of re-injecting its mail in the incumbent's network and considering all mail volume collected.

The following summarizes our basic approach:

1. The starting point is the monopoly situation: volumes per customer per zone.
2. Cost-based tariffs are fixed by incumbent, according to the assumed scope of the USO (and the equations as defined in Appendix).
3. The entrant determines the volume objective, unit costs following the cost model, tariffs per zone, volume delivery objective and corresponding investment in the network.
4. Cream-skimming competition is simulated by the demand model. For each demand class and each zone, cost-driven price competition adjusted by assumed loyalty parameters determines the total demand in the market and the share of it obtained by I and E (see the Appendix for details). Some iteration is required, since prices are set to average costs in each zone, given the delivery systems in place for I and E and the access prices.
5. When market equilibrium is reached, the mechanism yields end-of-year volumes and market shares.

6. On the basis of the volume and market share results, the entrant determines the extent of his distribution network for the next period. Mail remaining that had to be re-injected with a higher access tariff through access to the incumbent's network.
7. New cost-based tariffs are set.
8. Return to (4) above if the percentage variation of one tariff or demand is higher than the convergence criterion.
9. Continue until market equilibrium is reached.

The calculation is complete after ten periods (i.e., ten years), but typically marginal tariff changes become smaller than a convergence tolerance criterion after five or six periods.

The model describes the entrant taking away mail through bypass: this erodes the incumbent's economies of scale in those zones in which bypass occurs. Such erosion changes the volumes delivered by each operator in each zone and this determines average costs of both operators, according to the zones in which bypass occurs. The zone-specific impact of the entrant erodes delivered incumbent mail volumes, first in the dense, low-cost zones, thereby diminishing economies of scale and leading to a tariff increase in view of restoring eroded profitability. In the case of the entrant, the increase in volume decreases unit cost because of increased economies of scale, but the increase of volume in less dense zones increases unit costs.

3. RESULTS

First we summarize the assumptions made to calibrate our model about the standard country, the customers, the competitor and the access regulation. The number of items delivered per person and per year and for the population of the USA, the standard country, is introduced. The other parameters are listed in Table 2.

With these values the process converges. In a second step, the values of the mail delivery density are introduced corresponding to fixed intervals of fifty. In this way results corresponding to the sizes of most countries are obtained: in each case the model follows a process whereby scale obviously decreases for the incumbent with the entry of the competitor, and when the incumbent loses dense urban zones because of its high uniform tariffs. The entrant benefits both from increasing scale and from cream skimming the relatively denser delivery urban zones, lost by the incumbent. In Table 3, countries are placed in view of the corresponding scales. After five or six periods the model always converges, but the period reported is period ten. One should not interpret these results as final values for the countries since the calibration of the data used should still be considerably improved. However the large variations obtained in the results are of interest to understand the impact of economies of scale. Some of the basic findings evident from Table 3 are the following.

Table 2: Country, Delivery and Market Specifications

Country specification	
Urban area	80%
Rural area	20%
Household size	2.6
Hourly labor cost	20.32€
Delivery parameters	
Delivery frequency per week	
Incumbent	6
Entrant	3
Grouping index	
Urban area	2
Rural area	1
Delivery mode (in percent of routes)	
by foot	6%
by bicycle	0%
by park & loop	39%
by car	55%
Postal market parameters	
Market elasticity	-0.3
Proportion of retail customers	50%
Customer loyalty	
Retail	20%
Business	-10%
Substitution elasticity	
Retail	-0.75
Business	-1.25
Displacement ratio	1
Competitor behavior	
Freelance labor cost reduction	50%
Delivery network starting coverage	
Urban area	10%
Rural area	0%
Pricing regulation	
Access pricing	Accessed cost method
Tariff uniformity	
Incumbent	Yes, including on access tariff
Entrant	No

Given **economies of scale**, which differ country by country, when the market opens, what are the long term impacts of the chosen USO on tariffs, volumes and market shares? These variables of the converged model result are shown following the number of mail items per person and per year.

Unit cost variation under monopoly (unit cost = 1 for USA): the cost curve is non-linear. While the medium-sized countries, Norway and France, have a 4% to 10% handicap, Italy and Greece have a 135% to 276% cost handicap.

Table 3: Unit Delivery Costs as a Function of Mail Density

Country	USA	Norway	Austria France	Finland UK	Belgium	Ireland Japan	Portugal	Spain	Italy	Greece
Mail density	1.00	0.85	0.70	0.55	0.45	0.30	0.25	0.20	0.15	0.08
Unit costs	1.00	1.04	1.10	1.19	1.29	1.56	1.71	1.95	2.35	3.76

This is graphically presented in Figure 2.

Figure 2: Standardized Unit Cost as a Function of Scale

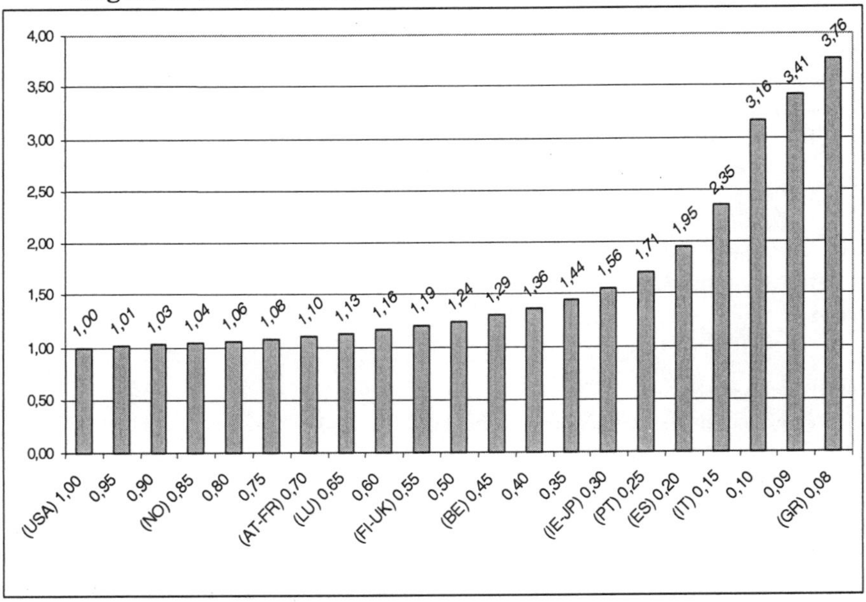

Horizontally: Number of items per person per year (scale), arranged in decreasing order with USA as standard (USA = 1.0)

Total volume variation after competition (volume after competition convergence divided by volume under monopoly): The impact of competition on reduced average tariffs and on general communication market substitution is positive and stronger in small-scale countries, the extremes varying from a 10% increase to a 25% increase.

Incumbent tariff variation after competition (incumbent tariff after competition convergence divided by incumbent tariff under monopoly): The tariff increase to be introduced by the incumbent as a consequence of the arrival of the entrant, the loss of size and of less costly urban zones, with relatively important results, but much more so in small-sized countries: the USA tariff increases by 53% while the French one increases by 72%, and the Italian by 126%. This corresponds to the price the retail customer has to pay for the USO after the opening of the market.

Entrant urban and rural tariffs after competition (entrant tariff in urban and rural areas after competition convergence divided by incumbent uniform tariff under monopoly): The discount given by the entrant is considerably higher in small-sized countries than in large-sized countries. Extremes vary between 66% and 39% in the urban zones and 36% and 29% in the rural zones; this also reflects a relatively more aggressive behavior of the entrant in the urban zones of the small countries. Scale is less significant in rural zones because higher unit costs prevent the entrant to capture market share.

Entrant collection market shares on retail customers after competition: Retail markets are more difficult for the entrant to capture than business markets are because of the loyalty of the customers and their lower tariff sensitivity. Again, though, small size is relatively more dangerous for the incumbent. In the smallest country, the entrant captures 48% of the retail market share for a 66% discount in the urban zones and a 36% discount in the rural zone versus 29% in the USA for a 39% discount in the urban zones and a 29% discount in the rural zone.

Entrant collection market shares on business customers after competition: Business markets are much easier for the entrant to capture than retail markets are because of the readiness of business clients to switch to the entrant and their higher tariff sensitivity. In small-sized countries, 100% market share goes to the entrant. In the larger ones, the incumbent only keeps 14% of the business market. Clearly the business market structure has been turned upside down with the assumptions made. It is understandable, because, from a methodological point of view, when in reality a 50% market share is reached, there is a duopoly: it is not possible to keep the same model assumptions about the market structure and parameters. For example, a game theory model should be used. The entrant's assumed fixed labor cost discount would not be realistic. No further study was done on this.

Financial resources needed by entrant to invest in its delivery network after competition (entrant's cumulative profit or account balance after competition divided by entrant's revenue after competition): It is interesting to see the impact of the market opening on the financial resources needed by the entrant to invest in a delivery network. It is obviously related to the importance of the delivery network created to take over a high delivery market share from the incumbent. In Italy, this amount corresponds to 105%

of the entrant's sales, in France 30%, in the USA only 18%. These results are acceptable in terms of the financial cost generated.

Table 4: Model results per country scale

Country	USA	Norway	Austria France	Luxemburg	Finland UK	Belgium	Ireland Japan	Portugal	Spain	Italy	Greece
Mail density	1.00	0.85	0.70	0.65	0.55	0.45	0.30	0.25	0.20	0.15	0.08
Unit cost	1.00	1.04	1.10	1.13	1.19	1.29	1.56	1.71	1.95	2.35	3.76
Volume variation	110%	111%	113%	114%	116%	117%	119%	120%	121%	122%	125%
Incumbent tariff variation	153%	160%	172%	177%	188%	193%	206%	212%	219%	226%	240%
Entrant urban tariff level	61%	59%	57%	57%	55%	52%	48%	46%	43%	40%	34%
Entrant rural tariff level	71%	71%	70%	70%	70%	69%	68%	67%	66%	65%	64%
Collect market shares entrant on retail	29%	31%	34%	35%	37%	38%	41%	42%	44%	45%	48%
Collect market shares entrant on business	86%	89%	94%	96%	98%	99%	99%	100%	100%	100%	100%
Financial needs entrant	18%	23%	30%	33%	40%	49%	68%	78%	90%	108%	146%

Legend:
Mail density = standardized mail density under monopoly where mail density =1 for USA scale
Unit cost = standardized unit cost under monopoly where unit cost =1 for USA scale
Volume variation = (Total Market Volume after Entry/(Total Market Volume under Monopoly)
Incumbent tariff variation = (Tariff I after Entry)/(Tariff I under Monopoly)
Entrant urban tariff level = (Tariff E in Urban after Entry)/(Tariff I uniform under Monopoly)
Entrant Rural tariff level = (Tariff E in Rural after Entry)/(Tariff I uniform under Monopoly)
Collect market shares entrant on retail customers = Market shares E Retail after Entry
Collect market shares entrant on business customers = Market shares E Business after Entry
Financial needs entrant = - (Cumulative Profit entrant after Entry)/(Revenue E after Entry)

Second, we show a number of variables of the converged model results according to **two dimensions:** not only **the scale,** corresponding to the number of mail items per person per year, but also the **mail delivery density** given by the average urban grouping index. The average rural grouping index is assumed to be 1. The urban grouping index, the number of delivery points per route, typically depends on the urban structure of the country, the number and size of apartment buildings compared to one family houses. It appears to be a crucial factor in the results obtained for unit costs. One finds a cost per item going from the cheapest (=1) for the standard country, the USA, to 1.31 in France and to 3.35 in Italy.

For the USA, with an urban grouping index equal to 2, this unit cost in standardized terms goes from 1 to 0.90 where the urban grouping index equals 6. For Italy, this standardized unit cost goes from 2.35 with the urban grouping index equal to 2 to 1.69 where the urban grouping index equals 6. These unit cost decreases are important to understand, as they influence both the impact of liberalization in the different countries as well as the scale.

Figure 3 shows the unit cost impacts of scale and density (the urban grouping index) obtained from model results.

Figure 3: Unit costs as a function of scale (mail delivery density) and the urban grouping index

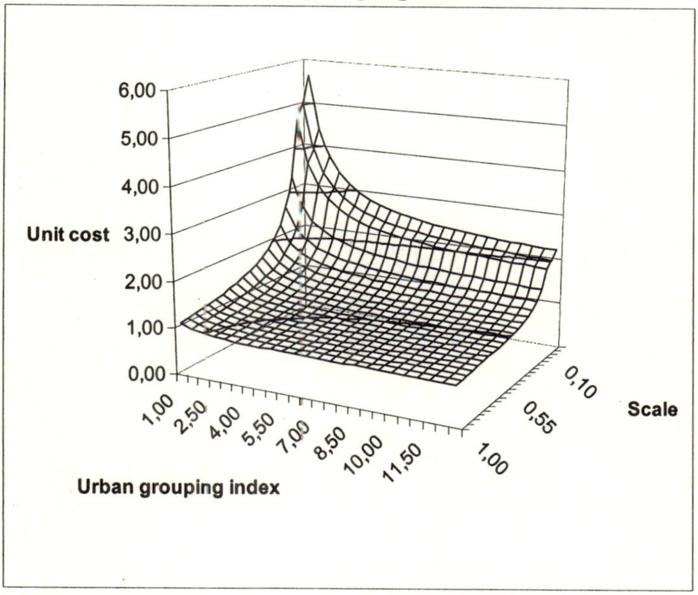

The higher the urban grouping index, the stronger the position of the incumbent. Figures 4 and 5 show the market shares obtained by the entrant in the retail and business markets. A higher urban grouping index makes the competitive position of the entrant more difficult and results in lower market shares: In the USA, 29% of the retail market goes to the entrant with $g_U = 2$ and 24% with $g_U = 6$. In the USA, 86% of the business market goes to the entrant with $g_U = 2$ and 77% with $g_U = 6$.

Figure 4: Entrant's retail market share as a function of scale and the Urban Grouping Index

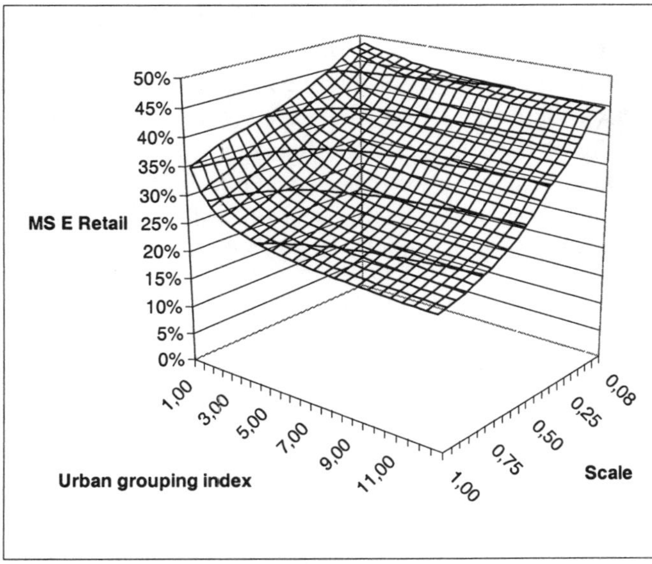

Figure 5: Entrant's business market share as a function of scale and the Urban Grouping Index

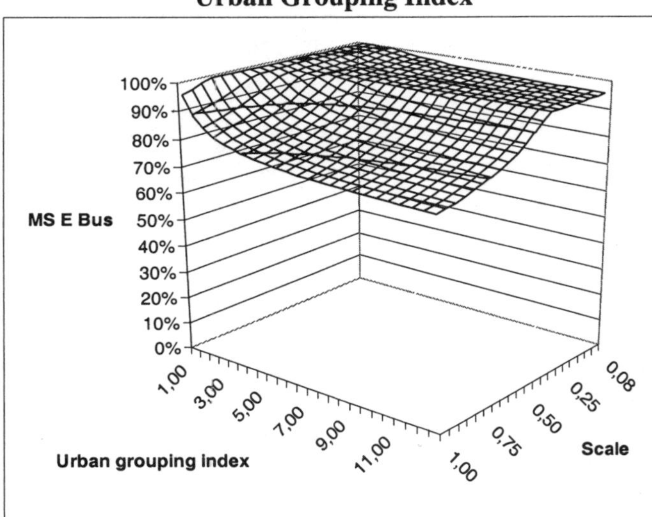

Let us now find another set of model solutions for a situation in which the incumbent must keep the tariff at the pre-opening level. The idea is to estimate the financial requirement needed by the incumbent to deliver the USO, under the assumption that the entrant captures an increasing part of the market share, starting with the dense mail delivery zones. Compared to the first set of model solutions, the entrant modifies its behavior and decides not to take any market share as soon as the unit costs go beyond the incumbent's tariff. The results are shown in Figure 6 below. We show (for the case where the grouping index equals 2) the financial compensation required by the Incumbent for breakeven operations as a percentage of revenues plotted against the number of pieces per person per year in the urban zone for the countries studied (those listed in Table 3 above), with the latter arranged in decreasing order of pieces per person per year along the horizontal axis. The USA requires a financial compensation of 17% of its revenues, while Italy requires 60%. Clearly, the result shows scale is a crucial factor.

Figure 6: Financial needs of Incumbent at constant tariffs in % of own sales

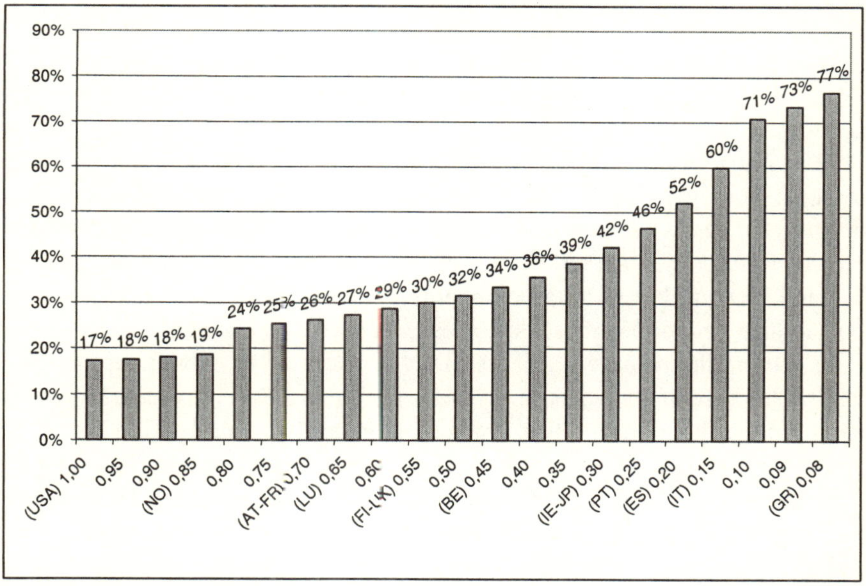

Horizontally: Number of items per person and per year in decreasing sequence, relative to the USA (USA = 1.0)

The numerical results are sensitive to many factors, which can be modified in the model:

1. Demand sensitivity: sigma, epsilon, the matrix of loyalty parameters *X* and price elasticities
2. The USO definition, including uniform tariffs for retail/business
3. Labor factor cost discount of the entrant (50% used in the current calibration)
4. Distribution frequency/service quality of the Entrant(s)

5. Retail customer ratio
6. Access tariff rules (uniform access costs were used in the calibration for the current results)

4. CONCLUSIONS

In a previous contribution (d'Alcantara and Amerlynck 2004), we demonstrated with a calibration approach that the order of magnitude for the financial losses caused by liberalization are a function of the scale of the postal operator. This study confirms the importance of economies of scale on financial viability of the postal operator using a bottom up collection and delivery cost model. Crucial determinants of the results were the constant tariff and the assumed annual fixed cost of the USO of the incumbent. These results imply that, in a liberalized situation, finances in the form of government subsidies or a compensation fund, necessary to cover the USO, should be a function of the economies of scale present in each respective country.

The impact of opening the postal market will depend on scale for many reasons: not only because of the total market tariff elasticity of the total demand for mail, which will determine the total volume of mail demanded, but also from the market shares of each operator, corresponding to the asymptotic equilibrium of the competitive market, since these market shares will reduce economies of scale for each operator and increase average unit costs. In addition, because of its direct connection to economies of scale, mail delivery density, in both urban and rural zones, is a crucial factor in determining the impact of liberalization in each country. The impact of competition is larger in small-scale and more urban countries. The increase in tariff to be decided by the incumbent for survival, resulting from market opening, is larger in small-scale and urban countries. The entrant will need more financial resources there to bypass the incumbent's network.

The financial loss of the USO provider, if not allowed to increase its tariff, is also larger in small-scale and urban countries than in large-scale and rural ones. A high urban grouping index lowers delivery costs. The incumbent's uniform tariff constraint implies a lower tariff in rural delivery zones and makes it more difficult to compete for the entrant. Therefore, the entrant abandons its rural network almost everywhere, except when the urban grouping index is small (relatively high delivery costs).

REFERENCES

Bernard, S., R. Cohen, M. Robinson, B. Roy, J. Toledano, J. Waller and S. Xenakis. 2002. "Delivery Cost Heterogeneity and Vulnerability to Entry." In *Postal and Delivery*

Services: Delivering on Competition, edited by M.A. Crew and P.R. Kleindorfer. Boston: Kluwer Academic Publishers.

Bradley, M., and J. Colvin. 1995. "An Econometric Model of Postal Delivery." In *Commercialization of Postal and Delivery Services*, edited by M.A. Crew and P.R. Kleindorfer. Boston, MA: Kluwer Academic Publishers.

Casals C., M. de Rycke, J. P. Florens, and S. Rouzaud. 1997. "Scale Economies and Natural Monopoly in the Postal Delivery: Comparison Between Parametric and Non Parametric Specifications." In *Management Change in the Postal and Delivery Industries*, edited by M.A. Crew and P.R. Kleindorfer. Boston, MA: Kluwer Academic Publishers

Cazals, C. and J-P. Florens. 2002. "A Comparison between Cross-Section and Dynamic Data." In *Postal and Delivery Services: Delivering on Competition*, edited by M.A. Crew and P.R. Kleindorfer. Boston: Kluwer Academic Publishers

Cohen, R.H., and E.H. Chu. 1997. "A Measure of Scale Economies for Postal Systems." In *Managing Change in the Postal and Delivery Industries*, edited by M.A. Crew and P.R. Kleindorfer. Boston, MA: Kluwer Academic Publishers.

Cohen, R., M. Robinson, G. Scarfiglieri, R. Sheehy, V. Visco Comandini, J. Waller, S. Xenakis. 2004. "The Role of Scale Economies in the Cost Behavior of Posts", to be published in the Proceedings of Wissenschaftliches Institut für Kommunikationsdienste GmbH (WIK), 8th Köenigswinter Seminar on *Regulating Postal Markets - Harmonised Versus Country Specific Approaches*, February 16-18, 2004.

d'Alcantara, G. and B. Amerlynck. 2004. "Financial Viability of the Universal Postal Service Provider under Uniform and Cost related Tariffs." In *Competitive Transformation of the Postal and Delivery Sector*, edited by M.A. Crew and P.R. Kleindorfer. Boston, MA: Kluwer Academic Publishers.

Jasinski, K. and E. Steggles. 1977. "Modelling Letter Delivery in Town Areas." *Computers and Operational Research* 4: 287-294.

Paternoster, A. 2002. *Labour Costs Survey 2000: Member States*, Statistics in Focus, Population and Social Conditions, Theme 3, 7/2003, Eurostat, European Communities.

Panzar, J. 1991. "Is Postal Service a Natural Monopoly?" In *Competition and Innovation in Postal Services*, edited by M.A. Crew and P.R. Kleindorfer. Boston, MA: Kluwer Academic Publishers.

Rogerson, C. and W. Takis. 1993. "Economies of Scale and Scope and Competition in the Postal Services." In *Regulation and the Nature of Postal Delivery Services*, edited by M.A. Crew and P.R. Kleindorfer Boston, MA: Kluwer Academic Publishers.

Roy, B. 1999. "Technico-economic Analysis of the Costs Outside Work in Postal Delivery." In *Emerging Competition in Postal and Delivery Services*, edited by M.A. Crew and P.R. Kleindorfer. Boston, MA: Kluwer Academic Publishers.

Chapter 4

On the Use of Cost Functions in the Assessment of the Impact of Liberalization on Postal Universal Service Burden

*Restricted versus Flexible Specifications**

Stefano Gori, Emiliano Piccinin, Simona Romito, and Gennaro Scarfiglieri
Poste Italiane

1. INTRODUCTION

The drive toward a single market for network industries (e.g. telecom, gas, electricity and postal services) in Europe has brought about in the past decades a series of directives aimed at creating more integrated and liberalized markets. Such a liberalization path has led to sector-specific legislation taking into account the peculiarities of the different markets (i.e., the revenue, cost, technology and nature of the services being provided).

Great emphasis has been placed on the concept of Universal Service provision, which encompasses ubiquity, quality and affordability of service, and on the cost stemming from its provision, with special emphasis on its financial sustainability in a liberalized environment.

Postal services are currently the network industry in which the financial sustainability of Universal Service is under scrutiny. The reserved area for incumbents has been progressively reduced over the last eight years, and studies are now being carried out on behalf of the European Commission in

---

* The views expressed in this paper are those of the authors and do not necessarily represent the opinions of Poste Italiane.

view of furthering the liberalization process, which might involve the full liberalization of the market.[1]

In recent years, two conflicting views about Universal Service sustainability in the context of liberalized postal markets have emerged. The first one, envisaged in the report to the European Commission by the consulting firm NERA (2004), claims that, "provided access to delivery networks is granted where necessary [in the European Union], we believe that the scope for competition in postal services is substantial." The second view was summarized in a recent paper (Cohen et al. 2004) by, among others, members of the United States postal regulator, the Postal Rate Commission (PRC). It claims that in some cases "special protections may have to be introduced along with liberalization …to avoid graveyard spirals …as entry could make the [Universal Service Obligation (USO)]'s geographical cross subsidies impossible to maintain."

We believe that the feasibility of a liberalization process – in the context of the USO – goes hand in hand with the flexibility of cost structures; i.e., the possibility for the incumbent to cut costs proportionally with the loss of market share to competitors. The higher such a flexibility, technically referred to as "cost elasticity to output," the higher the chance for the incumbent to adapt its cost structure to the new lower levels of activity. The lower the flexibility, the higher the chance for the incumbent to end up in an unsustainable financial situation, putting Universal Service provision at risk.

Both the NERA (2004) and the Cohen et al. (2004) studies provide cross-country empirical evidence that confirm their individual claims. And yet, the economic and econometric choices supporting their claims diverge: NERA (2004) uses a function that assumes constant elasticity of cost to output (known as Cobb-Douglas (hereafter CD)), while Cohen et al. (2004) use a function in which there is a positive fixed cost and cost is a linear function of output, i.e., where elasticities vary with output.

Overall the two studies represent a dichotomy from the point of view of: 1) the microeconomic analysis (constant versus varying cost elasticities), and 2) the econometric model (CD versus linear specification), which necessarily leads to 3) relevant regulatory implications (a uniform liberalization path versus a country specific liberalization path).

Both studies are based on a methodological approach that verifies *a posteriori* to what extent empirical data are consistent with their model, while in this paper we try to encompass the two studies through the use of a more general economic and econometric approach. In fact, both studies use specific cost functional forms (CD and linear) in order to fit empirical data.

---

[1] Particularly relevant is the late 2005 study of the impact of liberalization on Universal Service.

These impose restrictions upon the production structure. Instead, we use a flexible functional form, the Translog, which can be statistically tested to verify whether the underlying cost structure is consistent with more restrictive specifications (such as the CD).

Our results suggest that postal cost structure is characterized by increasing cost elasticity as volume per capita increases: therefore, cost structures are more rigid in low per capita volume countries. In these countries, volumes and revenues lost as a consequence of full liberalization may seriously jeopardize the financial viability of the Universal Service provider. The relevant policy implication of these findings is that full liberalization may not be the social optimum in these countries.

The paper is organized as follows: Section 2 introduces generalities about cost functions, Section 3 analyzes CD and Translog cost functions and their properties, Section 4 presents data we use in the empirical analysis, Section 5 the comparative results, Section 6 proposes a new approach towards cost elasticity estimation, and Section 7 summarizes the conclusions.

2. MICROECONOMIC FOUNDATIONS OF COST FUNCTIONS

In the modeling of the production behavior of firms under constrained optimization it is possible to use a production, or a cost, function. The cost function is the single most useful tool for studying the economic behavior of a firm, because it can handle multi-output productions, while summarizing all economically relevant information about the technology of the firm (Varian 1992, 49-63).

Let us consider a simple cost function[2]: if prices of input x_i are w_i, the total cost for the firm is:

$$C = \sum_{i=1}^{n} w_i x_i \tag{1}$$

The objective of the firm is to minimize costs (with an ultimate goal of maximizing profit) at the input prices w_i to produce a given level of output y:

$$C(y,w) = \min_{x_i \geq 0} \left[\sum_{i=1}^{n} w_i x_i : f(x) \geq y \right] \quad \text{or} \quad C(y,w) = \sum_{i=1}^{n} w_i x_i(y,w) \tag{2}$$

---

[2] The presentation will refer to a single-output production case but is easily extended to the multi-output case.

with $x_i(y,w)$ as a demand function for input x_i.

A cost function must satisfy six regularity conditions (Gravelle and Reese 1996, 197-229):

1. A cost function cannot be negative: $C(y,w) > 0 \quad \forall w > 0, y > 0$; hence, it is not possible to produce an output with no cost.
2. Input prices are monotonic: $w_1 \geq w \Rightarrow C(y,w_1) \geq C(y,w)$; if input prices rise, the production cost cannot decrease.
3. Output is monotonic: $y_1 \geq y \Rightarrow C(y_1,w) \geq C(y,w)$; if total output increases, total costs cannot decline, thus marginal costs must be non-negative. However, the average cost curve can increase or decrease with output.
4. Continuity and concavity in respect to w must be such that, if $\overline{w} = kw_1 + (1-k)w_2$, with $0 \leq k \leq 1$, then $C(y,\overline{w}) \geq kC(y,w_1) + (1-k)C(y,w_2)$; as the price of an input increases, the proportional increase in total costs should be no higher because of the substitution among inputs.
5. $C(y,w)$ must verify Shephard's Lemma (1970), which states that a small increase in the price of an input increases cost by an amount equal to the use of the input itself: $\dfrac{\partial C(y,w)}{\partial w_i} = x_i$.
6. $C(y,w)$ must be linear homogeneous in prices: $C(y,kw) = kC(y,w)$, $k > 0$. Linear homogeneity ensures that the cost-minimizing bundle does not change if all prices are multiplied by the same positive scalar, and, therefore, maintains the basic property that only the ratios of the inputs' prices affect the allocation of inputs (Segal 2003).

3. ECONOMETRICS OF COST MEASUREMENT

The econometric approach to production and cost estimation involves establishing a statistically significant relationship between output or costs and the factors determining them. As emphasized by the NERA (2004) study, a major advantage of the econometric approach (in cost estimation) is that it is able to control simultaneously for the impact of the different factors on costs and quantify the scope of the impact. The applied economics literature provides several functions, such as CD, Leontief and CES (constant elasticity of substitution). However, these functions place *a priori* restrictions on either the substitution possibilities among the factors of production or on scale economies.

In the area of producer behavior models, the classic paper by Arrow et al. (1961) called into question the restriction, inherent of the CD model, that all elasticities of factor substitution are equal to one. Since then several flexible functions have been developed, which allow substitution to be unrestricted, i.e., not even constant. The first of these was a Translog function developed by Berndt and Christensen (1972).

The most common restricted cost function, the CD, and the most popular flexible cost function, the Translog, and their respective properties, are presented below.

3.1 The Cobb-Douglas Cost Function

The CD cost specification can be expressed as:

$$C(y,w) = A\prod_{i=1}^{m} {y_i}^{\alpha_i} \prod_{i=1}^{n} {w_i}^{\beta_i} \tag{3}$$

or equivalently as:

$$\ln C(y,w) = \alpha_0 + \sum_{i=1}^{m} \alpha_i \ln y_i + \sum_{i=1}^{n} \beta_i \ln w_i \tag{4}$$

with $\sum_{i=1}^{n} \beta_i = 1$ (ensuring linear homogeneity).

Such a function satisfies all of the above mentioned regularity conditions, e.g., since the Hessian matrix of $C(y,w)$ is negative, the concavity of cost to prices is satisfied. Furthermore, as for the cost elasticity to output i, we have:

$$\frac{\partial C / C}{\partial y / y_i} = \frac{\partial \ln C}{\partial \ln y_i} = \alpha_i \tag{5}$$

If $\sum_{i=1}^{m} \alpha_i < 1$, there are increasing returns to scale: as the output increases, the cost increases at a slower pace. If $\sum_{i=1}^{m} \alpha_i > 1$, there are decreasing returns to scale: as the output increases, the cost increases at a faster pace. If $\sum_{i=1}^{m} \alpha_i = 1$, there are constant returns to scale.

Once α_i are determined, the elasticity of cost to output is constant at any output level, so that the share of the cost of the single output from the total cost remains constant; that is:

$$S_i = \frac{\partial C / C}{\partial w_i / w_i} = \frac{\partial \ln C}{\partial \ln w_i} = \beta_i \tag{6}$$

3.2 The Translog Cost Function

A flexible cost function can be defined as a second-order Taylor expansion, i.e., a local approximation to any cost functional form. The two general flexible functional forms are the general quadratic form and the Translog function (hereafter TL).

The TL function is the most frequently used flexible function in empirical work. The function was developed as a means of approximating the CES production function by Kmenta (1967) and has remained for decades the most popular and, by some experts, in particular Guilkey et al. (1983) and Greene (1993), the most reliable of several available alternatives.

A cost function, $C(y, w)$, can be articulated as a TL in the following terms:

$$\begin{aligned}\ln C(y,w) &= \alpha_0 + \sum_{i=1}^{m} \alpha_i \ln y_i + \sum_{i=1}^{n} \beta_i \ln w_i \\ &+ \frac{1}{2} \sum_{i=1}^{m} \sum_{j=1}^{n} \alpha_{ij} \ln y_i \ln y_j \\ &+ \frac{1}{2} \sum_{i=1}^{m} \sum_{j=1}^{n} \beta_{ij} \ln w_i \ln w_j \\ &+ \sum_{i=1}^{m} \sum_{j=1}^{n} \gamma_{ij} \ln y_i \ln w_j\end{aligned} \tag{7}$$

To satisfy linear homogeneity and symmetric Hessian matrix regularity conditions, the following restrictions must be imposed:

$$\sum_{i=1}^{n} \beta_i = 1, \ \sum_{j=1}^{n} \beta_{ij} = 0, \ \sum_{j=1}^{n} \gamma_{ij} = 0, \ \beta_{ij} = \beta_{ji} \text{ and } \alpha_{ij} = \alpha_{ji}. \tag{8}$$

Furthermore, the TL can be restricted to a consistency region where the function satisfies the above mentioned regularity conditions (monotonicity and concavity: Kjell et al. 1998).

A TL can easily be tested statistically to verify whether the underlying cost structure corresponds to more restrictive specifications.

A function is homothetic if it is separable in output quantities and input prices, i.e., if the elasticity of cost to output is independent of the price of the inputs.

In order to display this characteristic, a TL must satisfy the following condition:

$$\gamma_{ij} = 0 \tag{9}$$

A function is homogeneous of a constant degree if it is homothetic and displays a constant elasticity of cost to output. Homogeneity requires separability and that the elasticity of cost to output is independent of the level of output. In order to display homogeneity, a TL must satisfy the following conditions:

$$\gamma_{ij} = 0\,,\ \alpha_{ij} = 0 \tag{10}$$

A function is Cobb-Douglas if it is homogeneous and displays unitary elasticity of substitution among inputs. In order to display Cobb-Douglas characteristics, a TL must satisfy the following conditions:

$$\gamma_{ij} = 0\,,\ \alpha_{ij} = 0\,,\ \beta_{ij} = 0 \tag{11}$$

4. DATA

To conduct the empirical analysis on a sample comparable with that used by NERA (2004), we have collected data from European Union (EU) Member States. Belgium and Luxemburg were excluded as available information would not have allowed a reasonable estimate of postal business finances. No accession country has been considered in the data collection phase, because the ten countries that recently joined the EU have very different characteristics compared to the original Member States. This might have further complicated the estimation without improving it.

Indeed, NERA's report concluded similarly.[3] Furthermore, in presenting the results, NERA used coefficients applicable to the EU15 original Member States and added special terms that captured the incremental effect attributable to the "New Member State" status.

The time span covered by our data and that of the NERA sample is the same, i.e., from 1998 to 2003. Data was collected for the following variables: Mail Operating Cost, Postal Volumes, Unit Labor Cost, Number of Households, and Percentage of Population living in urban areas.

Data were not available for each variable in each country for every year. When necessary and possible we have interpolated or extrapolated data. The end result is a sample of sixty-three observations summarized in the following table:

Table 1: Country and year for sample data

Countries	2003	2002	2001	2000	1999	1998
Austria	√	√	√	√	√	√
Denmark	√	√	√	√	√	√
Finland	√	√	√	√	√	√
France	√	√	√	√	√	√
Germany	√	√	√	√	√	√
Greece	√					
Ireland	√	√	√	√	√	√
Italy	√	√	√	√	√	
The Netherlands	√	√	√	√	√	√
Portugal		√	√	√	√	√
Spain				√	√	√
Sweden			√	√	√	√
United Kingdom		√	√	√		

Consistent with the NERA (2004) procedure, data containing financial information (Mail Operating Cost and Unit Labor Cost) have all been reported at 2003 constant prices values[4] and also have been converted into as

[3] "The categorization that NERA believed would be most relevant was that between the EU15 and the ten countries which, when we started this study, were about to join the EU. First, these countries generally have lower volumes of mail per households. Second, these countries have had very much lower unit wage cost in the postal sector then countries in the EU15. Third, in the period covered by our data set (1998 to 2003) these countries where in the transition period to EU membership, in most cases towards a very much more market-based environment than the one in which they had operated in the past." NERA 2004, 121.

[4] Source: OECD Economic Outlook 76 database

comparable a form as possible through PPP 2003.[5] Original data were mainly in Euros but, when necessary, the average yearly exchange rate[6] has been used to convert other currencies into Euros.

As for the specific variables, data collection was as follows.

1. Mail Operating Cost was collected, when available, from annual reports, web sites, and the operators' answers to our questions. In some cases, however, we estimated mail costs consistent with mail volumes. In countries where we had no information on the division of total costs between letters, parcels, express and financial services we made broader assumptions, based on mail revenue divisions. When mail volumes or mail operating costs included parcels, we used Universal Postal Union (UPU) data on parcels volumes and calculated the implicit letter mail volumes or parcel operating cost.
2. Mail Volumes were collected from annual reports and web sites.
3. Unit Labor Cost data, defined as staff costs (including social security payments and pension costs) divided by the number of full time equivalent postal workers, were taken from NERA (2004, table 5.5).[7]
4. Number of Households was determined by the same method used by the NERA study: we used the variable "Dwelling Stock" that includes only conventional (permanent) dwellings, whether occupied or not.[8] For some countries we did not have the values for the whole period. In these cases we have collected data from the national statistical body of each country.
5. Percentage of Population living in urban areas data was collected from United Nations Economic Commission for Europe and integrated with data available on the Eurostat and World Urbanization Prospect web sites. [9]

5. RESULTS

The first cost function estimated is the same as the one estimated by NERA (2004). Specifically, we have estimated a CD function that expresses the log of mail operating cost (LNC) as a function of the log of output

---

5 Source: OECD, http://www oecd.org/std/ppp/

6 Source: The Italian Office of Exchange Rates, http://www.uic.it

7 The Netherlands data were not available on the NERA study, so we have determined the average labor cost using data from the annual report of the Dutch postal operator.

8 Source: the database model of Statistical Division UNECE/STAT- United Nations Economic Commission for Europe

9 Sources: UNECE/STAT, http://www.unece.org/stats/stats_h.htm; World Urbanization Prospect, http://www.un.org/esa/population/unpop.htm; Eurostat, http://europa.eu.int/comm/eurostat/

(LNVOL) and unit labor cost (LNW), controlling for the influence of two environmental variables, number of households (DW) and the percentage of people living in urban areas (URBAN). The estimation method was Ordinary Least Squares (OLS). The estimated equation is:

$$LogC = \alpha_0 + \alpha_1 * Log(Volumes) + \beta_1 * Log(Wage) + \delta_1 * Log(Households) + \delta_2 * (Urbanization\ Rate) + u_i, \quad (12)$$

where the u_i terms follow the Classical assumptions of the OLS. The results are presented in Table 2.

Table 2: Cobb-Douglas results

Regressor	Coefficient	Standard Error	T-Ratio	P-value
Constant	-1.6334	0.30454	-5.3633	[.000]
LNVOL	0.59205	0.029287	20.2156	[.000]
LNW	0.97248	0.075644	12.8561	[.000]
DW	0.40881	0.023901	17.1043	[.000]
URBAN	-0.12699	0.17619	-0.72075	[.474]
R-Bar-Squared .98921		F-statistic F(4, 58) 1421.5 [.000]		

As in the NERA (2004, table 8.1) case, regressor coefficients have the expected sign and are very significant, as probability values are well below 0.05.[10] The R-Bar-Squared is extremely high indicating a good model fit. The F-statistic can be used to test the probability that all the explanatory variables are simultaneously zero (i.e., they do not explain cost variance) and in our case it is close to zero. Results show also that the coefficient of the log of output is very similar to that obtained by NERA (2004): 0.59 versus a NERA estimate of 0.65. This coefficient is important, as it is a measure of what NERA defines as "Economies of Density", i.e., cost elasticity to output. In our estimation, through the use of a CD function, a 10% increase in volumes on a fixed network increases cost by 5.9%, while NERA estimated 6.5%, which is very close. Note also that, while the coefficient of the number of households is very similar in the two estimations (0.41 versus 0.40 in NERA), both being of the expected sign, the estimates of the other two coefficients are different. Thus, a first general result of our empirical

[10] The only exception is the significance of URBAN, which, although having the expected sign, has a large Standard Error.

analysis is that by using a CD functional form to fit our data sample we obtain results fairly close to those of NERA (2004).

The second cost function we have estimated is the TL case (i.e., the general, unconstrained version) of the CD estimated in the first model. The estimated equation is:

$$\begin{aligned} LogC = \alpha_0 &+ \alpha_1 * Log(Volumes) + \alpha_{11} * Log(Volumes) * Log(Volumes) \\ &+ \beta_1 * Log(Wage) + \beta_{11} * Log(Wage) * Log(Wage) \\ &+ \gamma_{11} * Log(Volumes) * Log(Wage) + \delta_1 * Log(Households) \\ &+ \delta_2 * (Urbanization\ Rate) + u_i \end{aligned} \tag{13}$$

where the u_i terms follow the Classical Assumptions of the OLS. The results are given in Table 3.

Table 3: Translog results

Regressor	Coefficient	Standard Error	T-Ratio	P-value
Constant	4.7161	6.2189	0.75835	[.451]
LNVOL	-0.31761	0.55109	-0.57634	[.567]
LNVOLVOL	-0.045991	0.029609	-1.5533	[.126]
LNW	-0.45786	2.8743	-0.1593	[.874]
LNWW	-0.37954	0.71272	-0.53252	[.597]
LNVOLW	0.3478	0.13312	2.6127	[.012]
DW	0.44641	0.024952	17.8905	[.000]
URBAN	-0.15692	0.16895	-0.92877	[.357]
R-Bar-Squared .99076		F-statistic F(7, 55) 950.3322 [.000]		

The R-bar squared and the F-statistics for this regression are very high, indicating that these variables do explain the variability of cost and that the specified model fits very well with the available data. However, the t-ratios are low, possibly indicating a high degree of variability in the estimates. The possibility of the variables not having enough explanatory power with respect to the dependent variable must be ruled out, due to the high values of the R-bar-squared and the F-statistics. Rather, it must be attributed to the presence of multicollinearity among variables, i.e., a high linear correlation coefficient among them. This, in turn, is the result of the fact that, like in any other TL construction, variables are derived one from the other.

It is crucial at this point to verify whether the appropriate statistical tests allow a researcher to restrict this TL function to a CD. In fact, if the statistical tests allowed the passage to the restricted form (e.g. CD), then the shortcomings associated with the Translog would be overcome: As we have shown in our first cost function, the restricted form produces coefficients with high significance. Otherwise, if the tests are not passed, the bias introduced by forcing a restricted form will counterbalance the advantages. It is important to stress that, if in a regression t-ratios are low but this is due only to multicollinearity (as indicated by a high R-bar-squared), the value of the coefficients is still the correct one, so that "doing nothing" is probably the correct way of proceeding. As pointed out by Studenmund (1997, 278):

> It is often best to leave an equation unadjusted in the face of all but extreme multicollinearity. Such advice might be difficult for beginning researchers to take, however, if they think that it's embarrassing to report that their final regression is one with insignificant t-scores. Compared to the alternatives of possible omitted variable bias or accidentally significant regression results, the low t-scores seem like a minor problem.

Therefore, "doing nothing" may well be the advised option when low t-ratios are due to multicollinearity. However, in our case, rather than an option, it has turned out to be a necessity, since none of the statistical tests for the passage to restricted forms have been passed, as all probability values are below the critical value of 0.05. The actual results are shown in the following tables:

Table 4: Test for homotheticity

Test		Ratio	Prob
$H_0 : \gamma_{11} = 0$	F(1, 55)	6.826	[.012]

Table 5: Test for homogeneity

Test		Ratio	Prob
$H_0 : \gamma_{11}, \alpha_{11} = 0$	F(2, 55)	4.6418	[.014]

Table 6: Test for Cobb-Douglas

Test		Ratio	Prob
$H_0 : \gamma_{11}, \alpha_{11}, \beta_{11} = 0$	F(3, 55)	4.2421	[.009]

Therefore, our second and third general results are that a TL is the appropriate functional form to fit our data sample and that statistical tests allowing it to pass to any restricted form are not satisfied.

In this respect, it must be noted that NERA (2004) ruled out the possibility of using a TL because "the results were not satisfactory…as many terms were highly correlated with the variables of volume and wages" but, surprisingly, they did not mention any hypothesis testing, which would have been the correct procedure to put forward. The absence of hypothesis testing has relevant policy implications: constant elasticity of cost means that one policy fits all countries, while varying elasticity of cost may signal the need to adopt different liberalization policies for different countries.

6. TOWARDS A NEW APPROACH

The third cost function we have estimated is an attempt to control for the relevance of per capita postal consumption as a determinant of the variability of cost. In fact, the Cohen (2004) study, under very general assumptions, shows that this variable can be used to predict very closely the unit cost of postal administrations in industrialized countries. To this end, we have built a variable that represents the yearly average number of postal items received, through the ratio of the log of volumes to the log of households. The function we have estimated is:

$$\begin{aligned} LogC = {} & \alpha_0 + \alpha_1{*}Log(Volumes) + \alpha_{11}{*}Log(Volumes){*}Log(Volumes) \\ & + \beta_1{*}Log(Wage) + \beta_{11}{*}Log(Wage){*}Log(Wage) \\ & + \gamma_{11}{*}Log(Volumes){*}Log\ (Wage) \\ & + \delta_1{*}Log(Volumes)/Log(Households) + u_i \end{aligned} \qquad (14)$$

where the u_i terms follow the Classical assumptions of the OLS.

The results are:

Table 7: New Translog results

Regressor	Coefficient	Standard Error	T-Ratio	P-value
Constant	-15.8548	12.7226	-1.2462	[.218]
LNVOL	1.6194	1.1198	1.4461	[.154]
LNVOLVOL	0.21566	0.058275	3.7007	[.000]
LNW	6.7235	5.9707	1.1261	[.265]
LNWW	0.032023	1.5356	0.020853	[.983]
LNVOLW	-0.73081	0.27003	-2.7064	[.009]
LNVOLDW	-0.040047	0.0071838	-5.5746	[.000]
R-Bar-Squared .95866		F-statistic F(6, 56) 240.5975 [.000]		

As in previous cases the R-Bar-Squared and the F-statistics are very high, showing a very high significance for the overall regression. The coefficients still suffer from the consequences of multicollinearity, but it should be noted that their significance is much higher than in the previous case.

We then checked whether it was possible to pass from the generic TL specification to a more restrictive one. Once again all of the tests rejected the correctness of adopting a more restrictive specification, as shown in the following table:

Table 8: Test for homotheticity

Test		Ratio	Prob
$H_0 : \gamma_{11} = 0$	F(1, 56)	7.3244	[.009]

Table 9: Test for homogeneity

Test		Ratio	Prob
$H_0 : \gamma_{11}, \alpha_{11} = 0$	F(2, 56)	11.1538	[.000]

Table 10: Test for Cobb-Douglas

Test		Ratio	Prob
$H_0 : \gamma_{11}, \alpha_{11}, \beta_{11} = 0$	F(3, 56)	8.2944	[.000]

Starting from the results of our regression we have then measured cost elasticity for each country belonging to the sample, according to the following formula:

$$Cost\ Elasticity = \frac{\partial Log(Cost)}{\partial Log(Volumes)}$$

$$= \alpha_1 + \alpha_{11} Log(Volumes) \qquad (15)$$

$$+ \gamma_{11} Log(Wage) + \delta_1 \frac{1}{Log(Households)}$$

Finally, we have regressed the obtained elasticities over volume per capita. As shown below, the interesting finding of this regression has been the presence of increasing cost elasticity as volumes per capita increase.

Clearly, our model is a first attempt and opens up the way for further research. The average cost elasticity is relatively high compared with those of previous studies and the reasons for this divergence should be investigated in the future.

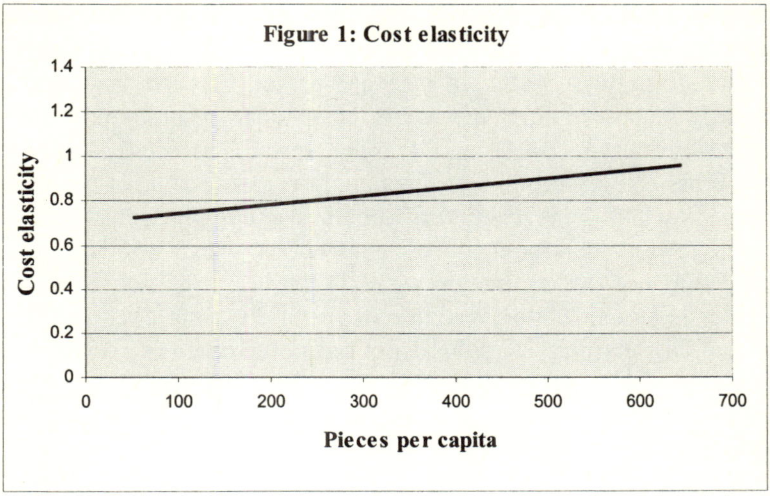

A variable and increasing cost elasticity to volumes has relevant economic and policy implications. The higher such flexibility, the higher the chance for the incumbent to adapt its cost structure to the new lower levels of activity (assuming entrants do capture market share in the liberalization process). The lower the flexibility, the higher the risk to the incumbent that it will end up in an unsustainable financial situation, putting Universal Service provision in jeopardy. Thus, the adoption of differentiated liberalization paths whose extent is set in accordance with cost elasticities should be carefully taken into consideration by policy makers.

7. CONCLUSIONS

Postal services are currently the network industry where the issue of Universal Service financial sustainability is under scrutiny. In recent years, two conflicting views about Universal Service sustainability in the context of liberalized postal markets have emerged, represented by two studies, one provided by NERA (2004) to the European Commission and another by members of the United States postal regulator and of postal operators (Cohen et al. 2004). A key element of divergence between these views is the flexibility of cost structures, i.e., the possibility for the incumbent to cut costs proportionally with the loss of market share to competitors. Both the NERA (2004) and the Cohen studies provide cross country empirical evidence that support their claims.

In this paper we have tried to address the diverging microeconomic and empirical issues raised by the two studies. Our results suggest that: 1) a flexible functional form satisfactorily fits the data; 2) postal cost structure is characterized by a varying, and not a constant, elasticity of cost to output, as none of the statistical tests allowing movement from an unrestricted flexible functional form to a restricted one are passed; 3) had we used a CD (restricted) functional form we would have found results similar to those presented by NERA (2004); and 4) much research is needed on finding a reliable cross country postal cost function. In response to this latter point, we estimated a wider generalization of previous works that constitutes only a first step towards this goal, opening up new research perspectives. Two major findings of this estimation were: 1) the high significance of volume per capita as an explanatory variable of postal cost, and 2) the presence of increasing cost elasticity as volume per capita increase. The relevant policy implications of these preliminary findings is that the adoption of differentiated liberalization paths should be taken into consideration more carefully by policy makers.

REFERENCES

Arrow, K.J., H.B. Chenery, B.S. Minhas and R.M. Solow. 1961. "Capital-Labor Substitution and Economic Efficiency." *Review of Economics and Statistics 43*(no. 3, August): 225-247.

Berndt, E.R. and L.R. Christensen. 1972. "The Translog Function and the Substitution of Equipment, Structures, and Labor in U.S. Manufacturing, 1929-1968." *Journal of Econometrics 1*(1): 81-114.

Cohen, R., M. Robinson, G. Scarfiglieri, R. Sheehy, V. Visco Comandini, J. Waller, and S. Xenaxis. 2004. *The Role of Scale Economies in the Cost Behavior of Posts.* Paper presented at the Wissenschaftliches Institut für Kommunikationsdienste GmbH (WIK), 8th Köenigswinter Seminar on Regulating Postal Markets Harmonised versus Country Specific Approaches, February 16-18, in Köenigswinter , Germany.

Guilkey, D., K. Lovell, and R.C. Sickles. 1983. "A Comparison of the Performance of Three Flexible Functional Forms." *International Economic Review 24*(no. 3, October): 591-616.

Greene, W.H. 1993. *Econometric Analysis*. New York, NY: Macmillan Publishing.

Gravelle, H., and R. Rees. 1996. *Microeconomics*. London, UK: Longman Publishing.

Kmenta, J. 1967. "On Estimation of the CES Production Function." *International Economic Review 8*(June): 180-189.

NERA. 2004. *Economics of Postal Services: A Report to the European Commission DG-MARKT.*

Salvanes, K.G. and Sigve Tjøtta. 1998. "A Note on the Importance of Testing for Regularities for Estimated Flexible Functional Forms." *Journal of Productivity Analysis 9*: 133-143.

Segal, D. 2003. "A Multi-Product Cost Study of the U. S. Life Insurance Industry." *Review of Quantitative Finance and Accounting 20*(no. 2, March): 169-186.

Shephard, R. 1970. *The Theory of Cost and Production*. Princeton, NJ: Princeton University Press.

Studenmund, A.H. 1997. *Using Econometrics: A Practical Guide*. Reading, MA: Addison Wesley Educational Publishers.

Varian, H.R. 1992. *Microeconomic Analysis*. International student edition. New York, NY: Norton.

Chapter 5

Questioning the Monopoly-Supported Postal USO in Developing Countries

Charles Kenny
The World Bank

1. INTRODUCTION

The monopoly-supported universal service obligation (USO) is usually defended on the grounds that the monopoly allows for cross-subsidy in letter services that in turn allows universal access to a service of great importance to all. This paper argues that letter delivery (as opposed to other services that may be provided by post offices) is not in universal demand in poor countries, that the size of the market in developing countries is such that USOs could not be met under the monopoly model, and that the monopoly carries heavy costs for sector development and consumer welfare. It proposes in the place of the postal USO a competitive approach involving universal access to a range of services that poor people have a need to access.

2. THE THEORY OF THE MONOPOLY-SUPPORTED USO

The European Union (EU) defines universal service to post in the following terms:

> "Member States shall ensure . the permanent provision of a postal service of a specified quality at all points in their territory at affordable prices for all users... the universal service provider(s) guarantee(s) every working

day... one delivery to the home or premises of every legal or natural person...[for] postal items up to two kilograms [and] postal packages up to 10 kilograms..."

Traditionally this USO has been linked with monopoly provision of services. The theory of the monopoly-provided USO can be summed up as follows. Mail delivery to the home is an important public service to which all should have access. For many low-volume or difficult to service users, however, the market price of mail services would be prohibitively high. In order to serve those customers while allowing for a financially sustainable postal network, a monopoly operator charges a single stamp rate for nationwide delivery, with "profits" made from the delivery of mail to high-volume areas and users (where the price of the stamp is higher than the cost of delivery) used to support "loss-making" delivery operations for low-volume areas and users.

Many developing countries have adopted the monopoly USO model for their own postal systems. They do not tend to have USOs as stringent as the EU's, while in many cases, the obligation is rather imprecise or undefined, it rarely involves home delivery, for example.[1] Nonetheless the general model holds that a provider will ensure one-price letter delivery across its national territory, funding loss-making routes with the revenues that it is guaranteed from a monopoly, over delivery on profitable routes.

The model has proven itself practicable (if not necessarily efficient) in many wealthy countries. However, its application in developing countries is likely to be inefficient, impractical, and inequitable. This paper argues that a narrow, mail-based USO should be abandoned and the postal sector opened to competition. In place of a mail-only USO, governments in developing countries might decide to extend access to a bundled range of services widely in demand by urban, rural, poor, and rich alike. These services might be delivered through post office franchises.

3. DO WE WANT A USO FOR LETTER DELIVERY IN DEVELOPING COUNTRIES?

Is there evidence that everyone in developing countries needs (or would use) letter delivery to a nearby post office every business day or every week? It is perhaps worth asking this question in the context of severe resource constraints that mean the goals of universal primary education or universal access to basic health care are far from being reached. To begin to answer

---

[1] Even within the EU there remain questions as to the nature of the USO—does it demand a uniform tariff, for example?

that question it is worth looking at demand for letter services in poor countries. Overall demand for postal services is very closely correlated with the size of an economy. Smaller (poorer) economies see lower mail volumes (letters per capita). Countries with a GDP per capita (PPP) of below $1,000 see mail volumes of below 1 per person per year—compared with closer to 100 per person in countries with a GDP per capita of above $5,000 (Table 1).

Constraints on demand due to inadequate or absent service delivery will be one factor behind low levels of use, but by far the dominant cause is demand related to income—as suggested by the results of both postal reform and extending access. Under reform, service quality improves, and this tends to increase use of the postal sector. But the usage increase, while impressive, is in the region of perhaps 100 percent, rather than the 10,000 percent differences between low income and high income country usage rates. For example, successful postal reform in Tanzania saw mail volumes increase from 0.87 to 1.26 letters per capita per year during 1994-98. This post-reform figure remains only approximately 0.17 percent of US per capita mail volumes. Regarding extended access, there does not seem to be a relationship between the percentage of the population covered by postal service and letter volumes per capita in developing countries—extending network access, like improving network quality, does not apparently uncover significant unmet demand for postal services (Kenny and Qiang, 2004). In Tanzania, for example, only an average of about 0.4 percent of the population within the catchment area of a post office visit that office each week (PWC, 2004).[2] Furthermore, it appears that demand for postal services is dropping in developing countries including Tanzania as alternate means of communication –especially mobile phones—spread (Souter et. al. 2005).

Table 1: Postal Structure and Development

Indicator	Average for GDP Per Capita (PPP) Band		
	<$1,000	$1,000-$5,000	>$5,000
Letters/Capita	0.9	4.6	98.4
Total letter volume	10m	634m	2,468m
KM2 per post office	4,702	1,738	458

Source: Calculated from UPU and World Bank data, 2001

The average consumer in poorer countries sends perhaps one letter per year—and we know that the great majority will neither send nor receive a single letter.[3] In particular, there is little demand from businesses (which account for as much as 80 percent of letters sent [Lee, 2004]) to deliver mail to the poorest in developing countries. This is because most do not have

2 In Malawi, the figure is closer to 0.2 percent.

3 At least not through the network captured by Universal Postal Union (UPU) statistics.

services that require billing (fixed telephony or electricity, as it might be), and they are hardly an attractive target for companies in terms of marketing purposes. If the majority of the population never receives a letter in the poorest countries, and might not even after significant postal reform, the concept of universal service is somewhat nonsensical.[4]

Overall, there does not appear to be significant demand for universal postal services even if they were to be a financially viable option. If universality was achieved using some sort of subsidy mechanism, given the direction of most mail towards business and the wealthy, this would constitute a regressive intervention.

4. COULD A LETTER USO BE SUPPORTED IN DEVELOPING COUNTRIES UNDER THE MONOPOLY MODEL?

Even if developing countries desire a monopoly-supported USO model, it appears unlikely to be sustainable in many countries. This section argues that developing countries, with small postal markets, cannot benefit from significant scale economies (which in turn drives up the per-unit cost of letter delivery) and face far more complicated environments in which to deliver mail. These factors combined mean that even a limited USO model supported by monopoly rights would be unsustainable in many low-income countries.

By and large (and with obvious exceptions such as China and India), absolute mail volumes in poorer countries are very small. Total mail volumes in countries under $1,000 GDP per capita average 10 million pieces, compared to 2.5 billion pieces in countries with a GDP per capita of over $5,000 (Table 1).

This is a problem because it is clear that there are fixed-costs associated with mail systems that make low-volume environments high-cost ones as well. Scale economies, due to factors such as automated processing and (more significantly) scale effects in delivery, will be one factor behind a relationship between total mail volumes and letters delivered per employee. Countries that see delivery of fewer than one million letters a year deliver on average below 4,000 letters per employee per year (such countries include Cape Verde, with just over 939,000 letters delivered by a staff of 3,947). This compares to over 60,000 per employee in countries where over 100 million letters are delivered a year (South Africa delivers nearly 2 billion

4 Regarding home delivery, many (most) poor and rural people do not live in households with a recognized address, so they could not receive mail if it were being delivered.

letters using a staff of 74,000, for example). This is a 15-fold productivity difference (Table 2).

Table 2: Cross-country Evidence of Scale Economies in Posts

	Average for Total Letters Delivered Band		
	<1,000,000	1,000,000 – 100,000,000	>100,000,000
Letters/Employee	3,587	20,693	59,739

Source: Calculated from UPU and World Bank data, 2001

We can see the impact of scale economies by looking at estimates based on the United States Postal Service (USPS) on the costs of a US-style service in lower volume environments with lower input costs. The USPS will differ dramatically from post offices in low-income countries in terms of automation, route topography, mix of mail, efficiency, and the nature of its customer base—and so the model is only an approximation (made less accurate by a weak proxy for input costs—that of GDP per capita). Thus, while Cohen et. al. show that their model inspired by USPS cost and demand conditions functions reasonably well in estimating features of rich country postal operations, it is very likely that the adjusted model will become increasingly inaccurate as a guide when looking at low-income postal markets (Cohen et. al. 2003).[5]

Figure 1: Estimated Relationship between Costs per Letter and Volumes

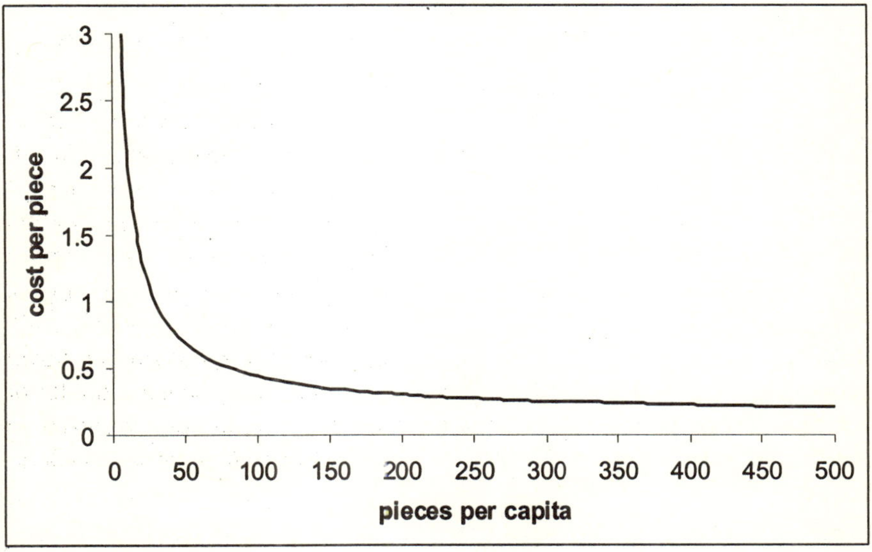

[5] It is also worth noting that UPU data suggests a fairly weak relationship between GDP per capita and total costs per letter (Kenny and Qiang, 2003). This is somewhat surprising

With those caveats, Figure 1 shows what the Cohen study and World Bank data suggests the cost of delivering a letter under United States' USO standards would be in countries with lower mail volumes. As the number of pieces per capita drop below 100 per year, costs rise dramatically above 50 cents per piece.[6] This may help to explain why the United States only mandated universal home delivery in 1958, when letter volumes were above 300 per person per year (Campbell, 2004).

Table 3: Estimated Cost Breakdown of USO Services in Low-volume Environments

	Cost of Mail/Piece ($)		
	Pieces/Capita		
	10	5	1
Mail processing	0.06	0.07	0.16
Transportation	0.02	0.03	0.07
Window service	0.08	0.13	0.34
Delivery	0.76	1.19	3.06
Other	0.44	0.69	1.77
Total	**1.36**	**2.11**	**5.40**

Table 3 suggests the breakdown of costs of US-quality delivery per piece of mail in a system of universal service in an economy where postal volumes per capita were low, based on data from the Cohen et. al. study and the World Bank. As seen, delivery would be expensive—over $0.76 per letter in a country with mail volumes of 10 per capita. Even without delivery to the door, the costs are high—over $0.60 per letter.[7] Again, this data only suggests orders of magnitude, as it is based on United States' postal data adjusting for input costs. Nonetheless, the point is clear that letter delivery becomes considerably more expensive in low-volume environments, not merely because of rising costs of home delivery, but also because the other

given evidence that poor countries in general see low volumes and so will benefit less from economies of scale, it may reflect lower quality and extent of service..

6 Cohen et. al. Provide data on prices for US quality USO at United States' input costs for various levels of letters per capita. To adjust (at a high level of approximation) for differing input costs (primarily labor), I used a regression of GDP PPP per capita on letters/capita to obtain estimates for GDP per capita at various levels of letters/capita. I then multiplied the "unadjusted" Cohen estimates by (predicted GDP)/(United States GDP) in order to get output cost estimates adjusted for input costs.

7 The procedure to adjust the Cohen et., al. estimates was similar to the above except that GDP per capita at a given level of letters per capita was calculated from a regression of GDP on letters per capita for countries with letters/capita values within 50 percent of those listed in the table (0.5 to 1.5 letters, 2.5 to 7.5 letters and 5 to 15 letters per capita respectively).

fixed costs of the network are divided up amongst far fewer stamp purchases.

Making this problem more acute is the fact that a far greater percentage of people in developing countries are difficult-to-serve rural customers—69 percent in low income countries (World Bank, 2002). Income density—an important measure of "demand for postal services per square kilometer"—is far lower in developing countries than rich ones—$39,000 per square kilometer in sub-Saharan Africa as compared to $658,000 in high income countries, for example (Kenny, 2002). Both of these factors suggest that even less stringent USO may cost more to meet in poor countries than they would in rich ones.

There is significant variation in all of these numbers—some postal operations are more efficient than others, and deliver more mail at the same level of GDP than others (Kenny and Qiang, 2003). At the same time, some developing countries have very large, very dense postal markets where delivery is far more straightforward. Nonetheless, the point remains that, in most cases, even less stringent USOs would be more expensive per letter than similar obligations in the developed world.

At the same time, the profitable market that might provide cross-subsidy is far smaller, because of the lower level of urban development and large corporate customers. Even in some of the richer, most population-dense, urbanized developing countries about 90 percent of routes are loss-making.[8] This situation would be worse in countries where only 31 percent of the population were urban (the case in low income countries). The cost and complexity of service delivery, especially in small markets, will help account for the fact that post offices frequently make significant losses in the developing world. Forty-five percent of countries with GDP per capita under $5,000 see revenues below operating expenses (let alone total costs).

Putting revenues and indicators of costs together suggests the scale of the problem. Low income countries will average total postal volumes lower than 10 million pieces a year. Imagine a national stamp price of $0.12.[9] National stamp revenues will bring in perhaps $1 million per year. This to support delivery to a population of about 10 million that is 69 percent rural and on average receives less than one piece of mail per year.

The price of delivery and the related costs of USOs can be significantly reduced from the hypothetical levels of Table 3, if the USO is realistically defined. In the United States, mail that is nondelivered (i.e., is picked up at post offices) accounts for 21 percent of volume and 67 percent of profits. In Italy, similar numbers are 14 and 42 percent. In other words, avoiding

---

8 Traffic is measured by revenues, in this case. British Postal Consultancy Service (2002)

9 Trinidad and Tobago's price after rate increases.

home-delivery dramatically reduces costs even in high-density environments such as in the United States (Cohen et. al. 2003). Abandoning home delivery for a post office box system (the de jure case in many developing countries, the de facto case in the majority) will greatly reduce costs. This has been done in Senegal, for example, where home delivery carries an extra charge. Asymmetric charging can also help raise revenues for rural access. Historically, differential charges applied in now developed markets (Ogilvie, 1893).[10] Furthermore, "universal service" does not have to mean uniform service. In Tanzania, the quality of service is lower in rural areas, with service only provided to post offices, and at D+4 rather than D+1.

Nonetheless, even differential service targets—as part of the USO—are unlikely to reduce costs to allow for a sustainable universal service, to be provided at a reasonable stamp price, on the back of the few profitable urban routes in low income countries. And so monopoly provision, even if efficiently run, would not garner the profits large enough to come close to true universal service provision.

5. AGAINST THE LEGAL MONOPOLY

The two arguments for monopoly provision in the postal sector are first, that the sector is a natural monopoly and second, that the monopoly allows for cross-subsidy of services and so meeting USO targets.

The first argument is not a good argument, even in theory, for enforcing a de jure monopoly. There are some reasons to believe that mail delivery services may be "natural monopolies". Mail delivery involves a network, and network externalities suggest that one big network serving a given area will, other things being equal, be more efficient than many overlapping networks providing the same service. In other words, if you leave a competitive postal market alone, it is likely that one competitor will eventually win out to control all, or nearly all, of the market.[11] But this is no justification for legally enforcing that market from the start. Quite the opposite. It is a reason to regulate the market so that a monopolist cannot take advantage of its position to squash competition and over-charge consumers for services.

Furthermore, the "natural monopoly" characteristic of posts, especially in developing countries, may be oversold. We don't need to go too far from basic posts to see that competition can work even in "networked postal" industries in developing countries—DHL, FedEx, and UPS demonstrate that

---

[10] The United States only introduced one-price delivery in 1885 (Campbell, 2004).

[11] This appears to be the case in a number of developed markets where competition has been introduced—for example, New Zealand and Sweden.

competition can flourish where obligations are few and prices can reflect costs. And in a developing country environment where total postal volumes are frequently too small to garner significant scale economies, the disadvantages of market fragmentation are reduced. Some evidence for this is that in many developing countries, a number of large postal users legally or illegally bypass postal incumbents to provide their own services (in Jordan, legal competitive operators provide services to deliver bills despite serious handicapping, for example).[12]

The widespread bypassing of incumbent postal providers in developing countries suggests that, whatever theoretical advantages to scale may exist, the inefficiency of monopoly government provision frequently outweighs them. Monopolies are likely to be less efficient and less innovative than competitive environments because the usual incentive to innovation and efficiency (the fear of losing customers to the competition) is not there. When the monopoly in question is operated by the government, the "theoretical" problem becomes even more acute. There is not even the incentive to maximize the quality and efficiency of services at a given cost in order to maximize (revenues and) profits. In an environment where the government monopoly service provider provides an inefficient, poor quality service, any "natural monopoly" advantages it should theoretically enjoy are frequently outweighed by the fact that post offices have not been run on sound business practices.

Not only are staffing levels frequently very high, but pricing structures suggest that the post office may even be losing money delivering to what should be their more profitable urban and corporate customers. A monopoly will only produce revenues to fund the obligation if prices, somewhere, are higher than costs. Given under-pricing and inefficiency of many government-controlled postal monopolies, this may be a questionable assumption. Furthermore, service standards remain low—as suggested by the low level of trust in many postal operators. In response to the question "do you trust your country's postal system sufficiently to have a friend mail a small package worth $100 to you?" the average survey respondent in Nigeria scored the post office 1.7 on a scale of one (no trust at all) to seven (complete trust) (Kirkman et. al. 2002).

In these cases, not only is an enforced monopoly failing to deliver on the promises of the USO, but by stifling competition, it is forcing people who use the post to use an inefficient and unreliable service provider. For little or

---

12 Andress (2004) notes that many developing countries with weak or non-existent regulatory structures nonetheless see more competition than developed countries with aggressively pro-competitive regulators such as the United Kingdom (where Royal Mail still has a 99.75 percent market share).

no benefit to the rural poor, the monopoly penalizes the corporate and urban user.

The practical example of the benefits of competition over monopoly in a poor developing country is Tanzania, where during a process of liberalization, total mail volume increased from 0.87 letters/capita/year to 1.26 between 1994 and 1998 as we have seen, while the postal company moved from loss to profit, and the number of post offices increased (UPU and WB 2001). Prices did rise closer to costs, but consumers were clearly willing to pay higher prices for a higher quality of services.

The second argument for monopoly is that if it were removed in a system of one-price national mail delivery, competitors unburdened by a USO would serve those routes that cost less to service than the price of a stamp. Once competitors had "skimmed the cream" from these routes, the USO provider would be left serving only (or mainly) routes that were unprofitable at the current stamp price, leading to significant losses.

The cross-subsidy under monopoly model is a terribly inefficient way to support access targets, however. We have seen that it is unlikely to provide significant resources in low-volume, largely rural low-income economies. Conversely, in rich countries, the value of the monopoly will be too much, in that the net cost to provide universal service will be very small while the benefit of operating free of competition is considerably larger. Even in (rural, low population-density) New Zealand for example, the incumbent is providing USO services without monopoly and at no additional cost to the government, suggesting that the benefits of universal coverage to the incumbent outweigh any costs even in a competitive environment.[13] The justification for the monopoly is not practicable, the results of the monopoly, especially in developing countries, are poor-quality services and low use.

It should be noted that the monopoly USO model can work. Trinidad and Tobago has increased household delivery to approximately 95 percent of population under the model, for example, as part of a broader reform effort that saw postal volumes and revenues approximately double, and quality of service and consumer satisfaction increase.[14] But even in a wealthier developing country, where the postal monopoly is delivering a comparatively efficient cost-related service and where the monopoly-funding-USO model may plausibly raise sufficient funds to support rural access, it is still far from the best way of extending access.

---

[13] Furthermore, such efforts appear fraught with computational difficulties in practice and require far more market intelligence than most developing country regulators (where there are such regulators) possess (see Andress, 2004).

[14] Walsh, 2001 and comments by Juan Ianni. From 1999 to 2003 delivery times fell from one week to nearly all mail by D+2, volumes rose 133 percent, revenues 75 percent, and a consumer satisfaction index went from 50 percent to approximately 85 percent.

6. A NEW MODEL

At the moment in many countries the "postal sector" is seen as coterminous with the post office. It may be more constructive to view letter and parcel delivery as the "postal sector". Under this model of market segmentation, some proportion of letters and parcels in developing countries are delivered via the post office, but the post office is but one of several potential service providers in the postal sector. The post office frequently also provides services in other sectors, including the financial and government services sectors.

It is important to make these distinctions because postal policy and regulation should be primarily involved with improving the performance of the postal sector, not the post office. Conversely, the post office frequently has roles in other sectors—it may be a vehicle for the delivery of a range of government services, for example. Ensuring the effective delivery of this wider range of services is the concern of many parts of government—the financial regulator for banking services, for example, or the transport department if the post office is involved in vehicle license issuance and delivery. Suggesting that postal policy and regulation should be about improved postal sector performance, and understanding that the post office's current and potential role spans many sectors, may help to clarify the roles and objectives for different parts of government and for the post office itself, allowing for a new model of both postal and government services delivery.

Whatever is decided about the services provided to every citizen, in the poorest countries the monopoly-supported USO for letter delivery is likely to be unworkable and damaging to consumers of postal services. The first two steps on a path to postal sector reform should be to abandon the monopoly and seriously reconsider the postal USO.

At the same time, in many countries, the most important social function of the post office is not as a letter delivery mechanism, but in delivery of pensions, financial services, or other activities. In many developing countries, postal payments represent over 50 percent of total postal revenues, and post offices remain the principal point of access to financial services for many in the working population (Walsh, 2001). Many post offices also act as the interface for government-to-citizen interaction such as license payments. Under those circumstances, what users most want is "universal access" to those services, not necessarily to letter delivery. Adding together this bundle of services that post offices frequently deliver, governments may well decide that it is vital for the great majority or all of citizens to be able to reach the service delivery point.

One possible model to deliver these services under a competitive regime might involve a system of local communications franchises providing customer services supported by a competitively-selected logistics firm providing delivery services both between franchises and with interconnection points to other postal and logistics companies.

At the local level, private franchises operated by a local entrepreneur would provide communications and services in every town or village with more than a minimum sustainable number of people. The government, as part of a participatory process, would set certain minimum services and standards that must be provided by the franchise. Such minimum services might include providing a PO box on the premises, sending a standard letter from one region to another, provision of basic banking facilities or issuance of pensions, for example. It is unlikely that delivery services would be part of this minimum basket, especially in poorer developing countries. The minimum (government-mandated) basket of required services offered by these franchises would be offered at prices that reflect costs, and these prices would be regulated where necessary. In addition, the franchisee would provide any other services it chose –perhaps photocopying services or Internet access, for example. The franchises (one per town or village) would be auctioned to the highest bidder or, if no one was willing to pay, a subsidy auction would be used.

Concerning inter-regional delivery, this could be done either by the national post office, or auctioned off to a private company, which would provide (comparatively infrequent, regular, sustainable) physical collection and delivery to the franchises, picking up mail from a set number of interconnection points. If a private company is used, this company would also be selected competitively, and it would receive a regulated (cost-based) amount per item delivered to or taken from the franchise plus (if required) an up-front subsidy. The company and franchises would have to provide letter delivery between post franchises at one price nationwide. Any of the private operators involved (local, regional or interregional) would be free to provide other postal services, but would have no monopoly on service delivery. By decoupling the service delivery function and making this a competitive function, one would avoid the problems of inefficiency and unsustainability of monopoly delivery apparent in low-income countries.

Of course, it is important to make the point that this paper has been based largely on generalities and averages. There will be developing countries where a monopoly-enforced cross-subsidy model is providing services of value to the rural poor and where they are doing so at some reasonable level of efficiency. Furthermore, the record to date of reform is patchy, suggesting we have more to learn about how to operationalize the competitive model.

Nonetheless, it is likely that moving from an unworkable monopoly model designed to deliver a service in low demand, to a functioning competitive model that delivers a range of services that poor people find important and that might have a dramatic impact on quality of life, at little cost in many developing countries. Even taking just the first steps of abandoning the monopoly postal USO would be significant progress.

REFERENCES

British Postal Consultancy Service. 2002. "Costing and Financing of Universal Service Obligations: Universal Service Costs and Estimates Report," PHARE Project 9728-02-01.

Campbell, J. 2004. "History of Universal Service in the United States." Presented at CRRI-Rutgers University's 12th Conference on Postal and Delivery Economics, June 2-5, 2004, Cork, Ireland.

Cohen, R.H., C. Pace, A. Rato, M.H. Robinson, R. Santos, G. Scarfiglieri, V. Visco Comandini, J.D. Waller and S.S. Xenakis. 2003. "Towards a General Postal Service Cost Function," mimeo US Postal Rate Commission.

Kenny, C. 2002. "Information and Communication Technologies for Poverty Alleviation: Costs and Benefits." *Development Policy Review* 20(2): 141-157

Kenny, C. and C. Qiang. 2003. "Developing the Postal Network –A Cross-country Analysis." Mimeo, Global ICT Division, World Bank.

Ogilvie, A. 1893. "The Rise of the English Post Office." *The Economic Journal* 3(11): 433-457.

PriceWaterhouseCoopers (PWC). 2004. "Postal Telecentres: Rural Development Through Internet Access in the South African Development Community." Report produced for the World Bank

Souter D, N. Scott, C. Garforth, R. Jain, O. Mascarenhas and K. McKemey. 2005. "The Economic Impact of Telecommunications on Rural Livelihoods and Poverty Reduction," mimeo, Commonwealth Telecommunications Organization

UPU (Union Postal Universelle). 2001. Letter Post Manual, Berne: UPU.

UPU. 2002. Postal Statistics Berne: UPU.

UPU and World Bank. 2001. "The Postal Industry in an Internet Age: Case Studies in Postal Reform." World Bank, Washington DC.

Walsh, T. 2001. "Delivering Economic Development: Postal Infrastructures and Sectoral Reform in Developing Countries." London: Consignia.

World Bank. 2002. "World Development Indicators." Washington DC: World Bank.

Chapter 6

Estimating the Net Cost of the USO

A Case Study of Colombia[*]

George Houpis, Almudena Lara and Mark Williams
Frontier Economics

1. INTRODUCTION

In common with many postal operators around the world, Adpostal - the state-owned operator in Colombia and bearer of the Universal Service Obligation - is required to provide a set of basic postal services throughout the country. A reserved area is also established by law giving Adpostal a monopoly over the collection and delivery of traditional mail products below 2 Kg. In practice, mail services are also provided by operators that are licensed to offer special mail services (e.g. courier services) and operators that do not have a licence at all. Adpostal therefore operates in a market which has effectively been liberalised and it currently has approximately 26% market share by value.

Another unusual feature of the postal market in Colombia is that a working Universal Service Fund, known as the Communication Fund (CF), already exists. Under this mechanism, licensed operators, including Adpostal, are required to make annual contributions to the Government operated fund. Revenue from this fund is then forwarded to Adpostal to support the financing of its USO services.

[*] We would like to thank Adpostal and members of the Steering Committee for the help and support received during our work. The views expressed in this paper reflect exclusively the views of the authors and not necessarily those of Adpostal or the Government of Colombia.

Operators' contributions to the Communications Fund are currently set at 4% of turnover from special postal services.[1] This figure was not set on the basis of an estimate of the actual net cost of the USO. The Government therefore required a calculation of the cost of the USO, as a basis for determining future contributions to the CF. This paper describes the methodology applied in carrying out such an exercise on behalf of the Government of Colombia and reports the results. We begin with a brief review of the literature of USOs in the postal sector and the implications of USOs in a liberalised market. This is followed by a description of the economic and regulatory context of the postal market in Colombia. We then go on to describe the approach that we adopted to calculating the net cost of the USO and the results of the calculation.

2. REVIEW OF THE LITERATURE

With the liberalisation of postal markets either planned or already taking place in many countries, considerable efforts have been made to understand the likely financial impact of liberalisation on an operator which retains a universal service obligation. In very general terms, this work has addressed two types of question: 'What is the net cost of the USO?' and 'What price would the bearer of the USO be required to charge if it were to remain financially viable in the face of competitive market entry?'

Panzar (2001) addresses the first of these two questions by providing a discussion of the concept of the cost of the USO and points out that any calculation of the net cost of the USO requires the specification of an unsubsidised counterfactual scenario. A general methodology for calculating the net cost of the USO is proposed which requires identifying two sets of customers: those who would be served, even if there was no USO, at the 'socially determined basic service rate'; and those which wouldn't.

The 'resource cost resulting from implementing the Universal Service Obligation' is the difference between the cost of providing services to these two groups. Panzar goes on to note that this approach "appears to require a great deal of data and analysis to implement", including estimates of penetration rates that would occur in the absence of a USO and the rates that would prevail.

Bradley and Colvin (2001) discuss methods for calculating the net cost of the USO that have been applied in the past. The Net Avoidable Cost (NAC) approach measures the losses arising from the components of the business where revenues are lower than costs, as a result of the USO. The Entry

[1] Special postal services are the courier services below 2Kg, provided either by the Adpostal or by licensed courier companies.

Pricing (EP) model approach, developed by Rodriguez et al. (1999), measures the loss of the ability of an operator to finance the USO when the reserved area is reduced or eliminated (i.e. the second of the two general questions identified above).

It was in the context of the second question that Crew and Kleindorfer (2000) introduced the concept of the Graveyard Spiral in which an operator with a USO would be required to raise its prices in order to finance loss-making routes as market entry takes place. This rise in prices could prompt further entry and possibly result in a 'graveyard spiral' in which the USO operator could not maintain financial viability in a liberalised market. The concept was explored further in Crew and Kleindorfer (2001) which considered the micro-determinants of market entry in a liberalised market, by focusing on customers as well as routes – the approach taken in previous papers.

The potential impact of market entry on an operator with a USO was also considered empirically in Cohen et al. (2004) for the US, d'Alecantara and Amerlynck (2004) for Belgium and Hill et al. (2005) for the UK. These models have a number of common features. They include a USO operator which has an obligation to provide services throughout the country at a uniform tariff and entrant(s) with no regulatory restrictions on the tariffs which they can set. The cost of delivery varies geographically and is usually modelled as two zones – one of which is high-cost and one of which is low-cost. Entrants can provide an end-to-end service or can deposit mail into the operator's system for delivery. The models also include some differentiation between products (i.e. mail types) and customers (e.g. business and residential).

The models are calibrated using actual cost data from operators in each country and are used to estimate the amount by which the operator will be required to raise its prices in the face of market entry, in order to cover its fixed costs and the losses made on providing services in unprofitable areas. Cohen et al. (2003) conclude that the graveyard spiral is unlikely to take place in the US. Hill et al. (2005) conclude that it is 'not the most likely scenario' in the UK, particularly in the short-run, but consider that it is more likely to take place in the long run. D'Alcantara and Amerlynck (2003) calibrate an empirical model for Belgium and, in their benchmark scenario, the entrant takes more than 50% of the market of retail customers and all business customers in the densely populated (i.e. low-cost) zone.

In the study by NERA (1998), the cost of the USO was defined as the "losses on those traffics that are handled at a loss".[2] They estimated this cost in nine countries in the EU, using two different cost concepts: Long-run Avoidable Costs in which they assumed that the costs of sortation, transport

[2] NERA (1998); Section 3.1.1, page 33

and delivery of mail would be variable if considered over a sufficiently long-period of time; and Fully Distributed Costs, in which the total costs of the mail business are included. The results of their estimation of the cost of the USO ranged from 14.3% of turnover in Austria, using the FDC approach, to 0%-0.5% in Denmark, Finland, France, Greece, Portugal and the UK using the NAC approach.

This study builds on some of the theoretical and empirical work that has already been undertaken but in the context of a market in which entry has already taken place.

3. BACKGROUND TO COLOMBIA

Colombia is the fourth biggest country in South America, with an area of 1.1 million km^2 and a population of approximately 44 million. It is a lower middle-income country[3] with a relatively urbanised population.[4]

Adpostal is the state-owned postal operator and bears an obligation to provide a set of postal services throughout the country, as agreed in the Inter-administrative agreement between Adpostal and the Ministry of Telecommunications (2004). In practice, Adpostal was already providing a basket of USO services throughout the country before 2004 and the agreement therefore served to regularise and clarify[5] a situation that already existed.

The agreement sets out the rights and obligations of Adpostal in relation to the USO delivery and specifies the services to be included in the USO. According to the agreement, Adpostal has the obligation to deliver in all the Colombian territory at geographically uniform tariffs: letters and postcards up to 2 Kg, prints up to 5 Kg, small packages up to 2 Kg, cecograms (special delivery for blind people) and packages up to 20 Kg. In addition, Adpostal is subject to the obligation to provide free postal services to certain governmental institutions, the tribunals and prisons. These services are referred to as 'franquicias'.

Although the Convenio Interadministrativo is relatively clear in its definition of the set of services included, there is, in practice, some scope for interpretation when carrying out the calculations of the net cost of the obligation. In particular, the Convenio is unclear as to whether the free services, the delivery of telegrams or the delivery of invoices should be included in the obligation.

---

[3] GDP per capita of US$6,702 in 2003; Current US$ (PPP); Source: World Development Indicators.

[4] Approximately 72% of the people live in urban areas.

[5] The definition agreed is in line with the UPU recommendations.

Mail services are divided into different groups: items above 2kg and items below 2kg. Items below 2kg can be further divided into traditional postal services and courier services.[6] The market for items above 2kg is fully liberalised and no licence is required to deliver these services. Adpostal has a statutory monopoly over traditional mail services, below 2kg, but express mail and courier services are open to competition. There are approximately 200 courier companies with licenses to provide courier services below 2kg. There are also a number of unlicensed operators that are active in the market.

Adpostal receives compensation for the provision of universal services from the Universal Service Fund, created originally in 1976 and then restructured in 1999 and 2000. The primary objective of the fund is to further plans, projects and programmes for facilitating access to telecommunications and postal services throughout Colombia. All licensed operators are required to contribute 4% of their gross revenues to the Fund. Total industry revenues are estimated to be c. 411 billion pesos (US$174.4m) in 2003.[7] Adpostal's postal revenues[8] of 105.6 billion pesos (US$ 44.8m) amounted to c. 26% of the total industry revenue. Licensed operators carried a total volume in 2003 of 270 million items, which is equivalent to 6.1 items per capita[9], of which Adpostal carried c. 14%.

4. GENERAL APPROACH

Two factors inform the decision on the methodology that is used to estimate the cost of the USO: the nature of the question that is being addressed and, importantly in Colombia, the data that is available for the calculation.

Unlike the majority of markets for which the EP model has been developed and applied, effective liberalisation and significant market entry has already taken place in Colombia. The Government has therefore focused on effective enforcement of the reserved area and improving the functioning of the USO Fund as a means of ensuring that the USO is financed on a sustainable basis. In both cases, the question facing the government is: what

---

6 Broadly, courier services are defined as mail services which have specified delivery times, tracking systems and require signatures on delivery. In principle, operators with courier licences are not permitted to use Adpostal's network.

7 The estimation of the actual size of the postal market is a challenging exercise because of possible underreporting by some operators and the existence of unlicensed postal operators. The 411 billion pesos figure is our best estimate of the size of the registered market, adjusted for potential under reporting by the operators.

8 Postal revenues exclude transfers from the government and any other non-postal revenues.

9 It is estimated an additional volume of unregistered mail in the market of 300 million deliveries in 2003.

cost is Adpostal incurring as a result of its obligation to provide USO services or what cost would Adpostal avoid if it did not have such an obligation? Ideally, this counterfactual situation would be specified through the legal definition of the USO and the legal provisions for estimating its cost. Unfortunately (and in common with the majority of countries) this is not the case. The first challenge faced in estimating the cost of the USO is therefore specifying the counterfactual.

The second issue that informs the choice of cost calculation methodology, as noted by Panzar (2001), is that of the availability of data. Adpostal is a state-owned postal operator in a developing country. It therefore has limited resources to spend on advanced management information systems and bespoke data collection exercises. Data on revenues and costs is only available at a high level of aggregation; data on revenues at the level of customers or routes and data on costs at product level is not available. These limitations place restrictions on both the type of calculation that can be carried out and the way in which it is done.

The approach taken to calculating the net cost of the USO within the limitations imposed by the available data was to apply the Net Avoidable Cost (NAC) methodology. As noted by Panzar (2001), this requires comparing the profitability of the USO operator with a counterfactual in which it does not have a USO. The counterfactual used in the analysis of the USO in Colombia was one in which the operator is not required to provide USO services in areas in which it is not able to profitably do so at a uniform price. However, in the areas where it provides the USO services, it is obliged to do so at the current uniform tariffs. This counterfactual is similar to the one applied by NERA in its study of USO costs in the EU.

Previous attempts to model the impact of market liberalisation on USO operators have been carried out using geographical zones, routes or customers as the basis unit of analysis. In Colombia, data limitations mean that the nine geographically defined zones in Adpostal's network is the only feasible unit of analysis. The application of the methodology involves several steps. These are summarised in Figure 1 and are described in more detail in the next section.

Another methodological issue in the calculation of USO costs in a postal network arises from interlinkages between zones of the network. For example, consider a network with two zones A and B. Some of the revenue generated in A arises from mail flows within the zone. Other revenue in Zone A is generated by mail flowing between Zone A and Zone B. If the operator ceases to provide services in Zone B because it is not profitable to do so, this will have consequences for the profitability of Zone A, since mail can no longer flow between the two zones. The model used to calculate the profitability of USO services in different geographical areas of the network should take these linkages into account.

Figure 1: USO cost modelling process

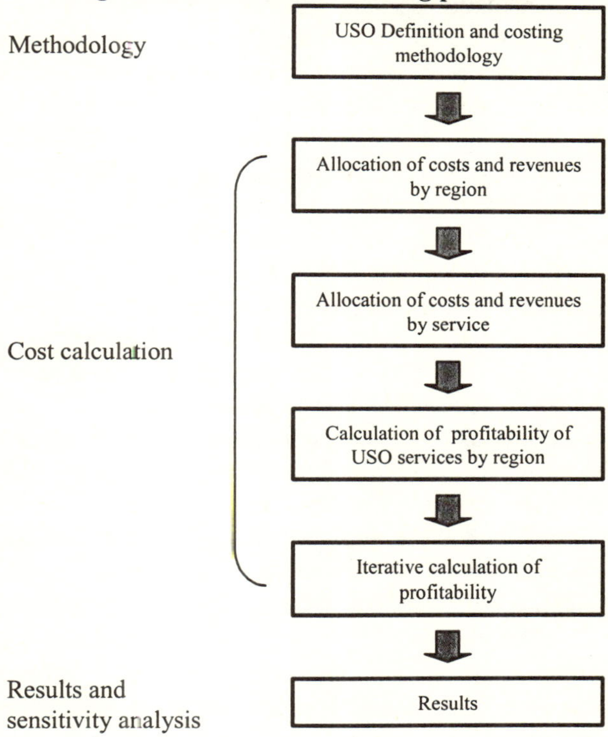

Finally, a view needs to be taken as to the relative efficiency of the USO bearer. We undertook a high level comparison of the relative efficiency of Adpostal compared to other similar postal operators, which indicated that the level of Adpostal's efficiency was broadly of the level expected, given the size of the country/operation and its level of development. Whilst this is only a very broad indication of relative efficiency, it indicated that the efficiency of Adpostal was not significantly lower compared to what would be expected when compared to other similar organisations.

5. THE NET COST OF THE USO FOR ADPOSTAL

5.1 Costs

In calculating the net cost of the USO, we consider long-run avoidable costs. Avoidable costs are those that are associated with production of a good or service, in this case, mail services. Costs which are not avoidable with respect to a service, are those that are required for the production of more than one service but which cannot be attributed to the service in question.[10] The avoidable cost concept means that the costs included in the calculation are both those which vary with the volume of output of a specific service, and those which are associated with the service but which are fixed in the short-run with respect to the volume of output of the service.

The use of the long-run cost concept implies that the business can be rescaled to adjust to a change in volumes. In practice, this involves the allocation of *all* costs to regions and products, including costs that may be sometimes regarded as fixed and common.

5.2 Allocation of costs between regions

The first step in the process is the allocation of costs between regions of Adpostal's network. Accounting data in Adpostal is collected at the level of nine 'regions'. Eight of these represent geographical areas of the network while one is 'planta central' which records central operating costs.[11] The accounting system can generate data on all operating and capital costs directly associated with these regions. This represents the costs of offices and building in each region, the labour costs of staff working in each region and the operating costs arising from collection, local sortation, local transport and delivery. However, it excludes all business overheads and central operating costs such as interregional transport costs and national level sortation costs. These costs are recorded against 'planta central' in the accounting system. Some of these costs are, in fact, related to the volume of mail services processed by the network and delivered through the regional offices. They therefore represent avoidable costs of mail services which were allocated to regions.

5.3 Pension Costs

The largest element of Adpostal overheads are pension costs. These accounted for 38% of Adpostal's total costs in 2003 and therefore warrant particular focus in the calculation of the net cost of the USO. These pension costs can be divided into two components. The first is contributions to the pension fund for current employees of Adpostal. The second is payment of

---

[10] Costs that are sometimes referred to as fixed and common costs.

[11] Planta Central also records some operating costs. This costs belong however to the operating area of Bogota, where Planta Central is based. The operating costs recorded in Planta Central were allocated to the operating region that generates them.

pensions to retired former employees of Adpostal or their dependents. These components have been treated separately in the USO cost modelling.

Pension contributions for current employees are a cost that is directly associated with employing staff in the business. If any of these staff were no longer employed, Adpostal would not be required to make pension contributions for them. They can therefore be regarded as avoidable for the purposes of calculating the net cost of the USO.

Pension payments to retired Adpostal staff are a fixed cost which Adpostal is required to meet, irrespective of whether or not it is satisfying its USO. Even if Adpostal was no longer obliged to serve all the regions of Colombia (i.e. if it was not subject to a USO obligation), it would still be obliged to meet its pension payments to pensioners. This would suggest that, when calculating the net cost of the USO on an avoidable cost basis, pension contributions for current employees should be included but pension costs for former employees should be excluded. However, there are also reasons why it might be appropriate to include these costs in the USO calculation. Adpostal's pension obligations are influenced by its position as a state-owned company whose employees retain some aspects of public sector pension rights. Adpostal's existing pensioners also have some of these public sector pension entitlements which are likely to be greater than private postal operators would incur. It is therefore possible that Adpostal would be unable to finance such pension obligations in a market in which it faces effective competition from private operators.

A second argument for including the cost of Adpostal's current pension obligation in the USO cost calculation is the fact that these costs were incurred in the past. The cost of current pensioners is a cost which was incurred in the delivery of postal services, including USO services, in the past. This pension obligation was not financed (i.e. no contributions were made into a fund to be used to finance future pension payments as the pension obligations were incurred) but Adpostal is required to finance it from current revenues. Payments for existing pensioners can therefore be thought of as deferred costs arising from the provision of USO services in the past.

Funding the USO on the basis of a calculation of the forward-looking net avoidable cost (i.e. excluding the cost of pension payments to former employees) would be correct from the point of view of economic efficiency. However, it is possible that, under such a system, Adpostal would be unable to finance its pension obligations, with significant consequences for the delivery of USO services in future. The impact of the pension costs on the estimation of the net cost of the USO was therefore considered as part of the modelling exercise.

5.4 Allocation of costs between products

Once costs have been allocated to regions, the next step is the allocation of costs between products. To begin with, cost elements which can be easily attributed to services that are not USO services are identified. For example, facilities or expenses dedicated to the provision of express services are eliminated from the cost calculation as they are clearly not related to the provision of USO services. Similarly, any costs incurred for the generation of non-postal revenues are also eliminated.

It is then necessary to allocate the remaining costs between USO and non-USO services. Accounting data captures cost data by services/activity (e.g. salaries) but not by product. In the absence of such data, we have allocated costs between USO and non-USO services in proportion to the volumes of USO and non-USO services, weighted by the unit cost of each service. Again, Adpostal had no data on unit costs of products and so the weighting factor used was based on experience of postal operations in other countries and cross-checked with Adpostal staff.

5.5 Revenues

The next step requires identifying the revenues that can be directly attributable to the provision of the USO services. Accounting information generally provides detailed information on the revenues earned by service. This level of detail facilitates the process of estimating the revenues earned by the USO operator in the provision of the services included in the USO. However, some practical problems arise in carrying out this exercise in Colombia due to the lack of full correspondence between the legal definition of USO services and the accounting categories. For example, the legal definition of packages for the purpose of the USO (i.e. up to 20 Kg) did not coincide with the definition in the accounts (i.e. up to 30 Kg). This required the estimation of the proportion of the total revenues from the packages services as recorded in the accounts that correspond to packages subject to the obligation. Similar issues arise from revenue categories (like the revenues from franking machines) that can, in principle, be attributed to USO or non-USO services, depending on the use being made of them. In our calculations, we explored the sensitivity of the results to different methods of allocating revenue between USO and non-USO services.

6. RESULTS

Once all costs and revenues have been allocated to region and then separated between USO and non-USO services, the profitability of USO services in each region, can be calculated. The sum of the net costs of USO services in each area is the total net cost of the USO. We tested two sensitivities in the calculation: the impact of excluding the cost of payments to existing pensioners from the calculation and the impact of different methodologies for allocating revenues between products. The table shows the results both including and excluding the historic pension costs. In addition, under Scenario I all revenues that are treated in the account system as common to USO and non-USO services are allocated to the USO for the purpose of the calculation. Under Scenario II, only a proportion of the common revenues are allocated to the USO services in the calculation. [12] The results of the analysis are shown in Table 1.

Table 1: Cost of the USO in Colombia under different scenarios, 2003

Historic pensions	Different allocation of revenues	Net avoided cost (billion pesos)
Included	Scenario I	37.2
	Scenario II	40.6
Excluded	Scenario I	4.1
	Scenario II	5.9

Table 1 indicates that, when the cost of historic pension payments is included in the calculation, the net avoidable cost of Adpostal's USO is between 37 and 41 billion pesos (US$15.7m – US$17.4m) which accounts for between 35% and 39% of Adpostal's postal revenues of 105.6 billion pesos (US$ 44.8m) and 9% of annual total postal sector revenues of c. 411 billion pesos (US$174.4m). However, if the pension costs are excluded from the calculation, the net cost of Adpostal's USO falls to a negligible amount. The role of pension costs is therefore clearly very important in determining the overall net cost of Adpostal's USO. The impact of the methodology used to allocate the revenues between products does not appear to have a significant impact on the results.

7. CONCLUSIONS

Colombia is an interesting case study of USO in the postal sector. Although the USO operator has a statutory monopoly over traditional mail services, it has lost a very significant share of the mail market to competition from both licensed and unlicensed operators. A calculation of the cost of the USO is therefore of immediate significance for both operators and the

[12] The proportion of revenues that should be attributed to USO services was agreed following discussions with Adpostal.

government and can be implemented through the mechanism of the Fund that already exists.

The methodology which can be used to calculate the net cost of the USO is constrained by the data that is available. In Colombia, this is from a traditional accounting system which does not allocate costs to individual products. Allocating costs to geographical units of analysis and products is therefore a key challenge in the USO cost calculation process. This is likely to be similar to postal operators in many other countries where internal network and financial information systems are limited in scope and resources are not available to carry out original extensive data collection exercises.

An important feature of the finances of Adpostal, which may also be shared with operators in many other countries, is the significance of overhead costs such as pensions. These have a major impact on the costs of the USO operator and must be borne in mind when calculating the cost of the USO. When they are included, the net cost of the USO amounts to approximately 9% of the sector turnover. When they are excluded, the net cost of the USO, when calculated using this methodology, falls drastically.

The exercise is also instructive because it raises a number of questions for policy-makers considering the implementation of USO Funds. One of these concerns the incentives that a USO Fund arrangement of the type found in Colombia provides to an operator that is the recipient of subsidies from a USO fund. The market for delivery of bills is highly competitive in Colombia as a result of extensive entry by both licensed and unlicensed operators. Many of these operators charge low prices and Adpostal has lowered its own effective prices through discounting in order to compete with them. In the absence of any detailed product cost data, it is not possible to determine whether these prices are below the incremental cost of providing such services. However, under the Universal Service Fund mechanism that is currently in place in Colombia, Adpostal could recover a proportion of any losses that it makes in providing USO services from other operators. The existence of a USO fund, based on actual profitability data from Adpostal may therefore encourage the recipient of such subsidies to price below incremental cost. This may have adverse implications for the long-term development of competition in the postal market. The optimal implementation of a universal service fund should therefore be accompanied by some regulatory oversight of the pricing of the individual USO services by the USO provider to prevent cross subsidies between services. This control would be helped by the implementation of an accounting system that allows computation of the incremental cost of the individual services.

A second question concerns the extent to which the conclusions from this study are directly relevant to other countries. There are a number of reasons why a degree of caution should be exercised in applying the conclusions of this study directly outside of Colombia. The definition of the USO in Colombia is based on the UPU recommendations but any comparison with another country would need to examine in detail the definition the scope in practice of the USO since this is obviously a primary determinant of the net cost. A second reason is that the cost structure of a postal business will vary between countries according to a number of factors, including the relative cost of labour and the geographical concentration of demand. Further country-specific analysis would therefore be required if the results of this study were to be applied in developed countries. On the other hand, the postal markets of many developing countries and emerging markets have features in common with Colombia. This study may therefore be instructive for policy makers in these countries considering the balance between promotion of competition and ensuring that it USO policy objectives are met.

REFERENCES

Bradley, M.D., and J.Colvin. 2001. "The Role of the Monopoly Product in the Cost of Universal Service." In *Future Directions in Postal Reform*, edited by M.A. Crew and P.R. Kleindorfer. Boston: Kluwer Academic Publishers.

Cohen, R., M. Robinson, R. Sheehy, J. Waller and S. Xenakis. 2004. "An Empirical Analysis of the Graveyard Spiral" In *Competitive Transformation of The Postal and Delivery Sector,* edited by M.A. Crew and P.R. Kleindorfer. Boston: Kluwer Academic Publishers.

Crew, M.A., and P.R. Kleindorfer. 2000. "Liberalization and the Universal Service Obligation in Postal Service." In *Current Directions in Postal Reform*, edited by M.A. Crew and P.R. Kleindorfer. Boston: Kluwer Academic Publishers

Crew, M.A., and P.R. Kleindorfer. 2001. "Whither the USO under Competitive Entry: A Microstructure Approach." In *Future Directions in Postal Reform*, edited by M.A. Crew and P.R. Kleindorfer. Boston: Kluwer Academic Publishers.

d'Alcantara, G. and B. Amerlynck. 2004. "Financial Viability of the Universal Postal Service Provider Under Uniform and Cost-Related Tariffs" In *Competitive Transformation of The Postal and Delivery Sector*, edited by M.A. Crew and P.R. Kleindorfer. Boston: Kluwer Academic Publishers.

Hill, R., R. Robinson and F. Rodriguez. 2005. "The Financial Equilibrium of Universal Service Providers in a Liberalized Postal Market." In *Regulatory and Economic Challenges in the Postal and Delivery Sector*, edited by M.A. Crew and P.R. Kleindorfer. Boston: Kluwer Academic Publishers.

NERA. 1998. "Costing and Financing of Universal Service Obligations in the Postal Sector in the European Union"

Panzar, J.C. 2001. "Funding Universal Service Obligations: The Costs of Liberalization." In *Future Directions in Postal Reform*, edited by M.A. Crew and P.R. Kleindorfer. Boston: Kluwer Academic Publishers.

Rodriguez, F., S. Smith and D. Storer. 1999. "Estimating the Cost of the Universal Service Obligation in Postal Service " In *Emerging Competition in Postal and Delivery Services*, edited by M.A. Crew and P.R. Kleindorfer. Boston: Kluwer Academic Publishers.

Chapter 7

Assessing the Cost of the Portuguese Postal Network

Practical Cost Evaluation of a Universal Service Obligation and Other Applications[*]

Ricardo Goulão Santos, Alberto Pimenta, and Sofia Beatriz Henriques
CTT Correios de Portugal S.A.

1. INTRODUCTION

In an increasingly competitive postal market, the issue of how to maintain a universal service of postal services is beginning to beg several questions. How can the profitability of the service providers be assured? How can the users be better served? What should the price/quality of service framework be? At what cost? Is it cost effective to deliver everywhere, at present price conditions? Subsequently, issues such as the cost of the Universal Service Obligation (USO), cross-subsidization, uniform pricing of a non-uniformly costing service, downstream access and the effects of entry are becoming increasingly important.

In this study we apply a cost model developed by CTT Correios de Portugal S.A. (CTT), the Portuguese Post,[1] in order to enable the calculus of

---

[*] The authors would like to thank Sacramento Costa for her invaluable help in the bibliographic review and also Antónia Rato for the definition of the Portuguese regulatory environment. We would also like to thank Michael Crew and Paul Kleindorfer for their initial support in proposing the current investigation. For the thought-provoking suggestions of our discussants at the postal conference in Antwerp, we also thank John Dodgson and Leon Pintzov. However, any inconsistencies are the full responsibility of the authors. The views expressed in this paper are those of the authors and do not necessarily reflect the views of CTT Correios de Portugal S.A.

[1] Although they are not different entities in themselves, CTT and the Portuguese postal network (PPN) are different concepts: the CTT, as postal operator, built and uses a postal

the cost of the postal network in its collection, transport, sorting and distribution activities. This model allows the assessment of the cost of each route of the Portuguese postal network (PPN) when providing D+1 and D+3 quality of service/time of delivery in each given year.

In this paper, we briefly present and discuss this model, and use it to evaluate the cost of the Universal Service Obligation (USO. The model then provides data for investigating the effect of the end to uniform pricing, an event likely to happen following market entry. Specifically, we measure the expected degree of price differentiation across Portugal.

In Section 2, we briefly present both the regulatory framework commanding the provision of postal services throughout the territory, and the geographical decomposition of mail traffic. These are the main constraints of the technological model of operation the CTT uses when providing its service. The former, the provision constraint, advocates homogenous service, while the latter, the geographical constraint, is based on postal demand, which is not homogenous. Hence, the CTT uses the model to determine how best to adjust to these 'contradictory realities.' In Section 3 we briefly present the cost model, which is used in the application of the USO costing methodologies discussed in Section 4. Section 5 presents the results. Section 6 concludes the paper, highlighting developments in the application of the cost model presented here.

2. UNIVERSAL POSTAL SERVICE IN PORTUGAL

2.1 The Regulatory Environment

The Portuguese Post, founded in 1512, has always been orientated towards universal service. Currently, CTT provides almost daily delivery of mail across Portugal, assuring next-day delivery of mail, if requested, to any domestic destination (the islands of the Azores or Madeira archipelagos being exceptions). Moreover, postal service is regarded as a fundamental human need, and thus its provision is bound by a strict affordability criterion. Consequently, CTT's service is one of the least expensive in Europe.

All these criteria are now clearly expressed in the law. Following the European Union's postal directive, Portuguese postal law defines universal service as the *permanent provision*, *throughout the Portuguese territory* at a *suitable level of quality*, and at *affordable prices* for *all users*.

---

network (the PPN) through which it provides its service. For now, the PPN coincides with the CTT's postal network. But with liberalization, this will not be the case. Additionally, Portuguese Post refers to the Portuguese postal operator, who is currently CTT.

According to current regulatory interpretation, the USO entails the provision of mail distribution services throughout the entire national territory, at geographically uniform and affordable prices. Strong political and social constraints practically impede any change in the governing framework of the postal service pricing policy.

These interpretations take a more formal expression in a concession contract binding the CTT as the Universal Service Provider (USP), with the obligation to perform collection and delivery at least once per working day according to pre-set quality-of-service targets. The CTT is also obliged to maintain and develop the post office and delivery networks, according to a public postal network development agreement.

Only during the last few years has it been possible to argue for the economic unfeasibility of a number of post offices, allowing for the raising of cost-sharing/opportunity-sharing solutions (partnerships) with local administrations and complementary services which require a capillary, i.e., small-unit, network such as the postal network.

2.2 Universal Mail Communication in Portugal

In order to serve the whole territory, the CTT deploys a widely capillary postal network, containing 995 post offices and two thousand agencies for clearance operations, 18,550 mailboxes, nine sorting centers, 405 postal distribution centers (PDC), and 435 transport routes where over 3,350 vehicles travel daily to provide universal postal services.

Table 1: Geographical distribution of mail

	Norte	*Centro*	*Lisboa e Vale do Tejo*	*Alentejo*	*Algarve*	*R.A. Açores*	*R.A. Madeira*
D+1 mail							
% mail sent	29%	14%	50%	3%	3%	1%	1%
% mail delivered	35%	14%	45%	2%	2%	1%	1%
D+3 mail							
% mail sent	23%	10%	61%	2%	2%	1%	1%
% mail delivered	37%	15%	37%	3%	4%	2%	2%

But, although the CTT is asked to provide the same level of quality of service in the delivery of any letter, whatever the destination, the need for mail communication, either from those who send or those who receive, is hardly geographically homogenous. In fact, as shown in Table 1, nearly 80% of mail communication in Portugal is driven by only two of Portugal's seven regions.

This concentration in mail mirrors both the concentration in population and income generated in the Portuguese economy,[2] as can be seen in the Table 2 below. It does not mirror, however, surface area coverage, with clear consequences on the operational and financial conditions that define universal postal service in Portugal.

Table 2: Geographical distribution of surface area, population and income

	Norte	*Centro*	*Lisboa e Vale do Tejo*	*Alentejo*	*Algarve*	*R.A. Açores*	*R.A. Madeira*
Surface area	23%	31%	3%	34%	5%	3%	1%
Population	29%	14%	45%	4%	4%	2%	3%
GDP	35%	23%	26%	7%	4%	2%	2%

Source: INE

Clearly all mail routes are not equal, either in mail volumes, revenue, or in cost. This is particularly noticeable if one compares the relative importance of mail volumes between the "Norte" and "Lisboa e Vale do Tejo" regions with their relative weight in costs, as presented in Table 3.

Table 3: Geographical distribution of postal cost

	Norte	*Centro*	*Lisboa e Vale do Tejo*	*Alentejo*	*Algarve*	*R.A. Açores*	*R.A. Madeira*
Mail sent from...	41%	17%	31%	4%	4%	2%	2%
Mail delivered to...	26%	12%	56%	2%	2%	1%	1%

The challenge of meeting USO, (i.e., the provision and financing of an undiscriminating, homogenous quality, uniformly priced), is growing with the advent of competition, in an increasingly liberalized market.

Assessing the cost of a postal network tailor-made to serve all the people throughout all the territory (even if nearly three quarters of the population lives in one quarter of the territory) is paramount in order to understand the nature of the USO cost and the impact of liberalization on the incumbent's capacity to finance it.

3. MEASURING COST

In order to assess CTT's cost for delivering D+1 and D+3 mail, we have developed a cost analysis model which decomposes costs in several functions and between the widest possible number of postal routes.[3]

---

[2] Thereby following the proverbial notion that mail flows from and to wherever money and people are.

[3] In order to help clarify concepts, we use the term 'transport route' to refer to each route used in transporting mail either from PDC to sorting centers (and vice-versa) or between

Following the collection of traffic data, we have built origin–destination mail-traffic matrixes, connecting different postal code areas, by 54,865 and 65,053 routes, for D+3 and D+1 mail, respectively. By using this matrix it was possible to fully divide all relevant costs between postal routes, according to mail traffic.

Each route cost was also decomposed according to the Postal Value Chain. A first decomposition is presented in Figure 1 below.

Figure 1: The Postal Value Chain

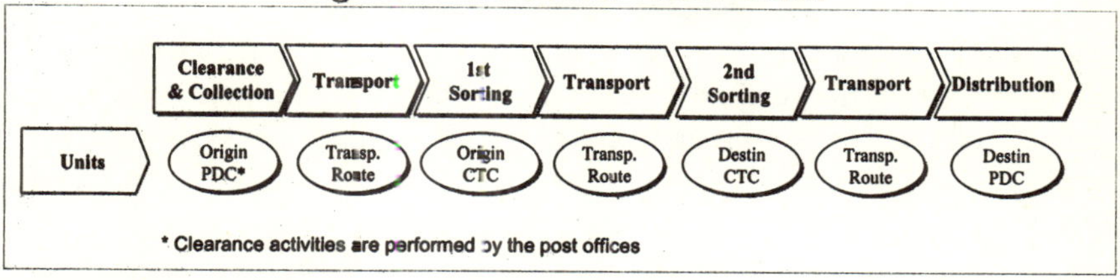

By mapping out which unit performed each particular function in each postal route, and using cost analysis information regarding product cost allocation in each of the units, it was possible to assign costs, by function, to each postal route. Adding to these costs are overhead costs, including the marketing, sales, administration, human resource management and financial support, which allows the service to be provided in economically efficient conditions.

Clearance activities were considered to be performed by the post offices inside each postal code area, where mail is then collected by postmen allocated to the relevant origin PDC.

Following preparation activities in the origin PDC (still encompassed in the collection function) mail is transported to the sorting centers through transport routes (secondary routes). These routes can be either unidirectional (concentrated) or bidirectional (mixed), i.e., in different time schedules they are used either to concentrate mail from origin PDCs to the origin sorting center or to disperse mail from the destination sorting center to the destination PDCs. The differing nature of the routes imply different cost allocations, with the cost of mixed transport routes being split according to transported mail volumes (both in this first concentration movement, from origin PDCs to origin sorting centers, as in the subsequent dispersion movement, from destination sorting centers to destination PDCs). The dynamic management of the transport function creates situations whereby mail flowing through one postal route can use alternative transport routes. In

sorting centers. The term 'postal route' alternatively refers to the full route from the sender's postal code to the receiver's, encompassing the full set of postal functions in postal service provision.

these cases, cost distribution between routes was done according to postal route mail volume.

Two sets of sorting operations occur in the sorting centers, involving both deck- and specific-sorting operations. The first set of operations concerns the handling of mail volumes received from origin PDCs in order to direct them to the correct destination sorting center. The costs related to those operations were allocated to the relevant postal routes according to inward mail volumes, i.e., those volumes that enter the sorting circuit from the origin PDCs. A second set of operations concerns the handling of mail received from several sorting centers to be distributed, through each PDC served by each particular sorting center, to each destination address. The costs related to this second set of operations were allocated to the relevant postal routes according to outward mail volumes, i.e., those volumes that exit the sorting circuit towards their respective PDCs for distribution.

Again, the secondary transport routes are used. This time, however, they serve the dispersion movement of mail. The cost allocation follows a similar set of rules as explained earlier. Finally, arriving to the destination PDCs, mail is distributed. The relevant per route costs in each PDC was also allocated according to mail volumes.

Table 4: Average variable costs by function, in 2002*

	Clearance & collection	*Transport*	*Sorting*	*Distribution*
D+1 mail				
Long run**	0.1124 € *(0.0059)*	0.0146 € *(0.0116)*	0.0340 € *(0.0074)*	0.2168 € *(0.1248)*
Short run	0.0410 € *(0.0026)*	0.0082 € *(0.0065)*	0.0144 € *(0.0035)*	0.0909 € *(0.0531)*
D+3 mail				
Long Run**	0.0370 € *(0.0049)*	0.0058 € *(0.0044)*	0.0203 € *(0.0039)*	0.1350 € *(0.0549)*
Short Run	0.0138 € *(0.002)*	0.0033 € *(0.0025)*	0.0086 € *(0.0016)*	0.0554 € *(0.0221)*

* Standard deviation in parentheses
** Assuming the units remain functioning and the technology remains fundamentally unchanged

A last level of decomposition was simulated, in order to compute the USO according to available methodologies. Costs were designated as being fixed or variable in the short run, and fixed or variable in the long run, according to their categories, as determined by accounting rules.[4] A summary of these costs is presented in Table 4, above.

[4] For example, some costs respond proportionally to changes in service provision, either in the short run or in the long run, while other costs do not. In some cases the distinction is not clear, but the criteria enabled a fairly non-distortionary classification.

With the direct results of our Cost Accounting model it is already possible to perceive a strongly unbalanced PPN.

In 2002, only half (43%) of the D+3 mail postal routes were profitable, nearly raising enough profit to support the loss incurred by CTT for the remaining half. A geographical decomposition shows that most of the Portuguese territory, corresponding to almost half (43%) of the mail volume distributed, is served at a loss. Overall, CTT incurred a loss of 12.7 million euros in the distribution of D+3 mail in economically unviable postal routes, financed through cross-subsidization. Figure 2, below, illustrates this result.

Figure 2: Universal service financial statement for D+3 mail

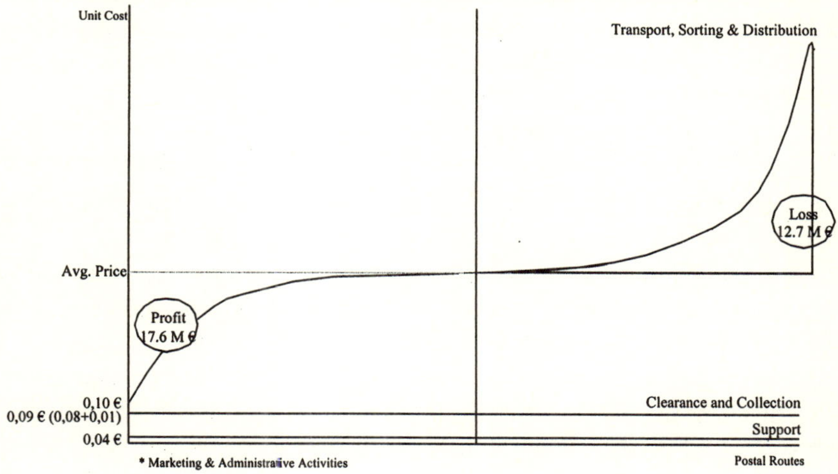

Figure 3: Universal service financial statement for D+1 mail

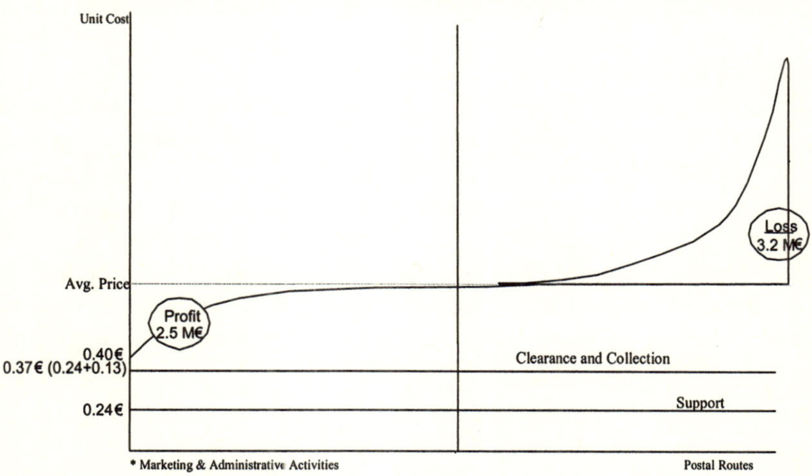

In the same year, the provision of D+1 mail service presented a grimmer[5] face, with the profit raised in the 45% profitable postal routes lagging from the needed to support the loss incurred by CTT in the remaining routes. Figure 3 illustrates these results.

Again, most of the Portuguese territory (44% of the mail volume) was being served at a loss. Overall, the Portuguese Post incurred a loss of 3.2 million euros in the distribution of D+1 mail in economically unviable postal routes. Direct product cross-subsidization, in this case, is not high enough to sustain the overall loss.

Given the information provided by the model, it was possible to simulate the calculus of the USO cost. To do this, we applied three alternative costing methodologies: Long Run Incremental Cost, Net Avoidable Cost, and Entry Pricing Cost. These methodologies are presented in the next section.

4. CALCULATING THE COST OF USO

The provision of universal postal service is a public obligation. This means that the government must ensure that anyone and everyone in the country's territory can use postal communications. The provision of services that meet this obligation, according to the Portuguese law and through a concession contract, was granted to CTT.

Universal service for CTT, or for any other incumbent, has two components: first, an economically-viable set of routes that subsidize a second, economically unviable, set of routes, the ones that truly are served because of the USO.[6]

Therefore, the USO implies a cost. More accurately it may imply a burden, calculated as the sum of losses in the economically-unviable postal routes. The consensus over the definition, however, does not apply to the best cost methodology to use.

Two different methodologies: (Total Element) Long Run Incremental Cost and Net Avoidable Cost can be used for valuation, but both assume status quo conditions. However, postal market liberalization implies the entry of competitors that will, necessarily, take a share of mail volumes. This competitive entry will occur where market conditions allow, i.e., in profitable routes. This implies an overall loss of financing capability for the USP to support the provision of postal service in unprofitable routes. To

---

5 Grimmer not due to the percentage of profitable routes but because the sum of profit is not enough to overlap the sum of losses in the unprofitable routes.

6 This is essentially equivalent to the Default Service Obligation, in fixed network industries i.e., the obligation to provide service where and to those from which no firm (not even the incumbent) derives economic value. See Crew and Kleindorfer (2002)

capture this effect, another methodology was applied: the Entry Pricing Approach.

4.1 Long Run Incremental Cost

When aiming to evaluate the incurred loss in economically-unviable postal routes, one way to do so is to account for gained revenues and increased costs derived solely from the provision of service on these routes. Consider a problem in which an established postal operator, operating all routes, and with full knowledge of the market and technology, wants to operate a new route. A calculation of the extent of cross-subsidization between postal routes in the provision of universal service would be carried out.

What in theory seems quite straightforward can, in practice, become an arduous task. As pointed out by Bradley et al. (1999), postal operators are big and complex organizations. Their complexity derives from providing a variety of products that are produced under scale and scope economies, and that use very different types of technology in providing mail delivery. In their paper, the authors review several studies and different methodological approaches, assessing their strengths and weaknesses.

Two major groups of methodological strategies for incremental cost appear. Top-down approaches rely on constant functional approximations to the technology. Bottom-up approaches begin by determining a product's incremental cost within each of the enterprise's individual processes and functions, and then aggregate the results over all processes and functions. These approaches usually rely on the engineering mapping of activities and their respective costs.

The approach used in this study resorts to a strong decomposition of costs according to postal routes and functions, through an accounting-inspired classification of costs as variable/incremental or fixed. We, therefore, do not follow an engineering process, as suggested by Soares et al. (2002). Instead, we use the Total Element Long Run Incremental Cost (TELRIC), treating each different postal chain function, j, in each route, r, as a cost-contributing element. Under this methodology, the USO cost was calculated as follows:

$$\sum_{r=1}^{R} \min\left[0, \left(p - \sum_{i=1}^{N} IC_{i,r}\right) * q_r\right], \tag{1}$$

with r=1,...,R being the different postal routes, p being average price, q_r being mail volume of route r and $IC_{i,r}$ being the unit incremental cost of function i (i=1,…,N) in route r.

As a proxy of incremental cost, long run variable cost, classified as such according to accounting criteria, was used.

4.2 Net Avoidable Cost

The Net Avoidable Cost (NAC) method was applied by Dodgson et al. (1998) to estimate the cost of the USO. In this methodology, the approach is not to calculate how much the cost/burden increment would be if the USO was to serve the economically-unviable postal routes, but how much cost it would avoid if, given the choice, it stopped provision on these routes.

Dodgson et al. (1998) identify two principal drivers of the unit cost of delivery: the cost of serving a particular address[7] and the volume of mail to be delivered to each address.[8]

A postal route is defined as unprofitable if the revenue earned from the items delivered in it does not cover all postal costs (collection, sorting, trunking, and distribution) and overhead costs. In these cases, one could argue that, by withdrawing from the routes, the postal operator would become more profitable, which, under the circumstances would signify greater efficiency.

However, one cannot assume that all cost is liable to disappear if the postal operator withdraws. There are partial, but not necessarily total, savings in costs, in any of the postal functions: clearance/collection, sorting, transport, and distribution costs. If the savings in these costs were to exceed the forfeited revenue, then there is an even stronger case against economic efficiency for providing postal services on these routes. The obligation of provision would then impose a burden, equal to the forfeited liquid savings.

In their study, Dodgson et al. (1998) propose that all costs should be interpreted with a long-run perspective, in which all costs, including capital costs, are said to be variable. However, when applying the theory, postal technology and the network are assumed to remain unchanged, due to lack of information.[9]

The approach used in this study for calculating NAC closely follows that of Dodgson et al. (1998). In this case, the Net Avoidable USO Cost was calculated as follows

---

7 This primarily depends on the density of points to be covered, which determine the number of delivery points that can be served per hour by foot, by cycle or by motor vehicle.

8 The more mail delivered to an address, the lower the cost of delivery per item.

9 If significant volumes were lost, in the long run, then the optimal sorting and transport network would be different, and could be redesigned to handle the lower volumes. Consequently, there would be cost savings, and we believe that these savings are relevant in determining total USO burdens.

$$\sum_{r=1}^{R} \min\left[0, \left(p - \sum_{i=1}^{N} \varepsilon_i * AC_{i,r}\right) * q_r\right], \tag{2}$$

with r=1,...,R being the different postal routes, p being average price, q_r being mail volume of route r, $AC_{i,r}$ being the average cost of function i (i=1,...,N) in route r and ε_i being the cost elasticity of function i, as presented in Cohen et al. (2003) (see Table 5, below).[10]

Table 5: Cost elasticity (USPS 1999), in Cohen et al. (2003)

Clearance (window service)	Collection & distribution[11]	Transport	Mail processing	Other
0.46	0.48	0.92	0.96	0.23

Entry Pricing Approach

The Entry Pricing (EP) Approach was developed by Royal Mail and PricewaterhouseCoopers and presented in Rodriguez, Smith and Storer (1999). This was a reply to the NAC USO approach, which fails to account for the effect of a changing market structure, resulting from liberalization. The NAC approach, in particular, fails to highlight the effects of liberalization on the USP's ability to finance the provision of universal service.

The EP USO Cost, according to Liddiard, Robinson and Rodriguez (1999), "measures the financial cost to the USP of meeting the USO where this is defined as the obligation it has to provide universal postal service at a uniform (geographically averaged) price." It can be calculated as:

$$\sum_{r=1}^{R}\left[\left(p - \sum_{i=1}^{N} IC_{i,r}\right) * \Delta q_r\right], \tag{3}$$

with Δq_r being the mail volume reduction due to entry. In this study, $IC_{i,r}$ was approached by $\varepsilon_i * AC_{i,r}$.

In order to estimate a plausible reduction in traffic, the Burns, Carlslake and Houpis (2002) model of entry with brand loyalty was used and adapted, considering each postal route as a market open to the competitive entry of a new operator.

In the model, we consider a single type of mail and two postal operators, the incumbent and the entrant. The entrant competes through product

[10] This choice was due to unavailability of estimated cost functions for CTT, a gap we intend to fill with further studies.

[11] An elasticity of 1 is assumed for distribution costs of any particular route if all routes destined to the respective postal area prove to be avoidable. It is, therefore, assumed that all distribution activities of the respective PDC are discontinued in the long run.

differentiation, allowing consumers to choose between the incumbent and the entrant as the provider of postal services for the delivery of each of their letters. As in Burns, Carlsake and Houpis (2002), price inelasticity is assumed, and, therefore, even if with entry there is an expected decrease in average market prices, the model assumes no changes in market demand (only shifts between postal operators).

As in Burns, Carlslake and Houpis (2002), the market is modeled as a Hotelling product differentiation market, with consumers' "placement" being defined according to their preferences regarding the differentiating characteristics of the services provided by the two operators in each specific market.[12] Each consumer values each item of sent mail with a value $x \in [0,1]$. Both incumbent and entrant will differentiate their specific service offer, locating themselves at points a and b respectively, $0<a$ and $b<1$.

By sending a letter whose intrinsic value for the consumer is x, the consumer will receive a benefit of either

$$U_i = \underline{S} + \beta - p_i - t(x-a)^2, \text{ if using the incumbent's service,}$$

or

$$U_e = \underline{S} - p_e - t(1-b-x)^2, \text{ if using the entrant's service,}$$

with $\underline{S}$ representing the intrinsic utility of the sent letter, β representing the incumbents (relative) brand value, p_i and p_e representing both the incumbent's and the entrant's prices. Representing "transport cost" is t, signifying the intrinsic cost, as perceived by the consumer, of failing to meet a service that completely matches the consumer's needs.

In this study, the value of β was determined according to the estimated brand value of CTT, in mail, relative to earned revenues, with a premium on D+1 mail. Therefore, for D+3 mail, assumed β was 23.0% of p_i and, for D+1 mail, 50% of p_i.

The choice of using either of these services requires that a participation constraint is met, that is:

$$U_i = S_o - t(1-x)^2, \tag{4}$$

with S_0 being the utility derived from consuming an outside service.

In a duopoly, the consumers will position their mail-sending options according to their intrinsic utility functions and differentiated service characteristics, so that point x, signifying the value of a letter whose sender

---

[12] It is conceivable to have a different entrant for each market. The incumbent, however, is always the same provider, the USP.

is indifferent between either postal operator, is such that $U_i=U_e$. Solving for x_i yields the market share of the incumbent:

$$x_i = \frac{p_e - p_i + \beta}{2t(1-a-b)} + \frac{1-a-b}{2} + a. \tag{5}$$

In a regulated duopoly, with a regulated uniform price for the incumbent's service,

$$p_e = \frac{MC_e + p_i - \beta + t(1-a+b)(1-a-b)}{2}, \tag{6}$$

where MC_e is the entrant's marginal cost.

In the calculus performed for this study, the model was calibrated as such:

Table 6: Model parameters

Variable	Value
MC_e	Short-run variable cost of CTT in each route
a	0.5
b	0
β	D+1=50%*p_i ; D+3=23.0%*p_i
t	0.1

5. RESULTS

5.1 Costing the USO

As it was presented in Section 3, CTT, with full distribution of costs, incurred a loss of 12.7 million euros and 3.2 million euros in the provision of D+3 and D+1 postal service, respectively, in economically-unviable routes. Table 7, below, presents a comparison between values estimated for the USO Cost, according to each approach.

A TELRIC approach to USO focuses on the increase in cost, net of revenues, incurred if the USP were to begin servicing a particular route, assuming all other costs are constant, (thus there is no need of a structural fit). As a result, incremental cost is strongly reduced, when compared with fully-distributed cost. Figure 4 presents an illustration of this reduction, for D+3 mail.

Under the TELRIC methodology used in this study, the USO cost would amount to 167,300 euros for D+1 mail and 518,300 euros for D+3 mail. These values correspond closely to three thousand routes for D+1 mail and

2,200 routes for D+3 mail, where CTT is clearly legally forced to perform mandatory 'dumping' (at least while uniform pricing is enforced).

Table 7: Approach comparison

	FDC approach	**TELRIC approach**	**NAC approach**	**EP approach**
D+1 mail				
Total Routes	Loss Generating	Long Run Inefficient	Avoidable	-
	39.076	3.087	3.368	-
Market Share Loss	-	-	-	8%
USO Cost	3.2 M €	167.3 t €	199.6 t €	2.2 M €
D+3 mail				
Total Routes	Loss Generating	Long Run Inefficient	Avoidable	-
	34.015	2.191	3.076	-
Market Share Loss	-	-	-	6%
USO Cost	12.7 M€	518.3 t €	745.4 t €	10.9 M €

If we assume a different stance on the relevant cost, i.e., not one that is increased by initiating an operation the USP already performs but one that can be avoided by retiring from a particular service, NAC is a closer depiction of the USP's dilemma. This, however, does move us away from a purist theoretical approach.

Figure 4: TELRIC USO cost for D+3 mail

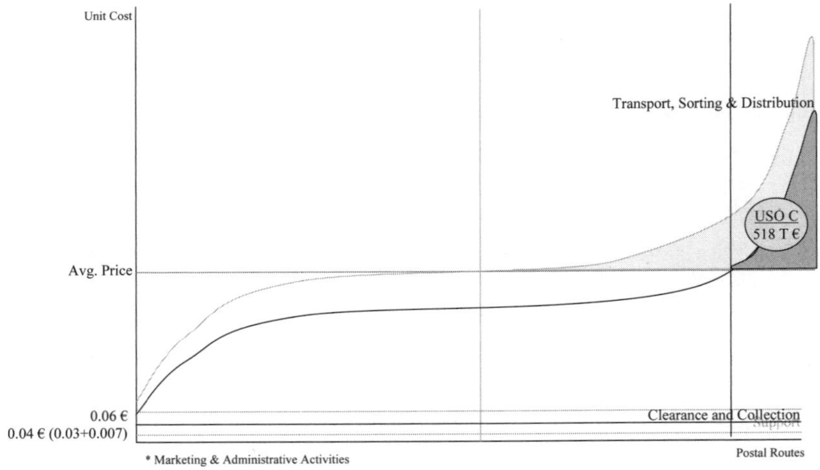

Still, by assuming that not all cost is avoidable, there is also a great reduction in Net Avoidable USO Cost, when compared to the financial loss calculated with full distribution of costs. Under the NAC methodology used in this study, the USO cost would amount to 199,600 euros for D+1 mail and

745,400 euros for D+3 mail. These values correspond closely to the 3,400 avoidable routes for D+1 mail and 3,000 avoidable routes for D+3 mail.[13]

Based on status quo competition conditions for D+1 and D+3 mail, TELRIC and NAC methodologies fail to illustrate the expected loss in the ability the USP has to finance the USO cost, through cross-subsidization. Under competition, and if the current USO regulation is to be maintained, the mandate to keep geographically-uniform prices, in particular, seriously hinders the USP's ability to maintain the universal service.

Given that it focuses on the loss derived from the requirement to provide geographically-uniform pricing in a liberalized market, rather than on the loss derived from inefficient or avoidable routes, the EP methodology depicts a different view of USO costs. This view is substantiated in the reduction of the financial sustainability of the USP, due to cream skimming.

Under the assumptions taken for the entry model and presented in Section 4.3, CTT would face an overall reduction of market share, both in D+3 and D+1 mail, although keeping a share of market in every route.. Average market share in D+3 would reduce to 94% and D+1 to 92%. The overall reduction of mail volume, with the less than proportional reduction of costs, would result in a overall loss of 10.9 million euros in D+3 mail net revenue and of 2.2 million euros in D+1 mail net revenue. Losses of these amounts would seriously affect CTT's ability to finance the provision of universal service, under current regulatory conditions.[14] As such, regardless of whatever loss incurred in inefficient or avoidable routes, the loss on profit in the most efficient routes, those that subsidize the loss-generating routes, is almost equivalent to the financial loss presented at the end of Section 3.

The EP methodology, therefore, adds a second source of USO cost to the one provided by the more comparable TELRIC and NAC approaches, but adds a much grimmer perspective on the expected effects of liberalization on the provision of universal service.

---

13 A sensitivity analysis was performed on the results of the NAC model. By autonomously changing every single elasticity under an interval of [-5%, +5%] for the Cohen et al. (2003) paper's values, the variation in NAC was not higher than 3.6%. A simultaneous increase of 5% in all elasticity values, which would express a significant technological change, would signify a change of up to 7.4% on Net Avoidable USO Cost. The highest estimated cost would therefore be close to 800,000 euros for D+3 and 220,000 euros in D+1 mail. The lowest estimated value would be close to 720,000 euros in D+3 and 188,000 euros in D+1 mail. NAC methodology, therefore, presents significantly robust results.

14 A sensitivity analysis was performed also on the results of the EP model. An important degree of sensitivity of USO cost on the variation of brand value was found. Due to the shifts of demand between incumbent and entrants, a variation of 4% in brand value in D+3 mail (as a percentage of price) would mean a 40%–55% variation in USO cost. A variation of 2% in brand value (as a percentage of price) would entail a variation of close to 35% in USO cost for D+1 mail.

5.2 The End of the Uniform Price

The EP Approach allows us to analyze the effect of liberalization and entry on the main regulatory restraint imposed on the incumbent on its ability to respond to entry — the geographically uniform price.

The proposition presented in this section is that, when assuming that all routes are open to competition, provided the incumbent serves each and every one of them with uniform prices, no such binding condition is placed upon the potential entrant. The entrant is free to choose whether or not to enter and to differentiate its service to better fit the market while reaping the highest possible profitability level. This is the accepted entry-regulatory framework, occurring in every regulated liberalized market.

The ultimate result, of course, is that, although the incumbent may be obliged to have geographically-uniform prices, the market is not. Therefore, it will not follow geographically-uniform prices, as Tables 8 and 9 illustrate for D+3 and D+1 mail, respectively.

Table 8: Geographic price index for D+3 mail[15]

Origin \ *Destination*	*Alentejo*	*Algarve*	*Centro*	*Lisboa e Vale do Tejo*	*Norte*
Alentejo	107	109	108	101	107
Algarve	107	108	109	102	106
Centro	108	109	108	101	108
Lisboa e Vale do Tejo	107	109	108	100	106
Norte	108	109	109	101	107

In an open market, there are reasons to believe that all D+3 mail addressed to the "Lisboa e Vale do Tejo" region will be priced at least 6% less than all D+3 mail addressed to different regions. It is also notable that those regions with less income, either in absolute or in per capita terms, will face the highest postal service prices for D+3 mail in an open market.

Table 9: Geographic price index for D+1 mail

Origin \ *Destination*	*Alentejo*	*Algarve*	*Centro*	*Lisboa e Vale do Tejo*	*Norte*
Alentejo	114	114	113	104	110
Algarve	114	114	112	103	110
Centro	114	114	112	103	111
Lisboa e Vale do Tejo	114	114	113	100	110
Norte	114	114	113	103	111

In D+1 mail, there are also clear geographic differences, with the regional penalization being even more noticeable. By forcing the incumbent

[15] I.e. the price index for D+3 mail sent from each region to the same or other regions, where the minimum price is the basis price index (100).

to geographically-uniform prices, regulation gives rise to an easier entry in the low-cost postal routes, probably allowing a bigger price reduction there. However, it also hinders the ability the USP has to rely on scale to reduce overall unitary costs and, therefore, to offer relatively lower prices in the high-cost routes.

In fact, a likely development, that may or not lead to a graveyard spiral,[16] is of a consistent increase in uniform prices, as suggested by Hill, Robinson and Rodriguez (2005), and a not-as-high increase in the highest prices, if differentiation is allowed.

Nevertheless, when full liberalization becomes a reality, it is very likely that a geographically-uniform price for mail in Portugal becomes a thing of the past.

6. CONCLUSION

Although USO mandates geographically-uniform quality and prices on the provision of postal services throughout most of the territory, the demand conditions for postal service in Portugal are hardly uniform. CTT would clearly face an uneven demand for mail services, with two regions (which represent only 25% of the territory), representing 75% of the population and more than 80% of both sent and delivered mail. This situation clearly allows for cross-subsidization, allowing the poorer and sparsely-populated regions access to postal services at a subsidized price.

The cost model developed by CTT, and used to support this study, allows us to identify the differences in cost when serving different postal routes, connecting senders and recipients across the country. It became clear that, for 2002, a relatively small (profitable) proportion of postal routes were financing the universal service.

The cost model was then trialed, through application of the USO cost calculations of three different methodologies. Focused on the variation of costs, by entry or exit, respectively, of burden-generating postal routes, TELRIC and NAC methodologies suggested that only a very small proportion of the incurred losses, 4% to 6%, should be deemed to be USO costs. The remnant would then be considered unavoidable or sunk cost.

Either way, the financial burden remains to be supported, and the EP Approach revealed that, under competition and the uniform pricing regulation, CTT would likely lose the ability to do it. In fact, expected loss of net income due to entry under uniform-pricing regulation would be much higher than estimated TELRIC and NAC calculations of USO and would almost equal the burden already supported in loss-making postal routes.

---

16 To be investigated in further research.

Finally, by furthering the analysis of the Entry Model's results, it becomes clear that the uniform pricing regulation is bound to become void by market action. Maintaining it would be an unfair restriction on the efficient provision of postal services by the incumbent, mostly hindering the needs of the less-dynamic regions of the country and their population.

Allowing relevant applications, the cost model proves to be a useful research and management support tool. Further developments on the calibration of models using cost elasticities estimated with Portuguese data may provide even more adjusted results in the application of USO costing methodologies.

Other prospective applications will be centered on an NAC and a TELRIC calculus under an entry scenario and the determination of the "graveyard spiral" risk on the provision of D+1 and D+3 postal services.

REFERENCES

Bradley, M.D., C.S. Brehm, J. Colvin, and W.M. Takis. 1999 "Empirical Estimation of incremental costs for the US Postal Service." In *Emerging Competition in Postal and Delivery Services*, edited by M.A. Crew and P.R. Kleindorfer. Boston: Kluwer Academic Publishers.

Burns, P., I. Carlslake and G. Houpis. 2002 "Brand Loyalty and Limited Entry in Postal Markets." In *Postal and Delivery Services: Delivering on Competition*, edited by M.A. Crew and P.R. Kleindorfer. Boston: Kluwer Academic Publishers.

Cohen R., C. Pace, A. Rato, M. Robinson, R. Santos, G. Scarfiglieri, V. Visco-Comandini, J. Waller, S. Xenakis. 2003. "Towards a General Postal Service Cost Function". Available at http://www.prc.gov/tsp/103/Cost_Function.pdf.

Crew, M.A., and P.R. Kleindorfer. 2002. "Putty-Putty, Putty-Clay or Humpty-Dumpty? Universal Service Under Entry." In *Postal and Delivery Services: Pricing, Productivity, Regulation and Strategy*, edited by M.A. Crew and P.R. Kleindorfer. Boston: Kluwer Academic Publishers

Dodgson, J., I. Senior, S. Estrin, P. Marks, M. Buckland, T. van Dijk, J.M. Rodriguez, L. Altinger, M. Begg, J. Müller and V. Visco-Comandini. 1998 "Costing and Financing of Universal Service Obligations in the Postal Sector in the European Union." Draft Final Report for EC DG XIII, N/E/R/A, London.

Hill, R., R. Robinson and F. Rodriguez. 2005. "The Financial Equilibrium of Universal Service Providers in a Liberalized Postal Market." In *Regulatory and Economic Challenges in the Postal and Delivery Sector*, edited by M.A. Crew and P.R. Kleindorfer. Boston: Kluwer Academic Publishers.

Liddiard, P., R. Robinson and F. Rodriguez. 1999. "Estimates of the Cost of the Universal Service Obligation using the Entry Pricing Approach". Available at http://www.postcomm.gov.uk/documents/competition/PostOfficeEntryPricingreport.pdf

Rodriguez, F., S. Smith and D. Storer. 1999. "Estimating the Cost of the Universal Service Obligation in Posts." In *Emerging Competition in Postal and Delivery Services*, edited by M.A. Crew and P.R. Kleindorfer. Boston: Kluwer Academic Publishers.

Soares, J., J. Confraria and A. Pimenta. 2002. "Postal Service Cost Modeling." In *Postal and Delivery Services Pricing*, edited by M.A. Crew and P.R. Kleindorfer. Boston: Kluwer Academic Publishers.

Access and Worksharing

Chapter 8

Establishing Non-uniform Access Prices in the UK*

Roger Hill and Richard Robinson
Royal Mail

1. INTRODUCTION

This paper discusses the pricing of access to a universal service provider's postal facilities. In particular it considers the derivation of non-uniform prices that reflect differences in the cost of serving different geographical areas and describes how Royal Mail has determined such prices.

The paper firstly describes Royal Mail's obligations and the history, so far, of the development of access services. It goes on to consider the theoretical concepts of how access prices might be de-averaged and then considers the practical issues encountered in implementing non-uniform prices. Examples from the resultant pricing structure are presented.

2. ROYAL MAIL'S LICENSE REQUIREMENTS

Royal Mail is the sole universal service provider (USP) in the UK and operates under a license issued by the Postal Services Commission (Postcomm) (Postcomm 2003). Condition 9 of this license mandates that Royal Mail is required to provide access to its postal facilities such that:

1. Access prices shall be based on a reasonable allocation of costs (and the determination of costs shall have regard to Royal Mail's obligation to provide a universal postal service in the United Kingdom)

---

* The authors would like to thank Frank Rodriguez and Paul Bates for their helpful comments on drafts of this paper.

2. Royal Mail does not unduly discriminate between persons having such access to its postal facilities or show undue preference towards any such person.

Taken together these requirements mean that Royal Mail must, in good faith, enter into negotiations with 'any person' requiring access to its facilities, whether a customer or a licensed postal operator. If negotiations fail then Postcomm can be requested to make a determination of the prices and/or conditions to apply.

Royal Mail's obligations to provide access to both postal operators and private customers reflect the requirements of Article 12 of the EU Postal Directive of June 2002 (European Communities 2002).

3. DEVELOPMENT OF ACCESS

It should be noted that 'access' – in the sense of avoiding part(s) of the traditional mails network operation - is not new. The concept of 'worksharing' developed in the late 1970s in the USA, since when mailers have been able to pre-sort mail and transport it (at least) part way through the network for handover to the USP (USPS in this case) for 'final mile' delivery. Prices are quoted as discounts from the public tariff and are based on avoided costs.

Since the late 1980s Royal Mail's range of Mailsort products has provided a similar opportunity to mailers with regard to the pre-sortation options, with a similar pricing basis. However, prior to the granting of Royal Mail's license there was no requirement to provide physical access at any 'downstream' point, and it is in this area that all recent developments have taken place.

Postcomm's decisions on Market Opening (culminating in Postcomm's document of February 2005 (Postcomm 2005a)) mean that, unlike in the USA, licensed postal operators can set up end-to-end postal networks, including final delivery. However, the inherent economies of scale of such an operation are likely to preclude the immediate establishment of delivery networks in many expensive to serve areas, thereby leaving Royal Mail as the sole (loss-making) incumbent operator in such areas. In some quarters, therefore, access to Royal Mail's delivery network is seen as an essential requirement to allow the development of competition. Such access can be used either nationally – in which case the competitor is focusing on the upstream part of the business – or geographically – in which case the competitor is also focusing on establishing its own network where it is economic to do so yet being able to offer universal coverage, although some competitors might offer a more widespread coverage at less than daily delivery frequencies.

In February 2004, Royal Mail signed its first negotiated access agreement with a licensed postal operator, UK Mail, to provide access at Inward Mail Centers subject to certain conditions (Royal Mail. 2004a). The details of this contract include an agreement on access prices for a number of product variants (differentiated in terms of the level of pre-sortation and format (letters v flats/packets)), a minimum volume requirement per Inward Mail Center (to ensure there is sufficient volume to cover fixed cost activities such as mail acceptance and verification), and a minimum coverage of Inward Mail Centers per day. The range of product variants was later extended to include machine-readable options. The access prices were uniform to all parts of the UK, but offered on the condition that the "fall-to-earth" of access mailings must be similar to the Royal Mail national average mail profile (based on the distribution of end-to-end mail). This condition helps to protect the Universal Service Obligation (USO) because it prevents access being used for a disproportionately high percentage of mail in high cost delivery areas.

The contract developed from this initial agreement forms the standard contract now available for access customers. A number of other licensed postal operators and also some large customers have now signed this standard contract – the latter use a third party to transport their mail to the Inward Mail Centers.

UK Mail started its operation in May 2004 and is by now operating at an annualized rate of approximately 250m items and remains on track for a 3% market share by the end of its third year (UK Mail. 2005).

During 2004/05 Royal Mail delivered around 100m access items and this is expected to increase significantly over the short to medium term. At this early stage it appears that access volumes are almost entirely the consequence of customers switching from existing Royal Mail end-to-end products, and that very little, if any, "new" volume has been generated in the market by the availability of access products, although this may change as the market develops.

However, the contract described above does not meet the requirements of some operators or customers. In particular, regional operators and customers necessarily cannot meet the 'national' mail distribution pattern or the Inward Mail Center coverage requirements, although they may be posting sufficient volume. In response to a request from such an accessor Royal Mail developed a set of non-uniform access prices that allowed the condition of requiring a national average mail profile to be avoided, which thereby increased the opportunities for access to its postal facilities. These prices and conditions are the basis of the contract signed in October 2004 and now form the second part of the generic access contract that is available to all. (See Royal Mail 2004b)

4. THEORETICAL CONCEPTS

Liberalization of the postal sector is still in its infancy in many countries, including the UK, and it is not yet known whether a liberalized postal market can fully support a non-subsidized USP that offers access to its facilities in the face of bypass competition. It is envisaged that entrants will choose to position their end-to-end (bypass) networks in the cheapest and most profitable to deliver areas. These areas tend to have a high density of businesses that send and receive high volumes of mail. The more expensive to deliver mail will be given to Royal Mail in places where it is unprofitable for the entrant to deliver itself. Royal Mail is therefore faced with a situation whereby the USO is under threat if it charges a uniform access price (based on national average costs) to all parts of the country. The threat is twofold –

Firstly, access mail will tend to be addressed to rural and outlying regions where the cost of delivery is in excess of the uniform access price. This in effect would mean that Royal Mail is subsidizing end-to-end competition.

Secondly, entrants can undercut the uniform access price in cheap to deliver areas and win an even greater share of profitable mail. This would start a vicious cycle, often referred to as a "graveyard spiral" (Crew and Kleindorfer, 2000), whereby Royal Mail receives a dwindling share of the profitable mail needed to subsidize its USO. Royal Mail might then be forced to increase its prices to sustain the USO, but this would allow entrants to undercut the uniform tariff in further delivery areas, and Royal Mail would be left with an ever-increasing burden of expensive to deliver mail.

Hill et al (2005) investigated the likelihood of a graveyard spiral occurring in the UK by modeling the impact of uniform access prices that are available to both entrants and customers, as well as the possibility of entrants offering end-to-end services. It concluded "a graveyard spiral is perhaps not the most likely outcome in the near term but one that remains a distinct and realistic possibility over the longer term". Nevertheless, the model results suggest that significant price rises would be needed to achieve financial equilibrium.

A number of recent studies have explored the setting of optimal access prices in the postal sector, including Panzar (2002), Crew and Kleindorfer (2002, 2004) and De Donder et al (2004, 2005). The studies share a common approach in that they develop models of a postal sector in which a USP offers access to its delivery network in both low cost (often simplistically referred to as urban) and high cost (often simplistically referred to as rural) areas. The USP also offers an end-to-end product that is uniformly priced to all destinations, which may or may not be optimally priced. The postal market also includes at least one entrant that can choose to compete in one or both delivery areas, using either access or bypass with potentially non-uniform prices.

Panzar (2002) identifies the possibility that access prices set on a uniform basis may fail to cover the average incremental cost of delivering to high cost areas, and hence users of access in such areas would be subsidized. A model is developed whereby access is priced on the avoided cost or margin rule version of ECPR, which given the existence of a uniform end-to-end tariff, produces the same access price in both urban and rural areas. It was found that as long as the distribution of access mail to each area is reflective of the pattern of end-to-end mailings, then the fixed network cost is recovered to maintain a break even financial position for the USP and inefficient entry is deterred. In the case where access mailings do not reflect the national average mail profile, and in particular when additional mail is accessed in high cost areas, then inefficient entry could occur and it is unlikely that a USP would be able to recover its fixed network costs to make a profit. It is noted by Panzar that this problem would not occur if end-to-end "postal rates were rebalanced prior to mandating unbundled access … so that the prices charged to all services and market segments were subsidy free". This is because the proposed ECPR "pricing rule would never result in unbundled access being priced below incremental costs". It is recognized however that access deals are likely to occur before the re-balancing of end-to-end services is accomplished, and therefore some de-averaging of access prices is needed in the interim to ensure that prices are at least as high as the average incremental cost of delivering to each area.[1]

Crew and Kleindorfer (2002, 2004) reach a similar conclusion and recommend some de-averaging of access prices even where end-to-end prices are uniform. They propose a pricing approach referred to as "delivery access pricing" (DAP), which can be represented in a simplified form by the following formula[2]:

$$p_i^{DA} = \min\left\{\max\left\{p_i^{DA/ECPR}, ac_i\right\}, p^{E2E}\right\} \tag{1}$$

where the access price to zone i, p_i^{DA}, is capped by the retail price, p^{E2E}, for each delivery area, and the calculated access price is the higher of the ECPR

---

[1] The 2 variants of access contract being offered by Royal Mail (uniform access prices for a national average mail profile, and de-averaged prices for a non-national mail profile) are closely aligned to the 2 cases considered by Panzar (2002).

[2] This is a restatement of the formulation shown in Crew and Kleindorfer (2005).

access price, $p_i^{DA/ECPR}$, and the average incremental cost of access, ac_i. Crew and Kleindorfer conclude "the DAP approach emphasizes the importance of charging for downstream access according to the work yet to be done by the (USP) and not only for the avoided cost upstream work accomplished by entrants".

The model developed by De Donder et al (2004, 2005) has a general pricing rule which is a modified version of ECPR, such that an access price p_i^{DA}, to zone *i*, is given by the following formula:

$$p_i^{DA} = d_i + \left(p^{E2E} - c^{UP} - d_i\right)\sigma_i + m_i \tag{2}$$

where the marginal cost of delivery to zone *i* is represented by the first term, d_i, the second term is the profitability cost of a displaced retail item (retail price p^{E2E}, minus upstream cost c^{UP}, minus the marginal cost of delivery to zone *i*) multiplied by the displacement ratio in that area, σ_i, plus a third term, m_i, which is a demand mark-up to ensure that fixed costs are recovered (to help achieve a break-even financial position) where bypass occurs.

The De Donder formula shares common elements with that given at (1). In particular, both emphasize the importance of some de-averaging of access prices to reflect differences in delivery costs in each area. The formulae also share the requirement to take into account the profitability cost of displaced items, as well as a mark-up to recover fixed network costs.

The theoretical approaches discussed above can provide some useful guidance when setting access prices. However, in practice, it is very difficult to follow a strict application of theoretical pricing formulae, not least because they include economic terms that are not easily measurable, especially before competitive entry occurs. The approach adopted by Royal Mail reflects the realities of a negotiated commercial agreement. Implicit is the idea that mail delivered to each zone represents a different "product", such that access prices should reflect the costs of work yet to be done in each delivery zone and so should be expected to vary across zones.

5. SETTING NON-UNIFORM ACCESS PRICES

The setting of non-uniform access prices had to satisfy a number of considerations for them to be accepted by our customers, operators and the Regulator.[3] Firstly and most importantly, the zonal prices must be cost reflective such that the access price of each zone is above the delivery cost

[3] Royal Mail could face Judicial Review if the terms of its zonal access contracts are felt to be anti-competitive or prejudicial.

of that zone. Secondly the number of pricing zones should be kept to a minimum to ensure the product is relatively easy to implement and not too complicated for accessors to understand. Thirdly the definition of zones should be in terms of Royal Mail's existing postcode structure to avoid unnecessary confusion, complication and duplication of addressing. Fourthly the mapping of postcodes to zones must be entirely transparent, such that a clear set of objective and measurable rules are applied in a consistent and mechanistic fashion. Finally the definition of zones and their access prices must be socially acceptable, and seen to be fair to customers, competitors and Royal Mail with its obligations as USP.

5.1 Cost Drivers of Delivery

Royal Mail provides access to its 70 Inward Mail Centers for a variety of configurations of pre-sorted and machine-readable mail. Figure 1 provides an overview of the activities through which the access mail is then processed before it is delivered. The activities are not necessarily completed in the order shown; for example, walk sorting may occur at the delivery office (after local distribution) if the mail is too large to be machine sorted at mail centers.

Figure 1: Major processing activities for mail accessed at Inward Mail Centers

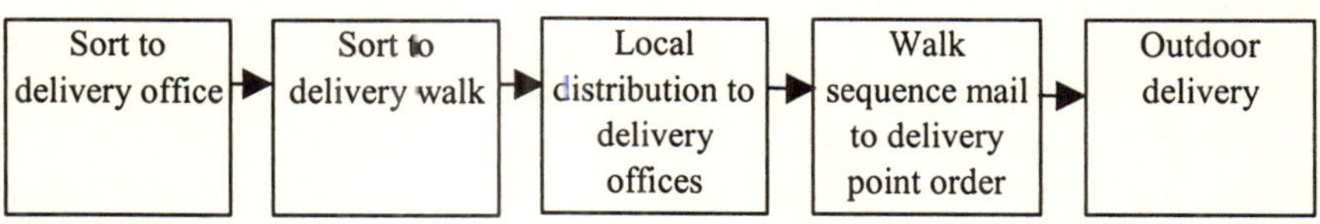

Unit staff costs for the 3 sorting activities (sort to delivery office, sort to delivery walk and walk sequencing) do not vary significantly by geography. These activity costs are driven by the unit time it takes to process each mail piece, which is mainly a function of the size and shape of the mail and the equipment in place to process the mail. The distribution of the size of mail is unlikely to vary significantly by geographical region, and cost differences due to the size/format mix of mail are reflected, to the limited extent possible within a weight based pricing structure, in the national tariff structure.[4]

A less significant driver of sorting costs is the proportion of large volume receivers of mail in a given area. These addresses, which typically are found in commercial centers, can warrant a direct selection in the primary sort stage. However, a small cost saving from a reduction in the number of

[4] Royal Mail will adopt a Size Based Pricing tariff structure ("Pricing in Proportion") from September 2006 and access prices will adopt this structure at the same time.

handlings may not be significant when taken alongside other causes of cost variation such as higher wage rates in London or differences in the mix of labor types due to local labor market differences.

Local Distribution is the activity of transporting mail from the mail center to delivery offices. The costs of this activity vary by geographical area, with unit costs for city centre areas being cheaper than for outlying rural areas. The average overall journey distance to a city center office is much less than that to rural delivery offices. Vehicle utilization is higher in city centers because these offices cover larger numbers of delivery points and high volume receivers.

Outdoor delivery is defined as the activity of traveling to each address and delivering mail through its door. Again the costs of this activity are variable depending on whether mail is delivered to city center, suburban or rural areas. City centers include a relatively high proportion of businesses that receive a large volume of mail per day and will require the use of a vehicle. This serves to increase the average cost of serving a business delivery point (both in terms of staff time and vehicle costs), but the per item cost is below average because of economies of scale resulting from high mail volumes.

Suburban deliveries are mainly by foot or cycle, with a high proportion of delivery points being detached residential houses with garden paths. Inter-drop travel distances are greater than in high-density urban areas and therefore fewer delivery points can be visited during the fixed-time span of a delivery route. This extra travel time per delivery point, together with the lower volumes of mail delivered to residential addresses, result in suburban unit delivery costs that are higher than in commercial city centers.

Inter-drop travel distances continue to increase as areas become more rural, to the extent that most delivery routes require the added cost of vehicle transportation. Whereas vehicle transportation in cities is cost justified on the basis of the large volumes being handled, vehicle deliveries in rural areas will typically serve low volume residential households.

In conclusion, the main differences in unit cost between geographical areas are due to the staff and vehicle costs associated with local distribution and outdoor delivery activities. Costs associated with sorting activities and buildings are relatively uniform across the UK, and in the case of buildings, the costs are relatively small.

5.2 The Definition of Access Pricing Zones

The most important factors that influence geographical cost variations are found to be the travel distance between delivery points, the average volume of mail per delivery point, and the remoteness of the area from major hubs.

It was important to identify robust data to measure these characteristics by postcode, and to be able to group postcodes with similar cost characteristics into zones.

The first major cost driver characteristic - average travel distance between delivery points – is a joint function of road distances and the number of delivery points in a postcode. Royal Mail has approximated this driver by measuring the Delivery Point Density (DPD) of each postcode, which is defined as total surface area (measured in square kilometers) divided by the number of delivery points.

Figure 2 shows the relationship between DPD and the average road distance between delivery points. When DPD is in excess of 100, the average road distance between delivery points is between 10-20 meters, which would enable most delivery points to be visited on foot or cycle. Road distances begin to increase significantly as DPD drops below 100, and there is a further "shift" in average road distance between delivery points when DPD falls below 10.

Figure 2: Relationship between delivery point density and average distance between delivery points

Measurement of the second major cost driver – volume per delivery point - becomes increasingly difficult as postcode areas are disaggregated into smaller areas, such that the resource needed to produce accurate volume measurements is unlikely to be justified on a cost basis. The measurement would also be unverifiable by outside parties and would therefore fail Royal

Mail's stated objective of transparency. An alternative proxy measurement is the proportion of delivery points that are registered as businesses[5] – business density (BD). Businesses tend to receive a much higher volume of mail than residential addresses, and hence, high BD postcodes have a high average volume per delivery point.

Figure 3 shows the relationship between BD and average volume per delivery point. Postcodes with an average BD below 10% receive about 80% of total UK mail, with the average delivery point in these areas receiving just over 2 items of mail per day. The daily average volume per delivery point increases above 10 items when BD approaches 60%.

Figure 3: Business density and its relationship to average volume per delivery point

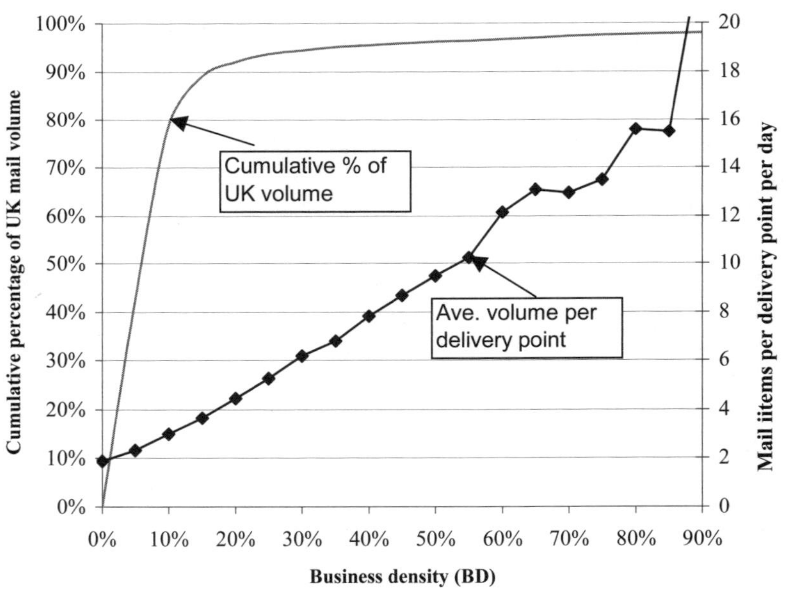

It is concluded that the vast majority of postcodes are predominantly residential with a low BD, and it is very difficult to separate these postcodes in terms of average volume per delivery point. However postcodes with a BD above 10% have a much higher than average volume per delivery point,

[5] Royal Mail uses a strict definition of what constitutes a business address. This includes a requirement for a sign outside the property to advertise the business as such. The business should also be recognized by the local council and be liable to pay the business rate of local property tax.

and typically are located in commercial centers that include the very largest receivers of mail.

The zone definitions take no account of the relative affluence of receivers of mail and are driven solely by the levels of BD and DPD, as it is assumed that the likely higher volume per delivery point of such receivers is balanced by the likelihood of having a greater distance and time between delivery points of such receivers. Any effects due to these factors would be difficult to compute, so in the interests of transparency and overall equity, no account of this has been taken.

DPD is also a good proxy for the third major driver of cost variations between geographical areas - the remoteness of the area from major hubs. This is useful because it avoids the need to add a third dimension to the definition of delivery zones.

Table 1: Cost driver characteristics of each delivery zone

	Zone 1: Commercial	Zone 2: High DPD	Zone 3: Medium DPD	Zone 4: Low DPD	Zone 5: Very low DPD
Definition	BD>10%	DPD > 1000	DPD <=1000 & DPD >100	DPD <=100 & DPD >10	DPD <= 10
% UK surface area	1%	3%	12%	52%	32%
% Surface area is urban	41%	74%	19%	4%	1%
% UK delivery points	8%	42%	33%	16%	1%
% UK mail volume	15%	37%	31%	16%	1%
Average MC to DO distance	3.9	6.7	16.4	34	87
Average road distance between delivery points (metres)	8.4	6.4	12	43.7	121
% Delivery routes are by motorised transport	25%	17%	28%	51%	79%
Average mail items per delivery point per day	4.5	2.2	2.4	2.6	2.6

The analysis above suggests 3 "breakpoints" for defining zones: at BD equal to 10%; and DPD equal to 10 and 100. A further breakpoint at DPD equal to 1000 was added to establish a middle zone with approximately the same unit cost as the national average access product. This was a practical consideration to ensure that one zone had the same price as the national average price, so that the zone could be a default option if information about a postcode's DPD or BD is missing.[6] Table 1 provides a description of each

[6] This might happen if the postcode is new or has recently been reconfigured. A full re-assessment of zones is carried out annually to avoid potential confusion and disruption to

delivery zone and a summary of its cost driver characteristics. Zone 1 accounts for less than 1% of the UK surface area, but 8% of delivery points and as much as 15% of national mail volume. In contrast, zone 5 accounts for 32% of UK surface area but only 1% of national delivery points and mail volume. Zones 4 and 5 have low DPD and therefore the road distance between delivery points is relatively great (43.7 meters and 121.0 meters respectively). These delivery zones are more likely to have motorized transport and this can double the costs of delivery.

Royal Mail has chosen to adopt its existing postcode system to define zones. This has the advantage of being readily available and maintained in databases used by mailers of pre-sort products, and is recognizable by customers and households. For the purposes of implementation, it does not make a significant difference whether zones are calculated at an aggregated or disaggregated postcode level.[7] However for the purposes of cost reflectivity, it is important that zones are configured using disaggregated postcodes to help ensure that geographical variability is not averaged out across large areas.[8]

Royal Mail has defined zones at a postcode sector[9] level of aggregation, of which there are approximately 10,000 in the UK, with an average of 2,700 delivery points in each. Postcode sectors have been tagged to one of the 5 zones according to DPD and BD calculations. If the mapping had been carried out at the more aggregated categorization of postcode areas, 94% of zone 1 delivery points would be re-tagged to different zones, and 74% of zone 5 delivery points would also be re-tagged.

The mapping is dependent on the specific characteristics of each postcode sector (DPD and BD) and is independent of both its location in the UK, and the characteristics of neighboring postcode sectors. This approach ensures that postcodes are not necessarily penalized if they are located in outlying parts of the UK. For example, of the 121 UK postcode areas, 117 contain a postcode sector in zone 1.

---

customers through continuous changes of zone definitions whilst ensuring that the definitions are reasonably up to date.

7 Some Royal Mail customers already presort mail to walk selection, which is a more disaggregated level of sortation than required for zonal access customers.

8 More aggregated categorizations of postcodes make it more likely that a rural area and a city area are grouped together. The average characteristics and cost of such a group would tend towards the middle, and hence an average price for this group would not be reflective of the different costs of delivering mail to city or rural areas.

9 A postcode sector is defined by the first 3 or 4 characters of the outward postcode plus the first character of the inward postcode. For example, SK7 2HE is in the postcode sector SK7_2. A postcode area is defined by the first 1 or 2 letters of the outward postcode, e.g. SK (Stockport) in the above example.

The mapping of postcodes to zones will not be constant over time. Royal Mail will review each postcode sector at least once per year to monitor whether DPD and/or BD have changed to the extent that the postcode should be mapped to a different zone. Possible reasons for a reclassification include an increase in the number of delivery points in a sector, e.g. after the development of a new housing estate, or a reduction in the number of registered businesses due to a recession.

It is important to note that postcodes are mapped to zones by reference to cost driver characteristics rather than the actual reported costs of delivering to specific postcodes. This ensures that zones are not influenced by whether delivery offices in a particular area are more or less efficient than average.

5.3 Access Prices by Zone

Zonal access prices are derived from the average uniform access price for a Royal Mail national average posting profile, and the access delivery cost of each zone compared to the national average delivery cost. The access price in zone i, p_i^{DA}, is given by

$$p_i^{DA} = p^{DA} + \left(c_i^{del} - c^{del}\right) \tag{3}$$

where p^{DA} is the national uniform access price, c_i^{del} is the access cost (i.e. the cost of the activities shown in Figure 1) in cost zone i, and, c^{del}, is the national average access cost. The approach ensures that the access price in any zone is above the access cost for that zone, provided that the national uniform access price is above the national average access cost. The national uniform access price can be expressed as the national average access cost plus a profit margin, and therefore (3) can be re-written to show the access price of each zone as a function of the access cost of that zone plus a profit margin,

$$p_i^{DA} = \left(c^{del} + \pi^{DA}\right) + \left(c_i^{del} - c^{del}\right)$$

$$p_i^{DA} = c_i^{del} + \pi^{DA} \tag{4}$$

where π^{DA} is the profit margin for the national average access product. It can be seen from expression (4) that the profit margin for all zonal access prices is identical, in absolute terms, to the profit margin for the national average access product. This means that the percentage profit margin decreases as the access cost of a zone increases. If the mark-up for each zone was proportional to the access cost of that zone, the difference in prices between zone 1 and 5 would increase above the current level.

Given the need for Royal Mail to test its policy on zonal pricing against competition law requirements (for example, to not be unduly discriminatory), a conservative approach to pricing has been adopted (minimizing the difference between the prices of zones 1 and 5). For similar reasons it was decided not to adopt a Ramsey type approach to pricing whereby profit margins are flexed in each zone to reflect whether the market in each zone is captive. Ramsey pricing would almost certainly result in higher profit margins (and hence inflated prices) in rural areas where competitors are less likely to develop bypass delivery networks to rival a Universal Service Provider offering a uniformly priced end-to-end service.

The access price of each zone can also be expressed as an avoided cost discount from a notional de-averaged E2E price. At the moment Royal Mail charges a uniform price on each of its E2E products, but this might change in the near future because some pre-sort products could be exempted from this pricing constraint by the Regulator. De-averaged prices for these E2E products would reflect the cost differences of delivering to each zone, and might take the following form

$$p_i^{E2E} = c^{avoid} + c_i^{del} + \pi^{E2E} \tag{5}$$

where p_i^{E2E} is the notional E2E price for mail destined to zone i, c^{avoid}, is the upstream cost that is avoided if customers access rather than purchasing E2E products, and π^{E2E} is the profit margin charged for E2E mail delivered to zone i. De-averaged access prices can therefore be rewritten by combining (4) and (5)

$$p_i^{DA} = \left(p_i^{E2E} - c^{avoid}\right) + \left(\pi^{DA} - \pi^{E2E}\right) \tag{6}$$

where the access price for zone i is a function of the notional de-averaged E2E price minus avoided upstream costs, and the profit margin differential between the E2E and access products.

5.4 Examples of Zonal Prices

Royal Mail has developed and published zonal access prices for a range of product variants, which are differentiated in terms of the level of pre-sortation and machine readability and most of which are broadly comparable to the range of end-to-end Mailsort products. All are handed over to Royal Mail at the Inward Mail Centers. All but the final two variants (1400(DO) sort and Walksort) require sortation at the Inward Mail Center. The variants are summarized in Table 2.

Table 2: Access product variants

Variant	Formats	Detail
120	Any	Sorted to Inward Postcode area (e.g. SK,TW)
120 OCR	Letter	Sorted to Inward Postcode area (e.g. SK,TW). Addresses must be machine readable by OCR
120 CBC	Letter	Sorted to Inward Postcode area (e.g. SK,TW). Items must have a machine readable barcode applied by the poster or upstream operator.
700	Letter	Sorted to Inward 'Machine Plan' (approximately 700 selections). Items must have a machine readable barcode applied by the poster or upstream operator.
1400 (DO)	Any	Sorted to Delivery Office(DO). After Revenue Protection activities the bags are transferred to the DO without individual items being sorted at the Inward Mail Centre.
Walksort	Any	Sorted to delivery route within bags sorted to Delivery Office. After Revenue Protection activities the bags are transferred to the DO without individual items being sorted at the Inward Mail Centre.

As an example of the prices Table 3 shows Royal Mail access and E2E prices by delivery zone for the 120 selection OCR product variant,[10] for the year 2005/06. The Mailsort 2 OCR 120 tariff of £0.174 is discounted from the 2nd class public tariff price of £0.21. In turn, the uniform access 120 OCR tariff of £0.13 is discounted against the equivalent Mailsort tariff, and this is equal to the zone 3 price under a non-uniform access contract. Zonal prices for the other zones i, reflect the differences in access cost between zone i, and the national average access cost. It is interesting to note that the de-averaged access price for zone 5 of £0.215 is higher than both the Pre-sort and Public Tariff equivalents for the E2E service. There is a possibility that this will encourage customers to segment their mail by zone, such that mail destined for zones 1-4 will be downstream access, whilst an E2E service will be used for zone 5. However Royal Mail has decided that the principle that access prices should be above zonal delivery costs is a more important consideration at this stage.

Zonal access customers are charged a price based on the "fall-to-earth" of their mail to delivery zones. If a customer accesses all its mail in zone 1, it is charged an average price for access 120 OCR of £0.111 per item. A more likely situation is that a customer accesses in all zones, in which case the

[10] A Mailsort 120 OCR mailing is presorted to 120 selections. This is broadly one per postcode area. All mail is required to be fully addressed and postcoded using an OCR (Optical Character Recognition) font.

average unit access price for a mailing would be somewhere between £0.111 and £0.215, and would tend toward £0.13 unless the customer has a non-national mail profile that is skewed towards city centre or rural delivery points.

Table 3: Royal Mail prices for access and equivalent E2E products, by delivery zone (2005/06 - UK pounds)

		2005/06 prices (0-60g/100g)[1]			
Zone (i)	$c_i^{del} - c^{del}$	E2E: Public Tariff 2nd class	E2E: Mailsort 2, 120	Uniform Access: 120 OCR	Zonal Access: 120 OCR
1	(0.019)	0.21	0.174	0.13	0.111
2	(0.005)	0.21	0.174	0.13	0.125
3	0.000	0.21	0.174	0.13	0.13
4	0.021	0.21	0.174	0.13	0.151
5	0.085	0.21	0.174	0.13	0.215
Average	**0**	**0.21**	**0.174**	**0.13**	**0.13**

[1]E2E prices apply up to 60g, Mailsort and Access prices apply up to 100g

At the commencement of the contract the customer's posting profile over the previous 12 months is used to determine the average price to be used for the forthcoming three months. This average price is recalculated every three months using the actual posting profile and adjustments made if necessary to ensure that the correct revenue has been collected. In the future, subject to technological developments, it may be possible to calculate the price at the time of posting, for each posting. The five individual zonal prices used in the calculation will be subject to review annually alongside other prices.

Table 4 shows a number of examples of how the average price varies depending on the fall-to-earth of a customer's posting. The examples cover a posting with a 'rural' bias and a posting with an 'urban' bias and it will be noted that the overall average for these hypothetical cases differs by the relatively small amount of 1p per item, although as previously noted the difference could be as much as 10.4p (zone 1 *vs* zone 5)

Table 4 : Examples of average prices for Access 120 OCR variant

Zone	Zonal price (p)	'National' Distribution	'Rural' Distribution	'Urban' Distribution
1	11.1	15%	5%	25%
2	12.5	37%	20%	45%
3	13.0	31%	46%	20%
4	15.1	16%	26%	9%
5	21.5	1%	3%	1%
Average		13.0	13.6	12.6

6. CONCLUSIONS

Royal Mail is required under the terms of its license to offer access to all its facilities such that access prices are based on a reasonable allocation of costs, and that Royal Mail does not unduly discriminate between persons having such access. The first access contract between Royal Mail and a licensed postal operator was signed in February 2004. The contract specified a uniform access price to all parts of the country, provided that access mailings have a similar "fall-to-earth" to the Royal Mail national average profile for end-to-end mail. This first contract has subsequently been agreed with a number of other postal operators and large customers, but it proved unsuitable for regional mailers that could not meet the national average mail profile.

A second access contract was therefore developed to meet the requirements of regional mailers, in which the requirement for a national average mail profile was not included, with prices for 5 delivery zones being related to the costs of transporting mail to, and delivering mail in, each zone.

Zonal pricing is still at an early stage of development in the UK. The derivation of prices, the zonal definitions themselves and some detailed aspects all remain under review; for example, the zone 5 price is currently above the corresponding retail price and the number of zones might be modified in the light of experience.

Developments in zonal access pricing are also likely to depend on the outcome of Royal Mail's current Price Control Review. Postcomm's initial proposals include access prices within the price control where they will be subject to pricing constraints that are yet to be finalized. (Postcomm 2005b)

Overall Royal Mail has taken a pragmatic, market led view in balancing the direction given by the theoretical concepts with the need to develop acceptable commercial responses to the legitimate requests from operators and customers for access to Royal Mail's key 'last mile' delivery operation.

REFERENCES

Crew, M.A. and P.R. Kleindorfer. 2002. "Balancing Access and the Universal Service Obligation." In *Postal and Delivery Services: Delivering on Competition,* edited by M.A. Crew and P.R Kleindorfer. Boston, MA: Kluwer Academic Publishers.

Crew, M.A. and P.R. Kleindorfer. 2004. "Access and the USO for Letters and Parcels." In *Competitive Transformation of the Postal and Delivery Sector,* edited by M.A. Crew and P.R Kleindorfer. Boston, MA: Kluwer Academic Publishers.

Crew, M.A. and P.R. Kleindorfer. 2005. "Competition, Universal Service and the Graveyard Spiral." In *Regulatory and Economic Challenges in the Postal and Delivery Sector*, edited by M.A. Crew and P.R Kleindorfer. Boston, MA: Kluwer Academic Publishers.

De Donder, P., H. Cremer, and F. Rodriguez. 2004. “Access Pricing and the Uniform Tariff in the Postal Sector.” In *Competitive Transformation of the Postal and Delivery Sector,* edited by M.A. Crew and P.R. Kleindorfer. Boston, MA: Kluwer Academic Publishers.

De Donder, P., H. Cremer, and F. Rodriguez. 2005. “Access Pricing in the Postal Sector: Results from a Model with Bypass and Customer Direct Access.” In *Regulatory and Economic Challenges in the Postal and Delivery Sector*, edited by M.A. Crew and P.R. Kleindorfer. Boston, MA: Kluwer Academic Publishers.

European Communities 2002. Directive 2002/39/EC of the European Parliament and of the Council of 10 June 2002 amending Directive 97/67/EC with regard to the further opening to competition of Community postal services. OJEC L176/21.

Hill, R., R. Robinson and F. Rodriguez 2005. “Financial Equilibrium of Universal Providers in a Liberalized Postal Market”. In *Regulatory and Economic Challenges in the Postal and Delivery Sector*, edited by M.A. Crew and P.R. Kleindorfer. Boston, MA: Kluwer Academic Publishers.

Panzar, J. 2002. “Reconciling Competition, Downstream Access and Universal Service in Postal Markets.” In *Postal and Delivery Services: Delivering on Competition,* edited by M.A. Crew and P.R. Kleindorfer. Boston, MA: Kluwer Academic Publishers.

Postcomm. 2003. License granted to Royal Mail Group plc. Issued 23 March 2001 and amended 1st April 2003.

Postcomm. 2005a. Giving Customers Choice: A Fully Open Postal Services Market. 18th February 2005.

Postcomm. 2005b. 2006 Royal Mail Price and Service Quality Review. Initial Proposals. June 2005.

Royal Mail. 2004a. “UK Mail/Royal Mail: Historic Agreement signed for Access to Postal Facilities”. February 10th 2004.

Royal Mail. 2004b. “Access to Royal Mail Postal Facilities,” found at www.royalmail.com, Terms and Conditions > Condition 9 Access Agreement.

UK Mail. 2005. Press Statement. May 17th 2005.

Chapter 9

Worksharing: How Much Productive Efficiency, at What Cost and at What Price?*

Robert H. Cohen, Matthew H. Robinson, John D. Waller, and Spyros S. Xenakis
Postal Rate Commission

1. INTRODUCTION

Worksharing refers to upstream postal activities, such as presortation and barcoding, performed by mailers or third parties to obtain discounts on postage for reducing the post's upstream costs. From a practical regulatory point-of-view the primary purpose of worksharing is to lower society's cost of production (i.e., to increase productive efficiency) by allowing customers and third parties to perform upstream activities when their costs are lower than the post's. Previous studies by the authors have shown that the increase in productive efficiency can be quite substantial (Cohen, et al. 2002, 2004).

Other studies by the authors have concluded that end-to-end competition is likely to have limited success (Cohen et al. 2000, 2005).[1] Thus, it may well be that upstream liberalization is the best way to increase productive efficiency in the postal market.

Prices for workshared mail are discounted from a base (non-workshared) rate. When worksharing discounts are designed to maximize productive efficiency, the resulting prices are called efficient component prices (ECP).

---

* The views expressed in this paper are those of the authors and do not necessarily represent the opinions of the Postal Rate Commission.

[1] This paper presupposes no competition in delivery. Other research indicates that with end-to-end competition, sustainability considerations may require worksharing discounts to be less than full ECP. *See* Billette de Villemeur 2002.

John Panzar has stated that ECP discounts "should be exactly equal to the cost the postal service would have incurred had it moved the mail through the non-delivery portion of its system" (Panzar 2002). The cost the postal service would have incurred by moving workshared mail through the non-delivery (upstream) portion of its system is likely to be less than it does incur for single-piece mail. Under these circumstances the ECP discount should be based on the cost of the mail most likely to convert to workshared status. This is the subject of Section 3.

Some observers in the U.S. have advocated a radical departure from using ECP for worksharing discounts. They call ECP a top down approach because it discounts from a single-piece or basic rate. Instead they advocate building rates from the bottom starting with a bare bones delivery rate and then adding charges for any additional services a mailer might require. They call this bottom up pricing. The authors believe that bottom up pricing would lead to productive *inefficiency* and would sacrifice the Pareto dominant feature of ECP pricing. Pricing of worksharing discounts is the subject of Section 4 and Section 5 summarizes our principal conclusions.

2. HOW MUCH PRODUCTIVE EFFICIENCY?

Worksharing discounts brought about a large growth of volume in the U.S. (Pearsall 2005, Cohen et al. 2002). This occurred especially in advertising mail[2] but also in First-Class and parcels. Worksharing expanded the number of categories of mail for each subclass where it was introduced. Advertising mail underwent the greatest expansion as it grew from two categories (prior to the first discount) to 178 today. First-Class Letters and Cards grew from two to 16. Analysis shows that when a new category was introduced there was a volume response that exceeded the response expected from ordinary own price elasticity (Pearsall 2005 and Cohen et al. 2002, 2004). We have concluded that when rate schedules are expanded to include more categories, mail becomes more useful and this causes volumes to increase.[3]

Initially worksharing consisted of simple presortation and it involved mailers substituting virtual sorting using computers for physical sorting by the Postal Service. Later it expanded to include bar-coding (including the associated address hygiene) and drop shipping. These changes have had a dramatic impact on productive efficiency. The discounts approved by the Postal Rate Commission (PRC) are based on avoided cost. We have

[2] Advertising mail consists of the Standard Regular and Enhanced Carrier Route subclasses.

[3] For example, worksharing gives mailers more control over the date of delivery. This adds value, especially in a geographically large country like the U.S.

calculated the value of the discounts for FY 2004 to be $14 billion. See Table 1. However, the cost to mailers of most worksharing activities is less than twenty percent of the discount (Cohen et al. 2004). Drop shipping is an exception. It costs less than half the discount. We do not know the cost to third party consolidators who physically sort First-Class letters and flats. Nevertheless, it can be estimated that about $11 billion of the $14 billion were net savings to the U.S. economy. Postal Service total expenses were $66 billion in 2004.

Table 1: Worksharing Avoided Costs and Value of Worksharing Discounts (2004 Millions)

Class of Mail	All Volume	Workshared Volume	% of Volume Workshared	Total USPS Cost Avoided	Value of Discounts
First-Class Mail	97,926	50,239	51%	$3,466	$3,440
Periodicals	9,135	8,731	96	1,485	1,396
Advertising Mail	95,564	89,762	94	9,297	9,121
Package Services	1,132	826	73	151	108
Other	2,349	-	-	0	0
Total	206,106	149,559	73	14,399	14,065
User Cost [a]					2,813
Mailers Net Saving[a]					11,252

a. User cost is assumed to be 20 percent of discount

While it might be hoped that introducing upstream competition would result in the incumbent operator increasing its own efficiency, this did not happen in the U.S. The Postal Service's total factor productivity increased a scant 1.5 percent over the ten-year period following the introduction of the first worksharing discount in 1976.

The increase of postal productive efficiency over time in the U.S. is the product of the growth of workshared volume and the increasing depth of presort and drop shipping into the network (i.e., the number of handlings that are eliminated). We first document volume growth due to worksharing and then show the trend of increasing depth of sort and drop shipping into the network. We also show how much of the upstream work remains in the hands of the Postal Service.

2.1 Volume Growth

The analysis of the causal connection between worksharing and volume growth that we present here is based on Pearsall's econometric model (Pearsall 2005). The model distinguishes between secular trends and growth due to worksharing. The impact of worksharing from the year before it began in each class to 2004 is shown in Table 2.

Table 2: Volume Growth Due to Worksharing Discounts (Year before Introduction to 2004)

Class	Year Before Introduction	Without Worksharing	From Worksharing	Total Growth
First-Class	1975	-3%	96%	93%
Periodicals	1977	-12	13	1
Advertising	1978	110	150	260
Parcel Post	1990	-71	294	223

The impact of worksharing was great for all classes save Periodicals. This can be explained by the fact that Periodical volume is driven by subscriptions which had started a per capita decline long before the advent of worksharing discounts. The impact of worksharing on advertising mail is of particular importance. Before worksharing the advertising share of total volume was 27 percent, today its share is 47 percent, the same as First-Class. So far in 2005 it exceeds First-Class.

2.2 Increasing depth of sort and drop shipping

2.2.1 Periodicals and Advertising Mail

Prior to the introduction of presort discounts for these two classes in the late seventies, mail was required to be presorted even though there were no rate incentives corresponding to the degree of presort. There was simply a uniform price. The introduction of presort discounts deaveraged the prices.

"Density" is the ratio of the volume of a mailing to the number of carrier routes included in the mailing. *Ceterus paribus*, the larger the volume, the greater the density, or the smaller the number of carrier routes included in a mailing, the greater the density. The latter is important, because it means that smaller volume periodical and advertising mailings can qualify for lower rates and this contributes to diversity in both industries. Worksharing discounts also introduced a new level of presortation, carrier route presort, that rewarded the most dense mailings. In 1991 a saturation tier was added that recognized the densest subset of carrier route.[4]

Presort discounts were powerful incentives for mailers to change their behavior by increasing the density of their mailings. Bindery lines were modified to allow separate editions of a magazine or advertisements to be combined into a single mailing and achieve greater density. The number of editions of publications that required separate mailings were reduced and efforts were made to speed up address changes and new additions to mailing lists so that subsequent (smaller volume) mailings of the same material

---

[4] In other countries most of this mail would be unaddressed mail. Because the Postal Service has a mailbox monopoly, it delivers much of this mail.

would not be needed. Advertising mailers chose more dense mailing lists when possible and advertising test mailings were also tailored to gain density. It is interesting to note that, unlike First-Class, there is little evidence of third-party consolidators combining advertising mailings to gain density.[5]

Table 3: Periodicals (Outside County) Presort Tiers (Percent)

Presort Level	1982	1983	1999	2002
Basic	35%	31	8	8
3/5-Digit	43	44	46	46
Carrier Route	22	25	46	46
Volume (billions)	8	8	9	9

Table 3 presents volumes and the changes in the distribution by presort levels for Periodicals over a 20-year period starting in 1982 when data were first available on the distribution by presort tier.[6] It can be seen that the response to the new carrier route category was substantial and that the basic level fell by over 75 percent by 1999 but then stabilized through 2002. Recently large printers have begun to increase co-bundling (i.e., merging different titles into the same bundle) to improve density.[7]

Table 4: Advertising Mail[a] Presort Tiers (Percent)

Presort Level	1979	1983	1999	2002
Basic	71%[b]	41	10	9
3/5 Digit	21	18	44	49
Carrier Route	8	41	31	27
Saturation			15	15
Volume (billions)	27	41	86	87

a. 1999 & 2002 distribution correct for migration of carrier route mail to 3/5-digit.
b. The data available for 1979 combined 3-digit with Basic.

Table 4 shows the volumes and changes in the distribution by presort levels for advertising mail. The data from 1979 is based on Postal Service estimates of what the volumes would have been if no worksharing discounts had been introduced in that year.[8] It can be seen that through 1999 the basic level declined dramatically.

Table 5 displays trends in drop shipping of commercial (excluding nonprofit) advertising mail. This is the category that makes the greatest use

---

[5] However, third parties are involved in the drop shipping of advertising mail.

[6] The table combines regular and nonprofit volumes and provides results for years in which data are available from omnibus rate case filings.

[7] They have also begun to co-palletize (i.e., mix bundles of different titles onto the same pallet) to allow drop shipping more deeply into the network.

[8] The data combines regular and nonprofit categories. The data in Table 4 also combines standard regular and enhanced carrier route for the years 1999 and 2002.

of drop shipping.[9] Discounts for drop shipping were introduced in 1991 so the data from 1989 provides a base line. It can be seen that mailers responded to the discounts and the percentage of mail that is drop shipped continues to grow and mail continues to be dropped more deeply into the network.

Table 5: Drop Ship Advertising Mail[a] (Percent)

	1989	1998	2004
No Dropship	85%	42	26
Bulk Mail Center (BMC)	1	24	27
Sectional Center Facility (SCF)	10	26	40
Destination Delivery Unit (DDU)	4	8	7
Volume (billions)	37	53	64

a. Only Commercial piece-rated mail.

2.2.2 First-Class

First-Class was a single-piece class prior to the introduction of the first presort discount in 1976. There were large *de facto* bulk mailers of First-Class, but no rate recognition was given to their mail. It was estimated that prior to the discount about 1.5 billion pieces (or about 3 percent) of First-Class was presorted (Postal Service 1976). It has grown to about 50 percent today. Because of economies of density, third party consolidators, who sprang into existence in every large city after the introduction of the first discount, frequently can work more mail to a greater depth of sort than individual mailers. Even very large mailers who prepare their own mail will give their residue (i.e., mail that they can not sort deeply) to a consolidator.

Table 6 shows that by 1993, 33 billion pieces of First-Class were presorted.[10,11] The nonautomation category is experiencing a steady decline in volume and receives a diminished discount.

Table 6: First-Class Mail Presort Tiers (Percent)

	1993	1996	2000	2004
Nonauto Presort	72%	28	11	5
Auto Basic Presort	1	4	12	12
Auto 3-Digit Presort	21	43	49	40
Auto 5-Digit Presort	6	25	28	34
Volume (billions)	33	38	47	49

[9] There is no incentive offered for drop shipping First-Class.

[10] The carrier route level may only be used for areas where the Postal Service has not installed automated sorting equipment and it is used by about one percent of presorted First-Class.

[11] First-Class also has a non-automation category (i.e., without mailer applied barcodes.) The remaining volume is referred to as "automation presort".

There is a continuing trend towards greater depth of sort as 5-digit gains share. We believe that this may be due in part to consolidation in the third party industry that allows the remaining players to achieve a greater depth of sort owing to economies of density. In addition, at least one firm, Pitney Bowes, is increasing its ownership of firms in the third-party industry and moves mail between facilities in order to achieve greater depth of sort. It can be seen that the volume of workshared First-Class continues to grow.[12]

2.2.3 Parcel Post

The drop ship program for parcel post was instituted in 1991. In the prior year, the volume of parcel post had reached a nadir of 128 million pieces after several decades of decline. As a result of the drop ship program, volume began to increase and in 2004 it reached 376 million including 275 million drop shipped. This program has allowed third-party consolidators to perform upstream activities with the Postal Service primarily doing the delivery to residences. Table 7 shows the distribution by level of drop shipment. It can be seen that nearly a third of the volume that is drop shipped is to the delivery unit.

Table 7: Distribution of Drop Ship Parcel Post Volume (Percent)

	2004
Origin Bulk Mail Center (OBMC)	5%
Destination Bulk Mail Center (DBMC)	62
Destination Sectional Center Facility (DSCF)	1
Destination Delivery Unit (DDU)	32
Volume (millions)	275

2.3 Upstream work that remains for the Postal Service

Table 8 displays the total piece handlings that must be performed by the Postal Service for each category of First-Class and Standard (advertising) letter mail and Standard flat mail. Two automated handlings are needed for sorting letters to the carrier walk sequence from the 5-digit level. In contrast, flats are sorted to carrier walk sequence manually by letter carriers and this sort is therefore not included in Table 8.[13,14] This accounts for the fact that letters require more handlings than flats. Despite the success of the presort program in the U.S., most of the work (i.e., 75 percent of piece

[12] Single-piece mail has been in a (non-monotonic) decline since about 1991.

[13] The Service is developing sequencing machines for flats.

[14] Notwithstanding, it costs less to sequence letters because it is an automated operation.

handlings)[15] remains in the hands of the Service. While some observers have spoken of a hollowing out of the Postal Service, this has not happened and judging from recent trends, it does not seem likely to happen.

Table 8: Total Piece Handlings (TPH) by USPS First-Class and Standard Mail Automation Presort FY 2004 - Excluding Nonprofit and Carrier Route Presort

	Total TPH per piece	Volume (000)	Pct. of Total Volume	Total TPH (000)	Pct. of Total TPH
First-Class and Standard Mail Letters					
First-Class Machinable Single-Piece	4.59	45,161,746	34	207,122,271	45
Automation Basic	3.86	11,282,055	8	43,568,784	9
Automation 3-Digit	3.22	42,348,465	32	136,383,474	29
Automation 5-Digit	2.23	35,035,250	26	77,963,744	17
Total Automation Letters	2.91	88,665,770	66	257,916,002	55
Total Automation and Single-Piece	3.47	133,827,516	100	465,038,274	100
Avoided by Automation Letters (vs. SP)	**1.68**			**148,725,843**	
Standard Mail Flats					
Basic Nonautomation	2.63	404,184	3	1,061,407	6
Basic Automation	2.43	424,369	3	1,032,145	5
3/5-Digit Automation	1.41	12,183,220	94	17,173,272	89
Total Std. Automation Flats	1.44	12,607,589	97	18,205,418	94
Total Automation and Basic Nonauto	1.48	13,011,773	100	19,266,825	100
Avoided by Std. Auto Flats (vs. Nonauto Basic)	**1.18**			**14,902,718**	

Note: Machinable First-Class (FC) single-piece is used as letter benchmark. FC bulk metered mail (4.60 TPH) would produce similar results, as would FC or Standard nonautomation basic presort letters (4.59 TPH and 4.60 TPH, respectively). For flats, presort level is adjusted to nonautomation mix for like comparison.

3. AT WHAT COST

Worksharing discounts send important signals to mailers who must decide whether the value of a discount outweighs the additional expense of the work required to qualify for it. Absent other considerations, it is important that discounts offered to mailers for reducing the Postal Service's workload accurately reflect the resulting cost reduction. Deviations from cost-based discounts will result in mailer decisions that are less efficient. The PRC has been criticized for setting worksharing discounts that are too small, leading to the subsidy of upstream activities of the Postal Service by the implicit price for delivery (Haldi et al. 2003). This criticism is based on the fact that the average worksharing discount for First-Class is less than the average upstream cost of single piece First-Class. It implies a significant departure from ECP, under which discounts and avoided costs for worksharing activities would be equal.

The evaluation of the cost of upstream activities is of particular concern for First-Class mail because it includes mail with a wide-variety of cost driving characteristics. The upstream costs of single-piece (non-workshared) mail reflect the fact that it is much more likely to be handwritten,

[15] USPS Total TPH divided by sum of USPS Total TPH and avoided TPH.

nonmachinable, inaccurately addressed, or weigh more than workshared mail. A presort discount, however, should simply reflect the (Postal Service's) costs saved by presortation. Using the raw differences between the average cost of single-piece and workshared mail as the basis for worksharing discounts would send the wrong price signal to mailers by encouraging the use of worksharing even if the mailer's cost exceeds the actual savings to the Postal Service.

As an example of the distortions that can be caused by using total cost differences to set worksharing discounts, assume that non-workshared mail costs an average of 23 cents for the Postal Service to sort, transport and deliver, while a subset of non-workshared mail with characteristics similar to workshared mail (non-workshared bulk) costs 20 cents to handle and workshared mail costs 15 cents. A discount equal to the 8-cent cost difference between non-workshared and workshared mail would result in upstream revenues equal to upstream costs, but it would not encourage the most efficient behavior.

Consider a hypothetical mailer of bulk non-workshared mail who must spend 7 cents to do the work needed to qualify for the 8-cent discount. This rate design encourages the mailer to do so and pocket the 1-cent difference. When this happens, the Service's costs are reduced by 5 cents, but its revenues are reduced by 8 cents. This is clearly an inefficient result. Not only will the lost contribution need to be recovered from other mailers, but also the total cost to society is increased from 20 cents (all work done by Postal Service) to 22 cents (15 cents by Postal Service plus 7 cents by mailer).

To encourage mailers to make the most efficient decisions, discounts must be set equal to the cost reductions that result from the behavior in question. In the example above, the worksharing discount must be set equal to the 5-cent savings from worksharing. If the cost differences within non-workshared mail are to be addressed, they should be through other rate elements. For example, nonmachinable mail is currently subject to a surcharge and it would, for example, theoretically be possible to impose an additional surcharge on mail with handwritten addresses to reflect the additional cost of processing it.

4. AT WHAT PRICE

The PRC selects unique markups over the attributable cost of each subclass in order to generate revenue to cover the institutional cost of the Postal Service. A feature of ECP is that otherwise similar pieces in each worksharing category within a subclass have the same unit (per piece) markup. This is the result of subtracting the cost avoided by each worksharing tier from the rate of the tier just above it or, in the case of the first worksharing tier, from the single-piece rate or the basic rate. A corollary of this feature of ECP is that the implied percentage markup of mail is higher when it is entered at lower presort tiers. Table 9 illustrates this.

Table 9: Illustration of Markups Implied by ECP

Non-workshared-piece attributable cost	10 cents
Non-workshared-piece rate (includes markup)	22 cents
Non-workshared-piece unit markup	12 cents
Implicit percent markup for single-piece	120 percent
Cost avoided by first tier of worksharing	2 cents
First tier worksharing unit attributable cost	8 cents
Rate for first tier	20 cents
Unit markup for first tier	12 cents
Implicit percent markup for first tier	150 percent

These features of ECP were important to the Postal Service at the inception of the program because it meant that it did not lose any institutional contribution because of worksharing. It was equally important to mailers that did not participate in the worksharing program because it meant that they would not be required to pay more in institutional contribution to make up for worksharing mailers who were paying less. ECP made worksharing a Pareto dominant move. No one was made worse off.[16] This was very important to the Postal Rate Commission because it was setting rates in a litigation environment and it wanted to ensure the broadest possible support for worksharing.

It is not surprising that some mailers who participate in worksharing and especially mailers who deeply presort, think that it is unfair for them to pay a higher percentage markup than others who do not presort or presort so deeply. They advocate that rates should not be discounted from the top as ECP requires. They would prefer a bottom up approach that starts with a bare bones delivery only rate to which an amount is added for each additional service that a mailing might require. The authors have not seen a full-blown bottom up proposal, but presumably it would include a markup

[16] If the starting point is averaged rates and disparate costs, then at the start institutional contributions are unequal. Under this circumstance deaveraging the rates will equalize the unit institutional contributions and some rates necessarily will increase. This was the situation for Periodicals when worksharing discounts were introduced. Prior to that, presorting was required but each presort tier paid the same averaged rate. When discounts were installed and ECP was used for pricing, rates were deaveraged. The problem did not emerge in First-Class or in advertising mail when carrier route was introduced because few pieces were being presorted in First-Class or presorted to the carrier route in advertising mail before the discounts were put into effect.

on each service element (perhaps an equal markup) that would lower the rates for the least workshared mail.[17]

It may be that bottom up pricing advocates are arguing for *de facto* subclass status (i.e., independent markup) for some of the worksharing tiers. If so, their argument would be about classification and not pricing. The Postal Rate Commission set forth in its MC95-1 decision its view that subclasses can be created from existing rate categories if it is shown that they have substantially different cost and market characteristics.

In contrast, 54 percent of carrier costs are fixed and this amounts to 52 percent of the total Postal Service institutional costs. They represent a significant cost that should be paid by every piece of delivered mail, regardless of the recovery of the institutional costs of other functions. In the previous section we showed that only ECP sends the pricing signal that leads to maximizing productive efficiency. Thus, to have workshare prices provide the proper incentive for the lowest cost producer to do the work, ECP should be used.

5. CONCLUSIONS

Worksharing may be the most effective means to increase productive efficiency in the postal sector. In the U.S., worksharing allowed the Postal Service to avoid over $14 billion in costs in 2004. We estimate that this results in productive efficiency increases (or net savings to mailers) that exceeded $11 billion in 2004.

In spite of the fact that 75 percent of the mail is workshared, the Postal Service still does 75 percent of all upstream total piece handlings. It is a myth that the Postal Service is being hollowed out by worksharing.

Efficient Component Pricing (ECP), which maximizes productive efficiency, requires that avoided cost be the basis of the discount. In a class with diverse costs, like First-Class, the benchmark must be the cost of the mail most likely to convert to worksharing. The cost of this mail is lower than the average cost of the non-workshared mail. Using the cost of the average piece will result in price signals that will lead to inefficient production.

---

[17] Bottom up pricing should not be confused with what is known as bottom up costing. Advocates of the latter object to the engineering models used to estimate the cost avoided by worksharing. They think that the engineering models have an *a priori* bias as to what costs are avoided. In order to get more reliable estimates, these advocates want to use the Postal Service's statistical sampling systems with improvements to estimate the cost avoided. They feel that having more reliable data is worth the increase in the cost of data collection because the increase would be very small in absolute terms compared to Postal Service total revenues.

Pricing that results in different unit contributions for worksharing tiers within a subclass would also give price signals that lead to inefficient production. It would turn the process of establishing worksharing discounts into a zero sum game. In contrast ECP pricing will give signals that maximize productive efficiency and allow worksharing discounts to be Pareto dominant.

REFERENCES

Billette de Villemeur, E., H. Cremer, B. and J. Toledano. 2002. "Pricing and Worksharing Discounts in the Postal Sector." In *Postal and Delivery Services: Delivering on Competition,* edited by M.A. Crew and P.R. Kleindorfer. Boston: Kluwer Academic Publishers.

Cohen, R.H., M. Robinson, R. Sheehy, J. Waller and S. Xenakis. 2004. "Postal Regulation and Worksharing in the U.S." In *Regulating Postal Markets – Harmonised versus Country Specific Approaches. To be published by Wissenschaftliches Institut für Kommunikationsdienste (WIK).*

Cohen, R.H., M. Robinson, R. Sheehy, J. Waller and S. Xenakis. 2005. "Will Entrants into a Liberalized Delivery Market Attract Investors". In *Regulatory and Economic Challenges in the Postal and Delivery Sector,* edited by M.A. Crew and P.R. Kleindorfer. Boston: Kluwer Academic Publishers.

Cohen, R.H., W.W. Ferguson, J.D. Waller and S.S. Xenakis. 2000. "Universal Service Without a Monopoly". In *Current Directions in Postal Reform,* edited by M.A. Crew and P.R. Kleindorfer. Boston: Kluwer Academic Publishers.

Cohen, R.H., W.W. Ferguson, J.D. Waller and S.S. Xenakis. 2002. "The Impact of Using Worksharing to Liberalize a Postal Market". In *Liberalisation of Postal Markets,* edited by G. Kulenkampff and H.Smit. Rheinbreitbach: Druckerei Plump KG.

Haldi, J., and W.J. Olson. 2005. "An Evaluation of USPS Worksharing: Postal Revenues and Costs From Workshared Activities. In *Competitive Transformation of The Postal and Delivery Sector*, edited by M.A. Crew and P.R. Kleindorfer. Boston: Kluwer Academic Publishers.

Panzar, J.C. 2002. "Reconciling Competition, Downstream Access, and Universal Service in Postal Markets. In *Postal and Delivery Services: Delivering on Competition,* edited by M.A. Crew and P.R. Kleindorfer. Boston: Kluwer Academic Publishers.

Pearsall, E.S. 2005. "The Effects of Worksharing and Other Product Innovations on U.S. Postal Volumes and Revenues". In *Regulatory and Economic Challenges in the Postal and Delivery Sector,* edited by M.A. Crew and P.R. Kleindorfer. Boston: Kluwer Academic Publishers.

Postal Service Staff Study. 1976. "The Necessity for Change", Appendix 3, Restructuring The Postal Service Classification Structure On Economic Principles, reprinted by the House Committee on Postal Service and Civil Service. Print No. 26, 96th Cong., 2nd Session.

Chapter 10

Regulating Access to Stimulate Competition in Postal Markets?*

Paul W.J. de Bijl, Eric van Damme, and Pierre Larouche
Tilburg University

1. INTRODUCTION

In European Commission (2005), the Commission's most recent progress report to the Council on the application of the Postal Directive[1], it is stated:

> "Competition has yet to develop in the addressed mail segment outside niche services, and this suggests that limited initial market opening combined with sometimes limited regulatory capacity or certainty, advantages enjoyed by incumbents, and regulatory asymmetries have all combined to deter entry ...The reasons for the continuously slow progress towards greater competition in fully liberalized postal markets are puzzling and deserve further analysis".

In this paper, we provide some elements for such an analysis. Clearly, with the market moving to a one-way distribution market and the abolition of legal barriers to entry (the reserved sector) in postal markets, the possibilities for competition increase, and we investigate whether effective competition is likely to develop on its own, or whether specific access

---

* The paper is based on the TILEC study "'Light is Right': Conditions for Competition and Regulation in the Postal Market' (June 2005) that was commissioned by Deutsche Post World Net and TNT. We thank the editors for helpful comments.

1 Directive 97/67 of 15 December 1997 [1998] OJ L 15/14, as amended by Directive 2002/39 of 10 July 2002 [2002] OJ L 176/21.

regulation is necessary or desirable in attaining this end.[2] We argue that in a liberalized postal market, besides legal and regulatory entry barriers, there are no significant natural entry barriers that could ultimately prevent profitable entry. We thus conclude that, as a result of the absence of monopolistic bottlenecks, a large section of the postal market will be accessible after full liberalization. Focusing on downstream access (competitors inserting mail at a point further down in the network of the Universal Service Provider (USP)), we argue that specific mandatory access regulation, on top of generic non-discrimination principles found in competition law and strengthened if necessary in sector-specific regulation, is not needed to facilitate competition and may be counterproductive. Not mandating access does not imply that access will be unavailable: the incumbent may offer it on commercial terms. Furthermore, regulating access may bias entry strategies towards a specific entry mode, thereby possibly limiting innovation.

The Postal Directive does not impose specific access rules. It refers to transparent and non-discriminatory access to the postal network, to tariffs and special tariffs having to be "geared to cost", and to the USP having to take into account avoided cost when setting special tariffs. Access is otherwise left to negotiations between market players. The European Commission (2005) states that access is an important issue that merits further analysis, that it appears premature to draw any conclusions at this stage, and that:

> "Access can help facilitate market entry for upstream consolidators. New competitors who want to establish a delivery network can also use access for a transitional period to build up customer relationships and volumes, before being able to compete end to end with the incumbent".

This no doubt is true, but it seems only one side of the picture. If mandating access at regulated tariffs makes access cheap, as compared to rolling out alternative infrastructures, then a natural development of full end-to-end competition may be hindered, or may be prevented altogether. As infrastructure competition typically offers more scope for innovation by entrants and provides stronger incentives for cost reduction, upsetting the balance by making available a mandated downstream access alternative may thus be counterproductive. In this paper we argue that, taking into account EC competition law and using the principles underlying the most recent

---

[2] This paper does not discuss the appropriateness of liberalizing the postal sector as such; hence, we do not consider the risk of a "graveyard spiral"; see Crew and Kleindorfer (2001). It is assumed that liberalization is justified and that the USO is adequately dealt with.

regulatory thinking (in particular the EC Electronic Communications Framework), downstream access should not be mandated via regulation. In our view, the absence of insurmountable natural entry barriers implies that a hands-off approach, a regulatory commitment to negotiated access, leaving the development of competition – and also of the *type* of competition – to the market, is most desirable.

Our conclusion, hence, differs somewhat from that reached in NERA (2004) and Moriarty and Smith (2005), in which it is suggested that regulated access to delivery networks may be necessary to have substantial scope for competition. We agree about the potential for competition, but in our view, given that delivery is not a monopolistic bottleneck, the incumbent will typically want to benefit from scale economies and, hence, find it to be in its interest to provide access, especially when a non-discrimination requirement is in place. Consequently, we argue for relying on 'freedom of contract', instead of obliging the USP to provide access at regulated terms. If it were nevertheless found that regulatory intervention could bring added value, we believe that the requirements of transparency and non-discrimination should be sufficient to establish a competitive postal market.

We note that our conclusion is in line with that of Van der Lijn and Meijer (2004). Our paper complements theirs, among others by providing a more elaborate legal perspective. We discuss the added value of our contribution more extensively in the concluding section, where we will also discuss related literature such as Crew and Kleindorfer (2002) and Panzar (2002).

The remainder of this paper elaborates our arguments. In Section 2, we set out the legal framework in Europe, leading to the conclusion that the presence of barriers to entry is a necessary condition for any intervention, whether under competition law or sector-specific regulation. In Section 3, we ask whether, in the postal market, there are natural barriers to entry, and we provide some indicative calculations to show that, already with a low market share, entry may be profitable. In Section 4, we explain the difference between natural monopolies, and monopolistic bottlenecks and argue that, even though segments of the postal market may be a natural monopoly, there is no economic justification for regulatory intervention on access as there are no monopolistic bottlenecks. In Section 5, we feed the results of the economic analysis into the legal framework and come to the conclusion that a hands-off approach is most desirable.

2. THE LEGAL FRAMEWORK IN EUROPE

2.1 The relationship between competition law and sector-specific regulation

With full liberalization, the reserved sector vanishes, and with it the need for detailed regulation to delineate and manage it. The whole sector is open to the workings of the market economy except for any regulation of the USP. So regulation must rest on solid economic analysis in order not to cancel the benefits of the operation of the market. Regulation based on technical characteristics should be discarded in favor of regulation based on economic analysis.

The design of economic regulation involves a consideration of two regulatory instruments, namely competition law (as a general form of economic regulation) and sector-specific regulation. At the outset, it should be underlined that the relationship between the two is conceived differently in Europe than in the US. In the latter, sector-specific regulation will usually be expected to include provisions to deal with conduct harmful to competition, and if it does, antitrust law is likely to be found inapplicable.[3] In the EU, in contrast, EC competition law is enshrined in the EC Treaty, and hence it is and remains in principle applicable irrespective of sector-specific regulation. The dominant view is that sector-specific regulation should thus concentrate on issues that are not adequately addressed via general competition law.

As this paper is concerned with the situation in Europe, the EU approach will be followed. In this respect, the conceptual and analytical principles of the new regulatory framework for electronic communications are very relevant: there is no need to re-invent the wheel. However, simply transposing the end-result of the regulatory process from one sector to the other is neither convincing nor responsible from an academic perspective. Rather, the main lesson to be drawn from the new framework in electronic communications lies in the significance of a principled approach to regulation, which starts from the fundamentals.

In line with the above, the electronic communications framework rests on a view of sector-specific regulation and competition law as complementary instances of economic regulation. Since competition law is generally formulated and applicable across-the-board, it also serves as a benchmark for sector-specific regulation. Sector-specific regulation is meant to be aligned with competition law in substance. This implies using economic analysis and following the well-known steps of market definition, market analysis and

---

[3] See *Verizon Communications* v. *Trinko*, Docket No. 02-682 (US Sup Ct, 13 January 2004)

remedies. Regulation which follows in the footsteps of competition law in substance is likely to be justifiable, whereas regulation exceeding the bounds of competition law should require a specific justification.

2.2 The starting point: competition law

In light of the above, it is useful to start by considering how competition law would apply to a liberalized postal sector. For the sake of argument, we leave aside market definition and the assessment of dominance, and simply assume that the incumbent would be found dominant on a relevant market comprising the provision of downstream services to competitors. The prohibition on abuses of dominant position at Article 82 EC implies then that the incumbent would be bound to refrain from certain types of conduct, or in other words, that it would be under certain obligations as to its conduct. Two types of obligation come into question here: access to facilities and non-discrimination.

2.2.1 Access to facilities

Access issues are sometimes brought under the keyword "essential facilities", but what matters is the test put forward in the case-law of the European Court of Justice (ECJ). In the case of physical facilities, the current test results from combining *Bronner* with *IMS*.[4] This test applies in order to judge whether a firm should be ordered to open up a facility (seen as a separate relevant market) in order to enable a competitor to compete with the firm on a secondary market. Before competition law can be invoked to force the opening of production facilities, four conditions must all be met:

a) the facility is indispensable to operate on the secondary market, i.e. it cannot be economically duplicated;
b) the refusal to give access to the facility is unjustified;
c) the refusal to give access prevents the emergence of a new product for which there is customer demand;
d) the refusal to give access is likely to exclude competition on the secondary market.

---

[4] The indispensability condition is not dealt with as a separate condition in ECJ, 29 April 2004, Case C-418/01, *IMS Health*, not yet reported, since the case deals with intellectual property, which is by definition not duplicable (or only within narrow limits in the case of copyright) and thus indispensable. It is covered at length in ECJ, 26 November 1998, Case C-7/97, *Bronner* [1998] ECR I-7791, which deals with physical property. For the rest, the tests put forward in the two cases are similar, with the *IMS* case specifying that the conditions are cumulative.

Conditions a) and d) appear most relevant here and will be reviewed in turn.

Indispensability of the facility. This condition was discussed at length in *Bronner*. That case is especially interesting since it is not only relevant as a legal precedent, but also on its facts. In *Bronner*, a small newspaper publisher in Austria (Bronner) wanted access (against reasonable remuneration) to the nationwide home delivery system of the largest newspaper publisher (Mediaprint), arguing that its own delivery method (using the Austrian post) was not competitive, and that it could not on its own (given its small circulation) create a parallel delivery system. The ECJ was asked by an Austrian court whether Mediaprint's refusal to grant Bronner access constituted an abuse of dominant position within the meaning of Article 82 EC. The ECJ started by recalling that the first step is market definition: there might be existing substitutes to Mediaprint's system, thus making the relevant market larger and possibly leading to the conclusion that Mediaprint is not dominant.[5] Next, on the issue of indispensability, the ECJ adds that even if the relevant market were made up by Mediaprint's system alone that does not suffice to make Mediaprint's nationwide system indispensable.[6] The ECJ notes that (i) there are other methods of delivery available (post, etc.) even if they are less advantageous[7] and (ii) competitors of Mediaprint can always, alone or in cooperation, set up a rival nationwide newspaper delivery system.[8] Very importantly, the ECJ adds that

> "it is not enough to argue that [creating a rival system] is not economically viable by reason of the small circulation of the daily newspaper or newspapers to be distributed… [I]t would be necessary at the very least to establish…that it is not economically viable to create a second [system] with a circulation comparable to that of… the existing scheme. "

Elimination of competition on secondary market. In sectors such as electronic communications or energy, entrants have a limited number of entry strategies, sometimes only one. In some cases, these strategies require access to the incumbent's facilities. In contrast, if there were a larger number of entry strategies, some of which would not depend on mandated or regulated access to the incumbent's infrastructure, there would be competition on the secondary market in any event. In that case, a competitor

---

5 *Bronner*, ibid., para. 34.
6 Ibid., para. 42.
7 Ibid., para. 43.
8 Ibid., para. 44.

requesting access to the incumbent facilities would thus not be invoking competition law in order to have a chance at all to enter the secondary market; rather, it would be trying to use competition law to support a specific entry strategy despite the existence of a range of other available strategies. Put in the balance against competing policy considerations – respect for property rights of the owner of the facilities – this would go beyond the role of competition law.

2.2.2 Non-discrimination

On the assumption that a dominant position has been found, the holder of that dominant position is typically bound by an obligation of non-discrimination, i.e. discriminatory treatment is likely to constitute an abuse. Non-discrimination implies first of all that the dominant firm treats all third parties on the same footing, i.e. by offering similar terms and conditions.[9] Only objectively justifiable differences in treatment are accepted, for instance rebates directly related to the volume of business. In a context of vertical integration, the Commission has taken a further step and claimed that "in general terms, the dominant company's duty is to provide access in such a way that the goods and services offered to downstream companies are available on terms no less favorable than those given to other parties, including its own corresponding downstream operations".[10] To this day, the ECJ has not expressly endorsed the Commission's view. We note that applying this latter extension of the non-discrimination principle may be difficult, or may require considerable (and costly) accounting adjustments. In any event, it should not be used as a backdoor to impose access obligations which cannot be imposed under cases such as *Bronner* and *IMS Health*, as discussed above.

An interesting feature of the postal sector in this respect is that part of the work involved in providing a postal service can also be done by the sender itself. Typically, large clients can involve in work sharing, carrying out some of the sorting operations themselves and then deliver the mail to the incumbent at some further point down the processing and transport chain. In return for doing part of the work, these clients obtain various rebates. The obligation not to discriminate under Article 82 EC implies that the rebates and other special conditions available to large clients should be available to

---

[9] See Larouche (2000), 218-230, relying on leading case-law, including CFI, 6 October 1994, Case T-83/91, *Tetra Pak II* [1994] ECR II-755, confirmed by the ECJ, 14 November 1996, Case C-333/94 P, *Tetra Pak II* [1996] ECR I-5951.

[10] European Commission 1998, para. 86. Here the main examples are to be found in telecommunications decisions.

competitors as well when they accomplish the same work and deliver mail in similar quantities.[11]

2.3 The role of sector-specific regulation

If regulation is put in place, it should be aligned with the competition law principles set out above, unless a strong justification to the contrary can be found.

As to whether there is any room for sector-specific regulation, the Commission put forward a three-part test when selecting which markets could potentially be regulated, in the context of electronic communications.[12] That test is framed in general terms and there is no reason not to follow it also in inquiring whether there is any room for sector-specific regulation in the postal sector. Pursuant to that test, regulation only comes into question on markets (i) with high and persistent barriers to entry; (ii) with no prospect of effective competition behind those barriers over time; and (iii) where competition law alone does not suffice to address the problems. All of these conditions must be fulfilled.

Furthermore, if and when these conditions are fulfilled for a given market, a number of principles govern the imposition of regulatory remedies upon firms found to be dominant on that market. These principles are now central to the new framework for the regulation of electronic communications, but they are not new: they correspond to general principles of EC law and as such are equally applicable to the postal sector. They are *adequacy* (the regulatory remedy must address the problem which was identified) and *proportionality* (the regulatory remedy must be likely to remove the problem identified, must not restrict the freedom of firms more than is necessary to achieve its aims and must be in proportion to the problem in question). These principles are reflected in the structure of the Access Directive for electronic communications,[13] which provides a range of remedies for regulatory authorities to consider: transparency, non-discrimination, accounting separation, access and price controls. Very importantly, this range increases in intensity, and in line with the principles of adequacy and proportionality, authorities must first look at the lighter remedies and consider the heavier ones only if the lighter ones can be proven insufficient.

---

[11] A point made by the Commission in its Decision of 20 October 2004, *BdKEP/Deutsche Post AG*, available on the DG COMP website (visited 20 May 2005), para. 86.

[12] European Commission (2003), Rec. 9. These threefold test is further developed in the Explanatory Memorandum accompanying the Recommendation.

[13] Access Directive: Directive 2002/19 of 7 March 2002 [2002] OJ L 108/7, Art. 9-13.

2.4 Conclusion on the legal framework

Whether it is to assess whether downstream access can be forced pursuant to EC competition law or to decide whether sector-specific regulation of downstream access is required, the key issue is whether substantial entry barriers are present. Only then are the *Bronner/IMS* conditions met and the first condition for the justifiability of sector-specific regulation fulfilled. We now address this issue from the economic point of view.

3. ENTRY BARRIERS AND ENTRY STRATEGIES

It is common to distinguish entry barriers into "natural", "strategic", and "legal" ones, where the latter category also includes regulatory barriers, such as regulatory uncertainty. As the objective of postal market liberalization is to gradually remove the legal entry barriers, we will leave these out of our discussion.[14] Strategic entry barriers, those resulting from the possible anti-competitive behavior of the incumbent USP, can be tackled by competition policy, and will also not be discussed here.[15] Our focus will, hence, be on natural entry barriers, originating in structural characteristics of the market.

As noted in NERA (2004), the economic literature on natural entry barriers is less developed than is desirable. The literature offers a range of alternative, non-equivalent definitions, the most well-known being those of Bain (1956) ("an advantage that incumbent providers in an industry have over potential entrants, that allows them to elevate their prices above the level that could be expected in a competitive market without inducing potential entrants to enter the industry") and Stigler (1968) ("a cost of producing ... which must be borne by a firm which seeks to enter an industry but is not borne by firms already in the industry.") According to both of these, sunk costs (costs associated with entry that cannot be recovered when the firm exits again), can be an important entry barrier. However, according to NERA (2004), sunk costs are negligible for most postal operations, specifically for those that build on computerized pre-sorting and manual sequencing; see also Panzar (2002), De Bijl et al. (2003)

---

[14] The VAT exemption for USO postal services supplied by the incumbent constitutes an important legal entry barrier, as stressed in Moriarty and Smith (2005). We note that, in the Netherlands, the exemption applies only for mail that is handled at regulated USO rates, thus lowering this barrier.

[15] See Jonsson and Selander (2005) for a discussion of strategic entry barriers in the Swedish market.

and the discussion in the next Section. Consequently, in the postal sector, sunk cost can effectively be ignored as a potential source of barriers to entry.

The two definitions, however, take a different stance as to whether scale economies are entry barriers: according to the Bain definition, they are, according to Stigler's definition, they are not. NERA (2004) shows that economies of scale (or economies of density, as they are called there) are very important in the postal sector: "When traffic increases on a fixed postal network, unit costs fall. In the original 15 Member States total costs would increase by 6.5 per cent if traffic on a fixed network were to increase by 10 per cent". We concur with Stigler that scale economies do not constitute a barrier to entry: if an entrant would have a superior technology, then it could make an offer to the large senders that would make all these senders better off and that would be profitable if it would be accepted by all these. To put this more precisely, scale economies *alone* do not constitute an entry barrier. It would only be impossible for the entrant to enter if the business senders were loyal to the incumbent, that is, if there simultaneously would be demand side inertia.

The same conclusion has recently been obtained, more generally, in McAfee et al. (2004). That paper, however, also concludes that scale economies *combined with brand loyalty* may produce an entry barrier. The intuition is easily seen: if customers display brand loyalty towards the incumbent, then the entrant can build up market share only slowly, hence, revenues will be lower at the start, and, if investments are lumpy and have to be incurred at the start of the operations, this may make entry unprofitable. The question thus is whether, in the postal sector, brand loyalty is so large, and investments so lumpy so as to induce an entry barrier in combination with scale economies. Direct evidence on the first issue is scant, but Moriarty and Smith (2005) show that, in the UK, costumer awareness of competition is low, thus inducing a kind of brand loyalty. We believe that this is a transitory phenomenon and that experience with liberalization in other sectors clearly shows that large costumers quickly switch to better offers when these are available. Secondly, the postal sector clearly demonstrates that entry can occur at different scales, and that investments can be postponed and carried out in a stepwise manner to match with demand. We conclude that scale economies do not constitute substantial entry barriers.

In other words, in our view, while theoretically some (non-artificial) entry barriers in the postal market may exist, these could only have a small effect. It is important to make a distinction between high and low entry barriers. The key question for policy is whether the entry barriers are so high as to make access regulation desirable. In order to assess whether it is justified to compel network access, it is important to determine the effects of possible entry barriers. In the process, one has to look at the alternatives; hence, one has to answer the question of what is the best way to do away with the limitations on competition resulting from entry barriers, if any. As we argue below, a large segment of the market is accessible for competitors: substantial entry barriers, that would justify regulating access to the USPs networks, do not exist.

In this respect, it is also important to note that entrants' customers can continue to avail themselves of the services of the incumbent postal operator (PO) for delivery zones or products not serviced by their competitive entrant. They can do this either directly themselves or through their entrant service provider, who can either use generic services of the PO for mail they do not wish to deliver themselves or negotiate special access agreements with the PO if volumes are sufficiently large to make this worthwhile for both parties; see Crew and Kleindorfer (2001, 2002).

Given scale economies in delivery, the natural question to address is how large a market share a 'reasonably efficient' entrant needs to obtain in order to reach cost parity with the incumbent. Although providing an answer is beyond the scope of this paper (as it depends on the precise details of the market under consideration, on the cost structure and the efficiency of the incumbent, on the wage premiums that it pays, etc.), we nevertheless provide a perspective by showing that the papers that have addressed this issue have come up with widely varying estimates.

Cohen and Chu (1997) were the first to calculate the critical market share that a competitor would need to capture in order to have the same unit cost as the US Postal Service. Their calculation is based on a cost function that is estimated on detailed data from the US Postal Services. They conclude that it is very difficult to enter the US market: an entrant that has a cost advantage of 50% and that delivers only one day a week would still need 15% market share in order to reach cost parity with the US Postal Service. An entrant that delivers two days a week would need 19% market share if it had a 50% cost advantage, and 23% if it had a 33% cost advantage. It seems that the critical market share for the US is relatively high.

A similar conclusion has been drawn for the UK in Postcomm (2004); also see Moriarty and Smith (2005). Annex 1 to the "Competitive Market Review" reports results from a model that has been developed by Royal Mail and concludes that significant volume may be required to compete profitably head to head with Royal Mail: "to match Royal Mail's present unit cost for delivery six days per week, and depending on the assumptions about new entrant's costs compared to Royal Mail, a new entrant might need to capture around 50% market share". As Chart A1.1 in that Annex shows, an entrant that delivers only one day per week would still need about 30% market share to reach cost parity.

Note, however, that the existing USP's cost function need not be very relevant for new entrants: they will not choose to mimic the business models and networks of incumbents. The latter originate from a time when the postal market was very different and they have been designed to fulfill the universal service obligation that is imposed on the incumbent. Entrants do not face such restrictions, and they will take advantage of the current situation. The postal market has moved away from a traditional two-way communications market, with businesses (rather than consumers) now being responsible for 80 to 90% of the mail that is offered. As single item residential mail is only a small segment of the market and as handling of it is costly, it is less attractive to entrants. They will predominantly focus on the B2B and B2C segments, both on high value mail as well as on bulk mail. Restricting ourselves to the latter, we note that entrants' ability to compete in this segment is enhanced by the fact that the market is relatively concentrated on the sender side. To illustrate, IG&H (2003) shows that, in the Netherlands, 50% of the mail originates from 500 to 600 large senders. Such mail can be pre-sorted electronically, hence, the entrant just has to focus on sequence sorting and actual delivery, where the first task can easily be done manually (hence, not needing costly investments) as long as the entrant serves a limited number of customers. Consequently, entrants can keep their operations straightforward and cheap by targeting a few large senders that generate sufficient volume. Indeed, several successful entrants in European postal markets, such as CityMail in Sweden, and Sandd and Selektmail in the Netherlands, seem to adopt models of this type.

The relevant question thus is what volume an entrant with such a business model needs in order to reach cost parity with the incumbent in delivery. As such an entrant will incur lower sequence sorting costs than a (traditional) incumbent that manually sequences the mail, we may focus on actual delivery. Obviously, to reach economies of scale, the entrant would like to limit the frequency of delivery as well as to restrict operations as much as possible to low cost, high-density areas; where its volume is thin, the entrant will prefer to hand the mail to the incumbent for delivery.

Studies for the Netherlands have concluded that an entrant's critical market share is low. Using the methodology from Cohen and Chu (1997), SEO (2003) concludes that an entrant to the Dutch market would only need 10% of the volume to be able to compete with the incumbent TNT Post (formerly known as TPG Post) on the basis of six delivery days per week, and that an entrant that limits delivery to 2 days per week only needs 3% of the volume. An appendix to SEO (2003) contains a separate analysis by the economic consultancy firm Nolan, Norton & Co that complements the Cohen and Chu (1997) methodology with data obtained from market parties and that discusses several alternative entry strategies. A green-field entrant, which has labor costs that are 60% of those of TNT Post, and that limits delivery to 2 days per week, needs 4% market share to reach cost parity with TNT. Such entrant would be very profitable if it would attract its business with a 10% discount as compared to the prices charged by TNT. In case the entrant already operates on related markets and hence can profit from economies of scope, entry (at existing prices minus 10%) would be profitable already with 1% market share, while cost parity would be obtained with 2% market share.

Given that the various estimates for the critical market share vary widely, it is important to complement the above model analyses with actual experiences. In the Netherlands, two entrants, Sandd and SelektMail, each had about 2,5% of the market in 2004 and each of them claims to make a profit. In Germany, PIN-AG, an entrant that started operations in 1999 and that focuses mainly on the Berlin area, claims to have reached profitability in 2003. Meanwhile, it has achieved around 20% of the local Berlin market. In Sweden, City Mail has been active since 1991, focusing mainly on delivery of pre-sorted bulk mail in urban areas. Jonsson and Selander (2005) report that CityMail has 7,5% of the overall market and that it has 25% of the market segment in which it is active. Also this company appears to run a profitable business. As the evidence shows, apparently, entrants in several countries can thus compete successfully even with relatively low market shares, thus showing the absence of 'meaningful' entry barriers.

In Section 2, we concluded that, according to current legal thinking in Europe, sector-specific regulation of downstream access would be justified only if substantial entry barriers are present. In this Section, we have concluded that there are no such barriers, hence, that regulation is not justified. In the next section, we will expand on the different types of entry strategies that entrants can choose from, and argue that regulation should try to avoid creating a bias towards certain entry modes.

4. NATURAL MONOPOLY, MONOPOLISTIC BOTTLENECKS AND ACCESS REGULATION

The reader may wonder how the above conclusion relates to the frequently made statement that the postal market is a natural monopoly (see, however, Ennis (2005) for a qualification to this statement). The answer is simple: although this statement may be true, it is misleading and hardly relevant for the discussion. While the term 'natural monopoly' is suggestive, the concept is associated with various misunderstandings. In particular, the following two statements are wrong in general: (i) "an industry that is a natural monopoly is best served if there is only one supplier"; (ii) "in an industry that is a natural monopoly, competition is not possible (viable), hence, such an industry will naturally be a monopoly."

To argue our claim, let us confine ourselves, for simplicity, to a single-product industry. In this case, the industry is said to be a natural monopoly if the cost function is sub-additive throughout, that is, unit costs are falling with output level. Consider statement (i). A monopolist would, presumably, have market power, leading to a higher mark-up, hence, a price above marginal and average cost. A successful monopolist may raise the price above the level that would result under competition, even though in the latter case, the cost would be higher. In other words, lower cost need not translate into a lower price. Furthermore, if the monopolist is shielded from competition, it need not have an incentive (or not as strong an incentive) to reduce costs. In other words, competition may lead to cost reductions that may not be (as easily) available in a monopoly. Put differently, taking a dynamic perspective, competition may lead to entry even if costs are sub-additive. Of course, regulation may limit the exercise of market power by the monopolist, hence, it may improve allocative efficiency, while maintaining (static) cost efficiency. However, regulation will not be perfect and will probably not be as effective as competition in reducing cost. Hence statement (i) is not necessarily true.

Statement (ii) – competition is not viable in naturally monopolistic industries – *is* true if competition takes the form of price competition in a setting of homogeneous goods, *à la* Bertrand. This is the most intensive form of competition that can be imagined: it assumes that providers do not differentiate their products, that consumers are fully aware of the prices and that they switch to a cheaper provider no matter how small the discount that this provider offers as compared to the incumbent supplier. For other forms of competition that are less intense than Bertrand competition, entry is possible and can be profitable in markets that are natural monopolies. An example is provided by quantity competition *à la* Cournot, or in a situation of price competition with horizontally differentiated goods. In such cases, competition is less intense, the price cost margin is positive and entrants can profitably enter. Consequently, statement (ii) is not generally true.

The above discussion is in line with the ''contestability' literature (Baumol and Willig, 1981) that showed that a natural monopoly does not in itself necessarily present insurmountable entry barriers, and also that, if a company does not have to sink costs in order to enter the market, the threat of competition will discipline the incumbent; it will refrain from demanding non-competitive prices because of the risk of being undercut by a potential entrant. In some industries, however, certain network elements are of such a nature that, in order to be able to provide services to the customers, access to them is essential: in railways and electricity, for instance, it is not economically feasible to reproduce the physical network. These cases involve a monopolistic bottleneck that a company must pass through if it wants to provide services, which provides a protective wall behind which the incumbent can hide.

Thus, the relevant question is not whether the industry is a natural monopoly, but rather whether entering the market requires specific sunk investments so that there is a monopolistic bottleneck. As we argued in Section 3, and more extensively in De Bijl et al. (2003), there are no essential facilities in the postal sector. Indeed, as Section 3 has shown, it is possible to enter certain (product or geographical) segments of the market while incurring only low sunk costs and still attain a stable market position. From there, the entrant can eventually grow further (still with only moderate sunk costs) and find a stable market position once it has reached a larger size, and so forth.

In short, there is room for various entry and growth strategies, and as a consequence, one does not have to help entrants get over a high entry barrier even at the expense of introducing at the same time a bias in the entrant's strategic choices and potentially curbing its incentives to innovate. The absence of sunk costs allows entrants considerable flexibility in the design of their organization and operations; this guarantees a high measure of allocative efficiency over time and promotes innovation. As noted above, the experience of several entrants to date illustrates that there are segments of the postal market in which a newcomer can enter and realize positive profits. To serve these segments, entrants can choose entry based on negotiated access with the incumbent USP or end-to-end competition by investing in their own facilities. They can also choose to target various market segments (geographical and customer type).

From telecommunications markets we know that regulation strongly affects the incentives on whether and how to enter the market (or a segment thereof) and that, since entry modes may depend, for their viability, on the regulatory framework, there is 'demand' for certain regulatory interventions. The question is, however, whether regulators should accept to satisfy that demand and attempt to foster certain types of competition, or let the market determine what works best. Access in the postal sector (in all its forms) is a complex good, which varies according to various idiosyncratic features such as mailing patterns and collection patterns. A mandatory access regime, since it makes access under the regulated parameters readily available, can pre-empt the determination of the most adequate terms and conditions of access by market parties. It could also lead to micro-management by the regulator, with additional frictional and transaction costs relative to the alternative of allowing entrants and the incumbent to negotiate the terms of access freely.

The postal market allows for a variety of entry strategies. In the absence of barriers to entry, the legal and regulatory framework should, therefore, aim to avoid creating a bias in the strategic decisions of entrants in favor of a business model fostered by the regulatory intervention.

In addition, it is important to note that entrants face regulatory uncertainty when deciding whether or not to invest. As a consequence, they may act more cautiously, to wait and see which regulation will apply in the liberalized segments, thus resulting in a delay of entry and investments, slowing down the maturing of competition: entrants choose a smaller coverage, or invest less in their own facilities, than without regulatory uncertainty. If investments are delayed in a particular segment, entry can also be delayed in other segments, in particular if entrants become active in a stepwise manner: entering the next segment only if entry in the previous one was successful. Hence, as a result of regulatory uncertainty, overall entry might be delayed and the strong position of incumbents might be maintained longer than necessary, increasing the need for heavy-handed regulation. In addition, regulatory uncertainty creates a bias towards entry modes based on access, and away from investments in their own facilities. In this respect, it would be best to settle the access issue once and for all.

In order to make access operational, both the incumbent and the entrant have to adapt their internal organization and processes. The incumbent has to create 'space' for the incoming mail volumes, both physically and with respect to capacity and planning. The entrant has to set up its processes such that they are in line with the incumbent's requirements for incoming mail volumes. The investments that the firms have to do to make this possible are specific for this activity only. This creates a mutual dependency among the firms. In the case of unforeseen events, such as an 'external event' causing a hiccup in the incumbent's sorting/delivery system or a failure by the entrant to deliver the agreed volume, the firms (or at least one of the involved parties) will try to renegotiate the charges and conditions of the access agreement. Given that their interests are not aligned, this will not be easy and will involve substantial transaction costs, for instance because the regulator, or perhaps a court, will have to intervene. Furthermore, given that contracts will always be incomplete, one can expect that these types of problems will arise sooner or later; see Hart (1995). An entrant that does not rely on access but invests in its own facilities will be facing a higher investment 'hurdle', but it benefits by not having to make asset-specific investments of the type needed in the case of access-based entry. Consequently, such an entrant will not be subject to a 'hold-up' problem and costly problems of renegotiation will be avoided when entrants do not rely on access. As the literature shows, in the case of complementary assets, investment and innovation is spurred by vertical integration, hence, stimulating end-to-end competition may yield dynamic benefits. Policy makers would be well advised to take the costs and inefficiencies caused by incomplete contracts and renegotiations into account when designing regulatory interventions.

It seems to us that, up to now, the two issues discussed in the previous paragraphs, regulatory uncertainty and incomplete contracting, might not yet have received the attention they deserve, and that due consideration of these issues may well reverse the preference from access-based competition over end-to-end competition. In any case, they strengthen our argument for a light-handed regulatory approach.

5. CONCLUSION

In this paper, we have sought to take a fresh look at European postal regulation in anticipation of the full opening of the market. We have focused on the regulation of relationships between competitors, and in particular on the need for regulation mandating downstream access. We have chosen to start from the fundamental questions and avoid the kind of shortcuts, which can be observed in some of the literature, whereby the outcome of regulatory processes in similar sectors is simply transposed over to the postal sector.

The starting point must be the economics of the postal sector. On the basis of theoretical considerations and practical evidence, we have seen that neither economies of scale nor economies of scope constitute a substantial barrier to entry. Furthermore, the postal sector is characterized by the absence of monopolistic bottlenecks so that any sunk cost advantages for incumbents are not very substantial. Rather, entry in the postal sector can take place at different scales, and here theory and practice concur in showing that a number of different entry strategies are available and potentially successful.

These findings have a number of consequences for the regulation. With the full opening of the market, regulation must be fundamentally rethought, and it must be firmly grounded in economic analysis. In the European context, any legal analysis must then start by considering competition law as a starting point, since sector-specific regulation must be aligned with competition law and would only be justified if the policy objectives could not be attained via competition law.

Under competition law, our finding that there are no monopolistic bottlenecks in the delivery chain implies that the essential facilities doctrine cannot be used to impose downstream access obligations upon the dominant postal operator. Following the reasoning of *Bronner*, competitors can create a rival delivery system and bypass that of the incumbent, and some of them are already doing so. That these competing systems are not or would not be identical to the incumbent's – whether in terms of coverage or frequency – does not turn the incumbent's delivery system into an essential facility. Finally, on the basis of *Bronner*, a competitor would have to show that, even with a volume of business comparable to the incumbent, it would not be "economically viable" to put together a competing postal delivery system. As was seen in Section 3, even with a volume of business substantially smaller than the incumbent's, competitors can already enter the market profitably on the basis of their own facilities. Accordingly, on the basis of the test in *Bronner*, downstream delivery does not constitute an essential facility. Furthermore, on the assumption that the incumbent postal operators would be found to hold a dominant position, competition law will apply to as to put them under a non-discrimination obligation.

Transposing these results in the regulatory discussion, this implies that *prima facie* there is no justification for heavy-handed regulatory intervention. This conclusion is strengthened when the analytical framework used to select relevant markets in the electronic communications sector is applied to the postal sector: in the absence of barriers to entry lasting over time (first condition of the three-pronged test), downstream access would not qualify as a candidate market for regulatory intervention. Should there be any intervention, the principles of adequacy and proportionality would also dictate that a light regulatory framework, centered on the non-discrimination obligation arising out of competition law, would be sufficient.

Caution is all the more warranted where, as in the postal sector, there is no obvious entry path, which would be dictated by economies of scale, network effects or other constraints. Because of the different cost structure (little or no sunk costs), a number of different entry strategies are possible in an open postal market. Furthermore, the incumbent postal operator and entrants are likely to have incentives to enter into negotiations on access, so that access will be granted as a result of relatively balanced negotiations. In the absence of any overriding reason, regulation should hence avoid influencing how competitors enter the market by facilitating a particular entry mode.

We conclude by briefly relating our conclusions to those reached by several other researchers in the field. In connection with deregulation of network industries in the US, there has been an extensive discussion on the conditions in which a dominant firm should be forced to unbundle and share its facilities (on non-discriminatory terms) in order to stimulate competition. There is general agreement that compulsory access should be exceptional and one point of view is that the incumbent should be forced to share only in case of essential facilities. In line with Panzar (2002) we have argued that, in the postal sector, an argument for mandating downstream access cannot be built along these lines as the local distribution network cannot be seen as an essential facility. Kahn (2001) has, however, argued in favor of a stricter requirement for mandatory sharing in which incumbents that have inherited facilities and consequent scale economies from their monopolistic past would be forced to allow entrants to share in the associated efficiencies. Along these lines, Crew and Kleindorfer (2002), Panzar (2002) and Moriarty and Smith (2005) have all discussed the pros and cons involved in mandating downstream access. While all of these authors agree that mandating downstream access may facilitate entry, most also write that such a policy may have costs as well: it may increase transaction costs, facilitate inefficient entry and inhibit facility based competition. Crew and Kleindorfer (2002) and Panzar (2002) also point to the difficulties of setting the appropriate regulatory rates, hence, the advantages of these rates being negotiated commercially. In this paper, we have pointed out that, in the European setting, competition law will always apply, hence, without sector-specific regulation, the incumbent will be forced to treat competitors in the same way as costumers, thus further tilting the balance in favor of negotiated access. Finally, in line with Kahn (2001) we have argued that mandatory access risks interfering with facilities-based competition and that the latter is to be preferred.

REFERENCES

Bain, J. 1956. *Barriers to New Competition.* Cambridge: Harvard University Press.

Baumol, W. and R. Willig. 1981. "Fixed Costs, Entry Barriers and the Sustainability of Monopoly." *Quarterly Journal of Economics* 96(3): 405-431.

Cohen, R. and E. Chu. 1997. ' A Measure of Scale Economies for Postal Systems." In *Managing Change in the Postal Delivery Industries*, edited by M.A. Crew and P.R. Kleindorfer, Kluwer Academic Publishers.

Crew, M.A. and P.R. Kleindorfer. 2001. "Whither the USO under Competitive Entry: A Microstructure Approach". In *Future Directions in Postal Reform*, edited by Michael A. Crew and Paul R. Kleindorfer. Boston, MA: Kluwer Academic Publishers.

Crew, M.A. and P.R. Kleindorfer. 2002. "Balancing Access and the Universal Service Obligation". In: *Postal and Delivery Services: Delivering on Competition*, edited by Michael A, Crew and Paul R. Kleindorfer. Boston, MA: Kluwer Academic Publishers.

De Bijl, P., E. van Damme and P. Larouche. 2003. "Towards a Liberalised Postal Market." TILEC, Tilburg University. (August).

Ennis, S. 2005. "When is Postal Delivery a Natural Monopoly?" Paper presented at CRRI - Rutgers University's *13th Conference on Postal and Delivery Economics*. Antwerp.

European Commission. 1998. Notice on access agreements in the telecommunications sector [1998] OJ C 265/2.

European Commission. 2003. Recommendation 2003/311 of 11 February 2003 [2003] OJ L 114/45,

European Commission. 2005. "Report from the Commission to the Council and the European Parliament on the application of the Postal Directive (Directive 97/67/EC as amended by Directive 2002/39/EC, Brussels, 23.03.2005, COM(2005) 102 final.

Hart, O. 1995. *Firms, Contracts and Financial Structure*. Oxford: Oxford University Press.

IG&H Management consultants. 2003. "Marktontwikkelingen en praktijkcases tonen toegankelijkheid van de Nederlandse postmarkt aan." (June).

Jonsson, P. and S. Selander. 2005. "The "Real" Graveyard Spiral: Experiences from the Liberalized Swedish Postal Market." In *Progress toward Liberalization of the Postal and Delivery Sector*, edited by M.A. Crew and P.R. Kleindorfer. Boston: Spinger.

Kahn, A.2001. *Whom the Gods Would Destroy, or How Not to Deregulate.* Washington DC: AEI-Brookings Joint Center for Regulatory Studies.

Larouche, P. 2000. *Competition Law and Regulation in European Telecommunications.* Oxford: Hart Publishing.

McAfee, P., H. Mialon and M. Williams. 2004. "What is a barrier to entry?" *American Economic Review* 94(2): 461-465.

Moriarty, R., and P. Smith. 2005. "Barriers to Entry in Post and Regulatory Responses." In *Regulatory and Economic Challenges in the Postal and Delivery Sector*, edited by M.A. Crew and P.R. Kleindorfer. Boston: Kluwer Academic Publishers.

NERA. 2004. "Economics of Postal Services; A Report to the European Commission DG Markt." (July).

Panzar, J. 2002. "Reconciling Competition, Downstream Access, and Universal Service in Postal Markets." In: *Postal and Delivery Services: Delivering on Competition*, edited by M.A. Crew and P.R. Kleindorfer. Boston: Kluwer Academic Publishers.

Postcomm. 2004. "Competitive Market Review." (September)

SEO. 2003. "Tante Pos krijgt concurrentie; effecten van de liberalisering van de postmarkt." Amsterdam. (September): 29.

Stigler, G.J. 1968. "Barriers to Entry, Economies of Scale, and Firm Size." In *The Organization of Industry*, edited by G.J. Stigler. Homewood, IL: Irwin.

Van der Lijn, N., and A. Meijer. 2004. "Is Mandatory Access in the Postal Sector the Key to Success?" In *Competitive Transformation of the Postal and Delivery Sector*, edited by M.A. Crew and P.R. Kleindorfer. Boston: Kluwer Academic Publishers.

Chapter 11

Enhancing Competition by Unbundling the Postal Administration

John Haldi and William J. Olson
Haldi Associates, Inc. and Olson Law Offices

1. INTRODUCTION

Attempts to bring the rigors of competition to postal authorities via de-regulation have stumbled repeatedly over the following dilemma: (i) the Universal Service Obligation ("USO") has powerful political support; (ii) the postal monopoly is asserted to be necessary to assure funding of the USO; and (iii) a fully de-regulated government monopoly is unacceptable. The unbundling model presented in this paper offers a solution to this dilemma. Although scope of the existing monopoly over delivery would not be reduced by this proposal, unbundling the upstream portion of the network would reduce substantially the amount of resources protected by the monopoly, while preserving the USO.

The concept of unbundling the United States Postal Service ("USPS") was posited over a decade ago in an unpublished paper by Rogerson and Treworgy (1994). That paper suggested bifurcating the USPS into two separate entities, one consisting of monopoly delivery services and the other of competitive non-delivery services. Such structural separation also was discussed briefly during debate over legislative reform of the USPS.[1]

Aside from the above-cited works, which received limited attention, the postal literature is devoid of discussion about unbundling the USPS, or any other postal administration, into separate entities. This void in the literature could stem from the fact that postal administrations have been structured as

---

1 Postal Service (2002), App. B, p. B-3.

unitary, vertically integrated networks for so long that it is difficult to imagine them being organized any other way.

Countries that have reduced or abolished the monopoly as part of postal reform have seen only limited entry by competitive delivery firms, largely because the need to replicate the delivery function on a wide scale presents a formidable barrier to entry. Unbundling the postal administration offers a more feasible and expeditious way to open a major portion of the postal network to effective competition.

Using the USPS as a prototype, this paper describes how an unbundled postal administration could operate. Particular attention is paid to the thorny issue of the USO. Separating contestable activities and opening them to true competition presents a feasible and meritorious option that deserves serious consideration by policy makers.

The paper is organized as follows: (a) the rationale and requirements for unbundling an integrated network are defined; (b) a restructured USPS network is described; and (c) the merits of such a restructuring are assessed.

2. RATIONALE AND REQUIREMENTS FOR UNBUNDLING AN INTEGRATED POSTAL NETWORK

A fully integrated postal network includes (i) acceptance, (ii) mail processing and transportation, and (iii) delivery. The portion of the network that provides daily delivery service to every address in the country benefits from extensive economies of scale and scope. Hence, that part of the network is viewed as having natural monopoly characteristics.[2]

The activities of acceptance, mail processing and transportation, on the other hand, are not subject to economies of scale or scope. Nor do any natural barriers preclude entry by would-be competitors. These activities are fully contestable and can be separated easily from delivery. They thus qualify as candidates to be split off into an autonomous entity, which would be subjected to full competition, while leaving the natural monopoly delivery function to be operated by the postal administration and regulated by the government.

---

2 In the United States, this natural monopoly is reinforced by laws that (i) prohibit access to mailboxes by anyone other than USPS carriers (the so-called "mailbox rule"), and (ii) give the USPS the exclusive right to carriage of low-priced letter mail. For information on the mailbox rule, *see* General Accounting Office (1997). For discussion about the nature and extent of economies of scale in delivery, *see* Cazals, *et al.* (2005a and 2005b) and the references cited therein.

The basic rationale for unbundling a postal network, as stated by Elcano *et al.* (2000), is the "underlying economic premise that increased competition ... results in increased quality, efficiency, and lower prices to the consumer." No approach to unbundling will reduce the scope of the natural monopoly over delivery. Given that fact, the best way to reduce resources operating under the protective umbrella of monopoly is to distinguish between (i) activities that can lay claim to natural monopoly (delivery) and (ii) all other activities that are contestable.

Transfer of all contestable activities to an independent for-profit private entity would increase substantially the resources subject to the discipline, risks and rewards of competitive markets. The entity's need to survive would instill cost-minimizing and profit-maximizing incentives into a large segment of the existing postal network.

In other network industries that historically were vertically integrated, such as telecommunications and electricity, unbundling is considered to have occurred after activities deemed potentially competitive were (i) restructured into a legal entity separate from those other activities that continued to function as a monopoly, and (ii) then spun off entirely, either to stakeholders or to a third party. The end result was that the continuing monopoly entity[3] ceased to exert any control over the newly created competitive entity. Legal separation of firms with vertically integrated networks either created or helped to expand intermediate markets that, prior to unbundling, may have been nonexistent. Creation of separate legal entities with different ownership interests also ensured that each restructured company would both (i) strive to be financially self-supporting, and (ii) independently set prices for their respective products or services at a level adequate, at minimum, to cover their own total costs.

In those industries where public policy has promoted unbundling, the stated objective was to achieve competitive efficiency, with prices of competitive services determined in competitive markets. Unbundling a postal administration in the manner envisioned herein would ensure that prices of mail processing and transportation services were determined in competitive markets. The monopoly portion would publish prices for its delivery services and establish access prices (within each subclass) available for use by all upstream competitors.

---

3 Or "entities" in the case of the old AT&T, from which several regional monopolies were created, along with a competitive long-distance operator. Subsequent mergers in the telecom industry have resulted in a certain amount of "re-bundling." Nevertheless, breakup of AT&T, coupled with technological developments (*e.g.*, cell phones, cable, the internet) have resulted in a more competitive telecom sector.

A postal administration can provide downstream access without restructuring along the lines described above.[4] Currently, the USPS allows downstream access by giving worksharing discounts, which correspond to implicit prices for upstream services.[5] When set in this way, however, prices can differ significantly from those likely to result from complete unbundling and full competition, as discussed in more detail below. This existing scenario will be referred to as a "partial liberalization" of rates, in order to distinguish it from a true separation of contestable activities.[6]

3. AN UNBUNDLED USPS NETWORK

As indicated above, a postal administration can be unbundled by separating it into two distinct units. The unit responsible for mail processing and transportation is referred to herein as the United States Mail Service ("USMS"). The other unit is referred to as the United States Delivery Service ("USDS").

The USMS would charge explicit prices for all mail processing and transportation services offered. Those prices would need to generate sufficient revenues to enable the USMS to be financially self-supporting.

The USDS would charge explicit rates for delivery, with the same rates being paid by USMS and other mail providers. Thus, the charge for delivery could not subsidize mail processing and transportation, or vice versa.

Separating functions in the manner described herein would necessitate certain changes that are considered integral to unbundling and are discussed below. A variety of other possible postal reforms, such as consolidating and transforming the retail network, revising the monopoly statutes, or changing the USO, are not integral to unbundling and are not discussed further.[7]

---

[4] The authors are not aware of any universally accepted definition of unbundling that necessarily requires creation of separate legal entities, so long as the necessary economic characteristics are present — namely, autonomous price setting by financially self-supporting entities, a competitive sector with no barriers to entry, and a level playing field for all competitors. De facto unbundling might be obtainable by restructuring a postal administration into autonomous (or quasi-autonomous) self-supporting divisions. Restructuring of The Post Office in Great Britain into three components — The Royal Mail, The Parcel Force, and Counters — illustrates such a possible restructuring.

[5] *See* Mitchell (1999) for discussion of worksharing discounts.

[6] For discussion of liberalization of postal markets, *see* Cohen, *et al.* (2001). Also *see* Crew and Kleindorfer (1995).

[7] For discussion of other possible reforms, *see* Postal Service (2002), General Accounting Office (2004) and Campanelli (2002). The model described herein focuses on the feasibility of splitting an organization that has been vertically integrated for centuries, and is widely viewed as a unitary institution. Only changes deemed essential for unbundling to succeed are discussed. This paper does not seek to resolve every operational issue that

Over time, full competition should reduce cost and improve quality of mail processing and transportation services. This would help to maintain — or even to increase — the total volume of mail delivered by the USDS.

3.1 The U. S. Mail Service

The USMS would be responsible for performing all contestable activities "upstream" of delivery; *e.g.*, acceptance, barcoding of originating mail, inter-city transportation, and all sortation other than sequencing mail for final delivery by carriers. Since these upstream activities would be open to competition on a level playing field and the USMS would have to be financially self-supporting, pricing of services provided by the USMS should be deregulated completely. Accordingly, the USMS would be subject to the same anti-trust laws as its competitors (*see* section 3.1.4, *infra.*).

Because the USMS necessarily would function in a highly competitive environment, it is essential that no part of the USO be imposed on the USMS. Every aspect of the USO should become the sole responsibility of the USDS. To survive and prosper, the USMS would need to be a lean, highly efficient operation, unencumbered by any significant requirement not also imposed on private competitors, and free of all restrictions placed on government agencies (*e.g.*, in the United States, compliance with the Davis-Bacon Act, veterans hiring preferences, etc.).

3.1.1 USMS Ownership

Since an autonomous USMS would compete directly with the private sector, it should replicate a private sector ownership model, preferably as a stock company. Initially, ownership could reside directly with the government or the newly created USDS. However, the most effective way to create a level playing field would be to privatize the USMS completely; *i.e.*, divest all of the stock. Some or all of the USMS stock could be sold to the public, analogous to what the Dutch and German governments have done with their postal administrations; proceeds from any privatization could be used to establish a reserve for unfunded liabilities of the USPS. So long as any ownership ties remain between the USMS and the government, absolute leveling of the competitive playing field would be difficult to achieve.[8]

---

might arise from unbundling upstream mail services. The purpose here is to demonstrate that such issues would be manageable.

[8] Government ownership would exempt USMS from all state and local taxes and fees. Offsetting such advantage, USMS employees might continue to be part of the federal retirement and health benefits system and be covered by the federal workers compensation scheme. For further discussion on level playing field issues, *see* Gibbons (2005).

Complete privatization would be the most assured way to eliminate political influence over what should be straightforward business decisions.[9] If the government retains links to the USMS, the concentration of employees around larger processing facilities could constitute a formidable political force to pressure Congress to override sound economic decision-making.

3.1.2 USMS Employees and Facilities

Following restructuring, most clerks and mail handlers, along with mail processing supervisors and other managerial staff at postal plants, would become employees of the USMS. Additionally, the infrastructure for letting and supervising transportation contracts would become part of the USMS. Of course, the USMS also would have its own management organization and overhead structure (*e.g.*, personnel department), entirely separate from that of the USDS.

The USMS would operate all existing USPS plants and distribution facilities, but no retail or delivery office. In an unbundled scenario, final sortation of mail into a carrier's route sequence would become a responsibility of the USDS. One obvious issue arises with respect to those facilities that now function in a dual capacity; *i.e.*, facilities that process originating, outgoing mail and also sort destinating, incoming mail into delivery sequence for carriers (only letter mail is machine-sorted into a carrier's route sequence at present).

Initially, the issue of dual-purpose facilities could be resolved in either of two ways. First, the USDS could contract with the USMS to use its facilities and employees to continue sequencing destinating letter mail. Alternatively, the USDS could lease the facility from the USMS during late night and early morning hours, and use its own employees to sort destinating (letter) mail into carrier sequence. Such alternative transitional arrangements could operate concurrently; *i.e.*, subcontracting in some places, while subleasing facilities in other locations. If either transitional arrangement proved highly efficacious in a particular location, it might continue indefinitely. Otherwise, in major metropolitan areas, the USDS in time should establish its own centralized facilities, used exclusively to accept and process destinating mail.

The USMS would need to have complete operational flexibility with respect to opening, relocating, consolidating and closing all mail processing

---

[9] The USMS could be structured as a quasi-autonomous, Government Sponsored Enterprise ("GSE"). Complete privatization would be preferable, but creation of a GSE might be one way to transition to privatization. Although GSEs such as Fannie Mae and Freddie Mac have operated quite successfully over a long time span, it would be naive to think that political considerations do not affect their decision-making.

facilities. In other words, facility decisions no longer would be influenced by political considerations, any more than are decisions by companies such as DHL, FedEx, and UPS. Managerial freedom to control this part of the network is integral to unbundling. In view of the way political considerations have constrained such decision-making by the USPS, especially closure of existing plants, complete flexibility ought to provide the USMS with a net gain in efficiency.

3.1.3 USMS Operations and Transportation

Standardized mailing requirements such as barcoding, electronic address verification, machine readability, packaging, etc., would be established by the USDS. The USMS would be required to prepare mail to meet all current and future USDS entry requirements on the same basis as any mailer or other provider that enters mail directly with the USDS. This is essential to creating a level playing field between the USMS and private sector competitors.

The USMS would be responsible for moving all mail that it handles from point of entry to the appropriate USDS delivery facility. Consequently, all USPS contracts for inter-city and long-distance transportation would become the responsibility of the USMS. All equipment currently used to transport mail between processing facilities would be transferred to and operated by the USMS.[10]

A competitive USMS would need to have complete flexibility with respect to negotiation of contracts with all transportation providers, including domestic and international airlines. Moreover, the USMS ought to be free to own and operate its own transportation equipment (as are FedEx, UPS and other competitors of the USPS), should that be deemed more cost-efficient. Such operational flexibility is considered integral to unbundling, and should be a source of net efficiency gains by the USMS.

3.1.4 Pricing of USMS Services

Establishing the USMS as a separate entity would change the manner in which prices are determined for many commercial and nonprofit bulk mailers. Not affected, of course, would be any mailer that already bypasses the entire upstream network and enters its mail at local USPS delivery units. For all other bulk mail, the USMS would charge separate, explicit prices for

---

[10] Outgoing international mail would bypass the USDS delivery network and flow directly to other countries. Incoming international mail from other postal administrations would be received by the USDS, which would contract with the USMS to process, transport and distribute it to the appropriate USDS facilities for delivery.

each service provided (as other third-party intermediaries currently do). Any mailer using USMS would pay those separate prices, plus USDS rates established for delivery. The USMS would continue to accept bulk mail, just as it does today, and then provide the mail with such transportation or processing as may be necessary to enter it at destination facilities of the USDS.

One major difference is that prices for all intermediate services would be unregulated.[11] Prices charged by the USMS for its services could be published or unpublished, uniform or nonuniform, negotiated or not subject to negotiation, as the USMS sees fit. As a deregulated entity, the USMS could change its prices whenever it elected to do so. Of course, all intermediate services provided by the USMS would be totally open to competition, so if prices for some USMS services exceeded the value of those services, competitors would be encouraged to offer those services at a lower price.

For example, for First-Class bulk mail, the USMS could charge a price that, when added to the rate for delivery, would equal the uniform rate charged for single-piece mail. Offsetting such USMS pricing freedom would be the requirement for the USDS to establish downstream access prices for all bulk First-Class Mail. Any attempt at aggressive pricing of bulk First-Class Mail by the USMS would attract considerable competition — like "bees to honey." Over time, competition can restrain and establish prices more effectively than regulation. Thus, for First-Class bulk mail, the USMS presumably would establish prices designed to keep bulk mailers' unit cost below the rate for single-piece mail, reflecting the fact that less work is required to process such mail.

USMS prices would need to be sufficient for the organization to recover its stand-alone costs. These would include all overhead costs necessary to operate as a separate, independent organization, as well as all existing attributable costs of mail processing and transportation (the Postal Rate Commission already treats most mail processing and transportation costs as attributable, hence those costs are reflected in the existing rates for each respective subclass of mail). The USMS necessarily would assume responsibility for some portion of the USPS's (non-attributed) overhead costs, thereby reducing the overhead burden on the USDS and allowing prices charged for delivery by the USDS to be reduced accordingly.

---

[11] Since USMS would be a competitive, financially self-supporting entity, classification distinctions would not be imposed on the USMS. It would have no more obligation than FedEx, UPS or other competitors to offer any kind of special price consideration for services provided to nonprofits, publishers, or any other mailers that heretofore have received favored treatment. Classification distinctions would continue to exist for the USDS (*see* Section 3.2.6, *infra*).

For example, the USMS would have its own senior executives and all attendant headquarters staff functions, such as legal, procurement, etc. All costs of supervising, managing and maintaining major facilities not currently attributed would become part of the USMS overhead. Similarly, although most transportation costs are attributed, any not now attributed would become overhead costs of the USMS. Although these overhead costs may not be attributable to any single class or subclass of mail, they relate directly to the upstream services provided by USMS. Consequently, they are part of the incremental cost of providing mail processing and transportation service, and would need to be recovered via a mark-up on the attributable costs of those services, as they no longer would be recoverable through a mark-up on the cost of delivery.[12]

Since pricing of USMS services would have to generate funds sufficient to recover stand-alone costs, some (perhaps many) explicit prices charged by the USMS for its mail processing services would need to exceed the current USPS implicit prices (*i.e.*, discounts) that have evolved under partial liberalization. Limiting such discounts to no more than avoided attributable costs means that, on average, USPS implicit prices fail to recover the full incremental cost of the services provided, quite unlike competitive pricing.[13]

The asserted rationale for limiting worksharing discounts has been the Efficient Component Pricing ("ECP") rule.[14] The ECP rule seeks to emulate competitive pricing within a regulated setting. It clearly states that prices for competitive services should equal average-incremental cost, which is neither the same as, nor equal to, attributable cost. Consequently, discounts that reflect only avoided attributable costs should not be viewed as conforming with the ECP rule found in the published literature.[15]

For upstream postal services, complete unbundling and abolition of all regulation is the only guaranteed way to assure competitive pricing. Unbundling would necessitate that the USMS charge competitive market prices that reflect the long-run marginal cost of services provided. Such

---

[12] As an independent entity, the USMS would need to have some means of determining the cost of each individual service that it offers. It might not opt to continue using attributable costs as currently defined. References to attributable costs here are a proxy for whatever other cost scheme the USMS might devise.

[13] Implicit prices for mail processing and transportation, in the form of worksharing discounts, fail to cover the USPS's own costs of doing the same work for which discounts are given; *see* Haldi and Olson (2003).

[14] For an explanation of ECP, *see* Baumol and Sidak (1994). For a critique of ECP, *see* Economides and White (1998) and Economides (2003). For a basic discussion of worksharing, *see* General Accounting Office (2003) and the references cited therein.

[15] Nowhere does the published literature on ECP refer to attributable cost, which is a term of art unique to the USPS. The ECP rule does not provide a rationale or theoretical support for any "rule" or pricing paradigm that limits worksharing discounts to attributable cost.

market prices are likely to differ from implicit prices (*i.e.*, discounts) that are based solely on attributable costs. Achieving the type of efficiency gains that come only from full competition will require that USMS prices for its different mail processing services be driven, over time, to the level of long-run marginal cost and competitive equilibrium. Moreover, it is reasonable to expect that prices would be driven to long-run marginal cost in short order, since numerous "hungry" competitors already exist.[16]

3.2 The U. S. Delivery Service

The delivery portion of the postal network would be the largest component of the USDS, along with retail outlets and various ancillary services. The USDS would accept mail for delivery at designated acceptance units. In general, all Destination Delivery Units (DDUs) would serve as acceptance units. In addition, in urban areas the USDS might establish centralized bulk mail acceptance units to service nearby DDUs.

All bulk mail accepted by the USDS would be required to meet stated requirements, including minimum quantities (the exposition here assumes that the existing minimums for bulk mailings remain in effect). Mail would be accepted at published rates (*see* Section 4.2.8, *infra*) from (i) the USMS, (ii) any firm or organization that enters its own mail, (iii) any letter shop or printer that prepares mail on behalf of others, or (iv) presort bureaus, consolidators or others providing intermediary sorting and transportation for mailers seeking better service and/or lower rates.[17]

Responsibility for meeting all aspects of the existing USO would fall solely to the USDS. To help the USDS finance its USO, the USDS would retain the existing statutory monopoly, which would be neither enlarged nor reduced.

In view of the USDS monopoly, all of its rates and fees for delivery would continue to be regulated by the Postal Rate Commission ("PRC"). The PRC would be charged with assuring that all USDS rates, fees, and other terms are fair and non-discriminatory, and do not favor any particular competitor or restrict competition among those that provide mail to the USDS. The PRC's responsibility would be to protect competition, but not any individual competitor, including the USMS. Rates and classifications, as they pertain to delivery, could continue to be set as they are today; *i.e.*, by

---

[16] Many firms now providing intermediary postal services are fairly substantial in their own right; *e.g.*, UPS, FedEx, DHL, Pitney Bowes (PSI Presort), R.R. Donnelley, Quad Graphics, QuebecorWorld, etc.

[17] Any firm that entered mail directly with the USDS could be viewed as "partnering" with the USDS, as described by Elcano *et al.* (2000) and Bizzotto (2003). However, firms that entered mail directly with the USDS would be viewed by the USMS as competitors.

means of a formal adversarial rate proceeding. Other rate-setting procedures, such as rate indexing, also could be used; the manner in which rates for delivery are established is neither integral nor a prerequisite to unbundling.

3.2.1 USDS, The Universal Service Obligation, and Single-Piece Mail

The USO consists of: (i) daily mail delivery to every route, regardless of volume; (ii) daily collection of mail from all collection boxes; (iii) operation of the retail network; and (iv) a uniform rate for single-piece letters. It is assumed here that the USO would continue unchanged. Since each part of the USO has unprofitable components (*e.g.*, unprofitable delivery routes, collection routes, or retail post offices) that a private enterprise firm might be motivated to reduce or eliminate, the monopoly and the USO go together. Consequently, the USDS would be responsible for providing all four elements of the USO.

Single-piece mail includes everything mailed by individual members of the public. Single-piece mail necessitates the expenses incurred to pick up mail from collection boxes and individual mailboxes, and to operate the retail network. Responsibility for single-piece mail thus is viewed as an integral part of the USO, hence is the province of the USDS. The general public would interface solely with the USDS, both at local postal retail facilities and at point of delivery. The USDS, therefore, would be responsible for meeting all service standards.

For single-piece mail, USDS would collect the full amount of postage, and then contract for it to be processed and transported. Initially, the sole contractor would be the USMS (to provide the USMS with a stable transition, the initial contract might be for an extended period, such as five or more years). The USMS would bring presorted single-piece mail to DDUs, the same service it performs today. However, if the USMS failed to control costs or meet service standards, the USDS could contract with other independent vendors to process and transport some, or even all, single-piece mail.[18] At the outset, the USMS might dominate the contracting relationship, at least for processing of ordinary single-piece letters. With respect to Express Mail, Priority Mail and parcels, however, even from the outset the USDS could consider contracting with others, such as DHL, FedEx, or UPS.

---

[18] Any contract for processing of single-piece mail would contain provisions to assure privacy and limit the allowable time for the contractor to process and transport the mail. In 1997, the USPS entered into such a contract for processing and transporting Priority Mail.

3.2.2 USDS Ownership

The USDS would continue to be owned and operated by the government. Governance of the USDS could be the same as the USPS, with a governing board appointed by the President and confirmed by the Senate. The governing board would hire the top full-time executives, who would serve at the pleasure of the board. The financial break-even requirement would be similar to the existing requirement for the USPS. Subsidies might exist for free-for-the-blind mail. Any such subsidy, however, would be for the benefit of blind persons, not to help support the USDS.

3.2.3 USDS Employees and Facilities

All city and rural carriers would be employees of the USDS, as would their supervisors, as well as clerks and mailhandlers needed to oversee, accept or handle mail at DDUs and any other facility operated by the USDS. Postmasters, retail clerks, and contract carriers also would be part of the USDS. The USDS would have its own management organization and overhead structure, including the Inspection Service, data processing centers, etc.

The USDS would own (or lease) and operate all retail facilities. It would rent post office boxes to the general public, and deliver mail to those boxes. It also would be responsible for distributing and selling stamps, including operation of freestanding kiosks and all contract post offices. The USDS would own (or lease) and operate any destinating delivery units (DDUs) that are not part of a retail post office.

As indicated previously, existing plants would continue to process both originating and destinating mail until the USDS decided to acquire and operate its own centralized, dedicated acceptance units in metropolitan areas. Having dedicated facilities that process only destinating mail may appear redundant. However, equipment and space costs are rather small in comparison to labor costs. Separate facilities would help reduce congestion at loading docks, and might improve service by reducing the volume of mail that for some reason becomes temporarily displaced, but ultimately gets delivered days or even weeks late.

3.2.4 USDS Ancillary Services and Transportation

The USDS would own, operate and maintain all address correction services, which would be available to all users on the same basis. Fees for use of such services would be paid by the USMS on the same basis as others.

The USDS would only be responsible for moving mail from a local, centralized acceptance unit to nearby DDUs. All trucks currently used for collection of mail and local transportation between centralized metropolitan destination facilities and DDUs would remain with the USDS, as well as all delivery vehicles currently operated by USPS carriers.

3.2.5 USDS Attributable and Residual Costs

The portion of the postal network which must provide daily delivery to virtually every route in the country, regardless of volume, has relatively high non-attributable (fixed) network costs which result in economies of scale and scope. As indicated previously, the USMS would assume some unattributed overhead costs, so the entire burden of existing overhead costs would not be incurred by the USDS. Nevertheless, after unbundling, the non-attributed overhead costs of the USDS likely would constitute more than 50 percent of its total costs and, for the USDS to cover the non-attributed portion of its cost structure, the systemwide mark-up on attributable delivery cost would need to exceed 100 percent.

3.2.6 USDS Rates, Acceptance and Payment

All rates for single-piece mail would be set by the PRC. As a matter of public policy, the PRC would be required to recommend a uniform rate for single piece letters, as it does now. Retail customers would be unaffected by unbundling in the manner described here.

One major change is that the PRC would have to recommend rates for bulk First-Class Mail entered at destination facilities of the USDS; *i.e.*, a downstream access price for bulk First-Class Mail. This would provide an incentive not only for drop shipping, but also for electronic transmission coupled with local printing and entry.

This discussion assumes that the existing classification structure would continue in effect, with rates for delivery continuing to distinguish between private correspondence, periodicals, for-profit and non-profit advertising mail, and packages. USDS rates for delivery would be determined by the PRC in accordance with criteria contained in the Postal Reorganization Act. These criteria would result in some products having higher mark-ups, while others would have lower mark-ups, as is the case now. However, PRC-established mark-ups would apply only to attributable delivery cost.

All intermediaries that handle bulk mail for others, including the USMS, would know that they must pay the USDS's published rates for delivery, adding to those rates their charge for such intermediate services as they provide. Collectively, rates charged by the USDS would need to cover its stand-alone costs, which would be reduced to the extent that the USMS became responsible for a portion of the existing pool of non-attributed overhead costs. At the same time, no USDS revenues could be used to enable the USMS to charge lower prices for any of its competitive services.

All mail tendered to the USDS for delivery, including all mail tendered by the USMS, would be subject to meeting uniform published standards and would be subject to inspection and verification before being accepted. The USDS would collect the appropriate rates from every organization tendering bulk mail for final delivery, including the USMS and mailers who tender their own bulk mail directly to USDS.[19] Whenever an intermediary (including USMS) tendered the mail of a business firm or nonprofit organization, the intermediary would be responsible for all payments due to the USDS.

4. MERITS OF UNBUNDLING AN INTEGRATED POSTAL NETWORK

Unbundling would maximize downstream access opportunities for competitors while preserving the USO. After unbundling, existing delivery, retail and collection networks would function uninterrupted, daily universal delivery service would continue unchanged, and single-piece letters would continue to be charged a uniform rate. Given this alternative, the current status quo (described previously as partial liberalization of rates) should be seen as an unnecessary compromise with the competitive standard.[20]

From the preceding discussion, it should be apparent that an upstream entity, such as USMS, is not integral to providing or preserving any aspect of the USO. Should the upstream entity fail to operate competitively, it could be replaced seamlessly by more efficient private sector competitors. Regardless of whether the upstream entity or its competitors prevail in the marketplace, using the competitive model to maximize efficiency in mail processing and transportation would increase mail volume and sustainability of the existing USO.

---

[19] In the case of single-piece mail, USDS would collect the full amount of postage and payment would flow from USDS to its contractor(s), which initially would be the USMS. If the USMS were to be restructured as an autonomous unit within the USPS, such payments would constitute transfer fees. Such fees should be identical to those charged to independent third parties; *see* Panzar (2002).

[20] The threat of a postal death spiral is not considered in this paper. Crew and Kleindorfer (2005), after examining several access and entry policies, found partial liberalization, with final delivery retained by the postal administration, to be the policy most likely to avoid a death spiral. Crew and Kleindorfer did not examine the unbundling and full competition model described herein.

Subjecting upstream services to the full rigors of a competitive market necessitates giving management complete flexibility over the upstream portion of the postal network. Thus freed, management at last would be able to reshape and improve the mail processing network without costly political constraints (which would doom an otherwise competitive USMS to economic failure). Importantly, it also would have strong, market-based incentives to do so.

Complete unbundling should be accompanied by total deregulation of pricing for upstream postal services for all bulk mail. All upstream services should be fully open to competition. Since the upstream entity would have to be self-supporting, it would need to price its services so that, collectively, the organization would recover its stand-alone costs. With the upstream entity no longer immune from the anti-trust laws, competition would drive prices to their long-run marginal cost, thereby protecting bulk mailers from monopolistic price-gouging. The USPS has resisted efforts to offer destination entry prices for bulk First-Class Mail. Having an unbundled delivery unit offer such prices not only would promote competition, but also would be an important efficiency-enhancing change that is long overdue.

It is submitted that unbundling upstream services and opening them to full competition on a level playing field constitutes the most significant and salutary reform possible in the current political climate. The increase in efficiency that could flow from such unbundling likely would be on par with, and even might exceed, increases in efficiencies that could be obtained from other proposed major reforms, such as reducing the number of delivery days required by the USO (*e.g.*, from 6 to 5 days per week in the United States), or reforming the retail sector (*e.g.*, closing or relocating thousands of money-losing retail outlets).

The discussion herein has demonstrated how an unbundling policy could be applied to the USPS, the world's largest postal administration. It should be clearly understood, though, that unbundling offers an important policy option for any country that desires to increase the level of competition in the postal sector. It should be an especially attractive option wherever a postal administration, for whatever reason, is encumbered by a high-cost mail processing operation. Inevitably, providing support for such high-cost operations imposes an unnecessary burden on the delivery portion of the postal network. This economically desirable and politically achievable approach deserves serious consideration in ongoing discussions about postal reform.

REFERENCES

Baumol, W.J., and S. Gregory. 1994. "The Pricing of Inputs Sold to Competitors." *Yale Journal on Regulation*, 2 (no. 1, Winter): 171-202.

Bizzotto, A. 2003. "Postal Worksharing: A Partnership with Our Customers," statement presented to the Presidential Commission on the U. S. Postal Service.

Campanelli, J. 2002. "The USPS – What Needs to Be Done." *Mailing Systems and Technology* 14 (no. 3., March-April): 34-37.

Cazals, C., F. Fève, J.P. Flourens and B. Roy. 2005a. "Delivery Costs II: Back to Parametric Models." In *Regulatory and Economic Challenges in the Postal and Delivery Sector*, edited by M.A. Crew and P.R. Kleindorfer. Boston: Kluwer Academic Publishers.

Cazals, C., and J.P. Flourens and S. Soteri. 2005b. "Delivery Costs for Postal Services in the U.K." In *Regulatory and Economic Challenges in the Postal and Delivery Sector*, edited by M.A. Crew and P.R. Kleindorfer. Boston: Kluwer Academic Publishers.

Cohen, R.H., W.W. Ferguson, J.D. Waller and S.S. Xenakis. 2001. "The Impact of Using Worksharing to Liberalize a Postal Market," Presented at 6th Koenigswinter Seminar on Postal Economics "Liberalization of Postal Markets" (February 19–21, 2001).

Crew, M.A. and P.R. Kleindorfer. 1995. "Pricing in Postal Service under Competitive Entry." In *Commercialization of Postal and Delivery Services: National and International Perspectives*, edited by M.A. Crew and P.R. Kleindorfer. Boston: Kluwer Academic Publishers.

Crew, M.A. and P.R. Kleindorfer. 2005. "Competition, Universal Service, and the Graveyard Spiral." In *Regulatory and Economic Challenges in the Postal and Delivery Sector*, edited by M.A. Crew and P.R. Kleindorfer. Boston: Kluwer Academic Publishers.

Economides, N., and L.J. White. 1998. "The Inefficiency of the ECPR Yet Again: A Reply to Larson." *Antitrust Bulletin* 43: 429.

Economides, N. 2003. "The Tragic Inefficiency of the M-ECPR." In *Down to the Wire: Studies in the Diffusion and Regulation of Telecommunications Technologies*, edited by A. Shampine. New York: Nova Science Publishers, Inc.

Elcano, M.S., R.A. German and J.T. Pickett. 2000. "Hiding in Plain Sight: The Quiet Liberalization of the United States Postal System." In *Current Directions in Postal Reform*, edited by M.A. Crew and P.R. Kleindorfer. Boston: Kluwer Academic Publishers.

General Accounting Office. 1997. *U. S. Postal Service: Information About Restrictions on Mailbox Access.* GAO/GGD-97-85 (May, 1997).

General Accounting Office. 2003. *U. S. Postal Service: A Primer on Postal Service Worksharing.* GAO-03-927 (July, 2003).

General Accounting Office. 2004. *U. S. Postal Service: Bold Action Needed to Continue Progress on Postal Transformation.* GAO-04-108T (Washington, DC: November 8, 2003).

Gibbons, M.A. 2005. "Universal Service Providers: Defensive Moves on the Level Playing Field." In *Regulatory and Economic Challenges in the Postal and Delivery Sector*, edited by M.A. Crew and P.R. Kleindorfer. Boston: Kluwer Academic Publishers.

Haldi, J., and W.J. Olson. 2003. "An Evaluation of USPS Worksharing: Postal Revenues and Costs From Workshared Activities." In *Competitive Transformation of the Postal and Delivery Sector,* edited by M.A. Crew and P.R. Kleindorfer. Boston: Kluwer Academic Publishers.

Mitchell, R.W. 1999. "Postal Worksharing: Technical Efficiency, and Pareto Optimality." In *Emerging Competition In Postal and Delivery Services*, edited by M.A. Crew and P.R. Kleindorfer. Boston: Kluwer Academic Publishers.

Panzar, J.C. 2002. "Reconciling Competition, Downstream Access, and Universal Service in Postal Markets." In *Postal and Delivery Economics: Delivering on Competition,* edited by M.A. Crew and P.R. Kleindorfer. Boston: Kluwer Academic Publishers.

Postal Service. 2002. *Transformation Plan* (April, 2002).

Rogerson, C.M. and D.E. Treworgy. 1994. "Refocusing the U. S. Postal Service Monopoly." Presented at Fourth Conference on Postal and Delivery Economics, Saltsjöbaden, Sweden.

Valletti, T.M. and A. Estache. 1998. "The Theory of Access Pricing: An Overview for Infrastructure Regulators." (March, 1998.) The World Bank Institute. Washington, D.C. and European Center for Applied Research in Economics. Brussels.

Liberalization and Quality of Service

Chapter 12

The Economic Implications of Quality of Service Regulation in a Liberalized Postal Market*

Tom Balogh,[1] Richard Moriarty,[1] Paul Smith,[1] Roisin Doherty[2] and Ian Leigh[2]
Postcomm[1] and Postwatch[2]

1. INTRODUCTION

The future shape of the quality of service regulation in the UK has received much attention recently as Postcomm, the regulator, develops proposals for a new price control for Royal Mail, the dominant supplier, to apply from April 2006. This includes financial incentives to achieve quality of service performance that meets customers' needs. Customers are keen that their voices are heard in the development of these proposals, and Postwatch, the statutory consumer council, has been leading efforts to understand what customers want from Royal Mail so new targets take account of customers' needs. Postcomm's price control review formally commenced in March 2004 and the control will apply from April 2006. It is proposed to last for four years. This represents the first concerted effort to put in place a quality of service regime for postal services in the UK based on empirical evidence from customers and will be based on customer research by MORI and consultation by both Postwatch and Postcomm.

This review takes place in a rapidly changing postal market. The UK postal market will be fully opened to competition from 1 January 2006. Competitors are beginning to enter the parts of the market already open to

---

* The views expressed in this paper are the authors' own and not necessarily those of either Postwatch or Postcomm.

competition (bulk mailings), offering products with different price and quality commitments than Royal Mail. At the same time as competition is introduced, Royal Mail's financial health is improving. Although its quality of service performance has been criticized by customers, the company has been working hard to improve its performance compared to the poor performance in 2003/4.

Therefore, the challenge for regulation is twofold. First, to ensure that quality of service targets, that meet customers' needs and are achievable by the company, are put in place. Royal Mail should be given effective incentives to meet these standards, including redress for customers if standards are not met. Secondly, to ensure that the new quality of service regime from April 2006 reflects conditions in a developing competitive market and continues to safeguard provision of the Universal Service.

This paper looks at how Postcomm, Postwatch and Royal Mail have reviewed quality of service regulation in the UK – both in terms of targets and incentives. Section two discusses why quality of service regulation is necessary. Section three explains the current quality of service regime for Royal Mail and section four summarizes the results of MORI's research into customer expectations of quality. Section five considers how a new quality of service regime should be created and maintained. The final section sets out our conclusions on the impact of quality of service regulation in a liberalized postal market.

2. WHY REGULATE QUALITY OF SERVICE?

It is generally accepted that price controlling a supplier with a powerful monopoly position in a market is necessary. However, more than prices must be controlled if a regulatory framework to meet customers' needs is to be created. If pricing was constrained but the company was free to provide whatever quality of service it wished, then the company might be able to maximize its profits by reducing spending on maintaining quality. A company's ability to profit maximize using this strategy would be constrained by impacts on demand of poor quality of service, e.g. switching to other media, as well as any scope for customers to exercise a choice of supplier if parts of the market are open to competition. Where customers have limited alternative options the scope for the company to maximize profits by reducing quality would be increased. Therefore, in general, if a company with a strong monopoly position is being price controlled, it also needs to have quality of service regulation[1].

The postal market for letters and small packets in the United Kingdom is currently a de facto monopoly dominated by Royal Mail. There is now some competition in the market, but the latest analysis by Postcomm showed Royal Mail still having a 99.3%[2] market share.

Despite fears about e-substitution, the postal market in many countries appears to be remarkably resilient to competition from new communications technologies and in some cases has actually benefited from new technology (packets are sent by on-line shoppers and text-messages have been used in Wales to alert householders to the fact that post has been delivered to their letter box). In such a market - where there are few possible alternatives for circulating written media and a real need for the services provided - the regulator would ideally act as a surrogate for the demands of a market. However, it is difficult to establish what these might be as it is necessary for the regulator to understand how a full range of customers value quality, including the receivers of mail (who do not pay the postage). Each customer can be expected to have a different willingness-to-pay as can each customer group. This means that a regulator must understand these groups in detail to ensure that it can simulate their wishes and apply greater pressure on price or quality as they would wish. This is especially the case with large volume mailers who are each likely to have very specific requirements for their mail. Since large businesses account for a large proportion of mail volumes, this can create difficulties for the regulator trying to mimic the individual pressures they would each apply to the regulated company.

Based on an understanding of how customers value quality, regulators should set quality levels, usually by creating explicit obligations within the license for dominant providers, requiring them to meet minimum standards of service that customers can expect to receive in the absence of significant competitive pressures. The regulator must use an economic achievability test for the company alongside assessing customer need when setting targets. Certain target levels might be unachievable at any reasonable economic cost. This approach has been adopted in other UK regulated sectors.

Regulators then need to provide the company with an incentive to meet these standards. The company's incentive to maintain demand levels and its reputation will provide incentives to maintain quality of service. However, these incentives are likely to need to be supplemented by specific financial incentives for failure to meet quality of service targets. The stronger the

---

1 The corollary of this is that only price controlled services should be subject to quality of service regulation.

2 Market share by volume, Quarter 3 year-to-date, 2004/5.

company's market position the more important will be financial incentives. In determining the scale of these financial incentives, regulators take account of both the costs and benefits associated with improvements in quality. Generally speaking, a regulator will seek to make it more profitable for a company to meet its targets - this means that the marginal reward for an improvement in performance must exceed the costs that the company incurs to make that improvement. Moreover, the regulator will also try to ensure that the marginal reward for improved service quality does not exceed the value that customers attach to that improvement, thereby deterring companies from spending more on quality of service than customers are ultimately willing to pay, e.g. gold plating.

Based on other regulators' experience in the UK the following basic principles should apply to postal services when considering incentives for quality of service performance. First, mechanisms that compensate directly those customers that experience poor quality of service generally represent the best protection for users. Second, automatic financial incentives should be put in place when it is not possible to compensate customers directly for poor performance. Third, enforcement of the license (either imposing financial penalties for non-compliance with the license or requiring the company to take certain actions) should be seen as a last resort and to deal with very serious performance failings only.

These principles can be seen in the approach taken by most UK economic regulators. Over time, the scope of these incentive mechanisms has expanded to capture more dimensions of service quality, especially in circumstances where research has demonstrated that customers place particularly high value on specific aspects of a regulated firm's service.

International comparisons in postal services reveal different approaches. There is very little regulation of quality of service other than transit time for mail items and where such standards are regulated, they are seldom subject to financial incentives, e.g. New Zealand. This may be explained by the fact that New Zealand has been liberalized for a far longer time than the UK market and so competition may now be strong enough to ensure that customers' needs are adequately met without regulation or it might reflect a different view about the circumstances in which regulation is required. Many countries perform quality of service measurement (this has been required of European Community countries since February 2005 under standards such as EN 13850). The Directive gives each member state scope to decide how to regulate in line with the directive. The principles above should be applied to the regulation of quality of service for post in the UK.

Mandatory compensation schemes should offer the best protection for users because they directly compensate customers for any poor quality of service. However, such schemes may not be enough. Direct compensation has disadvantages where it is not possible to identify individual users that have suffered from poor performance or where it is prohibitively costly to arrange payment. Senders of stamped mail, for example, cannot be traced. The low propensity of customers to complain also reduces the effectiveness of this incentive (in 2003/4, less than £1m was paid in compensation for delay while the bulk mail scheme returned £42m to customers despite the fact that roughly half of Royal Mail's revenues are derived from the retail products).

This means that further automatic financial incentives are necessary and a revenue adjustment mechanism ('C-factor') should cover retail products. While this does not provide direct compensation to customers on a personal, or even product-specific level, it does recover a certain amount of revenue from a defined basket of tariffs and so provides a link between the price that they pay and the quality of service that they receive. If set at the correct level a C-factor should mimic the market to simulate the revenue-drop caused by disaffected customers and so force the incumbent to maintain quality as it would were it not a monopoly.

It would be unreasonable for a regulator to take away more than the regulatory profit allowed as an automatic penalty. However, a penalty up to the regulatory profit is reasonable as, if a company's performance declined to such an extent that the full automatic penalty was applied, a competitive market might well penalize the company to this extent or more.

Where explicit license obligations, setting out minimum standards of service, are set, enforcement of these obligations can be an excellent tool to ensure that action can be taken if performance falls short of the level that the regulator has stipulated. Yet over-emphasis on the license can cause its own problems and should only be used for very serious performance failings when other means have failed. Postcomm's experience in regulating quality of service under the current price control is outlined below in section 3.

Compensation for service failure is important to all customers. However, it can be argued that, in circumstances where customers do not have choice in their supplier, compensation is even more important as customers are denied the opportunity to switch when faced with service failures. In monopoly circumstances compensation schemes resulting in financial or other recompense to customers can be an important incentive to improve quality and therefore should be regulated, i.e. the entitlement of customers to compensation made more prescriptive.

Operators in competition with Royal Mail will either seek to offer at least as good service quality as Royal Mail for similar prices (in which case Royal Mail is free to raise its own quality level – targets being minimum levels to be achieved) or will compete on the basis of either reduced quality of service for a lower price or improved quality of service for a slightly higher price. If the margins available to competitors are sufficient to enable them to offer significantly lower prices than Royal Mail then customers should be able to choose between competing products on the basis of their individual price quality trade-offs. Royal Mail might need flexibility to adapt its product range and quality standards at that point but that question is outside the scope of this paper. Where part of the competitive area is regulated, e.g. the scope of the universal service, an appropriate regulatory intervention would be to give license conditions to operators competing with the dominant provider requiring them to have a system adequate for recording, analyzing and responding to customer complaints, and to publish the number of complaints it has received (as Energywatch does in the UK gas and electricity supply markets).

3. QUALITY OF SERVICE REGULATION IN THE UK

The regulatory regime for postal services in the UK was transformed in 2000 by the Postal Services Act which created a new regulator, Postcomm and a statutory consumer body, Postwatch. Postcomm's first task was to grant a new license to Royal Mail, including quality of service provisions. In doing so Postcomm rolled Royal Mail's then internal targets into its license (the License) with the latter's agreement. The targets were retained in the 2003 price control (although the levels of some were adjusted).

Royal Mail's quality of service is currently regulated using a number of different conditions in the License. The most important of these conditions is Condition 4 (Service Standards and Compensation). There are four major aspects to what it requires Royal Mail to do. Firstly, to use reasonable endeavors to collect postal packets and to deliver the packets it receives within a reasonable time. Secondly, to specify minimum standards of service that are no less demanding than targets contained in its license. Thirdly, to use all reasonable endeavors to provide these standards of service and fourthly, to maintain a scheme to compensate users affected by a failure to meet the standards.

Other requirements relating to quality of service are found within Conditions 2, 5, 8 and 19 of Royal Mail's license. Condition 2 requires Royal Mail to provide a universal postal service, which must include at least one delivery and collection of postal packets every working day. This reflects the requirements of the Postal Services Act 2000 and the European Postal Services Directive. Condition 5 requires Royal Mail to establish transparent, simple and inexpensive procedures for handling customer complaints. Condition 8 requires Royal Mail to adopt and comply with procedures designed to minimize the risk of loss, theft, damage or interference. Finally, price levels and revenue adjustment (the C-factor) are dealt with in Condition 19.

The current price control includes two mechanisms that provide Royal Mail with incentives to meet its quality of service targets - compensation schemes for retail and bulk customers, and a revenue adjustment mechanism (C-factor) to induce Royal Mail to meet its quality of service targets. Enforcement action and the threat of this can also be taken under Royal Mail's license for poor quality of service performance.

The compensation regime in the UK was established in 2003 and provides for different forms of compensation for retail and bulk customers if license targets are not met. Under the scheme, retail users are entitled to free stamps or monetary payments if mail items are significantly delayed. For senders of bulk mail, compensation payments increase with the magnitude of any Royal Mail failure to achieve the quality of service target for each service. Customers of any service for which Royal Mail has failed its quality target by 1% or more, automatically get a refund of 0.1% of their spend on that product for each 0.1% failure, subject to a cap at 5% (needed so that the risk born by Royal Mail is not large enough to adversely affect its financial viability).

The revenue adjustment mechanism allows Royal Mail to recover more revenue if it achieves certain standards of quality. About 1% of Royal Mail's revenue for first and second class stamped and metered mail, and for standard parcels, is subject to this quality incentive.

If the financial incentives within the compensation schemes and the revenue adjustment mechanism have not led to satisfactory quality of service performance by Royal Mail, Postcomm reserves the ability to take enforcement action against Royal Mail under its license. This means that Postcomm could take enforcement action if Royal Mail had not used 'reasonable endeavors' to meet its quality of service targets. If Postcomm found that Royal Mail had failed to comply with the license requirement, the latter might face a financial penalty. When and how this license requirement will be enforced is more uncertain than automatic revenue adjustments, although Postcomm could provide guidance about when and how it would enforce the license requirement.

Enforcement action often includes financial penalties. In the United Kingdom penalties levied by Postcomm go to HM Treasury rather than affected users. If this is the case the link between customers and redress for poor quality of service performance is broken as the shareholder receives the financial penalty anyway. This reduces the incentive for the shareholder to put pressure on the company to improve and maintain quality of service performance, as it will receive the money as a financial penalty even if not as profit.

Royal Mail has never hit all of its 16 performance targets, achieving nine in 2001/2, three in 2002/3, none in 2003/4[3] and four in 2004/5. This has resulted in regulatory financial penalties on two occasions to date. In 2002/3, Postcomm imposed a financial penalty on Royal Mail for service quality failures for Postage Paid Impression and Response Services. In 2003/4, Royal Mail was allowed to recover £13m of revenue under the "C" factor rather than the £30 million it would have if all quality of service targets been met and paid out over £42m in direct compensation to business customers. The result was a total of £60m returned to customers for a year in which Royal Mail failed to meet any of its quality of service targets). This was about 25% of its price controlled operating profit (after provision for pension deficit payments).

Performance in 2004/5 was still below target; Royal Mail achieved four out of sixteen targets. Performance was considerably better than in 2003/4 but Royal Mail is still likely to face significant financial consequences for this failure from the statutory compensation scheme. Table 1 below shows Royal Mail's quality of service performance for key public tariff products since 1995/6.

Table 1 - Royal Mail's Historical Quality of Service Performance

	1st class (stamped & metered)[4] (%)	2nd class (stamped & metered)[5] (%)	Standard Parcels[6] (%)
1995/6	92.3	97.9	76.0
1996/7	85.9	96.2	78.0
1997/8	91.5	98.3	81.5
1998/9	91.1	98.6	85.0
1999/00	91.0	98.8	85.0
2000/1	86.5	97.3	85.0
2001/2	89.9	98.3	81.0
2002/3	91.8	98.6	88.5
2003/4	90.1	97.8	88.9
2004/5	91.4	98.5	89.7

3 When determining the appropriate level of compensation for customers, Postcomm accepted Royal Mail's argument that the fire at the Northampton mail centre should be considered a "force majeure" event. Taking this into account would mean that Royal Mail met one of its targets (Mailsort 3) for the purposes of determining the appropriate level of compensation.

4 The current target is 93%.

5 The current target is 98.5%.

6 The current target is 90%.

The table[7] above shows Royal Mail's recent performance in the context of its historical performance. While both Postcomm and Postwatch have stated that the current levels of service are not sufficient, they are still among the best achieved in the last decade. Against this background Postcomm, Postwatch and Royal Mail began to look thoroughly at quality of service regulation from first principles in 2004.

4. WHAT SHOULD BE REGULATED? - AN EMPIRICAL BASIS FOR A NEW REGIME

In reviewing the current targets and potentially putting targets in place for the future, the first step for Postwatch, Royal Mail and Postcomm was to carry out independent empirical research designed to establish customer requirements from universal and other postal services (in terms of speed of delivery, reliability, security etc), and to assess customer expectations of quality over the possible period of the next price control (up to 2011).

The research included customers from all sectors, both business and domestic, high value and low value, senders and receivers, across the whole of the UK. It looked at how Royal Mail's reputation varied across all customer groups. Analysis was undertaken to understand what was driving overall favorability towards Royal Mail and customer's preferences. The research also identified a set of customer expectations and opportunities for improvements. Results of the study are available in full on Postwatch's website.[8]

The research identified a number of critical service success factors for Royal Mail's customers. The most important factors (common to all customers surveyed) were reliability, delivery on promises, and trustworthiness. Keeping to schedule was also important for the top 500 and medium customers. The drivers of favorability differ a little by customer group. 'Meeting expectations' is a key driver for the top 500 and medium sized businesses, while 'reliability' is the key driver for both domestic and small businesses. This implies that the issue for customers is not the level of the target per se but rather achieving it.

The research also attempted to assess customer preferences by looking at the trade offs customers make between price and different service attributes.

---

[7] The measurement systems (and targets) for these targets have changed over the years (especially when the License came into being in 2001). The figures cannot therefore give a wholly representative picture of past performance.

[8] www.postwatch.co.uk, MORI. 2004. Royal Mail Quality of Service research study conducted for Royal Mail, Postwatch and Postcomm.

For domestic and small business customers three factors were considered – price, delivery time, and percentage of mail delivered within time targets.

The results are similar for small business and domestic customers. Both groups valued price and percentage of mail delivered within time targets slightly more than delivery time of day targets. Figure 1 shows these results for small business and domestic customers.

Figure 1: Small businesses are similar to domestic customers

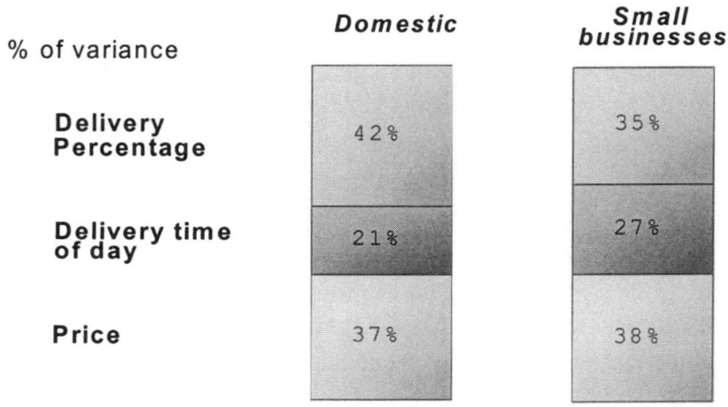

Base: Consumers (1879), small businesses (280), excluding R sq uared < 50%

MORI

The results also demonstrate that delivery percentage becomes even more important for those domestic and small business customers who mostly use first class mail and that small business customers using first class for most of their mail are more likely to favor service over price.[9] Conversely price is more important among small business and domestic users who have a greater propensity to choose cheaper second class services. This price sensitivity is more marked in older domestic customers. It also appears that domestic and small business customers place more value on an improvement to delivery time targets and delivery percentage than a price reduction.

A slightly more complicated set of factors was considered for business customers. These were price, the day items are delivered, the percentage of mail delivered, and non-delivery to addressee. The high level results are presented in the table below and reveal that in general the trade-off is between price and delivery on the target day. The importance of the percentage of mail that is delivered is constant across all the groups

---

9 MORI. 2004, Royal Mail Quality of Service. Ibid. See table 'There is differentiation in use of current services,' p.31.

considered and those using second class are only slightly more price sensitive than those using first class services or equivalent.

Figure 2: Relative importance by size of business

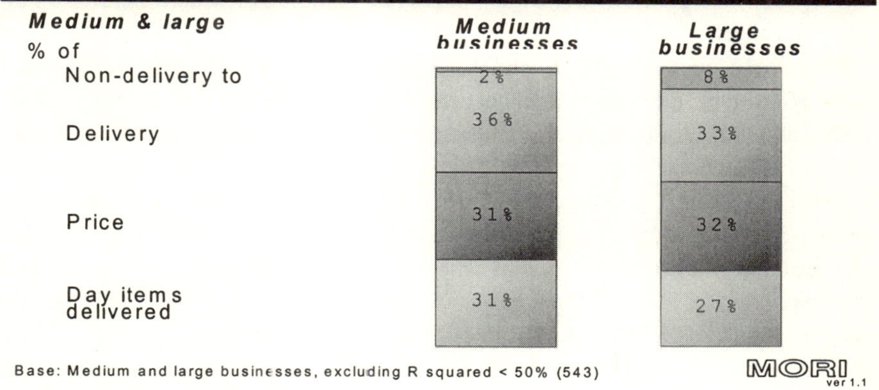

With regard to customer expectations, all customers surveyed shared the view that the basic necessity is for the mail to be delivered according to the service promise. Loss was also a critical factor for all audiences, and was viewed as unacceptable by the majority across all types of customers, no matter what the price of the service is. Only a small percentage of the top 500 and medium business customers disagree with this. These customers seem to trade off a small number of missing items with others factors such as price. [10]

Loss - Some customers would pay more to reduce loss. Users of first class services and those top 500 and medium business customers, who mainly use the post to send documents and business correspondence, would also be the most likely to accept an increase in price, should this mean a reduction of items going missing. More than half of small businesses (53%) and 61% of domestic customers would be prepared to pay more for the postal service should this lead to a decrease in the number of items lost in the system.[11]

Meeting delivery targets - Very few customers found a slippage acceptable in delivery of more than two working days after the target day. Three-quarters of domestic customers believed that all those items that missed their target delivery day should be delivered the following working

---

[10] MORI. 2004. Royal Mail Quality of Service, p.45, op. cit.

[11] MORI. 2004. Royal Mail Quality of Service, p.47, op. cit.

day, and a further 19% said these should be delivered within the next two working days. Those who used first class post for most of their correspondence were also more likely to say that items that miss their delivery day target should be delivered the following working day (78% compared to 69% who used this service less).[12] This is a significant finding given that the research found that over half of domestic customers use first class services.

Business customers also had high expectations about when the tail of mail should be delivered with virtually all small businesses believing that items which missed their delivery target should reach their destination within the following two working days.

Collection and delivery windows - Consistent delivery and collection times were particularly important for medium and top businesses – particularly those who use the mail for financial or general business correspondence. 40% of those who use the mail service mainly for financial purposes and 44% of those who use it for general business correspondence believed that the maximum acceptable window of mail is 20 minutes (i.e. approximately 10 minutes either side of the expected time). A further third in each of these sectors would not accept a window of more than half an hour. Across all top 500 and medium customers, two-thirds claimed that the maximum acceptable window of delivery is half an hour and very few (7%) were prepared to pay more to reduce the window of delivery time.[13] Tolerance was even lower when it comes to collection times. Half of all medium and top 500 business customers would not accept a window of collection time of more than 20 minutes and a further 31% would not stretch to more than 30 minutes. The great majority (87%) were not willing to pay more to reduce the window of collection times – though this is slightly lower among top 500 businesses (78%).[14]

Overall the research demonstrated that customers' experiences and expectations of quality rely on more factors than just how long it takes to deliver mail. This shows that standards should not only be based on transit time. Especially key to customer perceptions was reliability.

---

[12] MORI. 2004. Royal Mail Quality of Service, p.49, op. cit.
[13] MORI. 2004. Royal Mail Quality of Service, p.53, op. cit.
[14] MORI. 2004. Royal Mail Quality of Service, p.53, op. cit.

5. HOW SHOULD QUALITY OF SERVICE BE REGULATED?

There are three key ways to regulate quality of service - publishing performance, the creation of regulatory targets and the creation of financial incentives.

The primary aim of standards is to bring service into line with customer expectations, and ensure that the level of service is maintained. The measurement system must be robust enough to ensure that any increase is due to genuine improvements and that any decline is captured. The measurement system must also be independent. Consideration must be given to both the cost of individual targets and the overall burden of the targets – which should be kept to a number that is clear to customers and manageable. If there are any targets that do not serve the purpose they were designed for then it makes sense to ensure that they are removed, altered, or replaced. Resources should not be wasted on something that provides no benefit to the operator or customers.

Accordingly, there must be a clear mandate for an aspect of the service to be targeted. We would argue that when deciding what to target there should be a balance between factors which drive customer satisfaction and the financial viability of the universal service provider (in respect of which, in the UK, the regulator has a statutory duty). Customers must feel reassured that they are getting the service they pay for. Similarly, if the targets are the correct ones, performance measurement should provide an opportunity for the universal service provider to identify and correct problems. Targets should encourage more efficient processes and in the long term be of benefit to postal providers.

When considering the target level, experience over the previous three years indicates that having different target levels on products has had a minimal effect on performance. It is unlikely that simply raising or lowering target levels in 2006 would be the best way to encourage improvement. In any event no target can be set at 100% with any degree of confidence - quality of service measurement relies on too many variables for 100% of anything to be guaranteed.

It must also be possible to measure the standard set to ensure the targets are effective. European regulations insist that independent end-to-end measurement is maintained and audited. Customers must be able to understand and appreciate what is being measured; the results should be comprehensible and demonstrate either improvement or decline in a way that will reflect customer experience.

The first step in the UK process, set out in Condition 4 of Royal Mail's license, is for Postwatch and Royal Mail to negotiate and try to create an agreed proposal to submit to the regulator. After this, Postcomm has to consult on proposals, which may or may not be the same as an agreed package, before finally making proposals for amendments to the license for Royal Mail to agree and commencing the new regime.

Ultimately there was not enough agreement between Postwatch and Royal Mail to be able to recommend a new regime to Postcomm. However, Postcomm has more information than ever before to help it create its own package of standards to consult upon.

5.1 Proposals for a new regime

Products outside of the price control should not have a regulated quality of service target (Royal Mail should be free to measure and publish such performance and pay compensation as it considered appropriate), while products inside the price control should have a regulated standard to ensure that Royal Mail cannot circumvent the objective of the price control by reducing costs through lower quality of service. However, it is not necessary for each product to have an individual standard (the same one could apply to multiple products) nor for all standards to have the same type of financial incentives and enforcement options.

Currently Royal Mail either passes or fails each target. Even when the failure is by a small margin it is still deemed a failure. A new structure therefore needed to be looked at that better reflect the true quality of Royal Mail's performance. In Table 2 is a proposed system of ranges. In this, each range would be linked to the incentive structure so that the consequences of any level of performance were known in advance. This gives a level of certainty to the regulated company that allows it to understand fully the consequences of its actions. It also gives more certainty to the market.

Table 2 - Possible Framework for new quality of service targets

Product	Delivery aim	Excellent	Satisfactory	Needs improvement	Unacceptable
		No impact	No impact	Compensation or revenue reduction	Additional monetary penalties

Thus, if Royal Mail's performance was within the 'Satisfactory' band, there would be no financial impact but if it slipped into the band labeled 'Needs Improvement', it would face financial incentives to improve.

Royal Mail has not consistently achieved the targets set in the current price control, which it accepted. However, in most cases it has, at some stage, come very near to doing so. Therefore, the level of the new standards should match those set in 2003 as they have been accepted by Royal Mail previously, and appear in general to be achievable and valued by customers.

Quality of service incentives must be set in a way that encourages the business to achieve the levels of performance funded in the price control. The C-factor and bulk compensation scheme should therefore be calibrated in such a manner that compensation is payable to customers if performance slips materially below these levels. As the MORI research suggests that public tariff customers value quality as least as much as bulk mailers, we believe that the amount of revenue exposed under the bulk compensation scheme and C-factor should be equal. The research conducted by MORI last year demonstrates that all types of user place much greater monetary value on Royal Mail's performance than the relatively small exposure that the C-factor gave in the 2003 control would suggest. Further, the quality of service failure over the period of the control suggests that the incentives were not sufficient for target levels of service to be achieved and consistently maintained.

6. CONCLUSION – THE IMPACT OF QUALITY OF SERVICE REGULATION IN A LIBERALISED MARKET

Customers expect that postal service providers will deliver on the promises they make. Where a provider has a de facto monopoly, we believe that some form of quality of service regulation is not just desirable but necessary to ensure that customers get what they pay for. In this paper we have looked at the current position in the UK. We do not think it is appropriate to impose targets on competitors to Royal Mail. These will most likely seek to differentiate themselves on the basis of the service they provide to customers. While the market may not assist in the regulation of the dominant supplier, any other operators will have to compete with Royal Mail and this should provide strong incentives for them to meet customers' needs. However, robust and reliable information on the performance of licensed competitors is necessary to allow customers to make informed decisions.

Postcomm will need to assess the likely effect on competitors of any new or revised quality standards and compensation arrangements for Royal Mail when it makes its final proposals on prices and service quality regulation. The main impact of any quality regime for Royal Mail on competitors is likely to be the possibility of raising the barriers to entry by forcing Royal Mail to offer a level of service that is artificially higher than customers want. Postcomm will need to be careful to ensure that this does not happen. The MORI research provides an important tool to aid in this.

To conclude, there is a continued role for regulation of quality of service within the postal market due to the power of a de facto monopoly provider even after full market opening. However, except for the benchmarking effects of the dominant company's standards, it is not appropriate to set standards for competitors. Instead, standards on aspects of quality other than transit time are necessary and the MORI research highlights this with its focus on reliability rather than speed. Quality of service may require standards but the number of standards needs to be limited. Financial incentives help ensure that a provider achieves standards but as market forces grow, gradual deregulation should allow these to become the dominant factor in the regulatory regime.

Finally, we would like to highlight key areas where there is scope for further work. Postcomm, Postwatch and Royal Mail have done considerable empirical research into the effect on quality of service of four key variables. These are coverage, structure, level and incentives. We have looked at these in the context of the research and the discussions between the three organizations and have highlighted the principles key to a discussion of them. However, there is scope for further, more theoretical, work on how these affect the regulation of quality of service. Most importantly further work to assess cost versus quality needs to be done to allow customer needs to be better aligned with what the company can cost effectively achieve. While this work is difficult it would add considerable value to the setting of targets.

REFERENCES

Horton, G. 1998. "Utility Regulation: Regulation of Quality." Royal Economic Society.

Baker, B. and S. Trémolet. 2000. "Regulation of Quality pf Infrastructure Services in Developing Countries." NERA.

Civil Aviations Association. 2005. Proposals for NATS.

Office of the Rail Regulator. 2003. Final Conclusion of the Access Charges Review.

Royal Mail. 2005. Benchmarking Other Measures used by Postal Administrators.

MORI. 2004. Royal Mail Quality of Service research study conducted for Royal Mail, Postwatch and Postcomm.

Chapter 13

Estimation of Consumers' Willingness-to-pay for Quality of Service in Post*

Gregory Swinand and Siân Jones
London Economics

1. INTRODUCTION

While Postal liberalisation is underway in the EU, much of the postal market remains regulated. Regulation takes the form of both price and entry protection. Entry protection is believed to be necessary for incumbent universal service providers (USPs) who face significant burdens from unsustainable cross subsidies[1]. With both price and entry set exogenously by the regulator, quality of service naturally becomes an issue. Regulators are thus properly concerned about quality of service. At the same time, facing increasing competition from various forms of communication, Posts are also looking at quality of service from a commercial perspective. In fact, at recent international conferences on postal economics and universal service, speakers[2,3] have given quality of service a prominent position in discussions

* The authors are Divisional Directors with LE. The authors wish to thank colleagues at LE, the editors of this volume, and many thanks to An Post. Any opinions, errors, or omissions are purely our own.

[1] While opinions on this differ, we give no opinion on the burden of the USO. However, we point out that the existence of entry protection indicates some policy agreement on significance of the burden.

[2] This includes the dinner address by Donal Curtin, CEO An Post, at the recent 2004 Conference on Postal and Delivery Economics in Cork, Ireland.

[3] For example, see the comments of Mr. Mazou, the Secretary General of the UPU at the 2004 23rd World Postal Congress, Bucharest. He stressed that quality of service went hand-in-hand with network efficiency, and that increasing quality of service was the most

about the future of the postal service. Many posts are under pressure from falling volumes and enhanced potential for electronic substitution. Quality of service improvement is seen as one way of stemming this tide.

Economic analysis of quality of service, from either a regulatory or commercial prospective, requires information on the marginal costs and benefits of quality of service improvements/degradation. Rigorous econometric evidence on the cost/production side has been investigated. Previously, Swinand (2004) argued that quality of service was the endogenous variable in the postal production process, that a production function econometric model captured the production process well, and enabled the estimation of the costs of improved service quality. However, with notable exceptions (Reay 2002) little work has been done to date examining empirically the consumer side of quality of service.

This paper studies consumers' willingness-to-pay for additional service quality on first class letter mail in Ireland. An Post, Ireland's USP, has recently been consulting with the regulator, and from a commercial standpoint internally, on the appropriate levels of service quality. The paper uses the econometric approach of estimating demand functions with quality as a determinant of demand. The dataset used consists of a representative sample of international mail originating in Ireland. We note that preferences for quality and price tradeoffs may differ, of course, for international mail than for domestic mail. While this and other qualifications about the current study naturally limit the ability to extrapolate the results to other jurisdictions, we believe the methodology and approach presented do have some claim to generality.

The rest of the paper is organised as follows. Section 2 reviews previous research in willingness-to-pay for postal quality, section 3 sets out our methodology, section 4 discusses the data, while section 5 presents results. Our conclusions are presented in section 6.

2. PREVIOUS RESEARCH[4]

For many posts and businesses, judgements about consumers' willingness-to-pay for quality are based on market research. Marketing scientists have for many years now conducted studies on service quality and attributes for existing and new products[5]. One popular method of marketing research often focuses on surveying consumers and asking what amount they

---

likely way universal postal service providers should be seeking to combat substitution towards electronic communications.

4 We focus on the empirical issues of estimation, regulation, etc. There is a rich theoretical literature on regulation and service quality, including: Cremer et al (1997).

5 A good reference is Urban and Hauser (1993).

would pay (accept) to receive higher (lower) quality. While these types of methods are very useful and can be quite sophisticated, survey evidence may suffer from potential biases, and it is often important to cross-check results with alternative methods.

Recently, the European Commission studied quality of service in relation to the implementation of the postal service directive (2003)[6]. The main focus, however, was to determine standards and definitions for the measurement EU Postal quality of service, and to determine what level of regulation, if any, was needed at the EU level to support the development in the internal EU market. For example, there is the possibility of one post exerting externalities on other posts or potential competitors via the quality of injected or cross border mail, and the EU Commission would obviously see this as a potential hindrance to the internal market. While much of the EC study focused on the rationale for regulation of QoS, one part of the study did focus on the potential impact of QoS on demand, and so is of relevant interest for our current study (while we are interested in the impact on price, there is generally believed to be a monotonically decreasing relationship between price and demand (quantity)).

The EC study mainly relied of interviews of USPs, and did not obtain any concrete empirical results[7]. The study concludes, "General statements about the willingness-to-pay for improved transit time cannot be derived based on the survey results. We asked for the most important QoS issues which should be improved in the view of the customers/consumers represented by the associations. Within the present MS transit time has been classified as an important issue by 4 out of 13 associations. Additional willingness-to-pay has been stated by two associations (business associations of France and UK). 2 out of 8 associations from the AC (consumer association of Poland and a business association of Slovakia) have considered transit time improvements as an important issue and both have stated an additional willingness-to-pay for such an improvement."

The EC study also notes the case study of Italy, which recently introduced a priority first class service. At the time, the stamp standard price

---

6 http://europa.eu.int/comm/internal_market/post/doc/studies/200308-ups-report_en.pdf

7 The study states; "While some information exists about the price elasticity of demand with respect to postal services, the level of the quality elasticity is still not empirically analysed. ... In the course of the study besides USPs and NRAs a large number of customer and consumer associations were asked about their opinion with respect to QoS issues of postal services. The transit time of domestic and cross-border letters and parcels was one important subject in the questionnaire. Against the background that only a small number of associations answered the questionnaire the results are neither representative for the Community nor for one particular country."

was €0.62, but the service standards were J+1 and high (90% hitting target[8]). Consumers were generally satisfied with the service. However, volumes shifted from both the economy class *and* the express class, so it was not possible to tell if the new service was a "success" although *some* customers had switched from the lower grade service to the higher quality service, and been willing to pay for it. Of course, it is also useful to note that this depends on the performance of the economy class service.

PostWatch[9], the UK watchdog, recently commissioned consumer survey work of Royal Mail's prices and quality, among other aspects. The conclusions of their work were mostly qualitative, but include: importance of quality aspects regarding punctuality, reliability and speed varies considerably with mailing intention and company size; price is a key decision driver, and the trade-off between price and quality is broadly accepted; for large companies, price is not the only factor; cost savings from improved process efficiency are also of great importance.

Table 1: Summary Price Equivalence Table – Consumers
Value Equivalent to a 1p increase in price from 28p to 29p

All Consumers	**Delivery time-of-day improvement (12pm to 5pm)**	**Delivery % point increase from 92%**
	One Hour	**1.1% pts**
Under 25s	Half an hour	0.5% pts
Over 25s	One and a half hours	2.5% pts
ABs	One and a half hours	1.2% pts
DEs	One hour	1.0% pts
Opinion stayed the same or got better	One hour	1.2% pts
Opinion got worse	One hour	0.9% pts
Prepared to pay more ('tail of mail')	Half an hour	0.4% pts
Not prepared to pay more ('tail of mail')	One and three quarter hours	3.2% pts
Send up to half of post by 1st Class	Two hours	2.3% pts
Send more than half of post by 1st Class	One hour	0.9% pts

Source: PostWatch Survey

The survey also asked consumers in the UK how they would trade off service quality for price. The PostWatch survey also based an assessment of the 1p value of various changes in service level. These were further broken down by customer demographic segment, and are summarised in Table 1.

---

8 According to the Commission document, there is some dispute as to whether the actual performance is this high.

9 See Royal Mail Quality of Service -http://www.postwatch.co.uk/pdf/Research/June_July 04QoS_studyfor_RM_PW_postcomm.pdf

Similar research was undertaken in relation to business customers, with qualitatively similar results.

In another study, PostWatch took a different approach to the study of service quality. They looked into estimating the 'costs of delay' to business in the UK from service quality failures at Royal Mail. If it can be assumed that businesses could pay to avoid the delays, then these estimates are useful insights into the willingness-to-pay for higher quality of service. Data from the PostWatch study are found in the table below.

Table 2: Valuation for Changes in Advertised Day of Mail Delivery (pence).

Advertised delivery day	First Class	Mailsort 1	Financial Mailsort 1	Second Class	Mailsort 2	Financial Mailsort 2	Response Services	Mailsort 3
Day 1	0.0	0.0	0.0					
Day 2	-6.8	-4.0	-7.3	5.6	1.9	3.6	8.9	
Day 3				0.0	0.0	0.0	0.0	
Day 4				-5.6	-1.9	-3.6	-8.9	
Day 5								
Day 6								0.9
Day 7								0.0
Day 8								-0.9

Source: PostWatch

The table shows the marginal valuations for each extra day of delay beyond the service standard for various types of Royal Mail products. For example, on average Royal Mail customers valued an additional day delay in first class post at –6.8p, and for Mailsort 1 at -4.0p. These were values to 'delay' and so they are negative—for slower service the values are estimated for improvement or delay symmetrically. The first class estimates might be interpreted as symmetric, i.e., that someone also would have been willing to pay 6.8p in increase their post's speed from 2 days to 1 day, although empirical findings suggest consumers' often have asymmetric preferences with respect to expected losses and gains[10]. Of particular interest are the relative figures between categories. Mailsort are the various bulk categories. These are, for the most part, less time sensitive than standard stamped first class post. Second class post as well, values delay beyond the service standard by less than first class, as one would expect.

We calculate the increase for each mail category associated with a 20%-point increase in quality. Note that this would not be possible for Royal Mail, in most cases, as next day delivery for first class is achieved at about 89%; so the figure is purely for hypothetical purposes. Nonetheless, the exercise is interesting. The more interesting part is the variation across

[10] See for example, Hartman, Doane, and Wu (1991). A large and consistent body of empirical literature in behavioral economics suggests consumers' have *loss aversion* or *status quo bias;* their absolute value of WTP for reductions in quality exceeds the value of symmetric increases.

products. For first class stamped mail, the WTP is about 24eurocents, while for certain types of bulk mail, the figure is only 5cents. Interestingly, the figure for 2nd class mail is only 9cents.

Calculating a weighted average figure takes account of the relative size of each mail category. Response services, for example, are only about 1% of total mail volumes, and mail sort 1 is also a small fraction of total mail volumes. First class and mail sort 2 together make up over 50% of volumes, while second class is more or less about even in importance with first class. The weighted-average figure is about 12euro-cents for a 20 percentage point increase in quality. Applying this across weight steps and formats suggests that, for 500g packets, the figure is quite low, while for 50g letters, the figure is high.

Table 1: Marginal Values for Additional Changes in Reliability, i.e. Percentage of Post Delivered by the Advertised Day (pence)

	First Class	Mailsort 1	Second Class	Mailsort 2	Mailsort 3	Response Services
Pence per % point	0.82p	0.44p	0.32p	0.27p	0.17p	0.85p
Increase 89% to 95% -> 6% to €	€ 0.07	€ 0.04	€ 0.03	€ 0.02	€ 0.01	€ 0.07
Increase 20% points	€ 0.24	€ 0.13	€ 0.09	€ 0.08	€ 0.05	€ 0.25
Fraction of total volumes	0.25	0.1	0.26	0.24	0.15	0.01
Weighted-average	€ 0.12					

Source: LE analysis derived from PostWatch study

3. METHODOLOGY AND MODEL

Our methodology follows the econometric approach to the estimation of demand functions. Fundamentally, the methodology consists of following the well-established path of positing a demand function, developing a suitable data set, and investigating an appropriate econometric model. We assume the natural log of quantity demanded in the market is a linear function of the natural log of price and other explanatory variables.

The addition of quality changes or variables that represent quality as a determinant of demand requires some form of variable for quality. The estimation of a willingness-to-pay for quality is possible, even when the price of quality itself is not observable directly. This is akin to the well-known hedonic pricing methods, pioneered by Griliches (1967), and others. In the most fundamental sense, the technique is to regress output prices on product characteristics. The extent to which quality characteristics *explain* price movements, independent of other factors such as time trends, incomes, etc, is then interpreted as the marginal value, or price, of that particular quality attribute. Early studies, for example, Court (1939), focused on other sectors. Our method is very similar in spirit to the hedonic techniques.

In the case of postal products, quantity demanded, is assumed to be the dependent variable. Price is set by the regulator, and so is exogenous, while quality of service levels are also exogenously[11] determined by regulatory policy and production possibilities of the firm. Other factors are known to 'shift' the demand function in the price-quantity dimension. These factors are typically things such as income (aggregate), time, and product characteristics. Such factors like national income and country-specific effects are also properly specified as exogenous or independent in the model.

Estimation can be achieved econometrically by obtaining observations on price, quantity demanded, quality and other factors for postal products. Care must be taken to take account of, or statistically control for, as many factors that impact price and quantity demanded as possible[12]. Such a model can be written in equation form:

$$\ln Q = \sum_i a_i + b_1 \ln P + b_2 \ln w + b_3 \ln I + b_4 \ln qs + e \qquad (1)$$

Equation 1 is the basic form of our estimating model[13]. In the equation above, ln is the natural log of the variable; Q is quantity demanded or volume of mail; a_i is a series of dummy variables which control for country-destination-specific effects, format, type, class, etc.; P is price, w is weight, I is income; qs is the quality of service variable[14], and e is an assumed iid mean zero normal random error term. The letters b_1 – b_4, are parameter coefficients to be estimated. They represent the estimated marginal impact of a change in the independent variable on the dependent variable.

Since we are interested in the impact of quality of service changes on the prices consumers are willing-to-pay, the model above is not the final step. After taking expectations, we can solve for the proportional change in price with respect to an associated change in quality of service. After estimating, solving for ln$P$, and rearranging Equation 1 above gives:

$$\ln P = \frac{1}{b_1} \ln Q - \sum_i \frac{a_i}{b_1} - \frac{b_2}{b_1} \ln w - \frac{b_3}{b_1} \ln I - \frac{b_4}{b_1} \ln qs \qquad (2)$$

---

[11] We assume quality is exogenous with respect to the consumers' demands. Quality may be endogenous to the production process, but quality for international service is generally exogenous we argue.

[12] Even if some factors are omitted, however, bias might be small as long as the omitted factors are highly correlated with the included factors.

[13] Slight variations were estimated by including different regressors and different data for service quality, such as UNEX and UPU standards.

[14] The definition of this variable is discussed in more detail in the next section.

In equation (2) above, then the coefficients on the ln*qs* variable can be interpreted as the elasticity of price with respect to a change in quality of service.

The intuition for the above approach can be given in a number of ways. We proceed with a graphical approach. We assumed a functional relationship exists between price and quantity demanded. The quality variable adds another dimension. The quality variable 'shifts' the price quantity relationship. A three dimensional function can be graphed as a surface. The interpretation of the partial derivative is the estimate of the 'slope' or gradient of the surface in the price direction, for a given change in quality of service.

We demonstrate the effects and the shape of the surface in Figure 1 below. Here we depict 'contour lines' of quality in the space of quantity and price. Thus, 'higher ground' in terms of quality, shows shifts in the price-quantity relationships. Where the contour lines are close together, this represents a 'steep' gradient in the relationships. The arrow shows the positive sloping direction(s).

The figure is useful in showing how low volume items have a higher WTP for quality. Notice that close to the price axis, at low volumes and higher prices, increases in quality (moving across the contour lines) will give steeper rises in price (lines are close together).

Figure 1: Quality 'Contour' Lines – Quantity Demanded versus Price

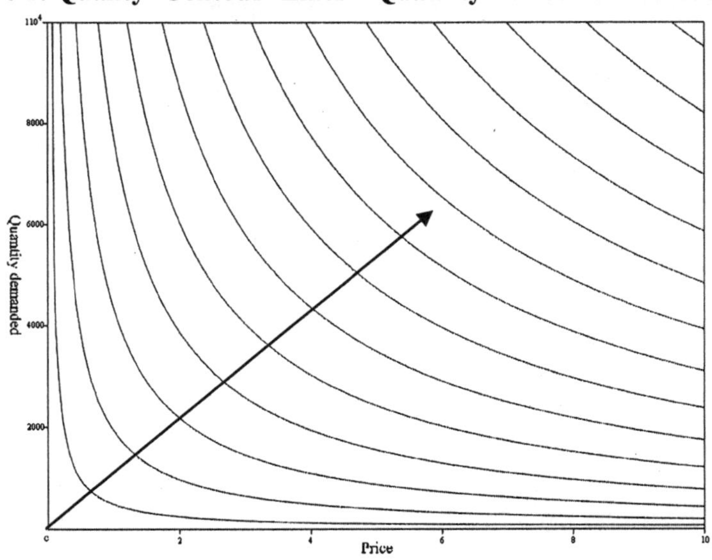

4. DATA

In relation to the model development, what is required are data that vary sufficiently in price, quantity demanded, and quality of service to be able to identify the functional relationships posited in the methodology section.

One particular difficulty in the application of our model for the case of An Post is due to several empirical facts concerning An Post's quality and service offerings. First, quality of service and prices do not change much over time for domestic mail. Thus, domestic mail volume changes with respect to quality changes are expected to be small. Further, due to economic operation, mail volumes have been rising, thus creating a further difficulty, as the estimation would need sufficient data and variation to 'differentiate' between the competing effects on volume (quality change—which has been small, and volume change which has been large). In addition, An Post does not offer a priority-economy or first and second-class service within the Republic – only next-day-target first class service is offered. Thus, the current mail consists of both time sensitive and less time sensitive mail, but there is no service-differentiated pricing as there is in, e.g., Royal Mail, where its two-tier system would allow a direct estimation of the valuation in the market of service quality differences.

Because of this lack of data for domestic mail, we base our estimates on international outbound mail data. A particular feature of the international tariff structure in Ireland enables us to exploit[15] a particular facet of the Irish mail system, that is, that international outbound mail to Northern Ireland is treated and priced as if it were domestic mail. That is to say, the prices, product and service offerings from the Republic to Northern Ireland are and have been exactly the same as service within the Republic.

International outbound provides an interesting dataset to estimate the impacts of quality on demand. Service quality levels vary by country of destination. We have data on price and quantity, weight, franking method, and whether the service is priority or economy, etc., each product for each country. Prices in fact vary by Zones 1 – 4, with zone 1 being NI, 2 Great Britain, 3 being the EU other than Great Britain, and 4 being the rest of the world. Mail to the USA, however, represents rest of world by a factor of about 10 to 1, so rest of world is for the most part the USA, with Canada, and Australia and Japan, making up the remaining 10%.

To obtain data on service quality levels, we used online published data from the UPU and UNEX[16]. The UPU data provide the service quality

---

[15] For detailed outputs provided to An Post, we were able to condition discrete price changes on the Northern Ireland data, and thus generate estimates of willingness-to-pay that varied by format (letter-flat-packet) and weight.

[16] For one country not available from this data, estimates were obtained from An Post.

targets for inbound[17] international for each country internationally (J + n), by service and class of mail. The UNEX data provide end-to-end service quality levels for first class mail in the EU. The UNEX data are particularly interesting because they provide data on a 'to and from' basis. Thus we have service quality levels in terms of % hitting J+3 'from Ireland', 'to the rest of the EU' for each country over time. The UNEX data also provide data on 'average delivery days'. The UNEX data are available over time for the last three years, while UPU data are the 'current levels' and standards, as per the UPU website, which has been recently updated.

Price and quantity data come from 1999-2003 revenue recognition models/accounts from An Post. An Post tracks revenue by product over time in these models. The models collect data on price (tariff) for each product delineated by weight, franking method, class, and destination.

We apply the service levels by country over time to the outbound international volumes and prices for products, which vary by class, format, weight and destination. We restricted our data to stamped mail, since we are interested in inferences about single piece mail for this study.

Thus, the data represent observations on aggregate demand in Ireland for outbound international mail by product by country over time. With cross classifying products by weight and destination over time, and adding variables such as income and dummy variables, we have about 40 variables in total in the data set with about 3616 observations. We treat each mail item with a different 'price' as a 'product' and then that, in each year, becomes an observation. The largest model estimated contained 22 regressors, including the constant, so the model has ample degrees of freedom for our dataset.

It is of note also that tariff changes occurred during the time period in question. The 25g stamped letter price increased from €0.38 to €0.43 over the period, with two discrete changes (there was an additional change in 2003.)

It is useful to look at the data in the price and quantity space in terms of a scatter plot. This gives an intuitive feel for the log-linear relationship that exists between quantity (volume) and price. These data are found in Figure 22.

It can be seen that most of the observations are clustered around low volume and lower prices. For the big volumes though, prices are very low. For high prices, volumes are very low. Converting the data by taking the natural log of each variable, gives an entirely different picture. The same data, converted by logs, is found in the figure below.

---

[17] That is to say, Belgium's inbound is Ireland's outbound to Belgium. The UPU standards are for delivery of inbound mail from the point of entry.

Figure 2: Scatter Plot of Relationship Between Quantity and Price

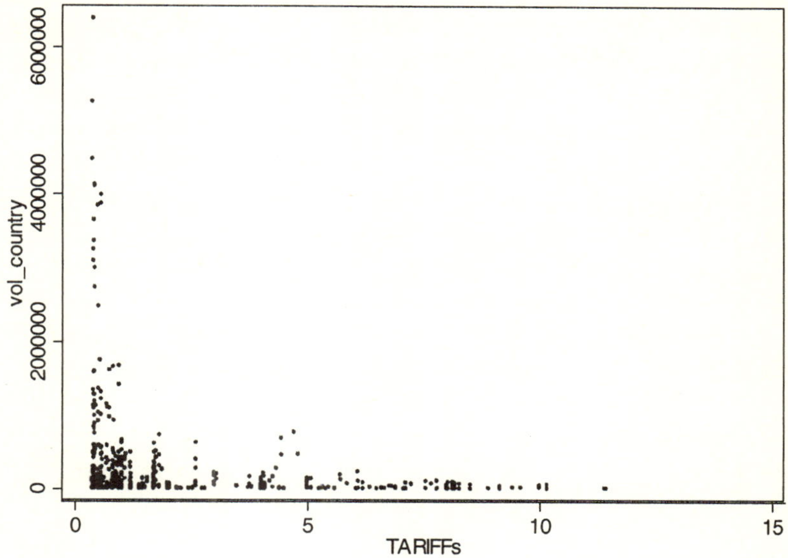

Figure 3: Log-converted Quantity and Price Data

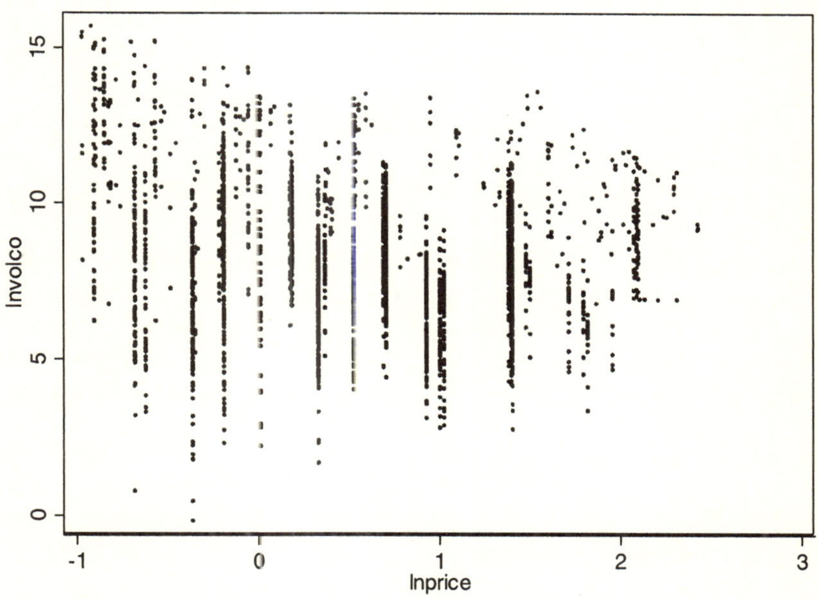

While graphical analysis of the data above is useful, the lack of clear pattern points towards more sophisticated methods. For example, there seems to be a downward sloping relationship between lnvolume and lnprice in the second figure. In fact, the estimated relationship is positive[18], however, when including variables for weight, class, zone, income, and quality, the relationship becomes negative as one would expect. The simple correlations are not unbiased estimates of the true relationships.

5. MODEL ESTIMATION RESULTS

We present results from the estimation of the equation (1). We present tables with the parameter estimates from each of two models, which varied by the definition of the quality variable. We omit some of the parameter estimates, such as dummy variables for country, etc.

A number of points deserve mentioning in relationship to the tables. Above all, we find statistically significant regression coefficient estimates for the parameters of interest; primarily, the parameters on price (lnprice), quality (depending on the model: lnavg_m_std, lnunex, dqual). Thus assuming the model is correctly specified, the observed sample data are unlikely to have been observed by random error[19].

The R^2 statistics are reported at the top of the tables. These statistics are estimates of the 'goodness of fit' of the model. An R-squared of above 30% is often considered good for cross sectional-time series or aggregated cross sectional time series data such as our data in our dataset. Model 1 has a slightly higher R^2 than model 2.

In both models, the variables with names that start with 'd' are dummy, or zero-one, variables, for flat, letters, zones, etc. About half the country and zone specific dummy coefficient estimates (not shown) were statistically insignificant. This is not too surprising, as many of the variables in the dataset, including price, do not vary with country of origin, but vary only by zone.

The first table, 4, is our preferred model. The results show that the quality variable has a statistically significant impact on the quantity variable, and of the expected sign. Thus the result shows that decreases in quality, all else equal, leads to decreases in demand[20]. The quality variable (lnavg_m_std) in this model is the average time (days) to delivery, minus the

---

[18] From the simple regression of lnvolume on lnprice; we do not present these results.

[19] The model passed standard statistical diagnostics for homoskedasticity and normality of the error terms.

[20] We are also assuming that price is completely exogenous. This is not usually true in demand estimation, but for postal products, it is likely to be a good assumption. Prices are set by a regulator or board, and not often changed.

delivery standard. So, the expected sign is negative, as when time over the standard increases, this is expected to have a negative impact on demand[21].

Table 4: Regression results: Model 1
R^2=48%

LnQuantity (dep. Var)	Coef.	Std. Err	t	P>|t|	[95% Conf.	Interval]
Dflat	-0.54	0.11	-4.97	0.00	-0.75	-0.32
Dlet	-1.82	0.15	-12.12	0.00	-2.11	-1.52
Dqual	7.69	0.22	34.24	0.00	7.25	8.14
Lnprice	-3.79	0.17	-22.72	0.00	-4.11	-3.46
Lnwgt	2.56	0.12	21.66	0.00	2.33	2.79
Lnincome	4.01	0.54	7.45	0.00	2.96	5.07
lnavg_m_st~d	-3.57	0.25	-14.20	0.00	-4.07	-3.08
_cons	-52.27	6.33	-8.26	0.00	-64.68	-39.85

Source: LE

The second table, 5, shows regression results from an alternative model; i.e., using a different quality variable. Here, quality is the % of letters hitting the standard as measured by the UNEX data (labelled 'lnUNEX'). Thus, an increase in the lnUNEX variable has a positive sign, as is expected. An increase in the percentage of letters hitting the standard has a positive impact on demand, and a positive impact on willingness-to-pay. Also of note is that the price variable is largely unchanged and remains statistically significant, similar to the previous regressions.

Table 5: Detail Statistical Output: Model 2
R^2=45%

LnQuantity (dep. Var)	Coef.	Std. Err.	t	P>|t|	[95% Conf.	Interval]
lnprice	-4.26	0.16	-26.56	0.00	-4.58	-3.95
lninc	2.74	0.53	5.14	0.00	1.70	3.79
lnwgt	2.85	0.11	24.93	0.00	2.62	3.07
lnunex	1.49	0.38	3.88	0.00	0.74	2.24
dqual	4.97	0.11	45.08	0.00	4.76	5.19
Dlet	-1.91	0.15	-12.80	0.00	-2.20	-1.62
dflat	-0.58	0.11	-5.37	0.00	-0.79	-0.37
_cons	-45.10	6.51	-6.93	0.00	-57.85	-32.34

Source: LE

The above parameter estimates can be converted into either elasticity estimates or actual € figures[22] for a given level of quality change. The

---

[21] Likewise, since the sign on lnprice is negative, then the (-) ratio of the coefficients, (from Equation 2) is negative. So a rise the in number of days to deliver over the standard leads to a negative marginal impact on price.

[22] With some algebra, equation (2) can be rearranged to give estimates that are conditional on the variables such as weight, volume, etc, but we do not present this here. Discrete or

elasticity estimates are more straightforward, and more general, as they are unitless. The elasticity is given as $-b_4/b_1$, where b_4 is the coefficient on the log-quality variable and b_1 is the coefficient on lnprice (Equation 2). For the first model[23], table 4, this leads to an elasticity estimate of -0.94, and for the second model, table 5, this leads to an elasticity estimate of 0.35. These are in essence estimates of the price elasticity of quality. Thus, a 10% increase in quality, which, in the UNEX quality definition, would be akin to about an 8-9 percentage-point increase in the percentage of mail hitting the standard, would lead to a 3.5% increase in price. By the first model, this would lead to a 9.4% increase in price. Many posts have basic stamp prices less than 50 euro cents. On a stamp of 48 euro cents, this would lead to an increase of between 1.6 (model 2) to 4.5 (model 1) euro cents. For heavier or bulky items, which could be as much as €10 to €25, the increase would range from about 35 euro cents to €2.35.

6. CONCLUSIONS

This paper has estimated consumer's willingness-to-pay for quality of service improvement. The model is an application of data for Ireland, for an often applied procedure of econometric estimation of demand. The demand function, the relationship between price and quantity is estimated, and other factors such as quality of service are included. The rate of change in price with respect to changes in quality of service is then calculated from the parameter estimates and converted to an elasticity. Qualitatively, our results suggest consumers are willing to pay small but probably significant amounts for quality improvements on standard letter items, and larger amounts for heavier items. Our results are quite similar to the limited previous research done in other jurisdictions and with other media types, such as the Postwatch research that suggested values between about one to seven euro cents for about a 6% increase in quality. Research in other network industries has come to similar conclusions. While the magnitude of some of our parameter estimates, such as the elasticity on price or the elasticity on quality may seem high, correct signs and the fact that the differing definitions of quality variable switched (as expected) signs, lend credence to the robustness of the findings.

The results suggest that consumers would be willing to pay seemingly small but not insignificant amounts for quality of service improvements of the order of 10% in existing single piece mail. Additionally, for higher

---

average changes and conditioning on the means of the data within Northern Ireland, over various ranges of the sample data (weight, format) will allow for € figure estimates that vary by weight and are consistent with Republic of Ireland tariffs.

[23] Again, recall that a decrease in the quality variable is an increase in quality in model 1.

value, lower volume, and higher weight items, consumers have a greater willingness-to-pay for improved quality. These results are generally consistent with An Post's own market research efforts using customer interviews and other such market research techniques.

In terms of directions for future research, it is important to note that we have used a particular dataset and a particular country and type of mail (international outbound). Additional research in other countries would be interesting. Further, developing panel data would enable country-specific characteristics to be studied. Additional or alternative data might also enable new modelling techniques or specifications. For example it would be interesting to see how quality would perform in a more formal model of consumer demand such as the AIDS (Deaton and Muellbaur1980). In addition, modeling techniques that did not restrict the model to a symmetric response for quality improvements verses degradation would also be interesting.

REFERENCES

Court, A.T. 1939. "Hedonic Price Indexes with Automotive Examples." In *The Dynamics of Automobile Demand.* New York, NY: General Motors.

Cremer, H., M. De Rycke, A. Grimaud. 1997. "Service Quality, Competition, and Regulatory Policies in the Postal Service." *Journal of Regulatory Economics* 11(5): 5-19.

Griliches, Z. 1967. "Hedonic Price Indexes Revisited: Some Notes on the State of the Art." *Proceedings of the Business and Economic Statistics Section, American Statistical Association*. 324-332.

Deaton, A., and J. Muellbaur. 1980. "An Almost Ideal Demand System." *The American Economic Review* 70(3): 312-326.

European Commission. 2003. http://europa.eu.int/comm/internal_market/post/doc/studies/200308-ups-report_en.pdf.

Hartman, RS, Doane, MJ, and Woo, C. (1991). "Consumer rationality and the status quo." *The Quarterly Journal of Economics* 106(1): 141-162.

Mazou. 2004. Plennary address, 23rd *World Postal Congress in Bucharest.* www.upu.org.

Postwatch. 2004. "Royal Mail Quality of Service" http://www.postwatch.co.uk/pdf/Research/June_July04QoS_studyfor_RM_PW_postcomm.pdf.

Reay, I. 2002. "The Welfare Economics of Universal Service Standards and Service Quality." In *Postal and Delivery Services: Pricing, Productivity, Regulation and Strategy*, edited by M.A. Crew and P.R. Kleindorfer. Boston: Kluwer Academic Publishers.

Swinand, G. 2004. "A Production Model of Service Quality at An Post." In *Competitive Transformation of the Postal and Delivery Sector*, edited by M.A. Crew and P.R. Kleindorfer, Boston: Kluwer Academic Publishers.

Urban, G. and J.R. Hauser. 1993. *Design and Marketing of New Products*. 2nd Edition, Englewood Cliffs, NJ: Prentice Hall.

Pricing Issues

Chapter 14

Pricing and Welfare Implications of Alternative Approaches to Setting Price Controls in the Postal Sector*

Philippe De Donder,[1] Helmuth Cremer,[1] Paul Dudley,[2] and Frank Rodriguez[2]
University of Toulouse, IDEI and CNRS-GREMAQ;[1] and Royal Mail Group[2]

1. INTRODUCTION

Within the postal sector, price controls are being developed and set to limit the scope for a universal service provider (USP) to increase prices and to provide incentives for improvements in cost efficiency (Correia da Silva et al, 2004). The provision of universal postal service, including setting geographically uniform prices within a country or member state, is an overriding requirement for the development of any policy decision in the postal sector, including that of setting of a price control. Further, some countries have moved away from a monopoly provision of postal service to one that is open, to varying degrees, to competition. The optimal structure for price controls within the economics literature is that of a global price cap (GPC) (see Billette de Villemeur et al (2003) and the references mentioned there), where all goods provided by the regulated firm are included in the computation of the price cap. This familiar result arises under conditions where a regulator is assumed to seek to maximise welfare while a regulated business maximises its profit and leads to optimal prices that are based on a mark-up on marginal costs. While GPC is the optimal structure for a price control also in the presence of competition, regulators have looked at alternative structures and approaches, at least in part as a means of

* The analysis contained in this paper reflects the views of the authors and may not necessarily be those of Royal Mail Group.

facilitating or promoting competition. For example, some have considered removing services that are deemed to be competitive from the coverage of the control (Dudley et al, 2005).

Our paper examines the implications of a regulator adopting alternative cost allocation and pricing rules for setting a price control in the postal sector and its focus is on this aspect of a price control rather than other areas such as the promotion of reductions in the level of underlying costs. A major issue with regard to cost allocation rules is the presence of significant fixed costs associated with the retention of geographic reach and provision of universal service (Cazals et al, 2005). This provides considerable scope for the potential allocation of fixed, network costs between products and means for trying to recover these and other costs through final postal prices charged by the USP. However, in a situation where a postal market is open or is in the process of being liberalised, this scope has the potential of being substantially curtailed by loss of mail volumes to competitors thereby limiting the ability of the USP to recover its fixed, network costs and remain financially viable. Through its consideration of alternative cost allocation and pricing rules, this paper aims to provide insights into the implications of potential regulatory decisions relating to the setting of a price control. Amongst other things, this highlights the need for consistency in cost allocation and pricing rules over time and the merits of the rules consistent with GPC that maximise economic welfare.

Our analytical model concentrates on the prices of a USP in the postal sector that are sufficient to recover network costs under conditions of entry. The ability to recover such costs is a central requirement of an effectively set price control. In the model the USP offers two products: a single piece product and a business mail product, the latter being treated as a bulk mail product requiring presortation of mail by the mailer.[1] This facilitates consideration of cost allocation rules consistent with a GPC (or "a single basket") structure for the control, alongside alternative cost allocation rules and two basket, non-GPC structures for the control. Although we do not consider the issue of the uniformity (geographical averaging) of tariffs explicitly in our analysis we note that single piece mail at a uniform tariff is used by most households and that its availability and price are of particular interest to regulators and policy makers.

---

[1] These can be thought of also as two groups of products. The defining difference between the USP's two products in our model is that entry is assumed to occur in the market for business mail but not for single piece mail. In order to restrict the model to just two goods we simplify and equate business mail with bulk mail. In practice, of course, some business mail does not require worksharing and it would be possible to develop a model which distinguishes between bulk mail and other types of business mail. However, the main insights from our model can be gained from the two good version developed in the paper.

We pay particular attention to two cost allocation rules which allow the USP to at least break-even overall which here implies that each product covers both its marginal cost and also share between them, through an allocation, the network cost incurred by the USP.[2] The first cost allocation rule results in the minimum price for the single piece product at which the USP breaks even overall.[3] The second rule results in the prices under GPC which not only allow the USP to break-even but also at the same time to maximise economic welfare. These rules together identify a range for the price of the single piece product within which the USP breaks even and economic welfare increases as the single piece product price rises towards its welfare maximising value. For prices below this range the USP does not break-even while for prices above this range the welfare maximising price is exceeded and there is a decline in welfare. Other cost allocation rules can then be applied to see if the resulting prices lie within this range. For example, we consider one other rule, equiproportional mark-ups (EPMU, see Sherman(1993)), which while neither welfare-maximising nor necessarily consistent with financial viability for the USP may be an option considered by regulators for the recovery of fixed, network costs.

The paper proceeds as follows. Our model is set out further in section 2. In section 3, we calibrate it with parameter values consistent with key characteristics of the postal sector outlined above and in section 4 we report results from our model calibrated with these values and test sensitivities. Section 5 draws out implications from our analysis for cost allocation rules, pricing and price control structures in a liberalised postal market.

2. MODEL

The model has three goods. The USP offers two goods (a single piece good labelled 1 and a business mail product which is assumed to be a bulk mail good labelled 2) with demands independent from each other. Note, however, that there is an effective floor to the single piece price which is the price of the bulk mail product plus the worksharing cost incurred by the sender in presortation and presentation of its mail to the USP. At any price below this it would be cheaper for the bulk mailer to use the single piece product so that all bulk mail would switch to the single piece product. Goods 1 and 2 can be thought of also as two baskets of goods rather than just as single goods. The consumer surplus derived from good 1 is given by $u(x_1)$. There is a global network (fixed) cost F which the USP incurs to meet its

---

2 Throughout this paper the term break-even is used to mean that the USP achieves a normal rate of accounting profit and so is able to be financially viable on a continuing basis.

3 A similar focus on the minimum uniform stamp price is developed by Panzar (2005).

obligation for the provision of universal service and constant marginal costs c_1 and c_2.[4] Entrants in the form of a competitive fringe provide a good, labelled 3, that is an imperfect substitute for good 2. The utility derived from those substitutes is given by $v(x_2, x_3)$. Good 3 is produced at a constant marginal cost c_3, with no fixed cost.[5] The price of good i is denoted by p_i and its demand function by $x_i(.)$. To simplify notation, we often do not write the argument(s) of the demand functions.

In terms of setting the price control and recovery of the network cost, we consider three possible pricing and allocation rules for the USP[6]: a global price cap (GPC), minimising the price of good 1 while breaking even overall and an equiproportional mark-up solution (EPMU). We first define the optimal second best prices and show that they can be decentralised using a global price cap where weights and average price have been suitably chosen. We then describe the other two pricing rules.

The second-best optimal prices are obtained when the regulator maximizes total welfare (the sum of consumer surplus and operators' profits) subject to the USP breaking even. Denoting by λ the Lagrange multiplier of the USP profit constraint, the regulator solves the problem:

$$\max_{p_1, p_2} u(x_1) + v(x_2, x_3) - p_1 x_1 - p_2 x_2 - p_3 x_3$$
$$+ (1+\lambda)((p_1 - c_1)x_1 + (p_2 - c_2)x_2 - F)$$

whose first-order conditions are

$$-x_i + (1+\lambda)(x_i + (p_i - c_i)\frac{\partial x_i}{\partial p_i}) = 0$$

which give the usual Ramsey prices

$$\frac{p_i - c_i}{p_i} = \frac{\lambda}{1+\lambda}\frac{1}{\varepsilon_i}$$

where ε_i is the demand own-price elasticity. Note that, as long as good 3 is provided at marginal cost, the formulas above are not affected by this good.

---

4 Fixed costs attributable to one particular good play no role in the analysis although the model could be extended to consider such a case.

5 Entrants are assumed to have no requirement to offer universal service. However, we assume in section 3 that the marginal cost of entrants' good 3 is higher than that of the USP's good 2 to allow for other costs entrants may incur in offering postal service.

6 The analysis of welfare-optimal (and other) cost allocation procedures was pioneered by Braeutigam(1980).

In other words, we will get the same formulas for the monopoly situation and for the case where the USP faces competition. The numerical values will of course be different, because the demand for good 2 will be more elastic when it competes with a substitute. Note also that we cannot exclude from the outset that, if competition is strong enough, the maximization program of the USP has no solution, i.e. there is no combination of USP prices that allows it to break-even.

The regulator can decentralize these Ramsey prices by using a global price cap formula. We assume that the USP chooses its prices in order to maximise its profit

$$(p_1 - c_1)x_1 + (p_2 - c_2)x_2 - F$$

subject to the price-cap

$$p_1 n_1 + p_2 n_2 \leq p^{\circ}$$

where n_i is a weight and p° the average price and both are set by the regulator. The first-order conditions are

$$x_i + (p_i - c_i)\frac{\partial x_i}{\partial p_i} = \mu n_i$$

where μ is the Lagrange multiplier of the price cap constraint. One can see that the regulator can decentralize the Ramsey prices by setting weights equal to (optimal) quantities, $n_i = x_i$, and by setting the average price appropriately. This level is such that the Lagrange multiplier of the constraint at equilibrium is equal to $1/(1+\lambda)$.[7]

Secondly, rather than using a global price cap, the regulator could fix the share of fixed cost α_i that each product has to cover, while the USP is just allowed to break-even, i.e. to post prices such that

$$(p_1 - c_1)x_1 + (p_2 - c_2)x_2 = F$$

with

$$(p_i - c_i)x_i = \alpha_i F \qquad (1)$$

$$\alpha_i \geq 0, \quad \sum_{i=1,2} \alpha_i = 1.$$

---

[7] This of course assumes that there exist prices p_1 and p_2 that allow the USP to break-even. If not, it is clear that no value of the average price, however large, can decentralise an allocation that does not exist!

The price of good $i=1,2$ is then given by

$$p_i = c_i + \frac{\alpha_i F}{x_i}.$$

Note that this formulation is implicit, since the demand function x_i in the right hand side of the equation depends on the price p_i. It is even possible that this problem does not admit any solution for a given value of α_i. For example, setting α_1 at zero means that all the network fixed cost should be recovered only by a mark-up on good 2, while good 1 is priced at marginal cost; depending on the calibration of demand and cost functions, the effective minimum for the price of good 1, and the respective sizes of the markets for goods 1 and 2, this may or may not be feasible. For instance, if competition is strong enough on the market for goods 2 and 3, even the profit-maximizing price for good 2 may not generate enough profit to fund the fixed cost F. In the rest of the paper, we consider solutions with the minimum value of α_1 since this yields the lowest price of good 1, p_1, that is compatible with the USP breaking even. A minimum value of α_1 of zero means that the totality of the fixed cost is funded by profit made on selling good 2. This does not imply that the USP posts the profit-maximising price of good 2, since we do not allow the USP to make a profit on good 2 greater than the amount of the fixed cost.[8] On the other hand, a strictly positive minimum value of α_1 implies that the USP posts the profit-maximising price for good 2 but that the maximum profit earned by selling that good is not high enough to fund the fixed cost.

Thirdly, the regulator could impose that each product's price exhibits the same proportional mark-up over marginal cost, while allowing the USP to break-even (see Sherman(1993)). Formally, the USP posts prices with a mark-up, k, such that

$$(p_1 - c_1)x_1 + (p_2 - c_2)x_2 = F$$

with

$$\frac{p_i - c_i}{c_i} = k$$

which is equivalent to

---

[8] Nor do we allow a negative value of α_1 which would entail a cross-subsidy from good 2 to good 1 or a value of α_1 below that consistent with the effective floor for the price of good 1 given by the price of the bulk mail product, good 2, plus the worksharing cost incurred by a bulk mailer.

$$k = \frac{F}{c_1 x_1 (c_1(1+k)) + c_2 x_2 (c_2(1+k), c_3)}.$$

Observe that there is no guarantee that such a value of k exists. If demand conditions (including the existence of competition for a subset only of the goods provided by the USP, as in this model) vary a lot between goods, break-even may require very different mark-ups over the different goods and a requirement of equiproportional mark-ups may prevent the USP from breaking even. The existence of an EPMU solution can only be assessed numerically after the model is calibrated.

Before going to the calibration of the model, we compare the three procedures presented above in terms of the share of fixed cost recovered by good 1 (the parameter α_l in equation (1)). The second procedure gives us the minimum value of α_l, and hence for p_l, compatible with the USP breaking even. The value of α_l obtained from the optimal price cap is always greater than this value, since the second-best optimal prices require a positive mark-up for all goods in our setting with a network fixed cost. These two procedures then determine a range of potential values of α_l compatible with the USP breaking even. Observe that increasing the value of α_l above its second-best value (i.e. raising the price of good 1 above its second-best value) would only generate a decrease in total welfare in the economy. We can also associate a value of α_l to the EPMU solution. If the EPMU solution is feasible (i.e. allows the USP to break-even), then this value of α_l is by definition above the minimum α_l computed above. On the other hand, it is not possible to say in general whether this value of α_l will be above or below the one corresponding to the second-best optimal prices. To answer this question, we first have to calibrate the model to which we now turn.

3. CALIBRATION

To calibrate the model, we start from the hypothetical situation where the USP does not face any entrants. We assume that the USP posts a price of 0.50€ for good 1, a single piece product, and of 0.40€ for good 2, a bulk mail product used by business. Quantities sold at those prices are, respectively, 2 billion and 8 billion items. We assume that the direct price elasticities of these two goods are, respectively, -0.2 and -0.4. A number of studies have estimated direct price elasticities for mail yielding values which are low and of about this order of magnitude (see Florens et al (2002), Nankervis et al (2002), USPS (2000)). Finally, we calibrate linear demands based on these quantities, prices and elasticities.

We need further information to calibrate the demand function for good 2 once good 3 is available from entrants. We use two types of information: the extent of entry for different price configurations and the substitutability between goods 2 and 3 for consumers. As for the extent of entry, we assume a significant level of brand loyalty to the USP and inertia in switching to competitor products.[9] In the main cases of section 4 entrants would capture 10% of the total market for goods 2 and 3 if the price of good 3 were set at the same level as the USP, and 50% of the market if entrants were to offer a 20% price discount over the USP. In section 4 also we study the sensitivity of our results to these assumptions and develop the case where, in the early phases of entry, the entrants' market shares are, respectively, 5% and 20% for an equal price and a 20% price discount.

The final element needed to calibrate demand for goods 2 and 3 is related to the substitution between those two goods. We measure it using the displacement ratio, whose formula is

$$\sigma = -\frac{\partial x_2 / \partial p_3}{\partial x_3 / \partial p_3}.$$

We fix the value of this ratio at 0.75, which means that three quarters of the quantities sold by entrants are effectively displaced from the USP, while one quarter represents additional volumes sold in the sector. We study the sensitivity of our result to this parameter by setting it at 0.9.

The marginal costs for the two goods offered by the USP are 0.30€ and 0.24€. The difference reflects higher sortation and collection costs of single piece mail. The worksharing cost of senders of bulk mail need not be the same as this difference but is likely to be of a similar order depending on the effectiveness of mailers in preparing and presenting mail in the this way. Accordingly, we assume for simplicity that the worksharing cost incurred by a bulk mailer is 0.06€ and that the effective minimum for the price of good 1 is the price of good 2 plus 0.06€. If the price of good 1 fell below this bulk mailers would find it cheaper not to incur the cost of worksharing and instead send all mail as single piece.[10] The fixed cost is 1.68 bn€ such that at these prices, volumes and marginal costs the USP breaks even under monopoly (including a normal rate of profit and equals 40% of revenue of 4.2 bn€). Two values are considered for the marginal cost of good 3, 0.32€

---

[9] There is limited evidence available on switching propensities. However, the calibration values used here are likely to be conservative and understate prospective switching.

[10] Clearly such a case could be modelled but is of little practical interest here where two separate goods are assumed to be offered by the USP. In practice, business mail includes also mail which is not presorted and here the effective minimum price for such mail is that for single piece and indeed may be the single piece product itself. As noted earlier the model could be extended to allow two business mail products, one requiring presortation and a second one of a higher price with no sortation requirement.

and 0.40€, and results reported for each to test the variation of our results to this parameter. As noted above, entrants do not have an obligation to offer universal service. While they do not face a fixed, network cost for this the marginal costs assumed are above those of the USP to reflect additional costs they may incur in offering a postal service.[11]

4. RESULTS

4.1 Monopoly Case

We commence our analysis by evaluating the position of the USP under monopoly and the prices, volumes and welfare under the three pricing or cost allocation rules set out in section 2. The numerical results from applying the calibration values set out in section 3 are shown in table 1. In the first column we report the output for the EPMU cost allocation rule which, in the monopoly case, allows the USP to break-even and was used to calibrate the model. Applying the calibration values set out in section 2, welfare is equal to 6.5bn€. The average price required by the USP under monopoly, given this cost allocation and pricing rule, is 0.42€. The share of the fixed costs of universal service provision collected from good 1 (α_1 using section 2's notation) is 23.8%, and so that raised from product 2 (α_2) is 76.2%.

Having calibrated the model for the EPMU case, the remaining columns in table 1 show the results of two further cost allocation rules under monopoly. These cases identify the range, as set out in section 2, of the minimum price for good 1 at which the USP breaks even at or above the price of good 2 plus worksharing cost for a sender of bulk mail (0.469€ in column 2) and the price for good 1 at which welfare is maximised subject to the USP breaking even (0.609€ in column 3). For the first of these, shown in the second column of the table, the USP breaks even with the good 1 price set at its effective floor of the price of good 2 plus the worksharing cost to a sender of bulk mail and a smaller share of the fixed cost is recovered from good 1, at 20.3%, than in the EPMU case. Given the price elasticities in the model, this results in slightly lower volumes in total from the two products so that the fixed cost is shared among a smaller number of items. The average price is marginally higher at 0.421€ and welfare lower relative to the values for these variables in the EPMU case.

For the welfare maximising prices achievable through a GPC, in the third column of the table, the mark-up on the product with the lower (absolute)

[11] A marginal cost of 0.32€ relative to 0.40€ reflects a lower cost and hence a situation where entrants are relatively more efficient. The marginal cost for the USP is lower still at 0.24€ though the USP also recovers the network cost of universal service provision.

price elasticity is higher than the mark-up on the product with the higher (absolute) price elasticity. Compared with prices under EPMU, the price of good 1 is higher and that for good 2 lower. Overall volumes rise and the minimum average price required for the USP to break-even and recover the fixed cost of universal service is lower at 0.417€. The allocation of fixed costs which maximises welfare and produces a lower overall level of USP prices leads to a greater share of the fixed cost being recovered from the lower elasticity product, good 1, at 35.1% rather than 23.8% under EPMU.

These results illustrate some points about the cost allocation rules that apply not only under monopoly but also more generally to the cases involving entry considered below. For prices of good 1 below that at the GPC outcome, three related points are evident from increasing the price of good 1, single piece mail, compared with good 2, bulk mail. First, with good 1 having a lower (absolute) price elasticity than good 2, the combined demand for the two products is increased which implies that there are more items of mail to share the fixed cost of universal service provision; secondly, the combined average price of the two products declines; and, thirdly, total welfare increases. Of the three rules, therefore, the cost allocation consistent with GPC produces the highest level of demand and total use of the network, the lowest average price and, as shown in section 2, the highest level of welfare. The alternatives to the rule consistent with GPC result in lower total volume, higher average prices and lower welfare. Nevertheless, in this instance, under monopoly the volume and welfare impacts of different price sets are quite small as are those on average price. In addition, the EPMU cost allocation rule results in prices that lie within the range between the minimum break-even price and welfare maximising price. The inference from this is that, under monopoly, there is a broad range of prices that are close to welfare maximising and include EPMU, which may also partly explain why a USP in moving from a monopoly to a competitive market may begin with prices that are far from welfare maximising prices.

Table 1: Prices, Volumes and Welfare Under Alternative Price and Cost Allocation Rules: Monopoly Case[1]

	EPMU	Lowest Price of Good 1 for Overall Break-Even	GPC
Prices,€ :			
- USP Good 1	0.500	0.469	0.609
- USP Good 2	0.400	0.409	0.373
Volumes, bn items			
- USP Good 1	2.000	2.025	1.913
- USP Good 2	8.000	7.930	8.219
- USP Total	10.000	9.955	10.132
Profit, €m	0	0	0
Welfare, €bn	6.500	6.493	6.510
Average Price, €	0.420	0.421	0.417
Share of Fixed Cost Recovered by Good 1, %	23.8	20.3	35.1

[1] Calibration values as follows: Marginal costs (USP good 1, 0.30€; USP good 2, 0.24€); fixed cost (1.68bn€ including normal rate of profit); price elasticities (USP good 1, -0.2; USP good 2, -0.4); relationship between prices (price of good 1 ≥ price of good 2 + 0.06€).

4.2 Entry: Central Case for Calibration of Demand for Goods 2 and 3

Unless entry represents completely new mail, it implies a decline in demand for the products of the USP. In our model we consider this through the effect on the demand for the USP's good 2, with which the entrants' product competes, with the demand function for the USP's good 1 remaining unchanged. If the prices of both products remain unchanged, reduced demand for good 2 due to entry results in a loss of contribution for each item of good 2 displaced by the entrants' product. A financial loss results and the initial set of prices and allocation of the network cost between the two products is no longer sufficient to allow break-even. In this subsection we apply our model to consider the implications of entry for our central case in calibrating demand as set out in section 3.[12] We do this for two alternative prices set by entrants to evaluate the effect of different degrees of entry. First, entrants' costs are assumed to be such that their price equals the initial price for the USP's product 2 (0.40€); this results in a limited amount of entry. Secondly, the entrants' price is 20% below this initial price; entry is then more extensive. Results for both entrant prices are reported in table 2.

[12] First, entrants capture 10% of the total market for goods 2 and 3 if their price were the same as that of the USP and 50% if they offered a discount of 20% over the USP; and, secondly, a displacement ratio, σ, of 0.75.

In the first case, results of which are reported in the first three columns of table 2, entrants charge a price of 0.40€. The lowest price for good 1 consistent with break-even after taking account of entry and losses of volume for the USP's good 2 is 0.54€. This is above the price of good 1 under monopoly which if unchanged at 0.50€ would result in the USP making a loss. Although the USP breaks even at the new equilibrium prices, the average price of its two products is higher than before entry (at 0.453€ compared with 0.42€) and welfare lower. While entry has led to overall market volumes growing slightly (by about 2%), those handled by the USP have fallen. The arrival of entrants decreases the quantity of good 2 sold by the USP at the monopoly price. This induces the USP to increase both its prices to make up for the lost revenue, which increases its average price and further decreases the quantities it sells. On the other hand, only one quarter of the entrants' volumes constitute an addition to the total market volume, and entrants offer good 3 at the same price as that of good 2 under monopoly (0.40€). This means that the consumers gain little from the availability of this new good, while they suffer from the increase in the prices of goods 1 and 2. Table 2 shows that the net effect of entry on the consumer surplus (and on total welfare) is negative, since total welfare is lower than under monopoly.

The second column reports the GPC solution. Compared with the previous column, the USP decreases its price for the more elastic good 2 and increases its price for the less elastic good 1. Given the high price of good 3, no entry occurs and the result obtained is the same as in the last column of table 1. The average price is again lower than that with the minimum price of good 1 and total welfare is higher. For this case of low entry, the range of prices identified by the outcomes associated with the minimum break-even price of good 1 and the GPC price has narrowed from 0.469€ to 0.609€ (in table 1) to 0.54€ to 0.609€ (in table 2). Nevertheless, this range includes EPMU which requires the USP to set prices at 0.541€ for good 1 and 0.433€ for good 2. Both prices are higher than before entry because, clearly it is the total volume of the USP's two products after entry that is relevant. Average price across the two products is higher (at 0.459€ compared with 0.42€ pre-entry) and welfare lower than under monopoly.

Table 2: Prices, Volumes and Welfare Under Alternative Price and Cost Allocation Rules: Entry Under Central Case for Calibration of Demand for Goods 2 and 3[1]

	Entrants' Price Compared With The Initial Price of USP's Good 2					
	Same			20% Less		
	Lowest Price of Good 1[2]	GPC	EPMU	Lowest Price of Good 1[2]	GPC	EPMU
Prices, € :						
- USP Good 1	0.540	0.609	0.541	0.847	0.996	0.524
- USP Good 2	0.427	0.373	0.433	0.386	0.316	0.419
- Entrants (Good 3)	0.400	0.400	0.400	0.320	0.320	0.320
Volumes, bn items						
- USP Good 1	1.968	1.913	1.967	1.722	1.603	1.981
- USP Good 2	6.442	8.219	6.266	5.036	7.476	3.910
- Entrants (Good 3)	1.785	0	1.965	4.097	1.600	5.248
- Total USP	8.410	10.132	8.233	6.758	9.079	5.891
- Total Market	10.195	10.132	10.198	10.855	10.679	11.139
USP Profit, €bn	0	0	0	0	0	-0.535
Welfare, €bn	6.238	6.510	6.204	6.142	6.339	5.897[3]
Average Price, €	0.453	0.417	0.459	0.503	0.436	0.572[4]
Share of USP Fixed Cost Recovered by Good 1, %	28.1	35.1	28.2	56.1	66.4	26.4

[1] Calibration values as follows: Marginal costs (USP good 1, 0.30€; USP good 2, 0.24€); fixed cost (1.68bn€ including normal rate of profit); price elasticities (USP good 1, -0.2; USP good 2, -0.4); displacement ratio (σ=0.75); extent of entry (10% of total market for goods 2 and 3 at entrant price equal to USP; 50% at price discount of 20% to USP); relationship between prices (price of good 1 = price of good 2 + 0.06€).

[2] Lowest price of Good 1 for USP to breakeven overall across both products.

[3] Using cost of public funds at 0.3.

[4] Including coverage of financial deficit at cost of public funds of 0.3.

In the second case, shown in the final three columns of table 2, entrants' prices are assumed to be 0.32€ so encouraging higher entry. As a result, the lowest price of good 1 which satisfies break-even is much higher at 0.847€ (in column 4) compared with 0.54€ (in column 1) while the price of good 2 at 0.386€ (in column 4) is below 0.427€ (in column1). Again, although market volumes increase, in this case by about 4%, those using the USP's network fall significantly. The average price of the USP products increases from 0.453€ to 0.503€ and welfare falls. The GPC price for good 1 is higher at 0.996€ and for good 2 somewhat lower at 0.316€. Entrants retain a significant share of overall volumes but, with the USP's total volume closer to that before entry, both the average price and welfare level improve towards their levels before entry. Given the high level of entry, no EPMU allocation allows the USP to break-even. The last column of table 2 reports the loss minimizing EPMU allocation, where the USP loss is 0.535bn€ and the contribution per item of good 1 to the fixed cost is 0.244€ while that from good 2 is 0.179€. In comparison, the minimum contribution on the USP's good 1 implied by the lowest price of good 1 to allow break-even is 0.547€ and that for good 2 is 0.146€. To facilitate comparison of the total welfare implications, it is assumed that outside funds are available at a cost of 0.3.[13] The average price of the USP's two products inclusive of this funding is 0.572€, well above that under the two other cost allocation rules. Consequently, in this case the EPMU cost allocation leads to the position of the USP being unsustainable or this loss is funded in some other way.[14]

Figure 1: Price of USP Good 1 and Welfare under Monopoly and with Entry at Entrant Prices of 0.32€ and 0.40€

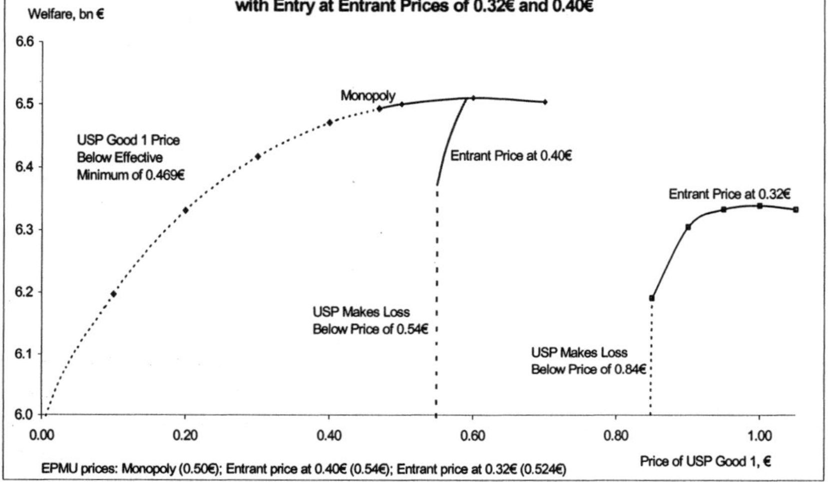

Figure 1 summarises some of these results and shows the relationship between the price of good 1 and economic welfare for the three cases of monopoly and entry at prices of 0.32€ and 0.40€. The unbroken part of each curve is the range from either the effective minimum of the price of good 1 given by the price of good 2 plus a bulk mail sender's worksharing cost (in the case of monopoly) or the minimum price of good 1 for the USP to break-even overall (in the two cases for entry) up to the GPC welfare-maximising price. The broken lines indicate the values of welfare which are below the

---

[13] Raising taxes generates distortions in the economy as soon as the government cannot use lump-sum taxes. Most estimates of the size of these distortions, called the cost of public funds, in developed countries belong to the range of 0.2 to 0.3. This means that, to raise 10 (million) euros, the government has to decrease the surplus of the agents who pay these taxes by the equivalent of 12 to 13 (million) euros.

[14] Other possibilities for funding such a deficit are not considered here but include changes to the service specification, taxes on entrants and a universal service or compensation fund (see De Donder et al (2002) for review). Where the USP is considered by its regulator to be less than fully efficient, price controls contain assumptions regarding the rate at which underlying costs should be reduced which would either increase contribution directly or allow lower prices leading to less entry and higher volumes. Implicitly the calibration values take account of this improvement which under incentive regulation may be overachieved. However, to the extent that a deficit would arise after such cost reductions then EPMU as a cost allocation rule would be inconsistent with financial viability.

sustainable price for good 1. The curves for the entry cases are much steeper than under monopoly indicating that welfare is much more sensitive to the price of the USP's good 1 where there is entry. This is due in turn to the impact of entry on the demand for the USP's good 2. The EPMU prices are recorded at the bottom of figure 1 and vary much less than the minimum prices of good 1 to allow the USP to break-even overall and hence respond only in a very limited way to the impact of entry. Figure 1 also highlights the impact of lower entrant prices and hence higher entry on welfare. As the extent of entry increases, welfare reaches its maximum at a higher price of good 1 and a lower level of welfare. A similar effect is apparent in the lowest price of good 1 to allow the USP to break-even overall such that the greater the degree of entry, the higher the accompanying level of this price and the lower the associated level of welfare.

4.3 Entry: Sensitivities on the Main Parameter Values

It is informative to understand the sensitivity of the results to the parameter values in the model. This can be achieved by changing one element of the calibration and comparing results from this with the original case. We report three comparative static analyses of this type in this subsection. First, the extent of entry in newly liberalised postal markets may be less than in a fully developed market. We examine this effect of a lower propensity of customers to switch in the near term by assuming 5% switch at equal prices (against 10% in the base) and that 20% switch at a 20% price discount (against 50% in the base). Secondly, one of the key parameters in the model is the extent to which traffic carried by entrants is new. In the base case, we assume that one in four items is new and three in four items displace those of the USP (σ=0.75). As a sensitivity, we evaluate a case where only one in ten items carried by entrants is new traffic (σ=0.9). The results from these sensitivities are reported in table 3. After this we consider a third sensitivity relating to the structure of demand in the central case, reported separately in table 4.

For lower initial entry, the comparison in table 3 is with the first three columns in table 2 where the entrants' price is the same as the initial price of the USP's good 2 (0.40€). With a lower propensity for the USP's good 2 traffic to switch to entrants, more of the network cost could be recovered under this cost allocation rule from good 2. The lowest price of good 1 is lower than in the case in table 2 and at its effective minimum of the price of good 2 plus the worksharing cost of 0.06€ for a sender of bulk mail. In addition, the GPC outcome remains close to that in the table 2 case. The EPMU cost allocation rule lies within this range and results in a smaller loss of good 2 volume allowing lower prices and higher welfare compared with the case in table 2. We conclude that with lower entry the range of cost allocations between lowest good 1 price and GPC is widened with the higher retention of volume helping to lower the average level of USP prices and raise welfare. Nevertheless, the EPMU rule remains with a lower welfare level than GPC.

Table 3: Prices, Volumes and Welfare Under Alternative Price and Cost Allocation Rules: Sensitivities Compared with Central Case for Calibration of Demand for Goods 2 and 3[1]

	Lower Entry[2]			Higher Displacement[3]		
	Lowest Price Good 1[4]	GPC	EPMU	Lowest Price of Good 1[4]	GPC	EPMU
Prices,€ :						
- USP Good 1	0.479	0.636	0.508	0.867	1.008	0.496
- USP Good 2	0.419	0.366	0.407	0.370	0.308	0.397
- Entrants	0.400	0.400	0.400	0.320	0.320	0.320
Volumes, bn items						
- USP Good 1	2.017	1.891	1.993	1.707	1.594	2.003
- USP Good 2	7.376	8.270	7.581	5.501	8.117	4.347
- Entrants	0.631	0	0.487	3.047	0.688	4.087
- Total USP	9.393	10.161	9.574	7.208	9.711	6.350
- Total Market	10.024	10.161	10.061	10.255	10.399	10.437
USP Profit, €bn	0	0	0	0	0	-0.606
Welfare, €bn	6.405	6.509	6.436	6.177	6.363	5.943[5]
Average Price, €	0.432	0.417	0.428	0.488	0.423	0.552[6]
Share of USP Fixed Cost Recovered by Good 1, %	21.5	37.9	24.7	57.6	67.2	23.4

[1] Calibration values as follows: Marginal costs (USP good 1, 0.30€; USP good 2, 0.24€); fixed cost (1.68bn€ including normal rate of profit), Price elasticities (USP good 1, -0 2; USP good 2, -0.4); relationship between prices (price of good 1≥ price of good 2 + 0 06€).

[2] Same as first case in table 2 (entrants' price, 0.40€, and displacement ratio, σ=0.75) but assumes entry equal to 5% of total market for goods 2 and 3 prices (10% in base) and 20% at a price discount of 20% (50% in base).

[3] Same as second case in table 2 (entrants' price, 0.32€; extent of entry (10% of total market for goods 2 and 3 at entrant price equal to USP; 50% at price discount of 20% to USP)) but assumes displacement ratio of σ=0.9 (σ=0.75 in base) or that 9 in 10 items carried by the entrants are displaced from the USP's good 2 and 1 in 10 items is new traffic.

[4] Lowest price of good 1 for USP to break-even

[5] Using cost of public funds at 0 3

[6] Including coverage of financial deficit at cost of public funds of 0.3

The second case in table 3 is compared with the case in the final three columns in table 2 with both assuming that the entrants' price is 0.32€. The only difference between the two cases then is that, against the original displacement ratio of $\sigma=0.75$, the corresponding parameter value is $\sigma=0.9$. This higher displacement means that the demand for good 2 is more elastic, and the USP reacts by decreasing the price for this product both in columns 4 and 5 (compared to table 2). The price of good 1 increases so that the USP breaks even. Faced with a lower price for good 2, the quantities sold by entrants decrease in both cases, and so does total quantity in the market. The impact on consumer surplus is a priori indeterminate: a higher displacement ratio means that goods 2 and 3 are closer substitutes so that consumers gain less from the introduction of product 3 in the market. On the other hand, consumers gain from the lower price for good 2 and lose from the higher price for product 1. With our simulations, the lower price for good 2 overrides the other effects and total welfare increases slightly. As for the EPMU cost allocation, increasing the displacement ratio does not enable the USP to break-even anymore than it did in table 2. On the contrary, the minimum loss attained under EPMU increases compared with table 2. This minimum loss is attained with lower prices than previously, both for goods 1 and 2. The net effect on welfare of a higher displacement ratio is composed of the positive impact of lower prices for goods 1 and 2 and of the negative impact of a higher USP loss and a less differentiated good 3. With our calibration, the net impact is slightly positive.

In table 4 we consider a third sensitivity. The structure of demand in the central case assumes that 80% of the USP's initial market is effectively open to entry either as presorted bulk mail or other types of business mail and that 20% of the market is not a realistic prospect for entry. For the sensitivity we assume that 90% of the USP's initial volume would face competition and hence a single piece share of only 10%.[15] All other parameter values are unchanged.[16] The first three columns of table 4 report results under monopoly. The pattern of results across the three pricing rules is very similar to those reported in table 1 for the central case. The EPMU rule is within the range of the two other rules and applying that rule leads to a price for good 1 such that it funds 12% of the network cost compared with 10% in the case of the lowest price of good 1 consistent with break-even overall and 19.2% in the case of the GPC. Welfare overall is lower (for example, in the case of EPMU 5.750bn€ compared with 6.500bn€ in the central case) as there is less of good 1 where consumer surplus is higher but again the differences in welfare between the three pricing rules are very small.

The two remaining columns in table 4 show the impact of entry for the case where entrants' prices are 20% less than the initial prices of the USP's good 2. The central case reported in table 2 produced a set of prices of the USP's two goods where break-even was feasible over a range of prices (for the USP's good 1 from 0.847€ to 0.996€). However, in the sensitivity, good 1 represents only 10% of the initial demand and table 4 shows that there is no pair of prices available to the USP which it can set to allow it to break-even overall. Instead we report the pair of prices which minimises the financial loss incurred by the USP. This sum is –0.081m€ and requires a significant increase in the price of the USP's good 1 to its profit-maximising level of 1.65€ and hence in the overall average price to 0.514€ compared with the prices under monopoly. As the best outcome is one of minimising continuing financial losses, this case is consistent with a "graveyard spiral"

---

[15] Single piece volumes have been declining in a number of countries in recent years. While 10% may be less than the share of consumer single piece and small business mailings in many countries currently, as e-substitution continues these segments of the market are likely to represent a declining share of future total mail volumes.

[16] The fixed cost and normal rate of profit implied by these parameters is slightly lower at 1.66bn€ compared with 1.68bn € in the central case.

unless an alternative means of funding is available to cover this deficit (Crew and Kleindorfer, 2000). As might be expected from the central case in table 2, the EPMU pricing rule produces a significantly worse financial outcome and a higher average price than that under the pair of prices for the USP's two goods which minimises financial losses.

Table 4: Prices, Volumes and Welfare Under Alternative Price and Cost Allocation Rules: Sensitivity of Single Piece Mail at 10% of USP Base Volume[1]

	Monopoly			Competition with Entrants' Price 20% Less Than USP's	
	Lowest Price of Good 1[2]	GPC	EPMU	Loss Minimising Pair of USP Prices	EPMU
Prices,€ :					
- USP Good 1	0.464	0.637	0.500	1.650	0.502
- USP Good 2	0.404	0.385	0.400	0.386	0.401
- Entrants (Good 3)	-	-	-	0.320	0.320
Volumes, bn items					
- USP Good 1	1.014	0.945	1.000	0.540	0.999
- USP Good 2	8.960	9.138	9.000	5.665	5.091
- Entrants (Good 3)	-	-	-	4.609	5.196
- Total USP	9.974	10.083	10.000	6.205	6.090
- Total Market	9.974	10.083	10.000	10.814	11.286
USP Profit, €bn	0	0	0	-0.081	-0.617 [3]
Welfare, €bn	5.746	5.756	5.750	5.083	5.190
Average Price, €	0.4101	0.408	0.410	0.514	0.549 [4]
Share of USP Fixed Cost Recovered by Good 1, %	10.0	19.2	12.0	44.5	12.3

[1]Compared with 20% of base volume in central case. Other calibration values as follows: Marginal costs (USP good 1, 0.30€; USP good 2, 0.24€); fixed cost (1.66bn€ including normal rate of profit); price elasticities (USP good 1, -0.2; USP good 2, -0.4); displacement ratio (σ=0.75); extent of entry (10% of total market for goods 2 and 3 at entrant price equal to USP; 50% at price discount of 20% to USP); relationship between prices (price of good 1 = price of good 2 + 0.06€).

[2]Lowest price of good 1 for USP to breakeven overall across both products.

[3]Using cost of public funds at 0.3.

[4] Including coverage of financial deficit at cost of public funds of 0.3.

5. IMPLICATIONS FOR PRICE SETTING AND STRUCTURE OF PRICE CONTROLS

In this final section we outline briefly the main implications from our model and numerical analysis for the setting of price controls in liberalised postal markets. In setting of prices and recovery through these of variable costs and the network or fixed cost of universal service provision, we have paid particular attention to the price of the product where entry is least likely (single piece mail or "good 1" in our model). Even though its price may not be affected by entry through a direct impact on its volume, it will be affected by entry to other segments of the market and the impact of this on the USP's total volume of mail. In this analysis we have concentrated on the range of prices for good 1 defined by the minimum price for that product to allow break-even for the USP and the welfare-maximising GPC price (which is always higher than this minimum since it calls for a positive mark-up on all goods). A price for good 1 in this range enables the USP to break-even and to enhance economic welfare by raising the price of good 1 and lowering that of the other product with a higher (absolute) price elasticity (bulk mail or "good 2" in our model). Of course, it may be the case that competition is so extensive, either because of the effect of entry on the demand for the USP's good 2 or the small size of the market for good 1 where entry is assumed not to occur, that no prices allow the USP to break-even.

Clearly the relevant volumes for the setting of prices and recovery of the network cost are those inclusive of the impact of entry. Entry reduces the mail volumes of the USP and so requires a different set of prices to achieve break-even. The higher the level of entry, the lower the volume of the USP to recover network costs and hence the higher the average price across products required by the USP to break-even. The increase in the average price due to entry also reduces the total level of economic welfare (having included the increase in welfare arising from the new products offered by entrants). If there is little entry, cost allocation rules such as EPMU result in prices that are likely to be within the range identified by the minimum price required for good 1 to allow break-even and the welfare–maximising GPC price. However, if entry is more extensive, cost allocation rules of this kind are increasingly likely to fall outside of this range and the cost allocation rule would need to be closer to that of the welfare-maximising GPC prices to enable the USP to break-even overall. At the limit, it may be that even complete price flexibility is insufficient to allow break-even and we consider a result of this type in the paper.

We find the following implications from our model for the setting of price controls. In terms of the overall level of prices required by the USP, our model shows clearly that this depends on the cost allocation rule. The level is lowest under GPC where welfare is also maximised and higher under alternative cost allocation rules (e.g. "lowest price of good 1" and EPMU). Consequently, in addition to assumptions made by a regulator relating to improvements in underlying cost levels of the USP, the overall level of prices set for a price control is contingent also on the cost allocation rule the USP is able to adopt for its pricing.[17]

---

[17] There may be some interaction between cost efficiency and the structure of prices. For example, the lower the level of the USP's costs, the lower its prices can be and hence the less entry will occur. This would widen the range of prices identified by the lowest price of good 1 to allow overall break-even and the GPC solutions and hence the range of cost allocation rules consistent with break-even.

Our model has incorporated two products for the USP although these can also be viewed as representing two groups of products. This facilitates consideration as to whether a single control or basket should apply as under GPC or whether the two products should be placed and controlled in two separate baskets. If the two products are price controlled separately, then this requires a division of the fixed, network cost between the two baskets. This cost allocation rule not only affects the degree of price rebalancing between baskets but also the average level of allowed prices, the overall level of welfare and the financial viability of the USP. The greater is the degree of competition, the more likely it is that any cost allocation rule, such as EPMU, will lie outside the range of prices at which the USP breaks even.

Where, as in our model, the fixed cost is common to both products, the interdependence of prices between the price controls on the two products is a key building block of the overall price control. This interdependence between different groups of products is unavoidable, particularly where entry is likely to be significant, as the overall requirement is for the two products jointly to recover the fixed cost. This requirement may be inadequately addressed by arbitrary cost allocation rules, like EPMU, if the degree of competition assumed in setting the price control is understated since in such cases the USP may be loss-making and ultimately unsustainable. Thus, cost allocation rules that are consistent with GPC and price control structures that facilitate the rebalancing of prices may be necessary to enable the USP to remain financially viable in the presence of competition provided a price solution exists.

We add two final comments. As noted in our introduction the focus of our paper has been on cost allocation and pricing rules within price controls rather than other areas such as promotion of reductions in underlying costs. To the extent that entry has a stimulating effect on service quality and/or the underlying cost level of the USP there are benefits which would need to be weighed with the areas covered by our paper. Secondly, in practice, there is uncertainty about the extent to which accounting costs should be treated as fixed or variable and, particularly, about the future volumes of USPs in a liberalised market. These informational considerations also suggest the benefits of allowing flexibility in terms of the setting of prices and facilitating this in the structure of a price control. To the extent that this is not allowed for and products are controlled separately, then it would be necessary for the regulatory framework to set higher allowed prices to accommodate the pricing rules implicit or explicit in the separate controls. That framework should include also the employment of tests and explicit means to underpin continuing financial viability where this becomes at risk.

REFERENCES

Billette de Villemeur, E., H.Cremer, B. Roy and J. Toledano. 2003. "Optimal Pricing and Price-Cap Regulation in the Postal Sector." *Journal of Regulatory Economics* 24(1):24-62.

Braeutigam, R. 1980. "An Analysis of Fully Distributed Cost Pricing in Regulated Industries." *Bell Journal of Economics* 11(1): 182-196.

Cazals, C., J.P. Florens, and S. Soteri. 2005. "Delivery Costs for Postal Services in the UK: Some Results on Scale Economies with Panel Data." In *Regulatory and Economic Challenges in the Postal and Delivery Sector,* edited by M.A. Crew and P.R. Kleindorfer. Boston: Kluwer Academic Publishers.

Correia da Silva, L., P. Dudley, L. Mautino and S. Richard. 2004. "RPI-X Price Control Regulation in the Postal Sector." In *Competitive Transformation of the Postal and Delivery Sector,* edited by M.A. Crew and P.R. Kleindorfer. Boston: Kluwer Academic Publishers.

Crew, M.A. and P.R. Kleindorfer. 2000. "Liberalisation and the Universal Service Obligation in Postal Services." In *Current Directions in Postal Reform*, edited by M.A. Crew and P.R. Kleindorfer. Boston: Kluwer Academic Publishers.

De Donder, P., H. Cremer and F. Rodriguez. 2002. "Funding the Universal Service Obligation under Liberalization: An Analysis of the Postal Market." In *Postal and Delivery Services: Pricing, Productivity, Regulation and Strategy,* edited by M.A. Crew and P.R. Kleindorfer. Boston: Kluwer Academic Publishers.

Dudley, P., H. Jenkins, L. Mautino, and S. Richard. 2005. "Competition and the Coverage of Price Controls in the Postal Sector." In *Regulatory and Economic Challenges in the Postal and Delivery Sector,* edited by M.A. Crew and P.R. Kleindorfer. Boston: Kluwer Academic Publishers.

Florens, J.P., S. Marcy, and J. Toledano. 2002. "Mail Demand in the Long and Short term." In *Postal and Delivery Services: Pricing, Productivity, Regulation and Strategy*, edited by M.A. Crew and P.R. Kleindorfer. Boston: Kluwer Academic Publishers.

Nankervis, J., S. Richard, S. Soteri and F. Rodriguez. 2002. "Disaggregated Letter Traffic Demand in the UK." In *Postal and Delivery Services: Pricing, Productivity, Regulation and Strategy,* edited by M.A. Crew and P.R. Kleindorfer. Boston: Kluwer Academic Publishers.

Panzar, J. 2005. "Combining Liberalisation and Unbundling Policies in Postal Markets." Paper presented to 13th Conference on Postal and Delivery Economics, Antwerp, Belgium.

Sherman, R. 1993. "Should Ramsey-Price Markups Differ?" *Journal of Regulatory Economics* 5: 217-225.

Tolley, G.S. 2000. Direct Testimony (sponsored by the United States Postal Service) as USPS-T-6 in Docket No R2000-01 before the Postal Rate Commission.

Chapter 15

Pricing the Last Mile in the Postal Sector*

Cátia Felisberto,[1] Matthias Finger,[1] Beat Friedli,[2] Daniel Krähenbühl,[2] and Urs Trinkner[2,3]
Ecole Polytechnique Fédérale Lausanne (EPFL),[1] Swiss Post[2] and University of Zurich[3]

1. INTRODUCTION

This paper explores whether it would be commercially interesting for historical postal operators to price the "postal last mile". By introducing the receiver pays principle it identifies an approach which could lead to a number of innovations in service arrangements and in financing the universal service obligation (USO).

Indeed, the way the postal last mile for the delivery of lettermail[1] has been defined, serviced and priced so far has historical origins and, as yet, has seldom been called into question. Today this question is attracting increased attention, driven by three considerations: first, mail volumes appear to decline, at least in the traditional letter market, leading to diminishing scale effects. Secondly, the changing consumer behavior resulting from new information and communication technologies is reducing the pressure on speedy delivery and prompting a redefinition of what constitutes a universal postal service. Thirdly, there is a growing debate about whether or not access to the incumbent's distribution network is to be granted to competitors.

---

* The views expressed in this paper are those of the authors and do not necessarily reflect the opinion of Swiss Post or EPFL. The authors would like to thank M. Crew and P. Kleindorfer for their helpful comments.

1 To facilitate discussion, this paper focuses on letter mail, considering that parcels have a somewhat different last mile problem. However, the models discussed here are, in principle, also applicable to parcels delivery.

Against this background and given the cost-sensitiveness of the last mile, postal operators are increasingly seeking ways to reduce costs at the distribution end of the value chain. They typically do so by delivering more efficiently or by reducing service levels. In contrast to these approaches, we look for possibilities to give *more* value to the last mile by introducing a delivery fee that receivers would have to pay when choosing traditional home delivery. In conjunction, we discuss a new way of financing the USO.

This paper models – for the first time, to the best of our knowledge – recipient pricing in the postal sector and tests it with Swiss data. In Section 2, we briefly consider the question of the last mile in other network industries to get a better understanding of the last mile issue and of whether and how it differs from other sectors. In Section 3, we look at USO service levels: as mail distribution remains a universal service obligation it is necessary to explore the leeway an incumbent actually possesses when exploring new options for the postal last mile. Section 4 describes principles, conditions, and fields of application of the receiver pays principle (RPP). We also outline its future potential for service level differentiation and for financing the USO. Section 5 presents and calibrates the model by looking at its implications in terms of both operators' profit and overall welfare. We present and discuss our results in Section 6 and conclude in Section 7.

2. THE PROBLEM OF THE LAST MILE

The "last mile" is a typical concept of network industries such as telecommunications, electricity, gas, and others. The last mile became an issue mainly because of the liberalization of these industries, where the owners of the networks have given or have been forced to give access to their networks. We briefly consider the debates in the telecommunications and electricity sectors and compare them with the postal sector.

In the <u>telecommunications sector</u>, the last mile is defined by the physical cable that links the individual household to the dispatching central. For economic reasons, it is generally not deemed efficient to duplicate this last mile. Therefore, the European Commission and national regulators have forced the historical operators to open up their last miles to competitors, who rent the last mile at a regulated price. More recently, technological alternatives such as television cable or broadband wireless access have emerged. It is therefore being increasingly debated whether access to the historical operator's last mile should be regulated at all, or whether technological and commercial competition is sufficient to serve consumers' interests and by doing so increase welfare. Most suppliers price their services with two-part tariffs (TPT)[2]. TPT means that the consumer pays a fixed plus a variable tariff. The first part of the tariff is a fixed participation fee that gives the right to make and/or to receive calls. The second part represents the actual usage of the phone line. Typically, callers are charged some fee per time unit consumed. From an economic point of view a TPT makes sense when the suppliers face a large amount of fixed costs (e.g., to set up and operate a telecommunications network). It enables the operators to charge usage fees close to marginal costs without making a loss. The special feature of the telecommunications TPT is that both the sender and the receiver have to pay the fixed fee. Therefore, we do not have a pure sender pays principle (SPP) in the TPT, because the fixed part (the connection fee) is equally distributed among the two parties. Figure 1 will later illustrate the pricing scheme in comparison with other network industries.

In the electricity sector, the discussion about the last mile is less advanced, yet, at least in the beginning of the liberalization process, very similar to the debate in the telecommunications sector. With the liberalization of energy production, local distributors remain monopolists in that they own the connection to the final consumer at the household level. Duplication of the incumbent's last mile is too expensive. Unlike in the telecommunications industry, no realistic technological alternative exists for local power distribution, which is therefore a typical example of a monopolistic bottleneck. Consequently, if consumers chose to purchase their electricity from a remote producer rather than from their local distributor, the local distributor is usually forced by the regulator to transport this electricity at a regulated access price. There exists a broad variety of pricing schemes for the final energy consumer, such as peak load pricing. Pricing schemes are mostly based on TPT and the receiver pays principle, as it is always the receiver who orders the power. Consequently, the receiver pays for both the power consumption (variable tariff) and the infrastructure needed to transport the power (fixed tariff).

In the postal sector, the concept of the last mile is used above all by analogy. Taking up this analogy, the postal last mile resembles the current situation in the telecommunications rather than the electricity sector. Although mail delivery has the properties of a natural monopoly

---

2 Although the TPT principle was known long before, it attracted renewed attention with the emergence of mobile phones. In the late 1990s the UK industry regulator claimed that the prices for calling mobile phones were too high. This triggered additional research. One of the findings was that the high prices stemmed from asymmetric incentives, where the originating party paid for the totality of the call. It was suggested that if instead the receivers were to pay for some or all of the call, mobile prices would be lower (Doyle and Smith, 1998). However, this might also lead to inverse effects. For instance, Schwarz-Schilling (2001) reports that the slower growth of mobile telephony in the US compared to other parts of the world could be attributed to the receiver pays principle.

(subadditive cost function), it can hardly be seen as a monopolistic bottleneck: the experiences of New Zealand, Sweden and the Netherlands indicate that the natural monopoly of letters delivery is contestable. To some extent this questions the rationale for the ongoing European discussions about regulated access. With emerging parallel delivery networks one can indeed expect a greater variety of pricing schemes and product differentiation. Yet, surprisingly, pricing innovations with regard to the last mile remain rare. Today, virtually all postal services apply the sender pays principle (SPP), where receivers do not have to pay anything to be connected to the postal network.

The core idea of the following sections is to explore whether, as in the telecommunications sector, advanced pricing models with TPT, RPP and SPP elements would make sense in the postal sector both from a commercial and a welfare point of view.

3. THE UNIVERSAL DELIVERY OBLIGATION

Historically, each European postal operator had its own definition and practice of the postal last mile. The EU Directive of 1997 (amended in 2002) states that the postal operator responsible for the universal postal service must deliver postal items *"to the home premises"*. However, it does not specify a series of issues, such as the exact point of delivery; it does not say anything about the exact time of delivery during the day; and it does not mention whether or not the operator may charge last mile delivery fees (e.g., subscription fees to the households or specific door delivery fees).

In other words, the European Commission allows for significant leeway when it comes to the requirements of downstream universal service, the "universal delivery obligation". A more detailed analysis of what universal delivery service means in different countries shows that, while there is significant similarity in delivery frequency, there remain differences regarding delivery point, time, and quality. Also, many countries grant exceptions to the universal delivery obligation, authorized normally by the regulator or exceptionally by the political authorities. In the case of Switzerland, house delivery is the standard. Exceptions can be decided by Swiss Post, though they must be notified to the regulator.

In conclusion, we can say that the downstream universal postal service and the pricing of this service as conceived from a political perspective generally remain quite vague – i.e., defined only by *"delivery to the home premises"* – yet almost no country seems to be taking advantage of this vagueness.

4. TOWARDS DELIVERY PRICING

Despite a number of structural similarities, it is the sender pays principle (SPP)[3] that prevails in the postal sector, whereas the receiver pays principle (RPP) or two-part tariffs (TPT) have gained widespread acceptance in other network industries. In those industries, technological advances and liberalization typically lead to new services, differentiated quality standards, and the unbundling of the value chain. We also find price differentiation with two or multi-part tariff schemes. This reflects growing competition, as well as demand and cost considerations: suppliers make use of market segmentation strategies with customer preferences being better reflected in the variety of product-price-bundles supplied. Generally, then, the presence of competition, along with high shares of fixed costs, leads to some sort of fixed access fee and variable usage prices.

A brief, non-exhaustive look at the literature shows that a large number of variables influences the choice of an optimal pricing model. In the telecommunications industry, for instance, there are differences between situations in which either party can initiate a message exchange and those in which only one party can do so. Other influencing factors are, amongst others: number of messages sent and received which have the same value for the respective senders and receivers; receivers' knowledge of the value of the message; degree of dependency between messages sent and received; cost relations between messages sent and received. Such model features have important implications for the choice of the welfare optimizing pricing model. By way of example, if an incoming message triggers an outgoing message of the same value in reply, then call externalities will be internalized in the demand for sending messages, if not, then a two-part pricing scheme might prove welfare optimizing. There are a number of papers analyzing such models. One important conclusion is that in the presence of call externalities RPP can increase both welfare and profits (Hermalin and Katz (2004)).[4]

Looking at the postal industry, we know of no case where RPP is currently in widespread use. We have to go back to the pre-Rowland Hill era to find RPP as a common means of payment.[5] However, the topic has been

---

3 The analogous term in the telecom industry is "calling party principle".

4 The results are, of course, subject to a number of model assumptions not discussed here. For further references see for example Jeon, Laffont and Tirole, 2004; and Kim and Lim, 2000.

5 For details on postal reform introducing the sender pays principle, see for example Hill and Hill, 1880. It is interesting to note that Hill proposed that a small additional charge be made either in advance or on delivery on the ground that, in some small places, the penny charge would not cover the cost of the delivery. However, he withdrew this suggestion

taken up again in the recent past. Owen and Willig (1981) stated that postal rates constitute a deviation from efficient marginal cost pricing. They proposed setting up a guaranteed basic service delivery and pricing additional delivery services to the receivers according to demand. Schwarz-Schilling discusses a number of reasons, among them *"operational costs, transaction costs and the relevance of distributional goals"*, for the fact that a two-part tariff (variable part SPP, fixed part RPP) *"has never been put into practice on a significant scale so far"* (2001:18). This conclusion relies on a set of theoretical considerations, yet the paper does not model or quantify costs or revenues.

Empirical evidence on the preference of receivers to pay for house delivery can be found in Elsenbast (1996). The author reports findings from a survey in which residents could choose between payable house delivery and free collection at a centralized P.O. box. He concluded – not surprisingly – that a majority (62%) of households preferred house delivery but – perhaps surprisingly – would, on average, also be prepared to pay for it.

Thus, there are potentially a number of welfare arguments in favor of such a "distributed two-part tariff", reflecting that both the senders and the receivers bear the costs of a piece of mail: the former paying the postage and the latter a fixed delivery fee. In Figure 1, the new pricing is illustrated in comparison with selected other pricing schemes.

Figure 1: Illustration of different pricing schemes in network industries

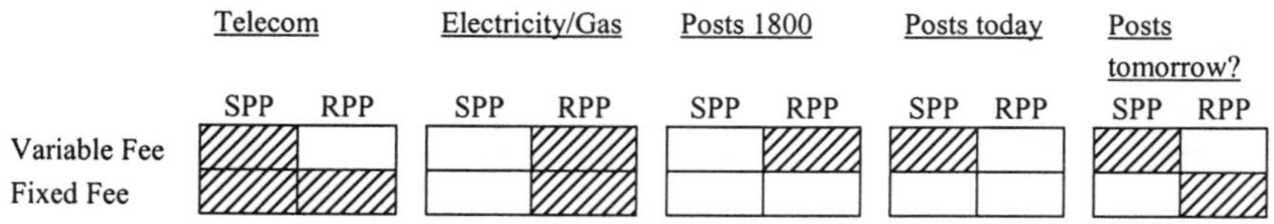

The four key arguments supporting such a combination of RPP and SPP in contrast to the pure SPP, as it is currently applied in the postal sector, can be summarized as follows. First, a two-part tariff scheme brings prices more in line with costs. Efficient pricing requires, in principle, that prices equal marginal cost. The postal network, though not a physical one, entails both fixed and variable costs. A large part of fixed costs can be associated with the delivery. Consequently, introducing a fixed and a variable price component would allow postal rates to come closer to marginal costs and thus also to economically more efficient pricing. Secondly, each network transaction implies that the message has a value for both the sender and the receiver. Hence, both the sender and the receiver should contribute to the cost of a message. Thirdly, a receiver contribution would allow for a

later (Hemmeon, 1912). For a more recent discussion, see for example Crew and Kleindorfer, 1991.

reduction of the sending tariffs. This, in turn, would stimulate volumes, which would positively influence economies of scale. Fourth, yet related to the third argument, a new source of financing the USO could be tapped.

From these four arguments we derive the following pricing model. The sender pays a variable fee for the mail sent. This includes collection, sorting, and transportation to easily accessible, low-cost locations. These may be centralized P.O. boxes at the post office, but also at, for instance, the city square or the road intersection, where the mail can be picked up by the receiver[6]. The receiver pays a fixed fee for any additional request, such as daily delivery to the doorstep[7].

The model can be used to varying degrees to cope with heterogeneity in delivery costs, which is the main cause of unsustainability of the USO in the face of entry. In other words, the model needs not to be applied to every address. Also, the model opens up a number of further options for service delivery. Receivers may wish to get their mail at the road intersection, at the house entrance, or at the doorstep, and pay differentiated prices accordingly. Moreover, once delivery is packaged and priced as a product in its own right, many additional features can be added, for instance in combination with redirecting mail, with different times of delivery, or in conjunction with electronic services. Yet, whatever model the postal operators offer to the households, it must be non-discriminatory.

In the remainder of the paper, we will focus on a stylized and simplified model as depicted in Figure 2.

Figure 2: Illustration of a stylized distributed two-part tariff

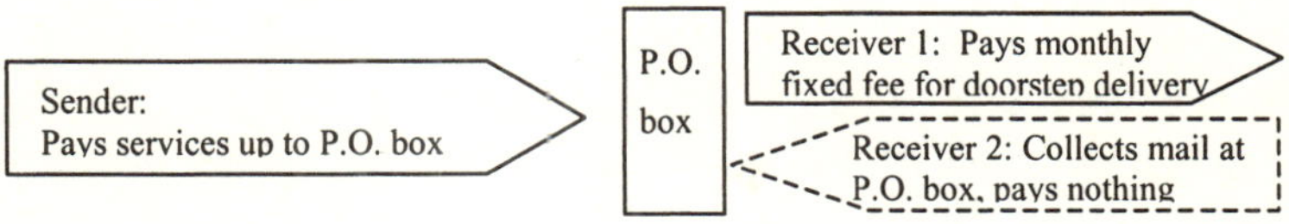

5. MODEL AND CALIBRATION

Our aim is to evaluate whether a combination of the SPP with the RPP performs better than the current SPP on its own, in terms of both operators' profits and overall welfare. We restrict ourselves to the study of the monopoly situation to reduce complexity.

---

6 A P.O. box is not necessarily located within a post office. P.O. boxes may also consist of large units with many individual delivery boxes. These units are located at places which are easy to reach for both the post office and the recipients who come to pick up their mail.

7 Note that receivers who are not willing to pay a "connection" fee are not cut off from the network altogether – unlike in the telecommunications sector.

Our model develops as follows. In the benchmark case, the SPP applies as it is today. Thus, the receiver does not pay for delivery. We compare this benchmark with the stylized distributed TPT as in Figure 2, which we call "*Delivery Flat Rate*" (DFR). The name *"Delivery Flat Rate"* stems from the fact that the receivers have to pay a yearly flat rate (*P*) to the postal operator if they want delivery at the doorstep. In other words, in order to receive the mail at the doorstep, the receiver has to pay *P* units of money per year. Nevertheless, customers also have the option of receiving the mail for free at a P.O. box (located at a nearby post office or another centralized location).

The DFR will allow the operator to reduce delivery costs and to have additional revenues (revenues associated with the flat rate that customers have to pay if they choose to receive lettermail at the doorstep). The operator can redistribute these additional revenues to the senders by decreasing the senders' price accordingly.

If receivers are not willing to pay the delivery fee and choose P.O. box delivery instead, they incur an opportunity cost (*OC*) of going to the P.O. box to collect the incoming mail. We assume *OC* to be a function of household income w, the search costs s to realize the opportunity income, and of time t needed to go from the household's doorstep to empty the P.O. box:

$$OC(w,s,t) = \alpha(w \cdot t)^{\beta} - s\,,$$

where α and β express the way customers value the opportunity money and time. Economic theory would state these two parameters to be 1. However, many factors are not directly covered in our opportunity function. For example, one could argue that the opportunity cost of going to the P.O. box also depends on the size of the household, on whether at least one member passes the point of centralized delivery each day, on age or health conditions of the members of the household, on whether the household receives newspapers separately from the rest of the mail, or on the number of mail pieces per day. It would be rather complex and arbitrary to introduce all these variables into our model. The two parameters α and β give us some flexibility to get an intuitive OC-distribution that corresponds to surveys made in Germany, as found in Elsenblast (1996).

The decision of the customer will depend on whether his opportunity cost of going to the P.O. box is smaller or bigger than the flat rate *P* he has to pay for delivery at the doorstep. If $OC \geq P$, then the customer will prefer to pay the flat rate and receive the mail at his doorstep. If $OC < P$, P.O. box delivery is chosen instead.

In order to analyze the welfare effects of the new DFR policy, we need to specify utility functions for senders and receivers, and a profit function for the postal operator. For the sender side we follow De Donder et al. (2001) and assume a representative sender with quasilinear preferences with respect to money:

$$U^S(q,\varpi) = aq - \frac{b}{2}q^2 + \varpi - pq,$$

where q represents the quantity of mail sent, p is the price per piece of mail the sender has to pay, and ω is the initial endowment of the customer. $a, b > 0$ determine the market size and the slope of the demand curve. $\varpi - pq$ reflects the amount of money the consumer spends on all other goods. The corresponding demand function of the representative sender is as follows,

$$q(p) = \frac{1}{b}(a - p).$$

For the receiving households $i \in 1 \ldots I$ we assume a constant individual utility V_i of being connected to the postal network. Thus, their (quasilinear) utility in the monopoly case is V_i. In the DFR case, they are worse off because delivery is costly now. Thus, in order to receive mail at the doorstep, the receivers need to pay the delivery flat rate P. If they choose the P.O. box instead, their cost is OC_i. Total receivers' utility can be written as

$$U^R(P) = \sum_i \left(V_i - \min(P, OC_i)\right). \tag{1}$$

Expression (1) offers an explanation why, so far, no postal operator has chosen DFR. If V_i is smaller than the cost of receiving mail, one would expect this person not to empty the P.O. box at all. We do not implement this possibility in our model by assuming that V_i is sufficiently large. Thus, everybody will be motivated to empty their mail box, and no network externalities are lost.

The postal service's costs are composed of both variable and fixed components, reflecting the existence of economies of scale in the mail processing. The profit function of the postal operator accordingly looks as follows:

$$\pi(\hat{p}, P) = (\hat{p} - c)q - F_u - F_d \underbrace{- F_{PO}(N - n(P)) + P \cdot n(P) + AC(P)}_{\text{Additional terms for DFR}}.$$

Parameter c denotes the variable costs per mail item, and F_u and F_d are the upstream and downstream fixed costs. F_{PO} are the operator's fixed costs for providing and billing an additional P.O. box. N is the total number of households in the economy, and $n(P)$ is the number of households who choose delivery at the doorstep as a function of the flat rate P. Consequently, N-$n(P)$ represents the number of households abandoning home delivery because the flat rate exceeds their opportunity costs for a self-service at the centralized point of delivery. $AC(P)$ are the avoided costs as a function of the flat rate P. In the benchmark case, P is zero and $AC(P) = 0$. If the flat rate was set to plus infinity in the DFR case, nobody would choose doorstep delivery and $AC(P) = F_d$. We assume that the postal operator redistributes all earnings and savings which are associated with the new policy to the senders by lowering the stamp price from p_0 to $\hat{p}$ according to the rule $\hat{p} = p_0 - \frac{P \cdot n(P) - F_{PO}(N - n(P)) + AC(P)}{q_0}$, where q_0 is the mail volume of the previous period.

Figure 3 provides additional intuition for the underlying cost assumptions. Following Cohen and Chu (1997), delivery costs can be split into three parts, i.e., "*route costs*", "*access costs*", and "*load costs*". Load costs are the costs of inserting the mail into the mailbox once the mail carrier reaches the mailbox. The profit function implies that we assume the load cost of a P.O. and mail box to be the same. These costs are included in c. Thus, only route and access cost are avoided when consumers switch to P.O. boxes. The total of route and access costs represent F_d.

Figure 3: Main Cost Drivers in Delivery

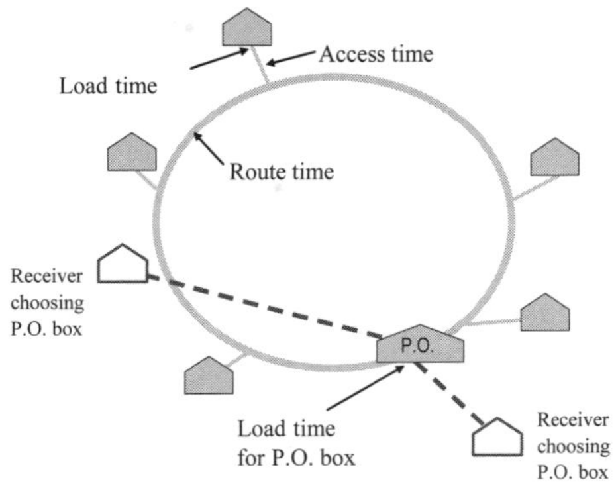

In order to compute overall welfare in the economy, we simply add up consumers' net utility and operator's profit. For DFR, we can find the consumers' net utility by subtracting the revenues associated with the flat rate and the total disutility of going to the P.O. box from the senders' surplus.

With this framework, we will have a positive mail volume impact for any negative value of price elasticity as long as $F_{PO}(N - n) < AC + nP$. This is because we assume that the postal operator redistributes earnings and savings entirely to the senders by lowering the stamp price p. With negative price elasticity, this leads to an increase in mail demand. Whether this translates into greater overall welfare depends on the avoided cost function and the switching behavior of the consumers, as determined by the distribution of OC in the population.

In order to assess the impact on welfare, we calibrate the model using Swiss data. Swiss Post stated in its annual report that approximately 2.86 billion pieces of addressed mail were delivered in 2004. Recent Swiss Post data suggest that overall price elasticity is approximately -0.3. Parameters a and b can be directly computed using prices, quantities and price elasticities of 2004. The expression for price elasticity is as follows

$$\varepsilon = -\frac{1}{b}\frac{p}{q}.$$

On the production side, we assume the same calibration as set out in Dietl et al. (2005). We estimate the operator's yearly outlay for a P.O. box (F_{PO}) to be CHF 35. A crucial point is the avoided cost function. The function reflects how delivery costs depend on the fraction of consumers choosing P.O. boxes instead of mailboxes. We assume a function of the following kind:

Figure 4: Avoided cost function

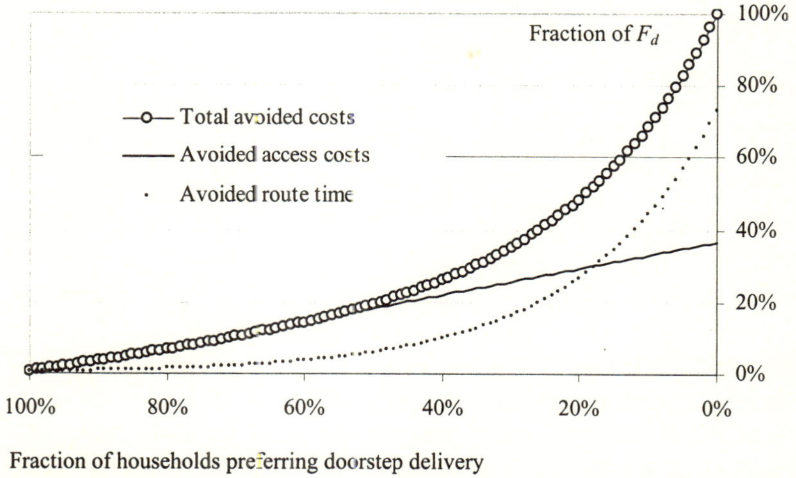

Total avoided costs break down into the two parts "avoided access costs" and "avoided route costs" (see Figure 3). When a consumer switches to P.O.

box delivery, the postal operator saves the access costs directly. These costs are related to the time the carrier saves with regard to reaching the consumer's mailbox from the prevailing route. This component is a linear function. The second component is the reduced route time, also called route costs. Route time decreases when a sufficient fraction of households switches to P.O. boxes and delivery routes can be optimized accordingly. We assume an exponential run of this curve.

In order to compute the distribution of opportunity costs, we have generated a random sample of 10,000 observations for each of the variables w and t. We assumed the households' income and distance from the P.O. box to be independent and to follow the lognormal distribution with the following means and standard deviations[8]:

Table 1: Mean and standard deviation of *w* and *t*

	Mean	Std deviation
w (CHF)	8.933	3.507
t (minutes)	8.78	2.48

Moreover, we assumed s = CHF 150, $\alpha = 1$ and β to be 0.7. Figure 5 depicts the resulting demand function for doorstep delivery.

Figure 5: Demand for doorstep delivery

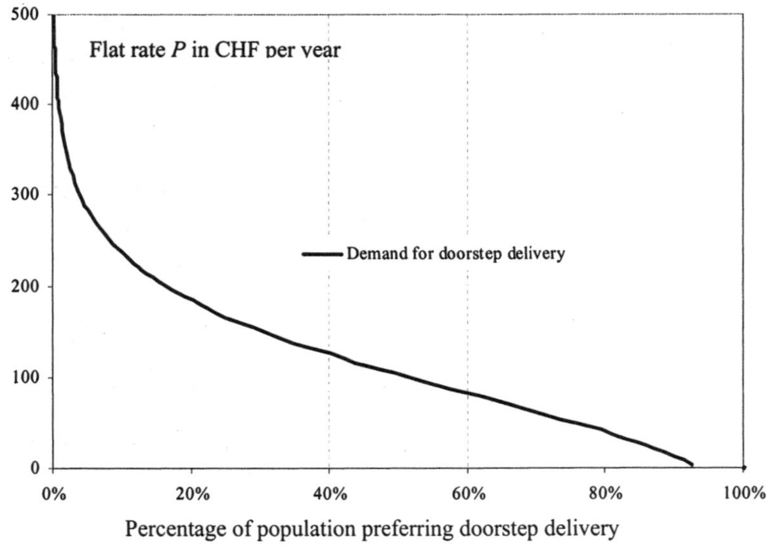

[8] Data supplied by the Swiss Federal Statistical Office and by Swiss Post.

6. RESULTS

It is a straightforward task to analyze the benchmark situation, i.e., the first stage before the introduction of the flat rate for doorstep delivery. The uniform price charged by Swiss Post was CHF 0.74 on average. The model yields a profit of CHF 196 million, a consumer surplus of approximately CHF 3.4 billion and total welfare of about CHF 3.6 billion.

If the new policy of delivery were introduced with a delivery flat rate of CHF 100 per year, without taking into account the costs of centralized delivery boxes for the operator (F_{PO}=0) and assuming that the postal operator applied an extensive redistribution of savings and earnings, the average price would drop by CHF 0.09 to CHF 0.65. Reduced prices would cause growing demand and accordingly increase operators' profit by CHF 44 million. Simultaneously consumer welfare would increase by 10% and total welfare by approximately 11%. Table 2 summarizes the results.

Table 2: Results for different flat rates, F_{PO} = 0

	Before flat rate	After flat rate (CHF) 40	70	100	130	160
Demand for doorstep delivery (%)	100	82	68	53	40	28
Average price (CHF)	0.74	0.69	0.67	0.65	0.63	0.62
Quantity (million letters)	2782	2837	2867	2889	2905	2920
Consumers' surplus (CHF million)	3423	3614	3707	3769	3816	3867
Profit operator (CHF million)	196	221	233	240	245	250
Total welfare (CHF million)	3619	3835	3940	4009	4061	4117
Welfare change (in %)		6.0	8.9	10.8	12.2	13.7

In Figure 6, we can observe how consumer welfare and operator's profit evolve for different values of the flat rate.

Figure 6: Impact of the flat rate on welfare and profit

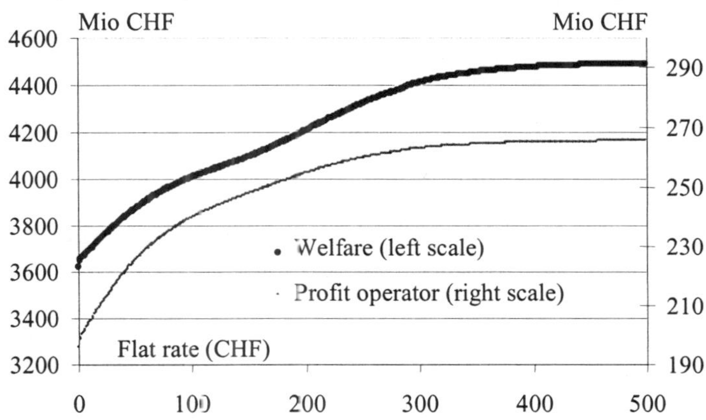

Assuming a flat rate of CHF 100 per year, we can see that irrespective of parameter α we will observe an increase in total welfare with the introduction of the flat rate (Table 3). All the remaining results are robust with regards to changes in α.

Table 3: Sensitivity analysis for α

	Before flat rate	Flat rate = CHF 100 per year				
		α				
		0.8	0.9	1	1.1	1.2
Demand for doorstep delivery (%)	100	28	41	53	65	74
Average price (CHF)	0.74	0.64	0.65	0.65	0.64	0.64
Quantity (million letters)	2782	2899	2889	2889	2892	2896
Consumers' surplus (CHF million)	3423	3893	3802	3769	3764	3770
Profit operator (CHF million)	196	243	240	240	241	242
Total welfare (CHF million)	3619	4136	4042	4009	4005	4012
Welfare change (in %)		14.3	11.7	10.8	10.7	10.9

So far, we have assumed that the provision of P.O. boxes was costless for the operator (F_{PO} = 0). Because of the redistribution of additional earnings and savings to the senders, this resulted in higher welfare whenever the flat rate was increased. In other words, there is no economic reason for doorstep delivery with this calibration of the model. Figures 7 and 8 show, however, how the results change if we take into account that the postal operator incurs the costs of building/providing an increasing number of P.O. boxes.

Figure 7: F_{PO} = 35, α = 1,2

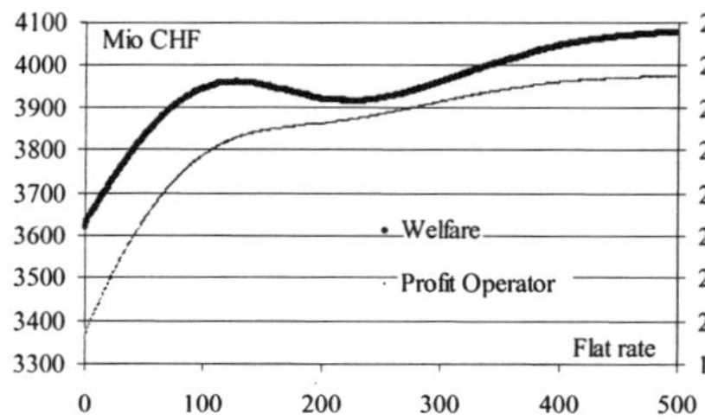

Figure 8: F_{PO} = 70, α = 1,2

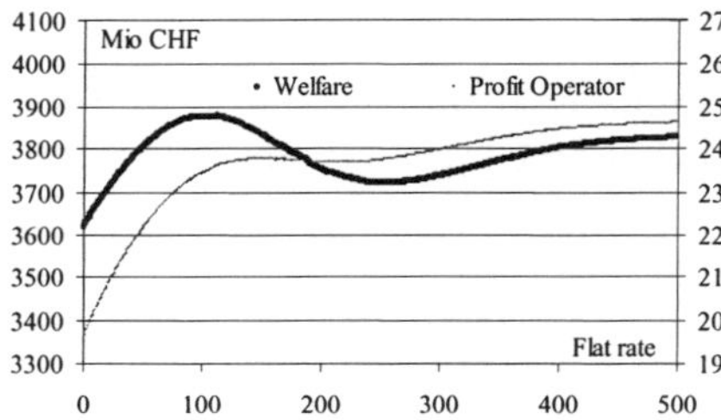

We now have a local maximum in overall welfare. This represents the point where an increase in the flat rate causes too many receivers to switch to P.O. box delivery. For about F_{PO} > CHF 50, the local maximum exceeds the border solution. In this case, the local maximum would equal the welfare maximizing delivery flat rate. To the right of the local maximum, exponential savings in route cost (cf. Figure 4) cause a local minimum.

However, the results should be treated with caution. One reason is the calibration of the demand function in Figure 5, which is more optimistic than the results from Elsenbast (1996) indicate. If one is thinking seriously about introducing a flat rate in Switzerland, the demand function should be derived empirically and matched with the corresponding demand parameters. Furthermore, the availability of P.O. boxes is probably not a linearly increasing function as implicitly assumed with the fixed provision cost per P.O. box.

7. CONCLUSIONS

Our purpose was to investigate and discuss a paradigm change in the postal value chain. We considered the question as to whom the bill for the service of the last mile should be presented, and explored the impact of combining the "Receiver Pays Principle" (RPP) with the traditional "Sender Pays Principle" (SPP) on welfare.

Our analysis leads us to the conclusion that a combination of RPP with SPP in the form of a modified two-part tariff increases overall welfare, in particular when the additional earnings and savings are redistributed to the senders. We predict an increase in mail demand, which is due to a decrease in the average stamp price stemming from the redistribution of the flat rate to the senders. Our results are based on the calibration of the demand for doorstep delivery and on the fact that we assumed a linearly increasing function for the availability of P.O. boxes. Accordingly, it is crucial to learn more about customers' perceived values and their buying patterns regarding last mile service options. Also, the implications of the introduction of RPP in a competitive environment must be further investigated.

However, the model opens the doors for mass customization in the last mile of the postal value chain. It is a starting point for seeing the recipient as a customer. Service bundles could be gradually and flexibly tailored and priced to recipients' needs. Incentives and decision making for service levels in the last mile would ultimately be transferred to those who expect and appreciate good services. Furthermore, the model provides a new and promising option for financing the universal service obligation – or, more precisely, the universal delivery obligation – of postal operators without abandoning the principle of solidarity between regions. Finally, RPP could be a suitable means of escaping from the dreaded "graveyard spiral" when it comes to a decline of mail demand. Thus, RPP could help tackling the challenges that postal operators will increasingly face in the future.

A number of questions remain unanswered, though. We hope to see postal experts launching supplementary surveys in order to help understand whether the model is indeed a viable solution for postal markets.

REFERENCES

Cohen, R. and E.H. Chu. 1997. "A Measure of Scale Economies for Postal Systems." In *Managing Change in the Postal and Delivery Industries*, edited by M.A. Crew and P.R. Kleindorfer. Boston: Kluwer Academic Publishers.

Crew, M.A. and P.R. Kleindorfer. 1991. "Rowland Hill's Contribution as an Economist." In *Competition and Innovation in Postal Services*, edited by M.A. Crew and P.R. Kleindorfer. Boston: Kluwer Academic Publishers.

De Donder, P., H. Cremer, J.P. Florens, A. Grimaud and F. Rodriguez. 2001. "Uniform Pricing and Postal Market Liberalization." In *Future Directions in Postal Reform*, edited by M.A. Crew and P.R. Kleindorfer. Boston: Kluwer Academic Publishers.

Dietl, H.M., U. Trinkner, and R. Bleisch. 2005. "Liberalization and Regulation of the Swiss Letter Market." In *Regulatory and Economic Challenges in the Postal and Delivery Sector*, edited by M.A. Crew and P.R. Kleindorfer. Boston: Kluwer Academic Publishers.

Doyle, C. and J.C. Smith. 1998. Market structure in mobile telecoms: qualified indirect access and the receiver pays principle. *Information Economics and Policy* 10: 471-488.

Elsenbast, W. 1996. *Die Infrastrukturverpflichtung im Postbereich aus Nutzersicht.* Diskussionbeitrag Nr. 162, WIK, Bad Honnef.

Hemmeon, J.C. 1912. *The History of the British Post Office*. London, Henry Frowde.

Hermalin, B.E. and M.L. Katz. 2004: "Sender or Receiver: who should pay to exchange an electronic message?" *Rand Journal of Economics* 35(3): 423-447.

Hill, R. and Hill, G.B. 1880: *The Life of Sir Rowland Hill.* London: Thos. De La Rue & Co.

Jeon, D.S., J.J. Laffont, and J. Tirole. 2004. "On the Receiver Pays Principle." *Rand Journal of Economics* 35(1): 85-110.

Kim, J.Y. and Y. Lim. 2000. "An Economic Analysis of the Receiver Pays Principle." *Information Economics and Policy* 13: 231-260.

Owen, B. and R. Willig. 1981. Economics and postal pricing. In *The Future of the Postal Service*, edited by J. Fleishman. Aspen: The Aspen Institute.

Schwarz-Schilling, C. 2001. Pricing Schemes in Liberalized Postal Markets. Presented at the Second Conference on "Competition and Universal Service in the Postal Sector," Toulouse, December 6-7.

Demand Studies

Chapter 16

Forecasting Swiss Mail Demand*

Urs Trinkner[1,2] and Martin Grossmann[1]
University of Zurich[1] and Swiss Post[2]

1. INTRODUCTION

The demand for mail is facing a great challenge. In recent years, substitutes such as e-mail and SMS (Short Message Service) have become a cheap, fast and convenient alternative. In the near future, new broadband-based services, the breakthrough of digital signatures, fully Web-based payment systems, and contracting solutions will further affect the mailing industry. In Switzerland, total addressed mail peaked in the last quarter of 2000, as shown in Figure 1. Since then, mail volumes have been shrinking. Yet it is not clear whether e-substitution has been the underlying cause or whether this was due to some other factor such as the economic slowdown in Switzerland between 2001 and 2003.

It is likely that e-substitution has the potential to change the long run trends of mail demand. In the past, in many countries, gross domestic product (GDP) could explain a large amount of the variation in mail demand. More recently, countries like the US, Finland, Sweden and the Netherlands reported that GDP is a less accurate predictor of first class mail streams. Nader (2004) concludes in his study of mail trends that "GDP and, more generally, economic activity is no longer as strong a determinant of mail volume as in the past."

---

* The views expressed in this paper are those of the authors and do not necessarily reflect the opinion of Swiss Post.

To get better insights about the e-substitution case in Switzerland we first look to the past. Using econometric modeling techniques, we analyze historical mail volume movements to identify trends and trend-breaks. Many authors have conducted such econometric studies previously. A brief summary can be found in Harding (2004). We apply a vector error correction model similar to the ones of Nankervis et al. (1995, 1999, and 2002) and Florens et al. (2002).

Figure 1: Quarterly mail demand (seasonally adjusted)

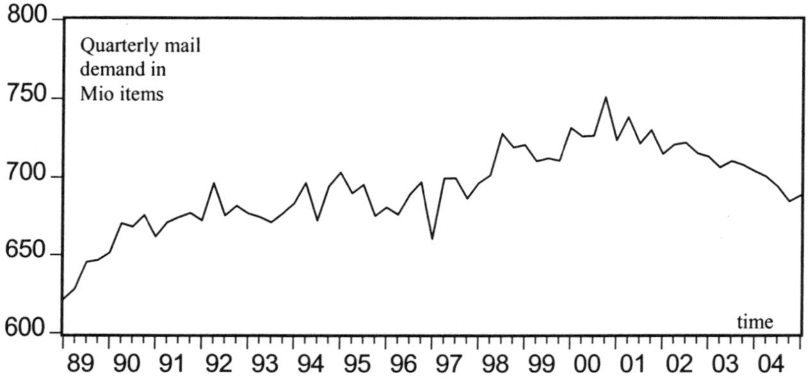

Probably all postal services assume that the various mail streams are affected in different ways by e-substitution. However, to analyze possible trend-breaks, we need long time series on mail demand. Unfortunately, such an extensive time series does not exist on individual mail streams in Switzerland. After Swiss Post introduced fast and slow mail in 1991, no distinction between mass mail and single-piece mail has been reported until 1996. Therefore, we need to analyze aggregated mail volumes in order to get a sufficiently long time series. Aggregated mail, hereafter referred to as "total traffic," includes first and second-class mail, but not unaddressed and registered mail.

Figure 2 presents the residuals of a static OLS regression of total traffic with only income (GDP) and price as explanatory variables.[1] The test statistics indicate the existence of an omitted variable. Note the autocorrelation at the end of the estimation period. The graph reveals a negative trend for the residuals after 1998. In other words, the model increasingly overestimates total traffic – a sign of e-substitution.

We proceed as follows: In Section 2, we introduce the data. Section 3 deals with possible revelations of e-substitution in time series analysis. Section 4 presents the applied error correction models including estimation

---

[1] The regression is not spurious, as the three $I(1)$ variables are cointegrated.

results. Section 5 deals with forecasting. We summarize and conclude in Section 6.

Figure 2: Residuals of static OLS regression, R^2=97%, DW=0.57

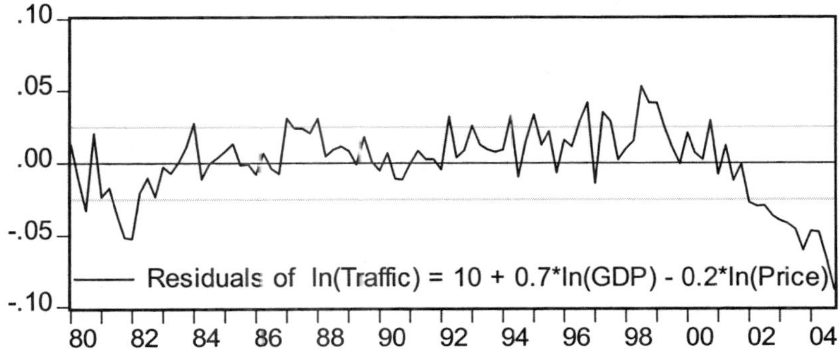

2. THE DATA

We analyzed quarterly data from 1980Q1 to 2004Q4. The main characteristics are summarized in Table 1. The last column contains the order of integration, according to the Augmented Dickey-Fuller unit root procedure.[2] Later, the order of integration will play an important role in setting up an error correction model. Traffic, GDP and all price indices are $I(1)$. Thus, the series are nonstationary, whereas their first differences $\Delta X_t = X_t - X_{t-1}$ are stationary. All the proxies for e-substitution are either $I(0)$ or $I(2)$.[3]

In the quarterly data set, the average growth in total traffic Q was about 1.7% per year. The growth rate between 1980 and 1990 was 4.1%, substantially larger than in the following decade (+1.4%). From 2000 on, the growth rate was negative (-0.9% per year). For real and nominal *GDP*, we observe a similar trend-break in the early 1990s, when Switzerland entered a recession followed by a period of low growth. GDP can be interpreted either as income or as economic activity reflecting a need for printed communication. The 'mail price index', *P*, reflects the price of a constant basket of various mail items of total traffic. The *CPI* (consumer price index) is issued by the Swiss National Bank. We use it to compute real measures and to account for inflation when regressing in nominal terms. The Swiss ministry for telecommunications has computed the

---

[2] Discussion of the theory underlying unit roots, cointegration, and tests for them, can be found in Florens (2002) or Hamilton (1994).

[3] Similar to those in Nankervis et al. (2002), the results of the unit root test for the e-proxies should be treated with caution. Some of the series start late in the data set, and some are interpolated with only a few observations.

telecommunication price index since 1993. We will call it the 'price of the substitute' (*PS*). It is a mixed index of telecommunications products including broadband Internet access prices. The series *PS* peaks in 1995 and is followed by a steady decline until 2000. Possible reasons for the decline are the various technological innovations and/or market liberalization. Important to us, the index reflects that substitutes, such as the Internet, e-mail, and SMS, became cheaper over time. However, properties of e-substitution other than price are hardly captured by *PS*. Table 1 does not list any variable for quality of service. We do not expect this variable to be a crucial point for our study because quality was never an issue in Switzerland.

Table 1: Overview of quarterly data set

Time series (in brackets shortcuts)	Data source	Average growth rate p.y.	Period of original data	Order of integration
Traffic and GDP				
Total Traffic (*Q*)	Swiss Post	1.7	1980Q1 – 2004Q4	I(1)
GDP nominal	SNB	3.9	1980Q1 – 2004Q4	I(1)
GDP real (*GDP*)	SNB	1.4	1980Q1 – 2004Q4	I(1)
Price indexes				
Mail price index real (*P*)	Swiss Post	1.3***	1980Q1 – 2004Q4	I(1)
Substitutes price index (*PS*)	BACOM	0.0	1993M5 – 2004M12	I(1)
Consumer price index (*CPI*)	SNB	2.5	1980Q1 – 2004Q4	I(1)/I(2)*
Substitution proxies				
% Active e-bankers (*eBank*)	Swiss Post		1998m9 – 2004m12	I(0)
% Internet users (*eUse*)	BFS		1994 – 2004	I(2)
% Internet buyers** (*eBuy*)	BFS		2000 – 2004	I(0)
% Broadband access** (*eBb*)	BFS		1999 – 2004	I(0)
% Overall e-index (*eIndex*)	Calculated		(artificial)	I(2)
% Mobile users (*mUse*)	BACOM		1991 - 2004	I(2)
Dummies and other				
dAB	Reflects the introduction of A- and B Post in 1991			
nDays	Deviation of number of labor days from their mean			

* I(2) due to Augmented Dickey-Fuller test, I(1) with Dickey-Fuller and Phillips-Perron tests.
** These series have been extrapolated with just a few datapoints.
*** The increase in real prices was mainly due to the introduction of first class mail and the abolishment of cross-subsidies from telecommunications products.

We did not include the substitute's price *PS* in the introductory regression. A modified static regression of the kind

$$\ln(Q) = \beta_0 + \beta_1 \ln(GDP) + \beta_2 \ln(P) + \beta_3 \ln(PS) \qquad (1)$$

reveals residuals similar to the ones in Figure 2. The main difference is that the negative trend of the residuals starts in 2000 instead of 1998. We treat this as an indication that the *PS* may not sufficiently reflect the various product innovations and increasing positive network externalities of all kinds of e-substitutes. As e-substitution cannot be measured directly, we use a set of proxy variables. Loosely speaking, a proxy is a series that is somehow related to an unavailable explanatory variable for which we would like to control (in our case for e-substitution).

Table 1 lists the proxies used in our analysis. 'Active E-Bankers' (*eBank*) contains the fraction of customers who actively use Swiss Post's E-Banking platform "Yellownet".[4] The data is available on a monthly basis. It is by far the most accurate measured proxy variable because the others are available on a semiannual basis at best, creating a need for extrapolation. Interestingly, *eBank* exhibits a constant linear trend in contrast to the other e-series, which are S-shaped (e.g., the cumulative normal distribution). The only semiannual series is the fraction of active Internet users in Switzerland (*eUse*). 'Internet Buyers' (*eBuy*) contains the percentage of the Swiss population that has used the Internet to buy goods. The data was collected on a yearly basis. The series start in 2000 with a high initial value of 23%. Because the available values have been close to the ones of eUse, we adjusted the series accordingly. The series *eBb* measures the percentage of the population with a broadband connection to access e-substitutes. Finally, the overall Index (*eIndex*) was constructed as the sum of the preceding series. The last variable *mUse* contains the fraction of the population with a mobile telephone. The proxy may reflect the substitution of mail through SMS.

3. E-SUBSTITUTION IN TIME SERIES ANALYSIS

E-substitution can reveal itself in various ways when performing time series analysis. A first form we encountered in Figure 2 where the plot revealed a negative trend for the residuals at the end of the estimation period. E-substitution is a straightforward explanation for this negative trend, as the e-proxies are highly significant when regressed against the residuals. A second and yet related indication for e-substitution could be that we cannot find a robust model over the whole time horizon without using any proxy for e-substitution.

If a model is estimated in natural logarithms, demand exhibits constant price elasticity. In equation (1), it equals parameter β_2 and is independent of Q and time. However, despite the legal monopoly of Swiss Post in the letter market, competition between physical mail and various electronic forms of written communication, such as e-mail, has evolved. In other words, one could expect increasing price elasticity and decreasing cross-price elasticity of mail demand over time. Therefore, a third way to detect e-substitution may be the estimation of model (1) over various time horizons. If price elasticity is consistently larger for samples closer to 2004, this may be a sign

---

[4] http://www.yellownet.ch

of e-substitution. Figure 2 shows the recursive estimates of equation (1) when the parameter for *GDP* (β_1) is restricted to 0.7 for all sample periods. The dotted lines represent +/- 2 standard errors[5]. 'Recursive estimates' is a procedure, in which the same equation is re-estimated for increasingly larger samples. For example, the first dot represents the estimate with a sample period from 1980Q1 to 1986Q1, whereas the last estimate has a sample period from 1980Q1 to 2004Q4. When moving to the right on the curves, the confidence bounds converge closer to the point estimates, because more observations are included in the respective estimation sample.

Figure 3: Recursive estimates yield increasing price elasticity

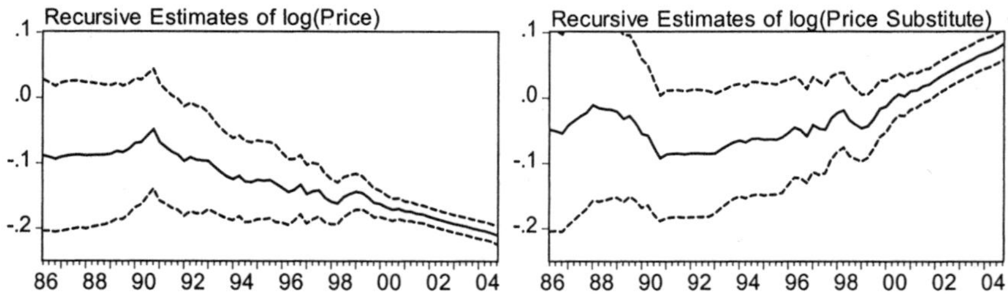

The depicted trends are in line with economic theory. With increasing competition between letters and the substitutes, prices become more important; customers get more price sensitive (price elasticity grows from -0.1 to about -0.2) and cross-price elasticity becomes significantly different from zero after 2002.

However, one of our objectives in this study is to forecast mail volumes in the near future. To do so, we need to find a robust model. This implies that it is not sufficient just to know that price elasticity may further increase over time.

4. LONG RUN MODELS FOR SWISS MAIL DEMAND

To forecast future mail demand it would be useful to know that the relation between mail demand, real GDP, and various other factors, such as price, availability, and quality of mail and its substitutes is stable. In the previous section we saw that all of the important variables are nonstationary $I(1)$ series. According to econometric theory, a long-run equilibrium relationship may exist for nonstationary series if they are cointegrated, i.e., that a stationary linear combination of the variables is $I(0)$. Under such conditions, a so-called (vector) error correction model (VEC) gives efficient

[5] A coefficient is significantly different from zero at the 95% confidence level if zero is outside the boundary.

estimates. In a VEC, the cointegrated series enter in levels.[6] The name stems from the underlying error correction mechanism shifting the equilibrium variables back to their long-run equilibrium.

We will estimate three models. The 'traditional model' does not include any of the e-proxies, whereas the two 'substitution models' do. This is the only distinction between the models. We specify for all models the same long-run dynamics such that mail demand, real GDP, and prices of mail and its substitutes represent a long-run equilibrium relationship. The Johansen Cointegration test in Table 2 indicates one cointegrating relation for all three models. If the test is performed for the four endogenous series alone, it reveals one cointegrating relation as well. We chose four lags, L, to include one year with our quarterly data.

Table 2: Unrestricted cointegration rank test

	Traditional-model		Substitution model 1		Substitution model 2	
Endogenous variables	*Q, GDP, P, PS* in natural logarithms		*Q, GDP, P, PS* in natural logarithms		*Q, GDP, P, PS* in natural logarithms	
Exogenous variables	*dAB*		*dAB, iBank*		*dAB, iUse*	
Cointegration specification	VAR and EC with constant, no trend		VAR and EC with constant, no trend		VAR and EC with constant, no trend	
Lags of VEC	4		4		4	
Johansen Cointegration test						
Null hypothesis H_0	Trace	Max E-V	Trace	Max E-V	Trace	Max E-V
0 cointegration relation	65.36*	27.53*	56.74*	38.43*	57.56*	36.27*
1 cointegration relation	21.12	21.13	18.30	10.63	21.28	16.01
2 cointegration relation	1.604	14.26	7.67	7.28	5.26	4.73

*Denotes 1 cointegrating relationship at 95% confidence level

The functional form of the VEC that corresponds to Table 2 is, for Q,

$$\begin{aligned}\Delta q_t = \alpha\overbrace{(1\cdot q_{t-1} - \beta_0 - \beta_1 gdp_{t-1} - \beta_2 p_{t-1} - \beta_3 ps_{t-1})}^{\text{Error Correction Term}} + \\ \gamma_0 + \gamma_1 dAB_t + \gamma_2 eproxy_t + \\ \sum_L \left(\gamma_{3,L}\Delta q_{t-L} + \gamma_{4,L}\Delta gdp_{t-L} + \gamma_{5,L}\Delta p_{t-L} + \gamma_{6,L}\Delta ps_{t-L}\right) + \varepsilon_t.\end{aligned} \quad (2)$$

We find the cointegrating relationship in the error correction term. If it equals 0 at some time t, we have been exactly in the long-run equilibrium in the previous period t-1 (i.e., the error term ε_{t-1} was 0). If the error correction term is nonzero, it will influence the latest prediction according to the speed of adjustment α.

---

[6] If cointegration was not found, a model in first differences would have to be specified to avoid spurious regression.

Table 3: Estimation results

Adj. sample size: 1982Q2 to 2004Q4	**Traditional model**	**E-substitution model 1**	**E-substitution model 2**
Long run equilibrium equation			
gdp (real)	1.09 [8.14]	1.10 [9.09]	1.12 [9.58]
p (real)	-0.27 [-4.12]	-0.27 [-4.52]	-0.22 [-3.53]
ps	0.17 [4.49]	0.05 [0.60]	-0.07 [-0.57]
Constant (β_0)	1.49	1.33	1.29
Short run equation			
α	0.19 [3.98]	0.13 [2.46]	0.12 [2.03]
dAB	0.00 [0.25]	-0.01 [-0.64]	-0.01 [-0.63]
eBank		-0.21 [-4.80]	
eUse			-0.09 [-4.42]
Δq t-1	-0.69 [-6.38]	-0.78 [-7.08]	-0.78 [-6.89]
t-2	-0.44 [-3.4]	-0.56 [-4.18]	-0.56 [-4.07]
t-3	-0.39 [-3.19]	-0.50 [-4.00]	-0.49 [-3.88]
t-4	-0.25 [-2.37]	-0.33 [-3.1]	-0.32 [-2.97]
Δgdp t-1	0.57 [2.07]	0.51 [1.91]	0.50 [1.84]
t-2	0.19 [0.65]	0.19 [0.67]	0.16 [0.57]
t-3	-0.02 [-0.06]	-0.05 [-0.20]	-0.06 [-0.23]
t-4	0.11 [0.43]	0.11 [0.43]	0.10 [0.40]
Δp t-1	-0.09 [-2.11]	-0.09 [-2.27]	-0.10 [-2.50]
t-2	-0.07 [-1.61]	-0.08 [-1.92]	-0.09 [-2.09]
t-3	-0.05 [-1.05]	-0.05 [-1.3]	-0.06 [-1.51]
t-4	-0.08 [-1.71]	-0.10 [-2.23]	-0.10 [-2.29]
Δps t-1	0.20 [2.21]	0.23 [2.65]	0.22 [2.51]
t-2	-0.23 [-2.41]	-0.21 [-2.25]	-0.22 [-2.39]
t-3	-0.09 [-0.86]	-0.08 [-0.81]	-0.08 [-0.87]
t-4	-0.12 [-1.25]	-0.11 [-1.23]	-0.12 [-1.28]
Constant (γ_0)	0.01 [1.23]	0.02 [2.93]	0.02 [3.99]
Test statistics			
R^2	57%	61%	60%
Adjusted R^2	46%	51%	49%
Log likelihood	271.24	275.96	274.87
F-statistic	5.26	5.86	5.63

The values in parentheses are the t-values. According to Wald tests all lags are significant and all endogenous variables satisfy Granger causation tests. Other e-proxies do not improve the model compared with eBank and eUse. We prefer them because of better data quality.

The only formal distinction between the three models lies in the choice of $eproxy_t$. In the traditional model, the term is not included at all. In the substitution models, the choice for *eproxy* will be *eBank* in Model 1, and *eUse* in Model 2.

Table 3 lists the results obtained from Johansen's two-step procedure. First, the long-run equation (the error correction term in (2)) is estimated. Thereby, the parameter of q is normalized to one. In a second step, the remaining parameters in equation (2) are computed.[7]

[7] We used Eviews for our computations in which the procedure is implemented.

The goodness of fit (R^2) of the three models is acceptable.[8] A graphical fit is shown in Section 4 In general, the coefficients have signs as expected and values that are in line with previous studies. The long-run price elasticity is highly significant and ranges between -0.22 and -0.27. This tells us that a 10% increase in price will reduce total traffic between 2.2 and 2.7% in the long run. However, the speed of adjustment α seems to be quite small and it is not clear, *a priori*, what the adjustment dynamics are. Figure 4 depicts the effect of a hypothetical 10% price increase at the beginning of year 2000 according to substitution model 1. The loss in volume converges to the prediction of the long-run price elasticity (as shown by the dotted line) after about three years. One would expect demand to be more price sensitive.[9]

Figure 4: Demand shock after a 10% price increase

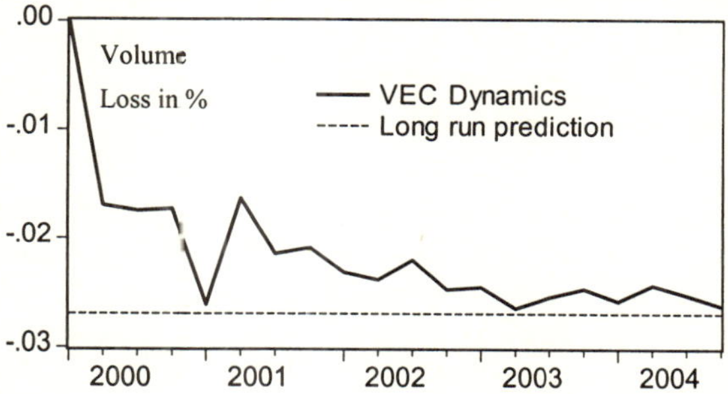

The main coefficient difference between the models is the long run elasticity of the substitutes' price *PS*; whereas the short run impact of a change in the *PS* is about the same among the three models, the long run effect is significant only in the traditional model. At the same time, the two e-proxies in the substitution models are highly significant. It appears that once *eBank* and *eUse* are included in the model, they provide a better approximation than the substitutes' price index does. An interpretation may be that the choice between writing a letter and sending an e-mail or SMS is dominated by other product properties than price.

---

8 If the same model is estimated with data that was not seasonally adjusted, R^2 and adjusted R^2 are between 97% and 99% when seasonal dummies are included. The large difference to the values given in Table 3 stems from the predictive power of the seasonal dummies. Without the seasonal adjustment, most of the variation in mail demand is caused by seasonality, which is well explained by quarterly dummies. To illustrate, a static regression for Q with only a constant, a trend, and quarterly dummies yields an adjusted R^2 of 84%.

9 See Cazals et al. (2002) for a theoretical treatment, of why time series models exhibit often lower elasticities than cross-section models.

5. FORECASTING FUTURE MAIL DEMAND

How do the three models predict future mail demand? One general possibility for forecasting with a time series model is to solve the previously estimated static model with one's own or a third party's expectations about future realizations of the independent variables for every t in the forecasting horizon $t+1 \ldots T$. This approach leads to two kinds of forecasting error: (1) erroneous expectations, e.g., the assumption of future GDP growth proves to be under- or overestimated; and (2) specification error of the previously estimated model. A second general possibility for time-series forecasting is to estimate a dynamic model in lags, so no expectations about future values of explanatory variables are necessary, at least for the one-step-ahead forecast at $t+1$. Either way, the forecasting interval for a given confidence level increases with the length of the forecasting horizon.

In order to predict with our vector error correction model we need to mix the two ways to some extent. Note that equation (2) does not include any values of the endogenous variables at time t. Thus, for predicting mail demand for the next period $t+1$, the model does not build on GDP_{t+1}: it only uses GDP_t. This property is useful for performing one-step-ahead forecasts because the model needs observed values of the endogenous variables only. Even multi-step-ahead forecasts are possible without making any forecast of the explanatory variables. To explain this, we return to equation (2). The complete VEC specification includes analogous equations for the other endogenous variables *GDP*, *P*, and *PS*. Thus, to perform a forecast for time $t+2$, we can use the predicted endogenous values from $t+1$. However, we still need to make our own expectations of the two exogenous e-proxies.

Both kinds of forecasts were carried out. The first kind is done by treating all endogenous variables, other than total traffic, as exogenous[10]. Thus, we need to predict all the explanatory variables manually. For nominal GDP, we assume 1.8% growth per year. Further, we assume nominal price stability of postal prices, and we extrapolate *CPI*, *PS*, *eBank* and *eUse* according to their past trends.[11] We solve the model stochastically to obtain confidence bounds. The results for the forecasting period from 1990Q1 to 2007Q4 are shown in Figures 5a, 6a, and 7a. The dotted line is the one-step confidence bound. From 1990Q1 to 2004Q4, the predicted values represent the model fit during the estimation period. The observations from 2005Q1 to 2007Q4 show the forecasts for the out-of-sample period. Observation 2005Q1 deserves special attention. It is the

---

[10] This means that ΔQ_{t+2} is computed with our own expectation of GDP_{t+1} instead of the VEC prediction $G\hat{D}P_{t+1}$.

[11] Taken all together, this is quite a large set of assumptions.

most recent realization of total traffic and enables an indicative reality check of the estimated models.

Figures 5b, 6b, and 7b show the results from the endogenous stochastic solution of the model, i.e., only *eBank* and *eUse* are determined outside the model. The forecasting period starts in 2005Q1. The dotted lines represent the multi-step confidence bounds. Note that the solution does not account for coefficient uncertainty in linked equations.

Figure 5a: Exogenous predictions TM

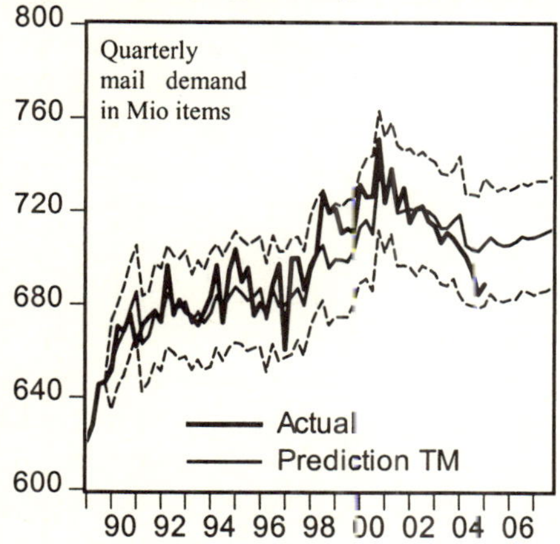

Figure 5b: Endogenous

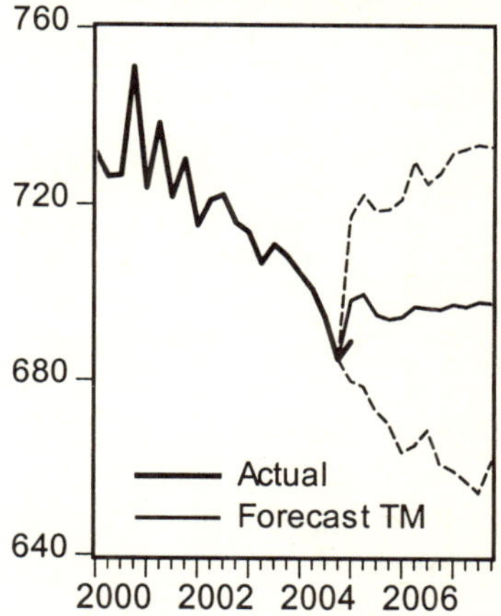

The traditional model (TM) gives by far the most optimistic scenario for future mail demand. According to the model's results shown in Figures 5a and 5b, mail demand has now entered a period of low but positive growth. Figure 5b reveals that the model fit for the realization 2005Q1 is not as good as those obtained from the substitution models. On the other hand, the predictions for the other endogenous variables are by far the most realistic ones (not shown here).

The most pessimistic outlook is given by substitution model 1 (SM1). According to the model, the decline in aggregate mail demand will continue at an accelerated speed (Figure 6b). The one-step-ahead forecast for 2005Q4 is quite accurate. However, the predicted dynamics for the other exogenous variables are quite unrealistic. According to the endogenous solution, Switzerland will enter a heavy recession soon.

Substitution model 2 (SM2) lies somewhere in between the other two. The exogenous solution states that the decline is slowing down (Figure 7a). The fit at 2005Q1 is almost perfect. In the endogenous model, the forecasts for GDP are again very pessimistic. This can be seen indirectly by comparing Figure 7a with Figure 7b; the decline is more severe in 7b, because the endogenous forecast for GDP is much lower than our expectation of 1.8% growth.

Figure 6a: Exogenous predictions SM1

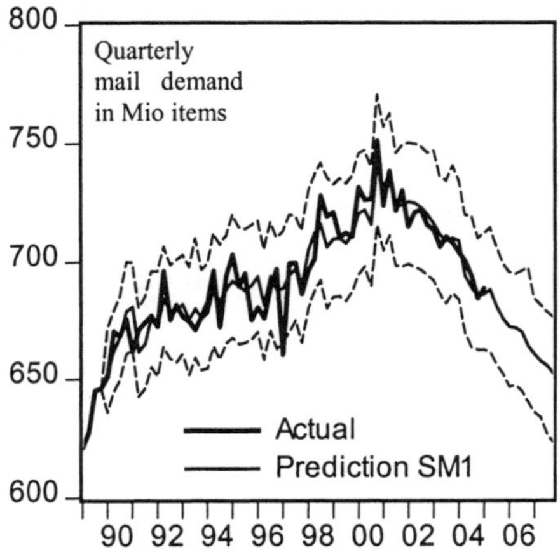

Figure 6b: Endogenous

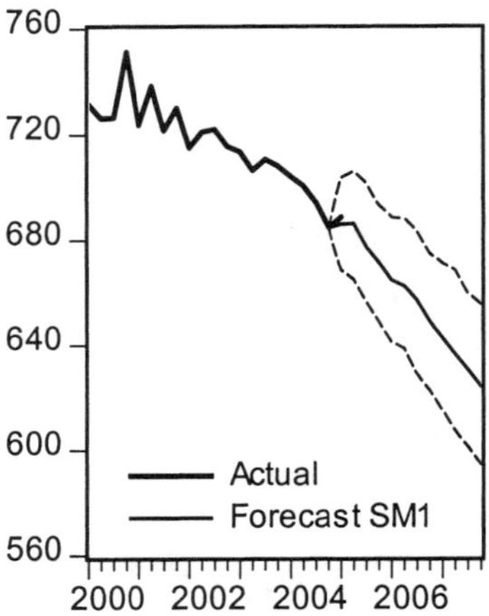

Figure 7a: Exogenous predictions SM2

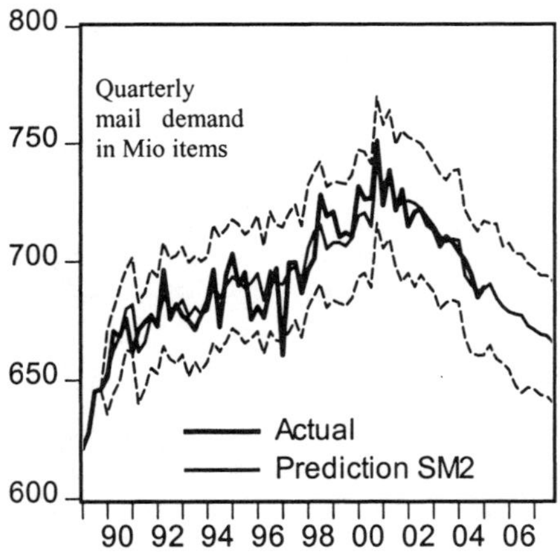

Figure 7b: Endogenous

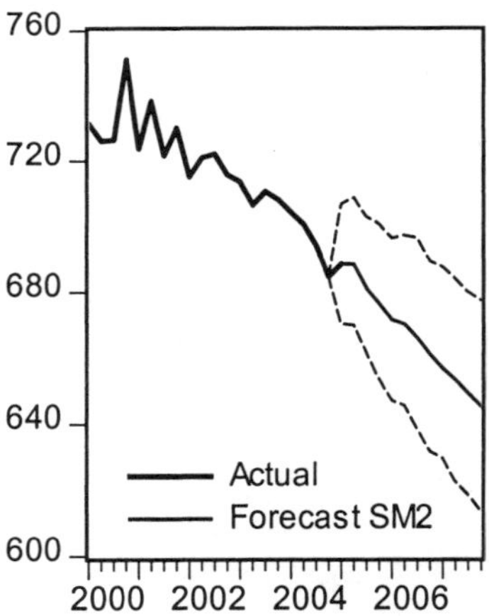

Comparing fit and forecast of the three models, each one has its own pros and cons. The traditional model exhibits the poorest fit, especially towards the end of the estimation period. As a direct consequence, the forecast performance at 2005Q1 is poor. Nevertheless, the endogenous predictions of GDP and prices seem to be the most realistic ones. Both substitution models predict an unrealistic negative development of future GDP. Still, they provide a better fit and a better one-step-ahead forecast.

6. DISCUSSION AND CONCLUSIONS

E-substitution is one of the most crucial issues in the postal industry. Most postal services heavily depend on their core business of delivering physical mail – once the only form of advanced long distance communication. The primary threat of e-substitution lies in the historical business model of most postal services. Over time, larger mail volumes increased economies of scale and enabled the postal services to keep postal rates low despite increasing labor costs and better service provision. A comparison between the development of real wages and real postal rates illustrates the historical postal business model. Whereas real wages grew exponentially, Swiss Post's real rates are today even lower than in the 1920s. E-substitution questions the stability of this business model. Moreover, the 'political universal service model' builds on growth of mail demand. The remarkable growth over the past 100 years enabled politicians to impose demanding service obligations on the postal services, i.e., nationwide coverage of home delivery, without undermining the financial viability of the postal service. Consequently, e-substitution also brings into question the stability of the political universal service model.

The intent of our research was to forecast future mail volumes and thereby to assess future e-substitution. We estimated three vector error correction models with quarterly data of Swiss aggregate mail demand. We found strong evidence that e-substitution has happened in the past few years. Moreover, two of the three models indicate that e-substitution will continue to undermine mail demand in the short and medium term. For the long term, we dare no prediction; we conclude that it is nearly impossible to make long-run forecasts with the applied techniques, because there is no unique proxy for e-substitution. Every such proxy yields another result, and combining or merging different proxies brings the same set of problems (or makes it even impossible to find a cointegrated long-run relationship). In addition, we do not know what kind of new substitutes will emerge in the near future and whether these substitutes are represented in our current proxies.[12]

Despite these limitations for long forecasting horizons, the short-run predictions seem to be accurate. Here we see the strengths of vector error correction models. They are powerful tools for forecasting the near future because they combine explanatory variables in levels, differences, and lags and still provide an economic interpretation of the results.

Inevitably, we do not know how severely e-substitution will affect mail volumes in the future. However, our model predictions are not optimistic,

[12] Other econometric methods such as discrete choice analysis could resolve the problem. Nonetheless, we believe that the design of a survey with choices over hypothetical e-products would cause similar problems as e-proxies do here.

ranging from accelerated decline to slow growth. We therefore recommend that postal services do not rely solely on their historical business models and that they prepare for the worst. In fact, many operators have initiated projects to respond to this uncertainty, e.g. with diversification into new product lines and with programs to make costs more responsive to (potentially declining) demand conditions. A key issue going forward will be for politicians and regulators to find universal service policies that do not increase the universal service provider's fixed costs.

REFERENCES

Cazals, C., and J-P. Florens. 2002. "Econometrics of Mail Demand." In *Postal and Delivery Services: Delivering on Competition*, edited by M.A. Crew and P.R. Kleindorfer. Boston: Kluwer Academic Publishers.

Florens, J-P., S. Marcy, and J. Toledano. 2002. "Mail Demand in the Long and Short Term." In *Postal and Delivery Services: Pricing, Productivity, Regulation and Strategy*, edited by M.A. Crew and P.R. Kleindorfer. Boston: Kluwer Academic Publishers.

Harding, M.C. 2005. "Mail Demand Models." Paper presented at the CRRI - Rutgers University's 13th Conference on Postal and Delivery Economics, Antwerp, June 4-7, 2005. Available at http://www.postinsight.pb.com.

Hamilton, J.D. 1994. *Time Series Analysis*. Princeton, NJ: Princeton University Press.

Nader, F. H. 2004. Mail Trends. Available at http://www.postinsight.pb.com.

Nankervis, J., and F. Rodriguez. 1995. "Aggregate Letter Traffic Demand in the United Kingdom and the Economy." In *Commercialization of Postal and Delivery Services*, edited by M.A. Crew and P.R. Kleindorfer. Boston: Kluwer Academic Publishers.

Nankervis, J., I. Carslake, and F. Rodriguez. 1999. "How Important Have Price and Quality of Service Been to Mail Volume Growth?" In *Emerging Competition in Postal and Delivery Services*, edited by M.A. Crew and P.R. Kleindorfer. Boston: Kluwer Academic Publishers.

Nankervis, J., S. Richard, S. Soteri, and F. Rodriguez. 2002. "Disaggregated Letter Traffic Demand in the UK." In *Postal and Delivery Services: Pricing, Productivity, Regulation and Strategy*, edited by M.A. Crew and P.R. Kleindorfer. Boston: Kluwer Academic Publishers.

Chapter 17

Generational Analysis of Mail Users*

Luis Jimenez, Elena Diakova, and Chrystal Szeto
Pitney Bowes

1. INTRODUCTION

The anticipated decline in the intensity of mail use by younger consumers belonging to the more recent generations is a commonly held conjecture. This belief is largely based on assumptions about the technological adroitness of younger consumers, which would seemingly drive them to electronic media and away from mail. The belief is also based on a perceived lack of preference of young people for paper media. Unfortunately, neither of these beliefs has been documented empirically, although it is broadly accepted that few person-to-person letters are being written. In contrast, studies show that future mail growth will be determined not by consumer-originated mail patterns, but primarily by business-to-consumer mail, over which consumers have little control. Advertisers, service providers and financial firms target consumers based upon the recipient's unique demographic characteristics, including age and income. However, research that identifies and quantifies a "generational effect" on the volume of mail received has not been available to date. This paper addresses the question: How much mail has been historically received by various age groups across time and what appear to be the determinants of

* The authors are indebted to Yohanna Suczek, Manager, Strategy Projects for an early draft of this paper, and to Shawn Flynn, Senior Analyst, for valuable input throughout the paper. The authors also appreciate the comments of Dr. Alan Robinson during his discussion of the paper at CRRI – Rutgers University's 13th Conference on Postal and Delivery Economics in Antwerp, June 2005.

mail receipt by generation of the recipient? The paper's analysis and conclusions rest on a wide-ranging review of the relevant literature, a statistical analysis of mail use by 31 cohorts[1] of adult U.S. households over the period 1987-2003, and the preliminary application of a demographic simulation model under development.

2. PAST PREDICTIONS ABOUT TECHNOLOGY ADOPTION

As technology improves, consumers are given greater choices about the methods by which they choose to send and receive information. Since the first radio transmission in 1895, entire generations have matured, each growing up with increasingly greater communications choices. Those who were ten-year olds in 1974, the year of the release of the Altair home computer, had no idea that their Millennial generation[2] counterparts would spend hours each day surfing the web and communicating via text message. Conversely, today's Millennials cannot likely envision a world without Internet-enabled instant messaging through their mobile telephones.

Just as it is difficult to predict future technology use, we suggest that it is also difficult to predict how future generations will use mail. Robust prediction models of communications media use have not, to our knowledge, been developed. Nevertheless, numerous previous attempts have been made to predict the fate of established media as new media have arrived.

When television was introduced, critics predicted the end of "radio, reading, conversation, and the patterns of family living" (The Future of Children, 2000). Others predicted that young people would abandon the cinema for television (Lee, 2000). Clearly, cinema, radio, reading, conversation, and traditional patterns of family living endure today although several waves of new technologies have since been introduced and adopted by consumers.

Even technology vanguards admit that it is difficult to predict the trajectory of technology. Intel's cofounder, Robert Noyce, once said in 1976:

> *Ten years ago [1966] it would have been difficult to predict that the calculator would displace the slide rule. Today, it is equally as difficult to predict what displacements are in store for the next decade or two. The capabilities of the microcomputer system, which can be purchased for the*

---

1 Cohorts are intact groups of people whose behavior can be tracked over time. Since our source used sample data for various age groups over time, our 'cohorts' are not as they are traditionally defined.

2 The Millennial generation includes those born between 1982 and 2001.

price of an automobile, are comparable to that of a medium-scale computer of a decade ago. And tomorrow the personal computer could become as much a necessity to the individual consumer as the automobile is today. ... With the proliferation of readily available inexpensive computing power, we can expect drastic changes in the future. [3]

Noyce predicted that by 2001, devices called auto-typewriters would largely displace the U.S. Postal Service, since the user's "completed letter is automatically typed out on the addressee's typewriter" (Olson, 2003). Although the "auto-typewriter" has yet to be invented, even the closest functional approximation to this device, email, has not materially eroded use of the U.S. Postal Service.

One reason why traditional media endure is because advertisers embrace new technologies by adding them to their existing media portfolio, co-consuming the new and the existing media (Media Info Center, 2004; Diakova, 2005). Simultaneously, existing media evolve to accommodate the new media. For example, even though the Internet has enabled users to send documents to each other free of charge, the facsimile machine has not disappeared. Fax machines are mainly used today to transmit documents that require legally binding signatures.[4]

Studies have shown that even children who have come of age in the digital world do not readily substitute traditional activities such as making telephone calls or listening to the radio with their more recent online equivalents. A US study found that only 4.1% of youngsters aged 15 to 17 had used the Internet to make a telephone call, while 63.8% of them had used the Internet to instant message, an activity whose purpose is largely different from that of a telephone call (US Department of Education, 2003).

Based on the theory of *functional equivalence*, this movement of social interaction and communication toward computers and the Internet should produce a measurable shift away from older communication technologies (Robinson, Kestnbaum, Neustadtl, and Alvarez, 2002). Generations of youth appear to adopt new technology by reallocating their time to the technology and medium most appropriate for each activity. Over time, older technologies cease competing for time in activities where they do not possess functional advantages and specialize in certain activities. However, most technological innovations do not do everything better than the old. As a result, every time a new communication tool is introduced, some people

---

3 Obtained via Olson, Sander (2003).

4 The validity of fax signatures is not generally questioned, but it has never been challenged in U.S. courts. Thus, there is a lack of legislative history that upholds their legality as a precedent that could be used in future litigation, should a recipient question the validity of the signature on a document, such as on an insurance policy, for example.

adopt and actively use it in combination with the old medium, whereas others stick to established communication tools (Chopra, 2005a,b).

3. LIFE-STAGE FACTOR AS AN INDICATOR OF MAIL RECEIVED

It is important to understand how the plethora of new communications media will affect the consumption patterns of future generations. Currently, the youngest adult consumers belong to the Millennial generation, born between 1982 and 2001 (Table 1). The generation born just prior to the Millennial generation is Gen X, or the Thirteenth generation. The members of this generation were born between 1961 and 1981. Baby Boomers from the Boom generation were born between 1943-1960, and prior to them were born the members of the Silent generation (Strauss and Howe, 1991). As each generation ages, the unique experiences of each generation shape its attitudes towards various life stage events and, as a result, each generation possesses a distinctive sense of self.

Table 1. Living American Generations

Living American Generations	Birth Years
Millennial	1982-2001
Gen X (Thirteenth)	1961-1981
Boom	1943-1960
Silent	1925-1942
G.I.	1901-1924
Lost	1983-1900

Source: Strauss and Howe, 1991

Generational affiliation and income are also determinants of whether a group grew up with technology. For instance, the 24 year-olds in the 18-24 year old group of 2004 were born in 1980. When they entered grade school in 1986, household PC penetration rates were around 20% (Technology Futures, 2002). By the time this segment of the population graduated from college and entered the workforce in 2003, household PC penetration had reached 75% (eMarketer, 2005b). Students of this group that grew up in high-income, technology-optimistic households likely had even earlier access to PCs at home or in wealthier school districts as initiatives adopted in the 80s provided school children with access to computers.

One might expect that consumers within the same generation would have a different mail experience based on their different experiences with technologies. However, the type of mail that a consumer receives is determined by his relevant demographic characteristics, including age, income, economic activity and life stage. As we shall show then, the recipient's adroitness with technology within a generational group has no incidence in the amount of mail he receives.

We have not found any studies or surveys that directly measure how youth allocate time for communication and social interaction between technologies such as telephone, e-mail and mail, nor have we found any complete studies comparing use of various communications tools by different age groups and generations. There are no studies that track and compare, for example, the computer, telephone and mail usage patterns of Boomers, Gen X'ers and Millennials as they mature. In contrast, an analysis of the USPS annual Household Diary studies that track changes in mail volumes from 1987 to 2003 provides the only solid data with which to study the mail receipt behaviors across generations.[5]

The USPS Household Diary study provides year-by-year weekly per-household mail volume in pieces by age of householder between 1987 and 2003. The graphical data in Figure 1 shows some minor variation within age groups over the period of the study. However, the long-term trend indicates stable patterns over the entire period of the survey. For Total Mail Volume, age of householder appears to be a reliable predictor of household mail consumption (Szeto, 2005).

Figure 1. Weekly Pieces per HH – Total Volume Mail Received by Age Groups Over Time

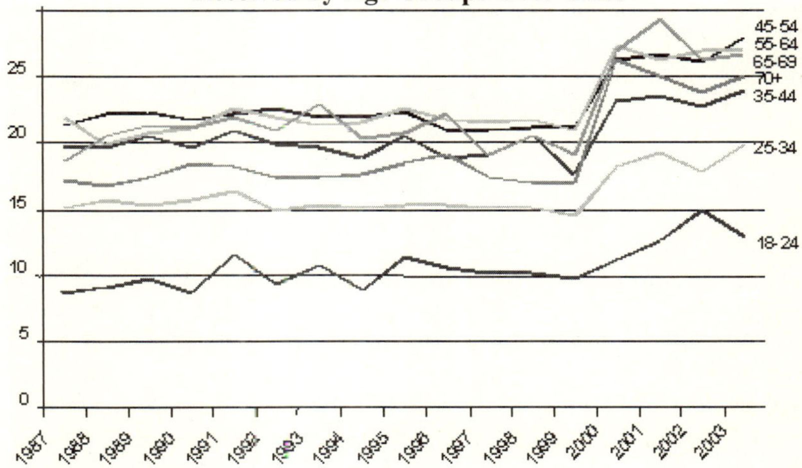

Source: USPS Household Diary, 1987-2003[6]

---

[5] The USPS Household Mail Diary study has been conducted annually since 1987. The annual sample size is approximately 5,000 US households. The small sample size and the relatively small historical base make the conclusions offered through this analysis preliminary and subject to additional verification.

[6] All data sets are available from the authors by request.

The significant increase in total mail volume from 1999 to 2000 across all householder age groups can be attributed to favorable economic conditions in the United States. To eliminate any exogenous factors such as the stage of economic cycle or postal rate increase that could influence mail growth or decline and compare only what happened between age groups and generations, the first step was to establish the Mail Volume per Household for each householder age group over the Mail Volume per Average Household. Using these normalized data we were then able to track how per-household mail volume received by each age group fares over time (Figure 2).

Figure 2. Total Mail Volume per HH Relative to Average Mail Volume per HH

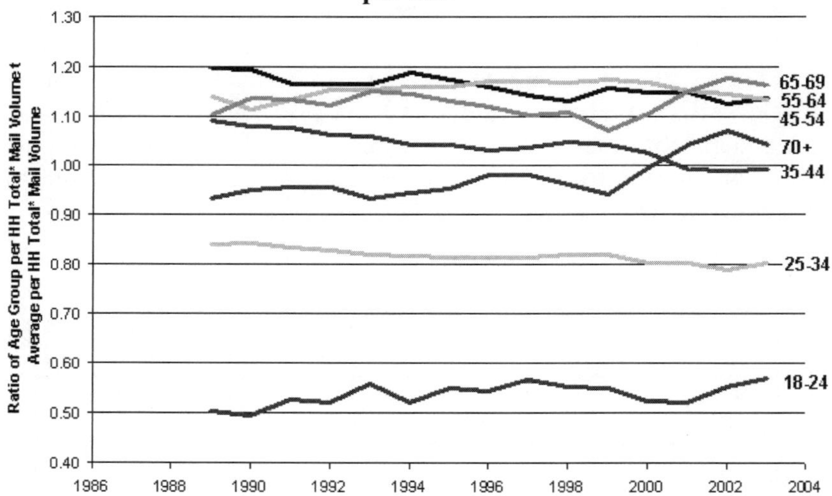

Source: Pitney Bowes analysis based on USPS Household Diary data, 1987-2003

The distribution of mail among age groups has remained consistent: young households (headed by people aged 18-24) receive, on average, approximately 0.55 pieces of mail for every 1 piece of mail received by a household headed by a 35-44 year-old. As the head of the household ages, his household's mail usage approaches the average. The consumer's peak mail consumption age is 45-54; these consumers receive roughly 15% more mail than that received by a household headed by a 35-44 year-old. As these household heads continue to age, their consumption gradually decreases until it again approaches the average.

To develop the analysis further, we identified 31 "cohorts" in the data available to us (Table 2). Each cohort is a group of people who are in a certain age group (e.g., 25-34 in 1987) and over time transition to a different age group in a different year in the future (in this case, they move to the 35-44 age group in 1997, or 10 years later). We call this group Gen X (10) because its members are of Generation X and it is the tenth cohort from that generation that we can track in our data.

Table 2. Cohort Grouping [7]

	1987	1988	1989	1990	1991	1992	1993	1994	1995	1996	1997	1998	1999	2000	2001	2002	2003
18-24	GenX (1)	GenX (2)	GenX (3)	GenX (4)	GenX (5)	GenX (6)	GenX (7)	GenX (8)	GenX (9)	GenX (9A)							
25-34	GenX (10)	GenX (11)	GenX (12)	GenX (13)	GenX (14)	GenX (15)	GenX (16)	GenX (1)	GenX (2)	GenX (3)	GenX (4)	GenX (5)	GenX (6)	GenX (7)	GenX (8)	GenX (9)	GenX (9A)
35-44	Boom (1)	Boom (2)	Boom (3)	Boom (4)	Boom (5)	Boom (6)	Boom (6A)				GenX (10)	GenX (11)	GenX (12)	GenX (13)	GenX (1) & (14)	GenX (2) & (15)	GenX (3) & (16)
45-54	Silent (1)	Boom (7)	Boom (8)	Boom (9)	Boom (10)	Boom (11)	Boom (12)				Boom (1)	Boom (2)	Boom (3)	Boom (4)	Boom (5)	Boom (6)	Boom (6A)
55-64											Silent (1)	Boom (7)	Boom (8)	Boom (9)	Boom (10)	Boom (11)	Boom (12)

Source: Pitney Bowes analysis based on USPS Household Diary data, 1987-2003

Each age group whose mail volume received could be measured over at least 2 points in time was identified as a cohort. Thirty-one cohorts were identified as shown in Table 2. Using these groupings, one can compare variations in mail volume per household between different cohorts as they move from one age group to the next. Figure 3 clearly shows the remarkable similarities in mail consumption behavior between cohorts. Although there is some variation in mail volumes between cohorts, each cohort falls within a relatively consistent range across all age transitions and the analysis strongly suggests that it is life stage (i.e., age group), and not generation, that determines mail reception patterns.

If there were a generational effect on mail received, then one would observe that households headed by people from earlier generations would receive, on average, more mail than later generations. For example, households from Gen X (2) who were in the age group 18-24 in 1988 and moved to the age group 25-34 in 1995 should have received on average more mail than households from Gen X (8), who were in the age group 18-24 in 1995 and in the age group 25-34 in 2001. In this case we should observe a monotonically decreasing slope instead of the random slope illustrated in Figure 4.

Figure 3. Comparison of Total Mail Volume per HH Relative to Average Mail Volume per HH as Cohorts Age[8]

[7] Key to Age Cohort Groupings: To follow members of an age group (cohort) as they move from one age group to another over time, select a cohort e.g., GenX (10) that is 25-34 yrs old in 1987. This same group will be in the next age group, 35-44, in 1997. However, the USPS source data does not break age groups into even 10 year or 5 year groups but rather creates one 7-yr group (18-24s), followed by four 10-yr groups, then one 5-yr group (65-69) and then an all others (70+). The result is overlapping 7-yr and 10-yr cycles.

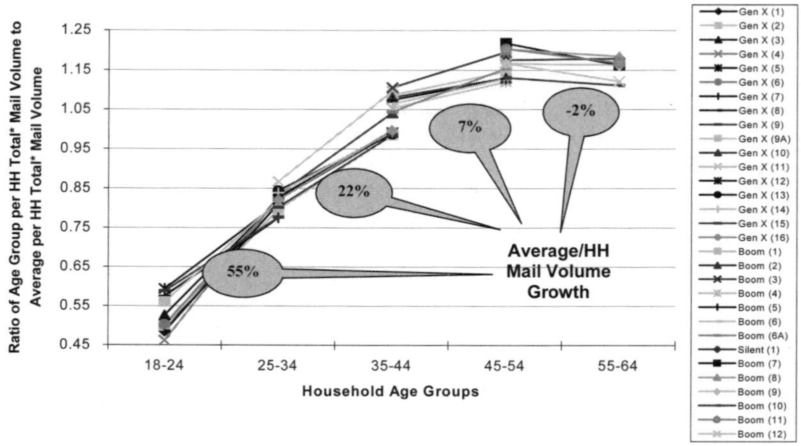

Source: Pitney Bowes analysis based on USPS Household Diary, 1987-2003

Figure 4. Actual Changes in Mail Volume Received by Gen X Households as They Aged from 18 - 24 to 25 – 35

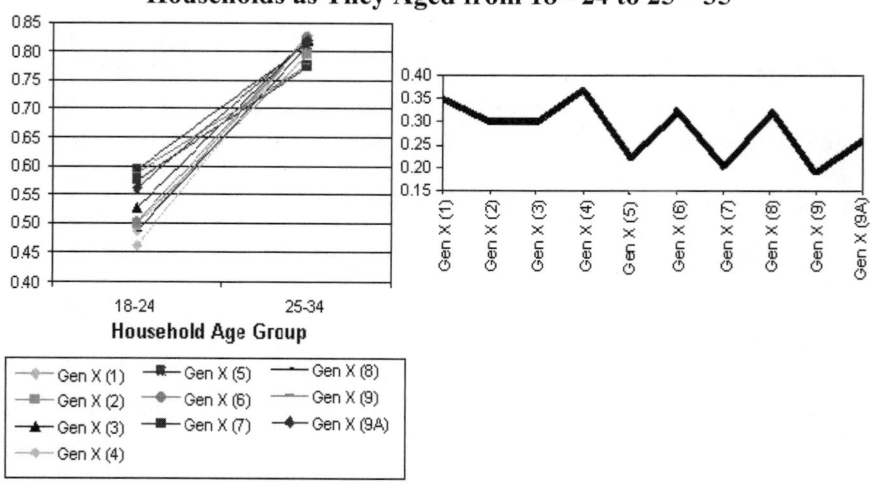

Source: Pitney Bowes analysis based on USPS Household Diary data, 1987-2003

However, actual data shows that there is no pattern of increase or decrease in mail volume received by age groups based on the years in which its members were born (Figure 4). For example, within a single generation the increases in mail volumes compared to average for cohorts Gen X (1)-Gen X (9A) as they move from the 18-24 age group to the 25-34 age group, stay within a 0.19-0.37 range and there is no pattern in the rates of change of

[8] Please see Szeto (2005) on www.postinsight.com for color-coded chart and cohort distribution across various age groups.

cohorts' mail receipt across years. The trend holds across all age groups. However, one cannot make the same comparison across generations, since only a limited seventeen-year data set is available, whereas a generation is characterized by a period of approximately twenty years.

Life stage, not generation-based, mail consumption patterns hold not only for the total mail volume, but also for all mail classes: First Class mail, Periodical mail, and Standard A mail[9]. For example, Figure 5 shows how First Class mail volume received by a household changes as the head of household ages. As a result, even though the percentage of change is different across various mail segments and household age groups, the age of householder can be one of the factors used in a model to determine mail volume received.

Figure 5. Comparison of per HH First Class Mail Volume Relative to Average per HH First Class Mail Volume as Cohorts Age[10]

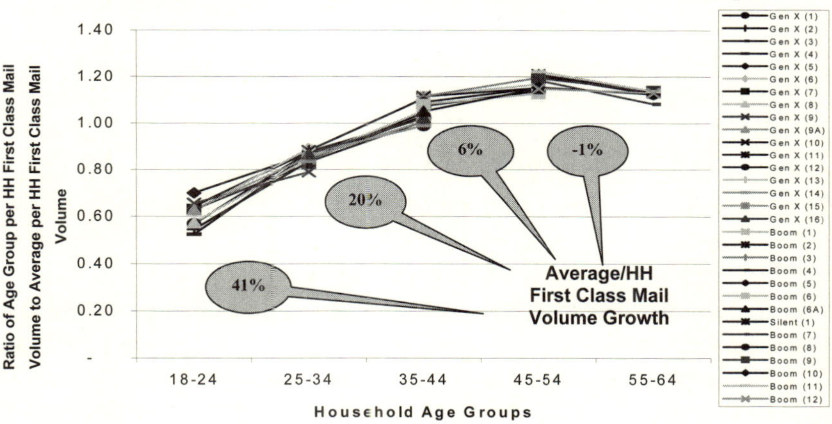

Source: Pitney Bowes analysis based on USPS Household Diary data, 1987-2003.

4. AGE OF POPULATION AS A PREDICTOR OF MAIL DEMAND

The previous analysis shows that although there is some variation in mail volumes between generational cohorts, each cohort's mail receipt volume falls within a relatively consistent range across all age transitions. Each cohort has a unique mailing experience, but this experience is correlated to a larger trend that is age related. Thus, we analyzed the data to assess if we

---

9 See extended Szeto (2005) on www.postinsight.com for findings for Periodical and Standard A mail segments.

10 Please see Szeto (2005) on www.postinsight.com for the color-coded chart and cohort distribution across various age groups.

could predict the volume of mail to be received by any one group based on the volume of mail received by its predecessor. A model with a single variable, *the actual mail volume received by the household age group 18-24*, has R^2 of 0.55 and thus explains 55 percent of *the actual mail volume received by the householder age group 35-44* (Table 3). In the regression both the intercept and coefficient terms are statistically significant, with a t-ratio of more than +/- 2.

Table 3. Summary of Fit: Response -Actual Mail Volume Received by HH in 35-44 Age Group Based on Predictor - Actual Volume Received by HH in 18-24 Age Group

R^2	0.56
R^2 Adj	0.53
Root Mean Square Error	1.27
Mean of Response	20.52
Observations	17

Source: Pitney Bowes analysis based on USPS Household Diary data, 1987-2003

When the authors conducted a multiple regression analysis to predict how much mail would be received by 35-44 year old householders based on the volume received by those in the 18-24 and 25-34 age groups, R^2 increased to 0.88, indicating that 88 percent of the variation in actual total mail volume received by the 35-44 age group can be explained by the volume received by the two age groups that immediately preceded it (Table 4).

Table 4. Summary of Fit: Actual Mail Volume Received by HH in the 35-44 Age Group Based on Predictors - the Volume Received by HH in the 18-24 and 25-34 Age Groups

R^2	0.88
R^2 Adj	0.86
Root Mean Square Error	0.69
Mean of Response	20.52
Observations	17

Source: Pitney Bowes analysis based on USPS Household Diary data, 1987-2003

However, the amount of mail received by households headed by a person aged 18-24 does not have a statistically significant influence on the response variable – the amount of mail that households received when headed by a person aged 35-44 (t- ratio is less than +/- 2 and thus the variable is not statistically significant after taking into account all the other variables.). This could be a result of a co-linearity among predictors, which is correlation between predictors in a regression model.[11] Although this study exhausts

---

[11] The scatter plot matrix shows strong linear relationships. The data and the summary of multivariate correlations analysis are available from the authors by request.

USPS Household Diary data, it should be noted that the data set is limited to a 17-year span with significant cohort overlap (e.g., the Gen X (1) cohort and Gen X (2) cohort share ~85% membership).

To eliminate any exogenous factors and compare only what happened between age groups and generations, the analysis was repeated using *the comparison of per household mail volume relative to average per household mail volume* instead of *the actual mail volume received by the household in any age group*. The result was not so impressive. Using the single variable *mail volume received by a household at 18-24 age group compared to average mail volume received by a household* in the regression, the model explains only 2% of mail volume received by households at the 35-44 age group compared to average mail volume received per household. One possible explanation for this result is that individually, the age and generational membership of the householder may not be factors that significantly influenced mail consumption.

By searching for other variables affecting mail consumption, the authors added one more predictor to the model - *the average income of a household at a particular age group*. Historically, economic activity has been the best indicator of household mail receipt volumes and it is affected by several factors, including household income and life stage of the mail recipient. Household income is tied closely with the life stage of the householder and reflects all activities in which people participate at particular points of their lives. A consumer's economic activity has been shown to increase until he reaches approximately 54 years of age. A UK Daily Telegraph article describes the years between 45 and 54 as the "discerning years," years when a consumer's tastes are at its "most extravagant" and can be likewise sated due to the departure of children from the family home (Barrows, 2005). Conversely, the years between ages 18 to 24 are the "burning years," years when money is disproportionately spent on leisure items. Although the proportion of income spent on leisure is great, the total money spent is relatively small.

The addition of the income factor produces completely different results. The R^2 has been increased to 61% and the income factor has a t-ratio of more than -/+ 2 (Table 5), whereas the comparison of the per household mail volume relative to the average per household mail volume factor remains statistically insignificant. Moreover, the model, which contains only the average income of a household at a particular age group as a predictor, has R^2 of 0.60. After running several regressions to predict mail volume based on average income of a household at a particular age group, the same pattern was observed: although the R^2 can vary, the total household incomes of householders at various age groups are statistically significant factors in predicting mail volumes received by households.

Table 5. Summary of Fit: Response - Mail Received by HH 35-44 Age Group Compared to Average Mail Volume based on the Predictors- the Average Income of HH at 35-44 Age Group and Mail Received by HH at 25-34 Age Group Compared to Average Mail Volume

R^2	0.61
R^2 Adj	0.56
Root Mean Square Error	0.03
Mean of Response	1.04
Observations	17

Source: Pitney Bowes analysis based on USPS Household Diary, 1987-2003 and US Census Bureau, 2005a data

Unfortunately, due to the way the data has been collected, it cannot be concluded whether or not the rates of adoption of various technologies among different generations are statistically significant factors influencing the mail volume. Fortunately for future analysis, data already collected includes mail use data preceding and following the introduction of personal computers and in-home consumer Internet. As the USPS collects and publishes mail-received information by households headed by the Millennial generation, particularly those who grew up with ubiquitous computer and Internet access, we can compare mail received by those cohorts with these of pre and post-PC Gen X cohorts.

Analysis of the data collected thus far shows no generational effect. Although the authors are limited by the 17-year data set, analysis shows that the average income of a household at a particular age group is a significant factor in predicting mail volume received by a household. Barring significant changes in income-based targeted advertising methods, mail receipt will not be significantly affected by generational affiliation.

5. DEMOGRAPHIC SIMULATION MODEL

Assuming that business processes do not change significantly in the near future and that average household income patterns will remain fairly constant, how will total mail volume received by US households change in the coming decades?

In this case, it is possible to estimate a consumer's mail receipt based on his or her life stage. Then, if life stage, and not generational identity is considered to be an indicator of mail receipt, even if only by way of the direct relationship between age and income earned, future household population demographics become instrumental to predicting future mail volumes. Using publicly available data collected through the US Census

Bureau's Current Population Survey between 1995 and 2003[12], it is possible to determine the frequency with which consumers in certain age groups have formed households in the past. Figure 6 below shows the changing mix of householder age as a percentage of total householder population. By plotting the households by householder age as a percentage of total households beginning in 1995 (the earliest date for which continuous and complete information is available), one can identify historical trends in the age of householder mix.

Figure 6. Householders by Age, as a Percentage of Total Householders

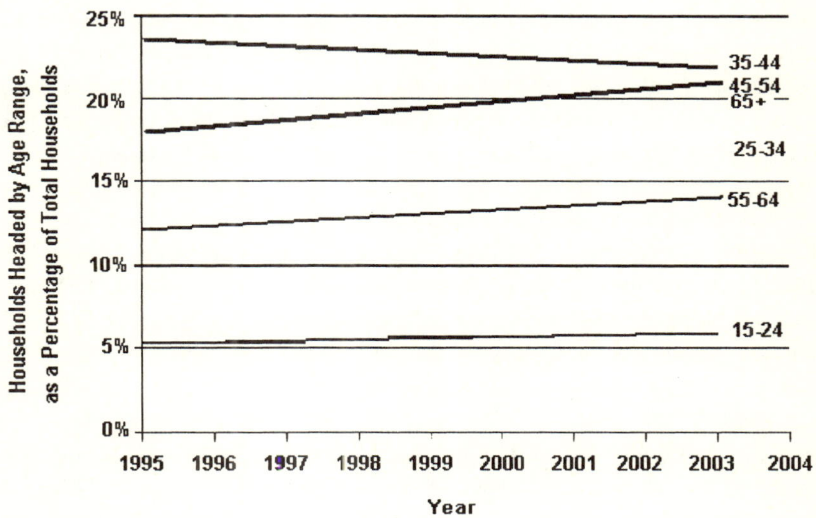

Source: PB analysis based on US Census Current Population Survey data, 1995-2003

From Figure 6, it is clear that as a percentage of total households, households headed by those that are between the ages of 45-54 and 55-64 have increased most quickly. Conversely, households, as a proportion of the whole, headed by those between the ages of 25 and 34 have fallen the most quickly (US Census, 1995-2003). Using householder age projections provided by the 1990 Decennial Census (US Census, 1990), age based household mail receipt patterns from the 2003 USPS Household Diary Study and household population estimations from the ongoing Current Population Survey, one can calculate and track average household mail volume of a particular householder age group over time to approximate the effect of changing population mix, business practices and patterns of mail use on total household mail receipt volumes by householder age.

12 Current Population Survey does not provide complete data for years prior to 1995.

In the case of changes in population mix, the most extreme predictions in the popular press tend to revolve around Millennials. However, Millennials are still quite young, few have formed households, and analysis shows that households headed by 18-24 year olds receive less mail than average households. Thus, even a dramatic decrease in mail volume received by Millennials may cause little deviation in total mail volume received by households in the near future.

Moreover, because of their size, the Baby Boomers are the generation to watch in the coming decades. As the population ages, population demographics suggests that mail volume growth will be increasingly concentrated towards the households with householders in the upper age ranges. The Boomers have been regarded throughout history as the generation to change the environment around them, both physical and spiritual, to suit their needs. Their spiritual, consumer and financial interests affect the marketplace around them. They designed concepts of self-religion, "immersed [themselves] in Tai-Chi, Zen," and dodged the draft, yet returned to more traditional values, even as they sought non-traditional, alternative medicines to stave off the aging process (Strauss and Howe, 1991). As consumers, Baby Boomers account for more than half of US consumer spending (Sivy, Kalwarski, and Gandel, 2005), most of which is spent on travel and healthcare. As a group, current Baby Boomers receive more periodicals than any other age group. AARP publications dedicated to those aged 50 and above (AARP Bulletin and AARP Magazine) have yearly circulations of over 40 million (Folio Magazine, 2004). It would not be surprising see economically active older consumers being heavily courted by advertisers and publishers in the years to come.

There is a tendency for business practices to adjust gradually[13] rather than quickly, and changes in business-originated mail volume caused by shifts in consumer preferences and behavior are not likely to result in the sudden cessation of mail to any single generation, especially as described of the Millennial generation. Conversely, a corresponding increase in mail volumes could be achieved by a similarly gradual shift towards mail-based communications due to data-security fears, or even the simple introduction of new services that require customer communications. Historically, the widespread adoption of consumer Internet and mobile telephones have generated new mail volumes. Additionally, any widespread shifts in consumer preferences are not likely to be constrained by the generational identity of the householder. Preference shifts of large magnitude are more likely to differently affect segments of all generations. It will become

---

[13] A case study of email adoption at Volvo revealed that it took five years and active support of management to achieve regular email use by a significant proportion of the company's workforce (Rogers, 2003).

increasingly important to track the mail receipt volumes of households on both ends of the spectrum: Millennial-headed households and Boomer-headed households.

Changing patterns of mail use will certainly affect mail volumes. However, widespread changes in mail triggered by the behavior and preferences of the Millennial generation will encounter resistance on two fronts: 1) the Millennial generation has not yet reached an age where its economic activity is great enough to alter the way advertisers and service providers will communicate with them and 2) the size and spending power of the Baby Boomer generation currently outpaces the Millennials' growth in both regards. Assuming no major changes in US business practices, one can change population growth and mail receipt variables assumed in the mail approximation methodology described above to forecast the direction of future mail growth. However, based on currently available data, it is not possible to draw conclusions about the direction in which mail receipt volumes will ultimately move.

6. CURRENT PREDICTIONS ABOUT FUTURE GENERATIONS' USE OF MAIL

Over the last ten years, William Strauss and Neil Howe have assembled and published a series of books and papers that describe how generations are formed by the cultural attitudes in place during their formative years (Strauss and Howe, 1991 and 2000). These cultural attitudes shape the behavior, character and expectations of each generation in different ways. The change from one generation to the next can always be identified by a larger cultural shift that alters the landscape in which the generation is formed.

Strauss and Howe identify one cultural attitude that shifted dramatically, ending the GenX generation and beginning the Millennial generation – *Society's Focus on Children*. In Millennials, Strauss and Howe document how during the formation and duration of the GenX generation's childhood years, American society as a whole reflected a marked disinterest in children. This generation began in the 60s, a time of increasing attention on individual fulfillment. This is the generation of the Latch-Key kid and benign neglect. During this generation's formative years, reproductive health science centered on birth control and produced the smallest generation in more than 100 years.

In contrast, the birth years of the Millennial generation were characterized by a society-wide fascination with children. Starting in 1982, the first year of this generation, society rediscovered their love for children. The 1980s produced the minivan, child focused product safety laws, baby on board signs, and celebrity moms (Strauss and Howe, 2000). Reproductive health science focuses on fertility treatments and women in their 40's and 50's are having babies. Society has renewed its interest in children, though its interest lies more in the new generation than the love of all children (Strauss and Howe, 2000).

According to Strauss and Howe, society does not alter its perceptions of a generation. If a generation is born into neglect, it will be neglected forever. Society had and continues to have very low expectations and respect for the GenX generation. They are perceived as a generation of 'no-good slackers.' If however, a generation is greeted with cheers and high expectations, society will continue to focus on them through out their lifetimes. Like the GI Generation, now known as '*The Greatest Generation,*' society expects great things of the emerging Millennial generation. Almost since their birth, this generation has been the focus of singular attention and expectation and as with the GI Generation, society will continue to bestow singular attention, respect and benefits onto this generation throughout its life.

The Millennial generation, the first generation to essentially grow up with computers will effect much of business-originated communications. Product mix, including magazine titles, may change over time to address the Millennial's current interests as they age and change. The volume of advertising mail sent to this generation is expected to increase over the volume sent to other generations. In order to accurately assess the impact of technology on their mail use, it will become necessary to track this generation's technology adoption rate across media as, for example, this generation's rate of internet penetration is significantly different from even that of their parents: by 2002, ninety-five percent of U.S. children between the ages of 5 and 17 had access to and used computers while only sixty percent adults had access to and used PCs. Virtually every child in the U.S. today, either at home or at school, has access to a computer (Dept. of Commerce, 2002). While the GenX generation was the first generation to grow up with exposure to computers, Millennials are the first generation to grow up with ubiquitous access to both computers and the Internet.

7. CONCLUSION

It is difficult to predict how the attitudes and behavior of future generations will affect mail consumption, especially since mail's unique demand nature dictates that the sender, not the receiver, determines receipt volume. If we believe that American society is as focused on the needs and wants of the Millennial generation as Strauss and Howe suggest, we can expect to see business-originated communications focused on this generation. We might also expect to see product mix, including magazine titles and television shows, change over time to address the Millennials' current interests as they age and change. We would similarly expect to see the volume of advertising mail sent to this generation increase relative to the volume sent to other generations.

However, the distribution of mail among age groups has remained consistent for the last seventeen years of rapid adoption of communications technologies. Corporations appear to be proportionately targeting the same demographics as in the past, as young households still receive, on average less mail than older households. A household's mail receipt approaches the average as the householder reaches 34-45 years of age and peaks as he reaches 45-54 years of age. As the householder continues to age, his household's mail receipt gradually decreases until it again approaches the average.

Comparing mail volume per household between different generational cohorts as they move from one age group to the next, we find remarkable similarities in mail consumption behavior. Although there is some variation in mail volumes between cohorts, each cohort falls within a relatively consistent range across all age transitions and the analysis suggests life stage, and not generation-based mail consumption patterns. Life stage, not generation-based, mail consumption patterns hold for all mail classes.

It also appears that the total household income of a householder at a particular age is a statistically significant factor in predicting mail volume received by a household. A household's income is tied closely with the householder's life stage and reflects all the activities in which he participates at particular points of his life.

However, it is not possible to categorically conclude that generational affiliation will not affect mail consumption, since findings are limited by data that have already been collected which is several years short of a complete generation. Therefore, the conclusions cannot be extrapolated outside of the data range with a high degree of confidence. Fortunately for future analysis, data that have already been collected includes mail received by consumers preceding and following the introduction of personal computers and the Internet. As the USPS gathers and publishes mail received information by Millennial headed households, who grew up with computer and Internet access, we can compare Millennial cohorts to pre and post-PC Gen X cohorts.

Certainly, consumers' adoption of new communications tools could alter communications habits and affect mail volume. However, the available data suggests that the changing demographic mix of the U.S. may lead to favorable conditions for the mail volume. As the population ages, a greater portion of households will be headed by Baby Boomers in the most economically active stages of their lives. Households headed by more economically active members of society receive more mail than average.

The size and spending power of the Baby Boomer generation currently outpaces the Millennials' growth in both regards. Even though the preferences of Millennials may affect the way in which businesses communicate, the Millennial generation has not yet reached an age where its economic activity is sufficiently significant to alter the way in which advertisers and service providers communicate with them. Moreover, changes in business practices that would result in a decrease total household mail receipt would take years to implement.

In recent history, neither the introduction of new technology nor affiliation with any generation inoculated one from following the general mail usage patterns of one's predecessors. Each generation witnesses the introduction of numerous new technologies, with the late Gen X and Millennial generations at a faster rate than ever. However, doomsday predictions about the fate of film, radio or television, in their respective eras, all proved untrue. While the introduction of each successive technology has changed the functions of its predecessor, none of the preceding media have disappeared. Just as radio has become a source for music and talk, and films have become both a visual and audio experience, mail's function and purpose will inevitably change and progress with the advent of new technology. As complete data on mail and media use across generations becomes available, it will be possible to draw more concrete conclusions about the factors that affect household mail receipt.

REFERENCES:

Barrow, B. 2005. "The Cost of an Adult Life is 1.5m" printed on April 26, accessed at http://news.telegraph.co.uk/news/main.jhtml on April 27, 2005.

Baughman, J.L. 1993. "Television Comes to America, 1947-57" accessed at http://lib.niu.edu/ipo/ihy930341.html on January 29, 2005.

Chopra, V. 2005a. "Emergence of Electronic Alternatives," A Pitney Bowes Background paper for the project "Electronic Substitution for Mail: Models and Results, Myth and Reality," http://www.postinsight.com.

Chopra, V. 2005b. "The Internet and Mail," A Pitney Bowes Background paper for the project "Electronic Substitution for Mail: Models and Results, Myth and Reality," http://www.postinsight.com.

Diakova, E. 2005. "Electronic Alternatives to Direct Mail Marketing," A Pitney Bowes Background paper for the project "Electronic Substitution for Mail: Models and Results, Myth and Reality," http://www.postinsight.com.

Divorce Magazine. 2005. "U.S. Divorce Statistics" accessed at http://www.divorcemag.com/statistics/statsUS.shtml on June 16, 2005.

Emarketer. 2004a. "53 Million in US use IM" Sept 8 accessed at http://www.emarketer.com/Article.aspx?1003031 on April 7, 2005.

EMarketer. 2004b. "US Household Penetration of Selection Telecommunication Services" Oct. 20, accessed at http://www.emarketer.com/Chart.aspx?41846 on June 9, 2005.

Employee Benefit Research Institute. 2005. "Facts from EBRI" accessed at http://www.ebri.org/facts/0701fact.htm on June 16, 2005.

Folio. 2004. "Blurring the Lines Between Custom and Traditional" accessed at http://www.m10report.com/July___August_2004.july040+M5ade7ba03be.0.html on April 25, 2005.

Friedlander, B.P. 1999. "Study: Poverty Touches 91% of African Americans During Adult Years," accessed at http://www.news.cornell.edu/Chronicle/99/4.8.99/poverty_study.html on June 16, 2005.

The Future of Children. 2000. Vol 10 No 2 Fall/ Winter.

Lee, L. 2000. *Bad Predictions*. Elsewhere Press: Michigan.

Media Info Center. 2004. Media Consumption Based on Hours per Person accessed at http://www.mediainfocenter.org/film/competition/consumption.asp on January 19, 2005.

Nie, N. H., and D.S. Hillygus. 2002. "Where does Internet Time Come From? A Reconnaissance." *IT & Society* 1 (Issue 2 Fall).

North Dakota DMV. 2005. "Drivers License and Traffic Safety" accessed at http://www.state.nd.us/dot/dlinfo.html on June 16, 2005.

Olson, S. 2003. Computer Predictions, Circa 1976 accessed at http://www.geek.com/news/geeknews/2003Oct/bch20031031022454.htm on April 25, 2005.

Pitney Bowes. 2004. US Mail Market Year in Review, Pitney Bowes Internal Document.

Robinson, J.P., M. Kestnbaum, A. Neustadtl, and A. Alvarez. 2002. "Information Technology and Functional Time Displacement." *IT & Society* 1(Issue 2 Fall).

Rogers, E.M.. 2003. *Diffusion of Innovations*, Fifth Ed. New York: Free Press.

Sivy, M., T. Kalwarski, and S. Gandel. 2005. "Playing the baby boomer trends" accessed at http://money.cnn.com/2005/03/25/pf/boomers1_0504/ on April 25, 2005.

Strauss, W., and N. Howe. 1991. *Generations: The history of America's Future, 1584 to 2069*. New York: Quill William Morrow.

Strauss, W., and N. Howe. 2000. *Millennials Rising: The Next Great Generation*. New York: Vintage Books.

Subrahmanyam, K., R. E Kraut, P. M. Greenfield, and E. F. Gross. 2000. "The Impact of Home Computer Use on Children's Activities and Development." *Children and Computer Technology* 10-2.

Suczek, Y. 2004. "An Analysis of Generational Changes and Their Impact on Technology Adoption, Media Use, and Communications," Pitney Bowes Internal Document.

Szeto, C. 2005. "The Impact of Age, Generation and Life Stage on Use of Mail and Media," A Pitney Bowes Background paper for the project "Electronic Substitution for Mail: Models and Results, Myth and Reality," http://www.postinsight.com.

Technology Futures Inc.. 2002. "Residential Broadband Forecasts" accessed at http://www.tfi.com/pubs/w/pdf/ti_broadband.pdf on June 9, 2005.

US Census Bureau. 2005a. Table H-10. Age of Head of Household: All Races by Median and Mean Income: 1967 to 2003, US Census Bureau website http://www.census.gov/hhes/income/.

US Census Bureau. 1995-2003 "Current Population Survey Reports" 1995-2003 accessed at http://www.census.gov/population/www/socdemo/hh-fam.html on April 25, 2005.

US Census Bureau. 1990. Table 3: Projections of Households by Type of Household and Age of Householder: 1995 to 2010, Series 1, 2, and 3 accessed at http://www.census.gov/population/projections/nation/hh-fam/table3n.txt on April 25, 2005.

US Department of Commerce. 2002. "A Nation Online: How Americans are Expanding their use of the Internet," February.

US Department of Education – National Center for Education Statistics. 2003. "Computer and Internet Use by Children and Adolescents in 2001," October 2003.

USPS.com. 2005. United States Postal Service, accessed at http://www.usps.com on June 16, 2005.

USPS Household Diary: The Household Diary Study Mail Uses & Attitudes, conducted annually by USPS from 1987 to 2003.

Veronis S.S. 2003. *Communications Industry Forecast & Report.*

The Wall Street Journal. 1987. "Computer Advances Improve Prospects for 'Paperless Office."

Watson, A. 2002. "e-business- Use the e-mail route and help save planet from paper waste," Birmingham Post, July 16.

Yahoo. 2005. "Majority of Teens, Young Adults Have Broadband Access" accessed at http://story.news.yahoo.com/news?tmpl=story2&u=/cmp/20050115/tc_cmp/57701552 on February 1, 20005.

Legal and Regulatory Issues

Chapter 18

The New EC Framework for State Aid to Public Service and the Postal Sector

Where Do We Stand Now?

Alessandra Fratini and Fabio Filpo
O'Connor and Company – European Lawyers

1. INTRODUCTION

When is financing of public postal services to be regarded as an advantage for the provider, therefore giving rise to the grant of State aid under EC law? Are public compensatory measures to be notified to the Commission and need they be approved before they can be put into operation? What are the conditions under which these measures can be allowed?

These are some of the questions which public authorities and service providers are confronted with when regulating or running public services. Some recent developments in EC State aid law and practice - the landmark Altmark judgment and the Commission new framework for the assessment of State aid to public services - are meant to provide the appropriate tools to answer the above questions. This paper reviews these most recent developments, with a view to appraising their specific implications for the postal sector.

2. THE STATE AID RULES AND THE "PUBLIC SERVICE EXCEPTION"

Under Article 87(1) EC, «[s]ave as otherwise provided in this Treaty, any aid granted by a Member State or through State resources in any form whatsoever which distorts or threatens to distort competition by favouring certain undertakings or the production of certain goods shall, insofar as it affects trade between Member States, be incompatible with the common market».

According to settled case law, the definition of State aid encompasses any advantage, i.e. every measure granted by public authorities, which, in various forms, mitigate the charges which are normally included in the budget of an undertaking.[1] To the extent that the aid is capable of affecting trade between Member States and distorting competition, it is incompatible with the internal market, unless it falls under the specific exceptions provided for in the EC Treaty.

As far as the advantage granted to the recipient is concerned, the case law has always referred to the concrete effect of the measure, disregarding its cause or the aim pursued.[2] To this purpose, the EC Courts have developed the so called "market economy investor principle (MEIP)", according to which public intervention does not constitute State aid when the State acts as a market operator, i.e. in line with the hypothetical behavior of a rational, profit-driven investor, operating under normal market conditions.[3]

Procedure-wise, Article 88(3) EC imposes the obligation to notify any new State measure falling within the scope of Article 87 EC, as well as the obligation to suspend temporarily the implementation of that measure (standstill provision), until it has been declared compatible with the common market. This provision creates a review mechanism, which rests within the exclusive competence of the Commission.[4]

Article 86(2) EC introduces an exception to the principle of incompatibility under Article 87 EC, providing that «[u]ndertakings entrusted with the operation of services of general economic interest or having the character of a revenue-producing monopoly shall be subject to the

---

1 See, for instance, Case C-387/92 *Banco Exterior de España* [1994] ECR I-877, paragraph 13; Case C-295/97, *Piaggio* [1997] ECR I-3735, paragraph 34.

2 It is settled case law that Article 87 EC does not distinguish between the measures of State intervention by reference to their causes or aims but defines them in relation to their effects (Case 173/73, *Italy v. Commission,* [1974] ECR 709 and Case 310/85, *Deufil v. Commission*, [1987] ECR 901).

3 Settled case law, e.g. Case C-305/89, *Italy v. Commission (Alfa Romeo)*, [1991] ECR I-1603.

4 Article 88(3) EC: «*The Commission shall be informed, in sufficient time to enable it to submit its comments, of any plans to grant or alter aid. If it considers that any such plan is not compatible with the common market having regard to Article 87, it shall without delay initiate the procedure provided for in paragraph 2. The Member State concerned shall not put its proposed measures into effect until this procedure has resulted in a final decision*». The procedural regulation (Regulation (EC) of the Council No. 659/99, OJ 99/L 83/01) sets up detailed procedural rules, according to principles developed earlier in the case law.

rules contained in this Treaty, in particular to the rules on competition, insofar as the application of such rules does not obstruct the performance, in law or in fact, of the particular tasks assigned to them. The development of trade must not be affected to such an extent as would be contrary to the interests of the Community».

Public service providers are exempted from the application of competition rules to the extent to which it is shown that their application is incompatible with the discharge of their duties (public service obligations). For the exemption to apply, Article 86(2) EC requires that: (i) the services constitute services of general economic interest; (ii) the services have actually been entrusted to the undertaking concerned by an explicit act of the public authority; (iii) the application of the Treaty rules hinders the performance of the particular task of the undertaking; (iv) this specific task cannot be performed by measures which are less restrictive of competition; (v) the measure has no substantial effect on intra-Community trade (i.e. does not affect the development of trade to an extent contrary to the interests of the Community).[5]

Procedure-wise, State aid must be notified and approved prior to its implementation, even where it qualifies for the derogation provided for in Article 86(2) EC.[6]

2.1 "State Aid Approach" vs. "Compensation Approach"

The application of the "public service exception" to State aid has always led to uncertainties. The crucial question is whether the "compensatory nature" affects the qualification of the measure: in other word, does it prevent the measure from falling within Article 87 EC, provided that it does not confer any advantage? Or does it relate instead to the aim of the measure, so that, in itself, it awards an advantage, which may be possibly justified on the basis of the "public service exception"?

This far, the EC case law has developed two different approaches in this regard. Under the so-called "State aid approach", any State funding granted to an undertaking entrusted with the operation of services of general interest constitutes, in principle, State aid within the meaning of Article 87(1) EC.

This approach distinguishes between situations where the State acts as a private operator in the market (where the MEIP applies) and situations where the State exercises public powers or prerogatives, such as the case at issue.

---

5 See opinion of Advocate General Léger, Case C-309/99, *Wouters*, [2002] ECR I-1577, paragraphs 157 to 166, with reference to previous case law. An exhaustive analysis of the matter is found in Buendia Sierra, "*Exclusive Rights and State Monopolies under EC Law*", Oxford, 1999, 346 sq.

6 Case C-332/98, *France v. Commission (CELF)*, [2000] ECR I-4833, paragraphs 27 sq.

In these cases, every intervention would go beyond the logic of a private operator and conclusively constitute State aid.[7] State aid may, however, be justified under Article 86(2) EC, if the conditions provided therein are fulfilled.

As to its procedural implications, the State aid approach implies the obligation to notify the compensatory measures and the application of the standstill provision of Article 88(3) EC.

Conversely, under the so-called "compensation approach", State funding of services of general interest amounts to State aid within the meaning of Article 87(1) EC only if, and to the extent that, the economic advantage which is conferred exceeds the costs of providing those services. This approach has been read as an attempt by the Court to limit the scope of application of State aid rules in an area which presents similarities to everyday sales and purchases in the market.[8] According to this interpretation, compensation for the costs of services of general interest may be compared to a "purchase of services" by the State.

From a procedural point of view, under the compensation approach State financing, falling outside of the scope of Article 87 EC, is not subject to the prior notification requirement and to the standstill obligation of Article 88(3) EC. This interpretation deals with the issue of compensation exclusively under Article 87 EC, depriving the derogation of Article 86(2) EC of any role in the context of State aid control.[9]

This approach has been developed in the Ferring judgment.[10] The Court, building upon some old case law,[11] revised what seemed to be the Court of

---

7 The CFI in particular, in two cases relating to the French public postal service and the Portuguese public broadcasting service, stated that compensation for public service obligations was to be regarded as State aid under Article 87 EC, even though it could be justified under Article 86(2) EC (Case T-106/95, *FFSA v. Commission*, [1997] ECR II-229, and Case T-46/97, *SIC v. Commission*, [2000] ECR II-2125). The ECJ took a similar approach in Case C-387/92, *Banco Exterior de España*, [1994] ECR I-877, and in the *CELF* judgment, quoted above.

8 Vesterdorf, Bo, "*A New Model drafted by the Community Courts?", in New Developments in European State Aid Law – Proceedings of the Experts Forum held in Brussels on 19 June 2003 (European State Aid Law)*: 13, p.17.

9 In fact, while proportionate compensation would fall outside Article 87 EC and would need not being justified under Article 86(2) EC, advantages exceeding the net additional cost of the public service would not be compatible with Article 86(2) EC (*Ferring*, quoted below, paragraphs 32-33).

10 Case C-53/00, *Ferring*, [2001] ECR I-9067.

11 Judgement in Case 240/83, *ADBHU*, [1985] ECR 531, where the ECJ stated that some indemnities granted by France to undertakings charged with the public service obligation of disposing of waste oils did not constitute aid within the meaning of Article [87 EC], but rather "*consideration for the services performed by the collection or disposal undertakings*".

First Instance's settled case law.[12] The Ferring case concerned a contribution imposed by the French government on the sale of medical products by pharmaceutical laboratories. Wholesale distributors benefited from an exemption from this contribution. The purpose of such exemption was to compensate the wholesale distributors of the extra charges deriving from certain public service obligations imposed to them by the French authorities.[13]

The Court, following the Advocate General's opinion,[14] stated that "provided that the tax [...] corresponds to the additional costs actually incurred by wholesale distributors in discharging their public service obligations, not assessing wholesale distributors to the tax may be regarded as compensation for the services they provide and hence not State aid within the meaning of Article [87] of the Treaty". In such a case, indeed, wholesale distributors would not be enjoying any real advantage.[15]

In its post-Ferring practice, the Commission has consistently adopted the compensation approach in a number of interesting decisions concerning the postal sector. In particular, the Commission held that State financing of public postal service in Ireland, Italy, UK and Belgium did not constitute State aid, since it was limited to the extra charges deriving from the mission of general interest entrusted to the companies concerned.[16] Conversely, the Commission found that State financing of the public postal operator in Germany was not proportionate to the additional costs of the public services.[17] The Ferring approach raised severe criticism, both within and

---

[12] In the nineties, the CFI had consistently followed the *State aid approach* (see footnote 7 above).

[13] Wholesale distributors were under a duty to keep in stock a range of medicines comprising at least nine tenths of all forms of medicines currently sold in France and to satisfy obligations related to the delivery time of those medicines.

[14] Opinion of Advocate General Tizzano of 8 May 2001 in Case C-53/00, *Ferring*, paragraphs 60-63.

[15] *Ferring*, paragraph 27.

[16] See e.g. Commission Decisions Case N 650 /2001 of 12 March 2002 - *Equity injection notification - An Post*; C 47 /1998 of 12 March 2002 – *Aid measures allegedly granted to Ente Poste Italiane*; C(2002)2402 of 2 July 2002 in Case N 749/2001 - *Posten AB giro payment service*; C(2002)3341 of 18 September 2002 in Case N 252 /2002 - *Reinvention of the urban post office network*; C(2003)1652 of 27 May 2003 in Case N 784 /2002 - *Post Office Limited (debt repayment, rural network support, loan for working capital)*; C(2003)2508 of 23 July 2003 in Case N 763 /2002 - *Augmentation de capital - Poste belge*.

[17] See Commission Decision C(2002)2144 of 19 June 2002 in Case C 61/99 - *Aid to business parcel activities of Deutsche Post AG*. The Commission found that the Government's measures compensated for costs related to services open to competition and were not strictly linked to public service obligations.

outside the Court.[18] It has been maintained that the Court had confused the issue of the "classification" of a measure as State aid with the (separate) issue of its "justification" under EC law[19] and that the Court's interpretation of Article 87 EC had deprived Article 86(2) EC of any practical effect ("effet utile"), since it would not have any further application in relation to State aid[20] and would favor inefficiencies in State aid control. Under the Ferring approach, indeed, control is limited to the proportionality of the measure and no attention is paid to the other conditions that otherwise should be met under Article 86(2) EC,[21] and especially the indispensability test, fundamental for the application of Article 86(2) EC.[22] The lack of prior notification, in particular, would deprive the Commission of an efficient means of surveillance.

In response to the above criticism, Advocate General Jacobs indicated a possible alternative approach in GEMO.[23] Trying to bring the inconsistent case law together, he distinguished between two different categories of compensatory measures. When there is a "direct and manifest link" between financing and obligations, so that the measures constitute a "quid pro quo" for clearly defined public service obligations, the measures do not grant any advantage and cannot constitute State aid. According to the Advocate General, this was the case when the Court followed the compensation approach.[24] Conversely, when there is no clear link between obligations and compensatory measures, the latter confer an advantage and are to be

---

[18] The first, and the strongest, criticisms came from Advocate General Léger, who in the two opinions he delivered in the course of the *Altmark* case firmly encouraged the Court to depart from the *Ferring* approach (opinions of 19 March 2002, "first opinion", and 14 January 2003, "second opinion"; the second opinion was due to the reopening of the oral procedure after the *Ferring* judgment, the parties' oral observations having been delivered before the judgment).

[19] Cfr. opinions of Advocate General Léger in the *Altmark* case. According to the Advocate General, the fact that the financial advantage was meant to offset the costs of the public service merely attained to the aim of the measure and consequently to its possible justification, rather than to its nature of State aid.

[20] See footnote 9 above.

[21] See paragraph 2 above.

[22] Castillo de la Torre, Fernando, and Keppenne, Jean-Paul, "*Ayudas estatales: jurisprudencia comunitaria en 2001*", in *Gaceta Jurídica de la Unión Europea y de la Competencia*, 217/2002,106 sq. and Nicolaides, Phaedon, "*The New Frontier in State Aid Control, An Economic Assessment of Measures that Compensate Enterprises*", in *Intereconomics*, July/August 2002: 194.

[23] Opinion of Advocate General Jacobs of 30 April 2002 in Case C-126/01, *GEMO*. The Advocate Generals interpretation has been defined as the "quid pro quo approach", as opposed to the "State aid approach" and to the "compensation approach."

[24] In particular, in the *ADBHU* and *Ferring* cases.

regarded as State aid. Their compatibility is therefore to be assessed under Article 86(2) EC, according to the State aid approach.[25]

3. THE NEW FRAMEWORK FOR STATE AID TO PUBLIC SERVICE

3.1 The Landmark Altmark Judgment: When Public Measures are not State Aid

The Altmark judgment was meant to clear the above inconsistency in the case law between the "State aid" and the "compensation" approach discussed above. The case was triggered by a preliminary ruling concerning the grant of licenses to operate regular bus local services to Altmark Trans, a local bus transport operator receiving public subsidies. The German High Federal Administrative Court asked the ECJ to determine whether subsidies granted by public authorities to offset the cost of public service obligations imposed on an undertaking operating a local passenger service constitute State aid.

In this respect, the Court stated that "where a State measure must be regarded as compensation for the services provided by the recipient undertakings in order to discharge public service obligations, so that those undertakings do not enjoy a real financial advantage and the measure thus does not have the effect of putting them in a more favourable competitive position than the undertakings competing with them, such a measure is not caught by Article [87](1) of the Treaty".[26]

However, the Court added that, for such compensation not to be State aid, four cumulative conditions must be satisfied:[27] (i) the recipient undertaking must actually have public service obligations to discharge, and the obligations must be clearly defined; (ii) the parameters on the basis of which the compensation is calculated must be established in advance, in an objective and transparent manner; (iii) the compensation cannot exceed what is necessary to cover all or part of the costs incurred in the discharge of public service obligations, taking into account the relevant receipts and a reasonable profit for discharging those obligations; (iv) where the undertaking which is to discharge public service obligations is not chosen pursuant to a public procurement procedure, which would allow for the

---

[25] This was the case, in particular, in the *Banco Exterior*, *FFSA* and *SIC* cases. Advocate General Stix-Hackl followed Advocate General Jacobs' approach in *Enirisorse* (opinion of 7 November 2002 in Joined Cases C-34/01 – C38/01, *Enirisorse*).

[26] Case C-280/00, *Altmark*, [2003] ECR I-7747, paragraph 87.

[27] *Altmark*, paragraphs 88 sq.

selection of the bidder capable of providing those services at the least cost to the community, the level of compensation must be determined on the basis of an analysis of the costs which a typical undertaking, well run and adequately equipped so as to be able to meet the necessary public service requirements, would have incurred in discharging those obligations, taking into account the relevant receipts and a reasonable profit for discharging the obligations.

Where all these conditions are met, compensation of public service obligations is not State aid and is not subject to the prior Commission's scrutiny. On the contrary, if one or more conditions are not satisfied, the compensation is State aid and shall be notified to the Commission pursuant to Article 88(3) EC, which may still authorize it under Article 86(2) EC.

Following the judgment, the Commission has applied the new approach in a number of cases. In very few cases (one of which related to a scheme for the security of supply in the electricity field, two other to development of broadband), the Commission found that all four of the Altmark conditions were met and, therefore, no State aid could be envisaged.[28]

In other cases, related to public broadcasting services, the Commission acknowledged that the Altmark conditions were not satisfied[29] but found that Article 86(2) EC was applicable.[30] The Commission appraised these cases according to the following reasoning. It first considered whether all the elements of Article 87 EC could be found and therefore whether the financing measure could, in abstract, constitute State aid. Secondly, it verified whether the Altmark conditions were met.[31] Where this was not the case, the Commission applied the conditions provided for by Article 86(2) EC, according to the specific features of the sector concerned.[32]

---

[28] Commission Decisions of 16 December 2003 in case N-475/2003 – *Ireland* ("*CADA*"); of 16 November 2004 in case N 381 /2004 – *Haut débit en Pyrénées-Atlantiques*; of 3 May 2005 in case N 382 /2004 – *Haut débit en Limousin – DORSAL* (decisions available on the Commission's website at: http://europa.eu.int/comm/competition/state_aid/register).

[29] In particular, the forth condition was not fulfilled in any of the cases; in addition, the second condition was also not met in some cases.

[30] See Commission Decisions of 1 October 2003 in Case N-37/2003 – *United Kingdom ("Digital Curriculum")*; of 10 October 2003 in Case C-62/1999 – *Italy ("RAI")*; of 15 October 2003 in Case C-85/2001 – *Portugal ("RTP")*; of 10 December 2003 in Case C-60/1999 – *France ("France 2 and France 3")* (decisions available on the Commission's website at: http://europa.eu.int/comm/competition/state_aid/register).

[31] In practice, the verification of the Altmark conditions constitutes an additional logical step that the Commission undertakes after having verified whether the "ordinary" elements of Article 87 EC are found.

[32] In the cases at issue, the Commission referred to its Communication on the application of State aid rules to public service broadcasting (OJ 2001/C 320/04).

In the light of the experience this far, it can be reasonably assumed that cases fulfilling all four of the Altmark conditions (in particular, the fourth one) are likely to be the exception rather than the rule.

3.2 The Complex Altmark Formula: The "Conditional Compensation Approach"

As discussed, when deciding the Altmark case the Court was confronted with the two different approaches, namely the "State aid approach" and the "compensation approach", which had been followed that far by the Court of first instance and by the Court itself.

In principle, Altmark confirms the Ferring's compensation approach, although in practice it introduced a set of "quasi-regulatory" conditions, aimed at limiting the application of the compensation approach to cases where there is a clear link between public service obligations and compensation. For this reason, the Altmark interpretation has been defined as the "conditional compensation approach".[33]

The Court, restricting the scope of permissible compensation, leaves scope for the application of Article 86(2) EC in the field of State aid, which had been excluded under Ferring's pure compensation approach. In fact, the diverging conditions under Altmark and Article 86(2) EC allow for a residual application of the latter. This is reflected in the Commission's post-Altmark practice and gives the way to further legislative intervention by the Commission.

The Altmark judgment, however, and in particular the application of the four conditions, raises some critical issues, amongst which the evaluation of the reasonable profit to be added to the amount of compensation for the public service obligations[34] and the assessment of the least cost to the community in case of selection of the public service provider through a tender. Moreover, the judgment introduces a sort of efficiency criterion, by requiring that the costs of the public service (to be compensated) be compared to those of a private undertaking, well run and adequately equipped to fulfill the task, thereby referring to a possible benchmark on the market.[35] The efficiency criterion evokes the market economy investor principle, whose application in the field of State aid is uncontroversial.[36]

---

33 Sinnaeve, Adinda, "*State Financing of Public Services: The Court's Dilemma in the Altmark Case,*" in *European State Aid Law* 3/2003: 351, 356.

34 The profit element had not been taken into account in the previous case law, neither applying the "State aid approach" (CFI's case law), nor the "compensation approach" (*ADBHU*, *Ferring*).

35 *Altmark*, paragraph 93.

36 See paragraph 2 above.

However, in most cases a benchmark can hardly be found in the market, and this is particularly true in those areas where the public service has historically been performed by a single operator making use of a public network.

It has also been remarked that the judgment marks out some specific situations which are not to be regarded as State aid although, according to some critics, they could still give way to possible advantage for some undertakings. We refer to specific situations where the mere conferral of a public service mission might in itself grant an advantage to the undertaking concerned,[37] or where even compliance with the "tender condition" might not be sufficient to exclude any advantage.[38] It may also be discussed whether the "profit element" could, in itself, constitute an advantage.[39] After Altmark, all these situations are to be left outside the scope of application of Article 87 EC, provided that the four conditions are met.[40]

The difficulties emerging from the application of the above conditions result in further uncertainties for the public service providers, increased by the risk of the possible violation of the standstill clause and the subsequent obligation to repay the aid received; in additional difficulties for the undertakings competing with the public service providers, which bear the burden of providing evidence of existing State aid before the national judges; and in additional risks for the Member States that public service is disrupted or endangered by ex post litigation.

---

[37] Merola, Massimo, and Medina, Caroline, "*De l'arrêt Ferring à l'arrêt Altmark: continuité ou revirement dans l'approche du financement des services publics*". In *Cahiers de droit européen*, v. 39, 5-6: 639, 670.

[38] See, for instance, the *London Underground* case (Commission Decision C(2002)3578 of 2 October 2002, Case N 264/2002 - *London Underground public private partnership*) relating to a public-private partnership, where the Commission considered that the fact that a tendering procedure had been put in place was, in itself, not sufficient to exclude any advantage and therefore undertook a detailed review of the procedure. See also Hankin, Robert, "*Final Conclusions from the Commission's Perspective*", in *Developments in European State Aid Law – Proceedings of the Experts' Forum held in Brussels on 19 June 2003 (European State Aid Law)*: 47, 551.

[39] The CFI case law under Article 86(2) EC, as well as the *ADBHU* and the *Ferring* judgments, do not allow any profit element to be taken into account.

[40] This aspect gives the way to criticism to the extent that since "*the criteria established by the Court represent sufficient* and *necessary conditions of qualification of (non) aid [...], (non)existence of aid would necessarily proceed not only from the object and amount of compensation, but also from procedural aspects*" (Santamato, Sandro, and Pesaresi, Nicola, "*Compensation for services of general economic interest: some thoughts n the Altmark ruling*", in *Competition Policy Newsletter*, 1 – Spring 2004: 17).

3.3 The Commission's Framework: What State Aid is Compatible

It had long been in the Commission's intentions to establish some regulatory framework for State aid to SGEIs.[41] However, given the uncertainties of the case law prior to the Altmark judgment, the Commission took the view that it was not possible to finalize any interpretative measure before further clarification by the Court.[42] Following the publication of the Altmark judgment, the Commission could complete its legislative initiative and adjust its administrative practice accordingly.

The long-awaited set of measures (the so-called "Monti Package"), which is meant to complete the framework created by Altmark, includes: (i) a Commission Decision on the application of Article 86 of the Treaty to State aid in the form of public service compensation granted to certain undertakings entrusted with the operation of services of general economic interest (hereinafter the "Decision"), (ii) a Community framework for State aid in the form of Public Service Compensation (hereinafter the "Framework") and (iii) a Commission Directive amending Directive 80/723/EEC on the transparency of financial relations between Member States and public undertakings (hereinafter the "Directive").[43]

These measures aim, on the one side, at establishing the conditions under which State financing of public service, which is State aid according to Altmark, can be automatically exempted from the requirements of Article 88 EC. On the other side, the measures aim at establishing the principles against which the Commission will assess public financing which, in so far as it does not satisfy the conditions for automatic exemption, will have to be notified and approved before it is implemented.

---

[41] In particular, as announced in its Report to the Laeken European Council – Services of General Interest (COM(2001) 598 of 17 October 2001, paragraph 28-29), the Commission's plan included a "Community framework for State aid granted to undertakings entrusted with the provision of services of general economic interest" to be issued in 2002. This framework was to be subsequently followed by a block-exemption regulation setting out the circumstances in which public funding would not be considered as State aid and defining the criteria under which public funding constituting State aid would be considered compatible with the EC Treaty. The foreseen measures were clearly based on the "State aid approach."

[42] See Report from the Commission of 13 December 2002 on the state of play in the work on the guidelines for state aid and services of general economic interest (SGEIs), published on the Commission's website.

[43] The measures, yet to be published in the EU Official Journal, have been posted on the Commission website (see http://europa.eu.int/comm/competition/state_aid/legislation/).

The Decision, making use of the Commission powers under Article 86(3) EC,[44] exempts from prior notification any measure which, while falling within the scope of application of Article 87 EC, is prima facie compatible with the EC Treaty under Article 86(2) EC. To this purpose, the Decision lays down a set of criteria that must be complied with.

Firstly, the service concerned is to be a genuine SGEI within the meaning of Article 86(2) EC and the public service task has to be entrusted by way of an official act, which specifies the nature of the public service obligations, as well as the undertaking(s) and territory concerned.[45]

Secondly, the compensation cannot exceed the costs of discharging the public service obligations, taking into account the revenue and a reasonable profit.[46] The costs include all the variable costs incurred in providing the SGEI, a proportionate contribution to the fixed costs (common to both the SGEI and other activities) and an adequate return on capital insofar as it is assigned to the SGEI. The revenue includes the entire revenue earned from the SGEI and must also include profit in excess of the reasonable profit generated by special or exclusive rights linked to another SGEI or by other "advantages granted by the State". The reasonable profit includes a rate of return on capital that must take account of the risk, or absence of risk and shall not exceed the "average rate for the sector concerned".[47] It may also depend on incentive criteria (relating, in particular, to the quality of service provided).

Provided that these conditions are fulfilled, the public support is ex se compatible with Article 86(2) EC when the public service provider's (gross) annual turnover (all activities included) does not exceed € 100 million during

---

[44] Article 86(3) EC: «*The Commission shall ensure the application of the provisions of this Article and shall, where necessary, address appropriate directives or decisions to Member States*». Some authors have highlighted an alleged misuse of powers by the Commission as to the choice of the legal basis of the Decision, which, in practice, corresponds to a "block-exemption" regulation. See, for instance, Rapp-Jung, Barbara, "*State Financing of Public Services – The Commission's New Approach*", in *European State Aid Law* 2/2004, 207, according to which the Decision "*introduces a further de minimis standard which, in contrast to existing de minimis regulation, would be based on Article 86*". Similarly, as the author notes, Article 86(3) EC as a legal basis to derogate from the notification duty under Article 88 EC could be contested (provisions exempting Member State from notifying have been so far adopted by way of Commission Regulations based on the Council Enabling Regulation (EC) 994/1998 adopted under Article 89).

[45] Decision, Article 4.

[46] Decision, Article 5.

[47] The Commission specifies that "In sectors where there is no undertaking comparable to the undertaking entrusted with the operation of the SGEI, a comparison may be made with undertakings situated in other Member States, or if necessary, in other sectors" (Decision, Article 5(4)).

the two financial years preceding the assignment of the SGEI and (ii) the annual compensation for the SGEI does not exceed € 30 million.[48]

Compensations granted to hospitals and social housings carrying out SGEI are compatible with the Treaty irrespective of the above ceilings,[49] while in the field of transport the Decision only applies to: (i) compensations related to air or maritime links to islands whose annual traffic does not exceed 300,000 passengers and (ii) compensations related to airports and ports whose annual traffic does not exceed 100,000 passenger (airports) or 300,000 passengers (ports).[50]

For all compensatory measures which would not fall under Altmark or under the Decision, and thus will have to be notified, the Commission has set up some evaluation guidelines. According to the Framework, State aid would still fall within Article 86(2) EC when the public service is clearly entrusted by way of an official act specifying, inter alia, the parameters for calculating, controlling and reviewing the compensation[51] and the arrangements for avoiding and repaying any over compensation,[52] and the amount of compensation does not exceed the costs of discharging the public service obligations (taking into account the relevant receipts and a reasonable profit).[53] Therefore, the aid that may be exempted by the Commission is the same as that falling, in principle, within the scope of the Decision, but exceeding the turnover and compensation ceilings fixed therein.

The Directive modifies the Transparency Directive,[54] with the aim of maintaining the accounting separation obligation for those undertakings which receive public service compensation and also operate outside the SGEI field, irrespective of the classification of the measure as a State aid. This is to prevent the new Altmark definition of State aid from affecting the

---

[48] Decision, Article 2(a).

[49] Decision, Article 2(b).

[50] Decision, Article 2(c) and (d).

[51] Framework, paragraph 10. These parameters may include specific costs borne by the undertakings in the regions referred to in Article 87(3)(a) and (c) EC.

[52] *Ibidem*.

[53] Framework, paragraphs 12sq.

[54] Commission Directive 80/723/EEC of 25 June 1980 on the transparency of financial relations between Member States and public undertakings (OJ 1980/L 195/35, as subsequently amended; see OJ 2000/L 193/75), which lays down conditions for ensuring a minimum degree of transparency in financial relations between the State and certain undertakings entrusted with the operation of SGEIs. The Transparency Directive requires Member States to ensure the transparency of financial relations between public authorities and undertakings which have benefited from public resources and to make available to the Commission all data concerning financial relations between the Member States and public undertakings.

obligation to maintain separate accounts for all companies receiving "public service compensation in any form whatsoever",[55] i.e. including compensations which, according to Altmark, are not State aid.

3.4 The New Framework: Clarity or Confusion?

As a first general remark, it is to be noted that none of the Commission's measures clarifies the application of the Altmark conditions. The Commission creates a complex parallel framework to be applied when the Altmark criteria are not complied with, i.e. when the measures concerned are State aid and fall under the Commission's scrutiny.

Moreover, practical difficulties are likely to arise in relation to the application of the additional criteria set up by the Commission, in particular with regard to the revenues and the reasonable profit to be taken into account when calculating the public service costs. While the pure costs' definition does not raise, in principle, particular difficulties (the Commission expressly refers to the Chronopost criteria),[56] the notions of "revenue" and "reasonable profit" are by some means contentious.

According to the Commission, the revenue to be taken into account must include the entire revenue earned from the SGEI concerned, excess profits from special or exclusive rights linked to other SGEIs and other (undetermined) advantages granted by the State.[57] While the reference to the revenues of the SGEI at issue is undisputed, this is less so in respect of revenues from special or exclusive rights linked to other SGEIs that generate excessive profit, or other advantages granted by the State, as well as "profits accruing from other activities outside the scope of the SGEI" if the Member State so provides.[58] In particular, it has been contested that the Commission analysis cannot extend to revenues or profits earned from another SGEI.[59]

The reasonable profit comprises a "rate of return on own capital that takes account of the risk, or absence of risk, incurred by the undertaking by

---

55 Transparency Directive, Article 2(1)(d), as modified.

56 See *infra*, § 3.5.

57 Obviously, to the extent that these constitute State aid.

58 Decision, Article 5(3).

59 See Rapp-Joung, Barbara, "*State Financing of Public Services – The Commission's New Approach*", quoted above, 211, who argues that the Commission has disregarded Article 86(2) EC, which only requires that the application of competition rules must not obstruct the accomplishment of the public service mission. The author also notes that the level of compensation should be assessed at the level of each SGEI and that the inclusion of revenues from activities other than those at issue is in contradiction with the EC rules on the unbundling of accounts (Transparency Directive) and with the still applicable broadcasting Communication (Communication from the Commission on the application of State aid rules to public service broadcasting, quoted above).

virtue of the intervention by the Member State, particularly if the latter grants exclusive or special rights". The rate "shall not normally exceed the average rate for the sector concerned in recent years".[60] It is evident that the assessment of what constitutes a reasonable profit entails a margin of discretion.

Finally, the criteria adopted by the Commission mirror the corresponding conditions in Altmark. However, the test related to the amount of permissible compensation is different, and quite substantially so. The Commission expressly refers to the Chronopost criteria.[61] This shows that it is aware that Altmark (reference to an efficient operator in the market) could be too hard a benchmark to apply in practice and that there are cases, which concern in particular network industries, where a broader standard may still guarantee the compatibility of the aid with the Treaty under Article 86(2) EC.

It follows from both the Altmark judgment and the Commission's measures that the applicable standard of permissible compensation is twofold. On the one side, the (objective) "Altmark criterion" (reference to an efficient operator on the market) guarantees that the State measure does not grant any advantage and is not State aid. On the other side, the (subjective) "Chronopost criterion" (total costs of the public service provider) allows State financing, which constitutes State aid, to be justified under Article 86(2) EC.[62] While the stricter standard would automatically apply, the broader standard would only apply under the Commission's scrutiny. Hence, the aid is automatically justified under Article 86(2) EC, pursuant to the Decision, when both the amount of compensation and the provider's turnover do not exceed the relevant amounts indicated therein. Conversely, when the aid exceeds these "de minimis" thresholds, it can be considered as compatible with the common market, under Article 86(2) EC, only by way of an individual Commission's decision following the procedure set out in Article 88(3) EC.

---

60 Article 5(4) of the Decision. In cases where there is no undertaking comparable to the undertaking entrusted with the operation of the SGEI, a comparison may be made with undertakings situated in other Member States or in other sectors.

61 Framework, paragraph 13.

62 See, for instance, Bartoshc, Andreas, "*Clarification or Confusion? How to Reconcile the ECJ's Rulings in Altmark and Chronopost*", in *European State Aid Law* 3/2003: 375, and Rapp-Joung, Barbara, "*State Financing of Public Services – The Commission's New Approach*", quoted above, 209.

3.5 The New Framework in the Postal Sector: Anything New?

Against the above background, the postal sector it is likely to fall outside the scope of application of the Altmark ruling.

The Chronopost case shows how difficult the analysis of the economic advantage may be, especially when it rests on the use of a network facility.[63] The Court had been called upon to decide whether the logistical assistance (use of the network) provided by the French public postal operator (La Poste) to a subsidiary operating in a competitive market constituted State aid. It maintained that in those situations where, given the absence of any benchmark on the market, the network is not a "market network" (and this was the case of the French postal network),[64] "normal market conditions must be assessed by reference to the objective and verifiable elements which are available".[65] Such objective and verifiable elements were constituted, in the case, by the costs borne by the network undertaking to provide the service.[66] The Court, therefore, introduced a sort of "second best" criterion to be used when, given the specificity of the sector, there is no benchmark available on the market.

---

[63] The *Chronopost* case began in the early nineties when SFEI, a French association of express courier companies, brought a complaint to the Commission. It claimed that the logistical and commercial assistance afforded by the French Post Office, La Poste, to its subsidiary SFMI (later renamed Chronopost) operating on a competitive market, constituted State aid, given that the remuneration for the assistance provided was allegedly more favourable than the normal market conditions. Subsequently, proceedings were also started before the Paris Commercial Court. The case brought at the national level originated a preliminary ruling to the ECJ (Case C-39/94, *SFEI*, [1996] ECR I-3547), while the complaint brought to the Commission originated a Commission decision (Commission Decision Case C 3/96 – *France*, OJ 1996/C 206/3), a CFI judgment which annulled the Commission decision (Case T-613/97, *UFEX*, [2000] ECR II-4055) and an ECJ judgment which repealed the CFI judgment (Joined Cases C-83/01 P, C-93/01 P and C-94/01 P, [2003] ECR I-6993). For an analysis of the case, see Fratini, Alessandra, and Carta, Andrea, "*Chronopost c. UFEX: la Corte di giustizia UE e le «relazioni pericolose» fra settori riservati e mercati aperti alla concorrenza*", in *Diritto del Commercio Internazionale*, n. 2 – 2004.

[64] *Chronopost*, paragraph 36. The ECJ explains that "*because of the characteristics of the service which the La Poste network must be able to ensure, the creation and maintenance of that network are not in line with a purely commercial approach*" and "*would never have been created by a private undertaking*".

[65] *Chronopost*, paragraph 38.

[66] I.e. "*all the additional, variable costs incurred in providing the logistical and commercial assistance, an appropriate contribution to the fixed costs arising from use of the postal network and an adequate return on the capital investment in so far as it is used for SFMI-Chronopost's competitive activity*"(*Chronopost*, paragraphs 39-40).

While not specifically related to public service financing, the Chronopost judgment provides some guidelines for the evaluation of the advantage element in the State aid scrutiny in the postal sector, which can be used outside the limited scope of the judgment. In this regard, a short comparison between Altmark and Chronopost proves that the strict benchmark introduced by the former for compensatory measures not to be State aid has very little scope of application where no market exists for the services at issue, as for the use of the postal network.

If, as Chronopost appears to suggest, the postal sector falls outside the scope of application of the Altmark judgment, it will be for the new Commission's measures to set the relevant benchmark for the assessment of State aid financing of the universal postal service. In this context, the ceilings that draw the line between the (automatic) application of the Decision and the (case-by-case) application of the Framework exclude the public postal operators from the scope of the Decision.[67] Thus, any public compensation of the universal postal service will be assessed by the Commission, on a case-by-case basis, under the Framework. In other words, no major changes from the current Commission practice can be expected to occur.

4. FINAL REMARKS: WHERE DO WE STAND?

In conclusion, the framework made up by the Altmark judgment and the above Commission's measures urges public authorities and public service operators to evaluate any measure granted to offset the costs of the service following a sequential analysis.

As a first step, it shall be assessed whether the measures at issue fall under Article 87 EC at all. To this purpose, the four Altmark conditions shall be considered, in order to appraise whether the measures confer a real advantage to the public service provider. Where the Altmark conditions are not met, the measures constitute State aid, but can still be justified under the Commission Decision.

In both cases, the measures are ex se compatible with EC law and are not subject to notification and approval.

---

[67] As it appears from the most recent State aid cases related to the financing of the universal postal services, public postal operators achieve turnover and compensation levels well above the Decision ceilings. See, for instance, N 183 /2003 - *Aids to the Greek post*, N 784 /2002 - *United Kingdom - "Government rural network support funding, debt payment funding and rolling working capital loan to Post Office Limited", N 763 /2002 – Belgique - Augmentation de capital de €297,5M de La Poste SA/NV.*, N 252 /2002 - *United Kingdom -Reinvention of the urban Post Office network.*

If the above criteria are not met, the aid can still be compatible if the requirements provided for in the Framework, which mirror to Article 86(2) EC conditions, are complied with. In this case, however, the measures have to be scrutinized by the Commission and can only be implemented following its approval. Measures which do not comply with these requirements constitute State aid incompatible with EC law. Where implemented, these measures are to be recovered from the recipient.

In the light of the Chronopost experience and according to the turnover and compensation ceilings set by the Decision, State measures for the compensation of the universal postal service will likely fall outside the scope of both Altmark and the Decision and need to be assessed case-by-case under the Framework. In other words, the compensation approach adopted by the Court will bring about no substantial bearing for the public service providers, the majority of which will be bound by the requirements of prior notification and clearance by the Commission.

To conclude, in spite of its complexity, the new framework will not bring substantial practical implications for the Commission's and Member States' practice in the postal sector. It looks like we stand exactly where we started in the early nineties: public service compensation requires a case-by-case assessment by the Commission under the conditions provided for by Article 86(2) EC.

Chapter 19

Postal Services Regulation In Europe

*A Comparative Study of the UK, the Netherlands, Belgium, France, Germany, Italy and Sweden**

Richard Eccles and Pauline Kuipers
Bird & Bird

1. INTRODUCTION

On 1 January 2006, the weight threshold of the reservable area under the EC postal services Directive 97/67 as amended by Directive 2002/39 (hereinafter: 'Postal Directive') reduces to 50 grams from 100 grams. The price threshold, which must also be met for mail to be within the reservable area, will be reduced from 3 times to 2.5 times the standard price for basic priority mail items. In most member states, the incumbent's statutory monopoly is expected to be reduced in line with the requirements and timescales of the EC Directive, with no definite plans as yet for full liberalization. By contrast, Sweden achieved full liberalization in 1993.

In the UK, the reservable area was abolished under the Postal Services Act 2000 subject to the requirement to hold an license to provide postal services, and the UK regulator, the Postal Services Commission ('Postcomm') has announced that it will grant licenses to all operators as from 1 January 2006 subject only to compliance with certain essential requirements, instead of only bulk mail providers and certain other special categories of postal services operator as at present. In the Netherlands, the

* The authors are grateful to their colleagues in Bird & Bird's various offices for their input into this paper concerning the regulatory position in their respective jurisdictions, as follows: Indiana de Seze (Belgium), Fleur Herrenschmidt (France), Georg Terhorst (Germany), Eutimio Monaco (Italy) and Henrik Nilsson and Josefine Jonsson (Sweden).

government has indicated an intention to assume full liberalization in 2007, subject to similar approach been taken in other member states, in particular the UK and Germany.

The ability of member state governments to reserve any part of the postal services market to the incumbent universal service operator is limited to what is necessary to ensure the maintenance of universal service under Article 7(1) of the Postal Directive. This paper will compare the status of liberalization, including the differential scope and approaches to definition of the universal service, in the UK and the Netherlands with the position in various other western European countries, particularly Belgium, France, Germany, Italy and Sweden.

These countries have been chosen because they represent various stages of liberalization against the background of the same EC regulatory framework. Sweden and the UK are (about to be) fully liberalized, although both maintain a universal service obligation for the incumbent postal operator. The Netherlands and Germany have chosen a more cautious pace of liberalization, but are both well ahead of the timetable provided for by the EC postal regime. The third category of Belgium, France and Italy consists of reluctant followers of the liberalization process, who take only those measures to the extent required by the Postal Directive and sometimes even postpone implementation where possible.

The liberalization process take place against the background of slightly increasing mail volumes in some member states and slightly decreasing volumes in others. In the UK, figures provided by Royal Mail and announced by Postcomm show that inland letter volumes grew by 1.5% in 2003/04, with expected market growth by at least 2% per annum for the following two to three years. By contrast, in the Netherlands, figures announced by the competition regulator OPTA for 2003 indicated decreasing mail volumes as a result of increased of electronic data traffic.

Any regulatory authority in the postal services sector needs to address four key areas of policy and to implement and/or apply rules in each of these four areas. These are: (i) the scope of the area of postal services reserved to the incumbent postal operator; (ii) the universal service obligations imposed on the incumbent postal services provider; (iii) the question of any price controls on the services provided by the incumbent universal service provider; and (iv) the extent and pricing of any required granting of access to competitors to the universal service provider's postal network. This is quite apart from the application of general competition law to an incumbent operator occupying a dominant position.

Each of these areas of policy is, or should be, interrelated. The ability of an incumbent to fulfill its universal service obligation depends on the extent of competition which it faces from other licensed operators. Its ability to counteract competition effectively whilst at the same time fulfilling those universal service obligations, depends on the degree of flexibility it is allowed in the pricing of its services. Moreover, due to the labor intensive nature of postal services, full network competition is in practice unachievable outside the urban areas, without competitive service providers being granted downstream access to the incumbent's network. On the other hand, this specific characteristic of postal networks also raises the question whether network access is essential for the development of competition in the postal services market. This in turn focuses on the key question of the price and terms on which an incumbent is required to grant such access, which in turn directly impacts upon it the ability to generate revenue and cover the costs of the universal service.

2. THE STATUTORY POSITION

2.1 EC legislation

The Postal Directive provides for a step-by-step opening of the European market for postal services, in which each step represents a significant but controlled reduction of the reservable area while on the other hand the continuity and quality of the universal service can be ensured.[1] A first significant step was taken in Directive 97/67/EC, which required the EU member states to impose obligations on the universal service provider and to reduce the reservable area (statutory monopoly for the incumbent) to items of domestic and incoming cross-border correspondence.

In July 2002, Directive 97/67/EC was amended by Directive 2002/39/EC, which provides for two further steps in the liberalization process. Article 7(1) as amended provides that the member states should have reduced the weight limit for reserved services to 100 grams and a price of not more than three times the tariff for an item of correspondence in the first weight step of the fastest category from 1 January 2003 on. As from 1st January 2006, it further reduces the combined thresholds for the area that can be reserved to the universal service provider to 50 grams and two and a half times such tariff as from 1st January 2006. However, such services can only be reserved to the extent necessary to ensure the maintenance of the universal service. Furthermore, all outgoing cross-border mail should be open to competition from 1 January 2003 (i.e. an additional 3 % market opening to competition), although exceptions are possible where these are necessary to maintain the universal service - for example if revenue from cross-border mail is

---

[1] See consideration 14 of Directive 2002/39/EC

necessary to finance the domestic universal service - or where the national postal service in a given Member State has particular characteristics.

With respect to the provision of non-reserved services, the Postal Directive offers the member states the choice between a general or no authorization, i.e. no approval required before starting the activity, and an individual license requirement. Of the member states discussed in this paper, only France and the Netherlands have opted for a general authorization system. The other countries all require a license of some form, although some only for certain letter post services (UK, Germany and Sweden) and other for all universal services (Belgium and Italy).

Like Directive 97/67/EC, Directive 2002/39/EC stipulates that the reservable area relates to 'items of correspondence' (which includes any communications in written form on any kind of physical medium to be conveyed and delivered at the address indicated by the sender on the item itself or on its wrapping, with the exception of books, catalogues newspapers and periodicals). However, the amended Article 7(1) of the Postal Directive provides that "to the extent necessary to ensure the provision of universal service, direct mail may continue to be reserved within the same weight and price limits". Although this means that member states may still include direct mail (which in practice constitutes the bulk of B2B and B2C mail volumes) in the reserved area, it puts a burden on the authorities to be able to justify that it is necessary to ensure the provision of the universal service.

The requirements of the Postal Directive dictate the minimum pace of liberalization in the member states until 2006. With respect to future developments, the European Commission has announced that it will investigate the possible completion of the internal postal market by full liberalization in 2009 and is expected to present its conclusions to the Council and the European Parliament before 31 December 2006. However, a number of member states, such as Finland, Sweden, UK, Germany and The Netherlands, are planning (or have already implemented) full liberalization of their postal services before 2009.

As already mentioned, the exclusive or reserved area rights granted by a member state to a universal service provider cannot extend beyond the scope of the universal service itself. This follows from the ruling of the European Court of Justice ('ECJ') in the landmark *Paul Corbeau* case[2] that exclusive rights in favor of a universal service provider are not justified under Articles 86 as regards specific services which are dissociable from the universal service itself (the service of general interest), where these meet special needs of economic operators and call for certain additional services not offered by the traditional postal service, and can be performed without compromising

---

[2] Case C-320/91, ECR (1993) I-2533.

the economic equilibrium of the service of general economic interest. Express mail services are an example where the specific dissociable services do not, taking into account their nature and the conditions in which they are offered, affect the *economic equilibrium* of the universal service provider[3].

The Corbeau test was restated by the ECJ in May 2001 in it judgment of *TNT Traco SpA and Poste Italiane SpA*[4]. The ECJ held that the imposition by a universal service provider of postal dues (based on universal service postage prices) on the provision by independent operators of express postal services, could only be justified with reference to Article 86(2) if the maintenance of such rights was necessary for the universal service provider to be able to perform its public service tasks or to perform them under *economically acceptable and financially stable conditions*. Further, the ECJ concluded that compatibility with Articles 82 and 86 meant that the proceeds from the postal dues may not exceed the amount of the losses incurred in the operation of the universal service by the universal service provider, that the universal service provider must also be required to pay the same dues when itself providing an express mail service not forming part of the universal service, and that none of the costs of that service may be subsidized from the universal service.

2.2 Statutory position in the member states considered

Various member states failed to take the necessary measures by the required date 31 December 2002 to implement the Directive 2002/39 into national law, although all member states have since done so. France was the last one to implement the EU Directives, with its law of 20 May 2005, after the European Commission initiated infringement proceedings in the European Court of Justice against France concerning non-implementation of the Directive and also France's alleged failure to appoint an independent national regulatory authority for postal service sector in accordance with the Postal Directive. This power/duty has now been granted to the independent telecommunications authority, which has now become the ARCEP, by the Law of 20 May 2005.[5]

---

3 The European Commission similarly drew a distinction regarding Spanish legislation, between basic letter services and international express services: *Commission Decision 90/456/EEC, OJ (1990) L233/19.*

4 Case C-340/99,ECR (2001) I-4109.

5 The government minister originally appointed also had certain responsibilities in connection with state property in the French incumbent operator *La Poste* as well as responsibilities for *La Poste's* economic and financial performance, so was not considered by the Commission to be independent.

Despite attempts on EC level to steer the path of liberalization of the postal sector, there are large differences in the extent and pace of liberalization in the EU member states. The Swedish and UK approaches to postal services regulation are more pro-liberalization than most member states. Liberalization in countries like the Netherlands and Germany is also ahead of the pace provided for in the Postal Directive. Belgium, Italy and most notably France seem more reluctant to open up their postal markets to (foreign and domestic) competition. The following table gives an overview of the regulatory position in the countries discussed:

	Letters reserved?	Direct mail reserved?
Belgium	Y	Y
France	Y	Y
Germany	Y	Y
Italy	Y	Y
Netherlands	Y	N
Sweden	N	N
UK	N	N

All countries which have a reserved area extend the scope of the reserved services to what is maximally allowed under the Postal Directive. Notable exception is the Netherlands, which has excluded direct mail from the reserved area and which has a more restricted definition of 'letter mail' instead of the definition of 'item of correspondence' in the Postal Directive that further narrows the scope of the reserved area.

The Commission recently published a report on the application of the Postal Directive, in which it considers the status of the transposition of the Postal Directive, its effect on the market opening in the European Union and the road ahead. Particularly interesting is the Commission Staff Working Paper underlying the Report, in which the transposition of the various provisions of the Postal Directive in the different member states is analyzed.[6]

---

6 Commission Report on the application of the Postal Directive, SEC(2005)388 and the underlying Commission Staff Working Paper COM(2005)102 final, both of which are published on the Commission's website http://europa.eu.int/comm/internal_market/post/studies_en.htm

3. REGULATORY OBLIGATIONS ON INCUMBENT POSTAL OPERATORS

3.1 EC legislation

The Postal Directive requires all member states to ensure the universal service includes, as a minimum, the clearance, sorting, transport and distribution of postal items of up to 2kg; the clearance, sorting, transport and distribution of postal packages of up to 10kg (with an option to increase this to 20kg); the delivery of postal packages received from other member states weighing up to 20kg and services for registered items and insured items.

The Postal Directive requires member states to ensure that the universal service provision complies with the "essential requirements", i.e. the need for confidentiality of correspondence, security of the network as regards the transport of dangerous goods and, where justified, data protection, environmental protection and regional planning. The Postal Directive requires the universal service offered to be identical to all users under comparable conditions, to be made available without discrimination, to be provided on an uninterrupted basis, and to evolve in response to the technical, economic and social environment and the need of users.

The Postal Directive contains various provisions concerning pricing and accounting for the universal service[7] and specifically in respect of the reservable services. Member states must ensure that, as regards the universal service, prices are affordable such that all users have access to the services, cost-orientated, transparent and non-discriminatory. The application of a uniform tariff must not exclude the right of the universal service provider to conclude individual agreements on prices with customers (i.e. in practice a lower price for example for bulk mail under transparent and non-discriminatory conditions). Universal service providers are required to keep separate accounts for the following: each of the services in the reserved area, non-reserved services which are part of the universal service, and services outside the universal service. Internal accounting systems must operate on the basis of consistently applied and objectively justifiable cost accounting principles.[8]

---

7 Articles 12-15.

8 Article 14(3) contains detailed provisions on cost allocation, whereby costs that can be directly assigned must be so assigned and common costs should be allocated on the basis of the origin of the costs, or if this is not possible on the basis of any indirect linkage to another cost category, failing which they must be allocated on the basis of a general allocator computed by using the ratio of all expenses directly or indirectly assigned or allocated, to each of the reserved and non-reserved services.

Accordingly, the main regulatory obligations on incumbent universal service providers can typically be divided into the following categories:

a) Obligations to provide a universal service and accompanying definitions of the scope of the universal service;
b) Quality of service requirements;
c) Financial requirements including transparency of tariffs and separation of accounts for universal service and other activities, and only the reserved area and for other universal service operations respectively, in accordance with the Postal Directive;
d) Pricing controls;
e) Obligation of non-discrimination;
f) Obligations to ensure a uniform tariff for the universal service.

The need to safeguard the universal service is both a fundamental objective and a source of limitations on licenses granted to other operators, under the UK regime. Moreover, under the Postal Directive, the need to safeguard the universal service is a pre-condition for granting any reserved area to the incumbent universal service provider. Until now, there has been no clear definition either at EC level of what is included within the universal service and what is not.

3.2 Regulatory obligations in the member states considered

Each of the member states considered imposes a universal service obligation complying with these minimum requirements. However, it is noteworthy that the approaches to defining the scope of the universal service differ as between EC member states. Other obligations are similarly imposed in all member states considered, sometime even without a requirement to do so in the Postal Directive. For instance, the universal service provider is required to apply a uniform tariff in each of Belgium, France, Germany, Italy, the Netherlands, Sweden (for single items of mail only), and the UK.

For the non-reserved services, some require a license for all postal operators, while others allow any company to carry out non-reserved postal services. Also, the authorization regimes differ greatly in the various member states.

Moreover, some member states have made use of the possibility provided for in Article 9(4) of the Postal Directive to set up a compensation fund to compensate the universal service provider for any undue financial burden which arises as a result of the universal service obligation. The relevant member states that have provided for such a compensation mechanism have done so, for example, on the basis of the other provider's turnover exceeding a minimum level (as in Belgium) or on a *pro-rata* basis (as in

France and Italy). In Germany, the incumbent, Deutsche Post AG ("DPAG"), can demand compensation from the regulatory authority where it can prove that the cost of providing the relevant universal service sufficiently exceeds the income from that service.

For the countries considered, the following overview can be given.

	License required?	Compensation for USO?
Belgium	Y	Y
France	N	Y
Germany	Y*	Y
Italy	Y	Y
Netherlands	N	N
Sweden	Y*	N
UK	Y*	N
* for some (universal) letter post services only		

As for the obligations imposed on the universal service provider, it appears that all member states considered have imposed regulatory obligations concerning reasonable, affordable, cost-oriented and uniform prices, non-discrimination, accounts separation for reserved and other universal services, quality of service levels, some form of pricing controls, and secrecy of letter mail. However the precise extent of the obligations differs somewhat per member state, within the boundaries set by the Postal Directive.

In the UK, the license obligations on Royal Mail not to show any undue preference or discrimination for or against any person or categories of persons have to some extent been clarified by means of an investigation carried out by Postcomm in late 2004 and concluded by means of a decision of 20 January 2005 adopting certain commitments of Royal Mail: *Investigation into Royal Mail Catalogue and Advertising Mail Promotion Scheme, Postcomm Decision dated 20 January 2005.* The investigation concerned a trial promotion undertaken by Royal Mail with 12 catalogue mailing customers during July and August 2003, with the aim of verifying whether it was feasible to launch a wider catalogue and advertising market promotion with a view to growing the overall catalogue mailing market. This raises the issue of whether the granting of discounts to customers by reference to their incremental mailings as opposed to the absolute volume of their mailings, can constitute undue preference or discrimination, in so far as it could result in different prices after discount being applied to customers mailing equal volumes. Postcomm questioned whether such a policy could ever be implemented by a company with the dominance of Royal Mail, in a way that is acceptable in practice, but did not reach any conclusion, stating rather that it would be disproportionate to prohibit Royal Mail from seeking to introduce schemes intended to develop incremental mailing. In the present case, Postcomm considered that the evidence indicated that growing the postal market was not the only aim of the promotions and that Royal Mail had not taken adequate safeguards to ensure that in practice account handlers only applied the available discounts to incremental mailings, as opposed to using the discounts to grant incentives to customers to switch mailings from a competitor of Royal Mail.

In order to close the case, Royal Mail provided assurances to the effect that any new promotions launched by Royal Mail would first be subject to a promotion approval process involving regulatory and competition law approval at a senior level and that Royal Mail would pro-actively involve its Compliance Officer in this process. The Compliance Officer is required to be appointed under condition 13 of Royal Mail license for purposes of facilitating compliance by Royal Mail with competition regulatory provisions of the license.

4. PRICING CONTROLS

4.1 EC legislation

The Postal Directive imposes a basic requirement that tariffs for each of the services comprised in the universal service must be affordable, ensuring that all users of access to the services, and be cost-orientated. Against this background, various member states have imposed specific price controls on the incumbent universal service provider as regards the provision of the universal service, and especially as regards the provision of reserved area services.

4.2 Pricing controls in the member states considered

The predominant basis of price controls on the universal service provider in each member state now considered, can be summarised as follows:

	Inflation (Prices/Costs Index)	Cost – orientation
Belgium	✓	
France		✓
Germany		✓
Italy	✓*	
Netherlands	✓	
Sweden	✓	✓
UK	✓	
* combined with quality of performance criteria		

In France, the Competition Council condemned La Poste, in November 2004, for proposing tying rebates bundling services in competition. La Poste was reproached for two types of practices:

(i) the application of a "global tying rebate" for purchases of all products open to competition: La Poste granted its clients rebates on the basis of the total turnover achieved on the services opened to competition (non-addressed mail, catalogues, B2B packages), thus inciting them (by using its wide range of products) to concentrate their purchases with La Poste.

(ii) the application of a "fidelity rebate": La Poste granted rebates based on the increase of the clients' purchases from one year to the other.[9]

5. THE PROVISION OF DOWNSTREAM ACCESS TO POSTAL NETWORKS

5.1 EC rules relating to network access

As the Postal Directive does not provide for any regulatory obligations concerning access to the postal networks, this is left to the member states. Some member states consider access to the postal network as a fundamental element of liberalization, while others regard access to postal networks unnecessary for the entry of new postal operators to the market. This is very much due to the fact that a postal network is not a physical infrastructure network like telecommunications or energy networks. Within a densely populated urban area giving rise to considerable volumes of inner city mail, it is arguably not unduly difficult to replicate a localized collection, sorting and delivery network. However the establishment of long distance conveyance and sorting networks capable of reaching remote areas involves much greater investments in infrastructure and, the wider the overall area and the more remote the individual delivery destinations, the greater the possibility that the postal network has the characteristics of a natural monopoly or "essential facility" for competition regulation purposes.

The Postal Directive (Article 12) provides that where a universal service provider grants access to its network by providing a service consisting of less than the complete range of features offered for the clearance, transport, sorting and delivery of postal items, for example to businesses, bulk mailers or consolidators, the universal service provider shall (in addition to applying the principles of transparency and non-discrimination) set tariffs which take

9 Decision 04-D-65 of 30 November 2004 (http://www.conseil-concurrence.fr/pdf/avis/04d65.pdf)

account of the avoided costs, as compared with providing the full clearance, transport, sorting and delivery service. Further, the tariffs and conditions must apply equally both as between different third parties and as between third parties and universal service providers supplying equivalent services. Any such tariffs must also be available to private customers who post under similar conditions, i.e. those who carry out an equivalent degree of mail preparation for an equivalent volume of mail items.

The European Commission took a very significant decision in the application of Article 86(1) combined with Article 82 concerning *La Poste of France* "on the lack of exhaustive and independent scrutiny of the scales of charges and technical conditions applied by La Poste to mail preparation firms for access to its reserved services".[10] The Commission decided, following the reasoning of the ECJ in *GB-Inno-BM*[11], that the French Government had allowed a situation to persist in which the public undertaking La Poste was faced with a risk of conflict of interest as the monopoly provider of basic postal services, in relation to determining the terms of access to its reserved services and especially its postal network, because of its activities as a competitor on the upstream market for mail preparation services. In such circumstances, it was the responsibility of the State to ensure an effective monitoring system so as to re-establish effective competition on the upstream market by ensuring that the drawing up of technical specifications and the monitoring of their application would be carried out by a body which is independent of La Poste as the relevant public undertaking. French legislation gave La Poste the power to set its own technical and financial conditions for access by mail preparing firms to its network, including for example conditions as to volume and standard presentation of the mail produced. These conditions were subject to only partial scrutiny by the relevant French public authority, which was not sufficiently independent and neutral in relation to La Poste. The Commission considered that La Poste was in a position to set technical and financial conditions for access to its network that, whilst apparently non-discriminatory, would in fact put La Poste's competitors at a disadvantage as compared with La Poste's subsidiaries. Also, there was the possibility that La Poste could apply the rules less strictly to its own subsidiaries than to competing mail preparers, as regards enforcement of its rules on quantity, format, presentation and times and places of delivery. These factors had a direct impact on the competitive conditions under which the mail preparation firms operated, whilst La Poste was itself and through its subsidiaries a competitor in the upstream mail preparation business. The Commission

---

[10] Decision of 23 October 2001, OJ (2002) L120/19.

[11] Case C-18/88, GB-Inno-BM (1991) ECR I-5941.

concluded that the conflict of interest on the part of La Poste itself constituted an abuse without need to show commitment of an actual abuse in order for there to be an infringement of Article 86 (1) EC.

It is clear that in the *La Poste* case, it was a material factor that lack of satisfactory independent monitoring and regulation of La Poste in relation to the imposition of terms of access for mail preparation firms to its downstream network, would involve discrimination between the conditions applied to La Poste's own subsidiaries and the two competing independent mail preparation firms, both as regards the specific terms and conditions applied and as regards the strictness with which they are enforced.

This European Commission decision has since been followed by a similar decision of the Commission under Article 86 EC against a provision of the German Postal Act, in October 2004. The European Commission concluded that certain provisions which prevent commercial mail preparation firms from earning discounts for handing over pre-sorted letter post at DPAG's sorting offices induced DPAG to discriminate against such mail preparation firms. The discrimination resulted from the fact that individual large users (senders) were allowed to feed self-prepared mail directly into sorting offices and receive volume-related discounts, whilst postal consolidators or intermediaries were prevented from obtaining comparable discounts for mail preparation.[12] However, at the time of writing, Germany and DPAG have filed appeals with the European Court of First Instance claiming that the Commission's decision infringes Article 82 of the EC Treaty and the Postal Directive.[13] The appellants argue that the Commission has wrongly assumed that the relevant provisions of the German Postal Act extend the DPAG's dominant market position in reserved area postal services into the upstream mail pre-sorting market (to the detriment of mail preparation firms). They also argue that it is not discriminatory for DPAG to be allowed to grant volume-based discounts to individual large users (mailers) for pre-sortation, whilst not granting such discounts to commercial postal service providers (i.e. intermediaries or consolidators).

5.2 Access regulation in the member states considered

To date, only Royal Mail (in the UK) and Deutsche Post (in Germany), but none of the postal service incumbents of any of the other member states now considered, are subject to specific regulatory obligations concerning the

---

[12] European Commission press release IP/04/1254, 20 October 2004. Decision is not yet published in the Official Journal, but the draft is available on the Commission's website: http://europa.eu.int/comm/competition/antitrust/cases/decisions/38745/en.pdf

[13] Case T-490/04, Germany v Commission and Case T-493/04, Deutsche Post AG v Commission, OJ (2005) Sec 31/29.

grant of access to their postal sorting, conveyance and delivery networks. In Italy, the Ministry of Communication is empowered[14] to take regulatory measures to promote access to the postal network. However, no time period is specified for the introduction of such regulations and no such measures have so far been announced by the Ministry.

By contrast, in some member states such as the Netherlands and France, there are specific rules on the incumbent in respect of granting access to P.O. boxes in post offices to other postal operators, as opposed to granting access to the main postal network.[15] Such access must be granted on transparent, non-discriminatory and reasonable terms to be negotiated between the incumbent and its competitors, under the supervision of the postal regulator.

In the Netherlands, the government expressly considered that further network access was not necessary for competition, provided that TPG Post accepts pre-sorted bulk mail from its competitors on equivalent terms to those applied to its large customers. In Sweden, there is no access obligation to Posten's postal network. Downstream access has been considered, but the committee advising the Swedish government concluded that such sector-specific legislation would be too far-reaching and would create an unreasonable administrative burden on the supervisory authority[16]. In addition, it considered that the matter should be dealt with on Community level.

In Germany, a postal services operator with a dominant position in the relevant market is obliged to offer access to parts of its overall postal services and to invoice accordingly. This obligation is subject to competitors' demand. Furthermore, the terms of any agreement reached on the basis of this obligation must be economically reasonable for the dominant operator. Finally, the dominant operator must be factually able to perform to the request, and the necessary capacity must be available[17].

In the UK, Royal Mail's license (condition 9) requires it either to agree a code for a grant of access to other postal operators to its network, or to negotiate the grant of access with such other operators, with a view to agreeing terms for such access. Such terms must be on prices that are based on reasonable allegation of costs and must not unduly discriminate between persons having access to Royal Mail's postal facilities. In the event that negotiations fail to lead to agreement, either of the parties can appeal to Postcomm to issue an direct to Royal Mail concerning the terms of access.

---

14 By Legislative Decree No. 269.99

15 A similar obligation with respect to access to P.O. boxes also applies to Deutsche Post in Germany.

16 Swedish Government Office Report SOU 2005:5

17 See sections 19 to 28 of the German Postal Act.

Royal Mail agreed downstream access with three competing operators in late 2003 or early 2004, UK Mail (December 2003) and a TPG Post, UK Ltd and Deutsche Post (April 2004), each of which agreements were hailed by Postcomm as a significant step forward for competitive innovation in service delivery. Each of the agreements involved the application of geographically averaged prices for mail deposited at Royal Mail's inward mail centers.

By contrast, Royal Mail has more recently agreed the grant of access to another operator (on 14 October 2004) a price which are geographically – averaged), i.e. the price varies depending on the geographic mail profile (know as 'zonal pricing'). This resulted in complaints by UK Mail, TPG Post, and Express Limited, prompting a Postcomm investigation which commenced on 7 January 2005. Postcomm is specifically investigating whether the system of zonal or de-averaged prices is unduly preferential or discriminatory for or against either the new entrants granted the de-averaged prices or the existing new entrants already granted access on geographically averaged prices, or whether such terms are duly preferential or discriminatory for or against Royal Mail's own downstream businesses. Further issues include whether or not Royal Mail may have obtained a commercial advantage from the disclosure of information gained as a result of granting access to its network and/or whether Royal Mail has properly complied with requirement to notifying published details of any zonal access price offer.

6. CONCLUSIONS

The UK and Sweden (and also Finland) have taken the fastest progress towards full liberalization of the postal services sector, given that Sweden has already liberalized in 1993 and full liberalization of the UK postal services sector is now little more than six months away, on 1 January 2006. Meanwhile, the Postal Directive requires further reduction of the reservable area, to a 50 gram weight threshold, in other EU member states on the same date. The process of liberalization raises important questions for the performance of the universal service. Whilst a pro-liberalization, pro-competition approach to postal services regulation, as seen in Sweden and the UK, may appear justifiable at the present stage of market development, with incumbents yet to face significant levels of competition, important competition regulatory issues need to addressed.

The national law and regulations of all the member states now considered impose a uniform tariff for the universal service. Each of the member states now considered also impose some form of specific price controls or caps on the incumbent universal service provider. Approaches differ to the means of controlling prices. Such controls are to a large extent inflation related, being based on a prices index or costs index, for example in Belgium, the Netherlands and the UK (or a combination of inflation and quality criteria as in Italy), whilst being more based on costs in France and Germany. The approach taken under the price index or cost index form of controls presupposes that the incumbent will, through its own efficiencies, prevent its costs escalating in excess of the rate of inflation from year to year, whilst the UK "RPI-X" approach requires the incumbent to achieve such efficiencies, measured by reference to the "X" factor.

As regards the compulsory grant of downstream access to the incumbent's postal network (as opposed to P.O. boxes) only the national regulatory systems of Germany and the UK (of the countries now considered) impose a specific obligation to grant such access. Other countries, like Sweden and the Netherlands have explicitly considered that specific regulation of downstream access is not necessary to establish competition, provided that the incumbent accepts, without discrimination, pre-sorted bulk mail from its competitors and large customers alike. It is in some ways surprising to find such disparity between the member states. This partly reflects the different approaches to liberalisation in the various countries, and it also may reflect a difference in views as to the extent to which a postal network could be replicated without undue difficulty and therefore whether or not it is a natural monopoly or "essential facility".

Further, the issue raised in the UK of whether the granting of access could in effect be treated as part of the universal service obligation, is of fundamental importance. Insofar as the provision of network access is granted to competing upstream postal services providers, the service is not provided, or at least not directly provided, to end users and therefore should not be treated as falling within the universal service obligation. However, as shown by the recent proceedings brought by the European Commission against Germany under Article 86 EC and by the *Bundeskartellamt* against DPAG under German competition law, the service to bulk mailers of accepting pre-sorted mail on a discounted basis is in essence a similar service. Insofar as the grant of downstream access should or were to be regarded as coming within the universal service obligation, this would mean that the associated universal service obligations would apply, including in particular the requirement for a geographically uniform tariff. This, in turn, would have certain implications, for example, as to whether Royal Mail should be entitled to impose a geographically de-averaged price for network access, which question is currently being investigated by Postcomm. It may well be that the appropriate and correct analysis is that downstream acceptance of pre-sorted bulk mail into the network on more favourable terms for users who wish to undertake pre-sortation represents, as regards such bulk mailers, an agreed departure from the universal service, rather than being an extension or part of the universal service itself.

In any event, where an obligation is imposed on an incumbent universal service provider to accept pre-sorted bulk mail into its network in return for work-sharing discounts, and the incumbent is required to do so on a non-discriminatory basis as between individual bulk mailer users and postal services intermediaries or consolidators, the result is in effect the same as imposing an obligation of downstream network access. This is the position recognised in the Netherlands, for which reason the Dutch legislator deemed it unnecessary to impose an obligation of downstream network access on TPG Post.

It is clear from the European Commission's decisions of October 2001 and October 2004 that where downstream access is provided at discount prices to large users who feed pre-sorted mail into the network, there should, under Articles 82 and 86 EC, be no risk of discrimination either as between the incumbent operator's own subsidiaries and competitors, and no discrimination as between large users carrying out pre-sortation and independent mail preparation firms or consolidators.

Based on these considerations, and in view of the increasing competition which incumbent universal service providers in EC member states can be expected to face as liberalization is progressed further, the following key issues arise:

In the face of an expected increase in competition, especially if fuelled by a cost-plus basis of pricing downstream access to an incumbent's network, the question must be raised of for how long it will be appropriate to require the universal service to be performed at a geographically uniform tariff. Such a uniform tariff obligation deprives the universal service provider of the flexibility to take reasonable steps to protect its position in the face of competition, by adjusting its prices to make them more cost-reflective and to respond to specific competitive threats in relation to particular geographic areas of classes of customers. The case law of the European Court of Justice on abuse of dominant position does allow generally a dominant operator to take proportionate steps to protect itself in this way.

As regards price controls, the question must be asked whether, if competition takes hold as intended by the EC and national regulatory authorities, will there be a need for continuing pricing controls? The regulatory rationale for price controls is, or should be, to provide a surrogate for the price-constraining effects of competition. The greater the penetration of new entrants, arguably the less the need for price controls on an incumbent's services.

As regards the terms of downstream access, the retail-minus or "avoided costs" approach to setting the price of access is expressly required to be taken into account under the Postal Directive. Once full competition has become established, the application of a cost-plus basis of charging for access to the network could in effect deprive an incumbent universal service provider of its ability properly to exploit its assets, especially if it would at the same time be required to bear the continuing burden of universal service provision. In the UK, Royal Mail has taken a practical approach and agreed with its competitors UK Mail, TPG Post, and Deutsche Post a structure of access charges which seems to resemble retail-minus charging. Postcomm has allowed this, or at least not prevented it, stating instead that it welcomes the voluntary conclusion of access agreements. It is to be noted that even though the approach to access pricing in Germany is largely based on the incremental costs, the approach actually applied by Royal Mail in the UK, and also the approach required under Dutch legislation for pre-sortation or "work-sharing" discounts, in each case applies the avoided costs principle. A cost-plus basis of pricing, based on the incumbent's costs of the downstream services actually provided, may fail to cover the costs to the incumbent universal service provider of maintaining and renewing the network. This is a feature of the cost structure to which an access seeker should properly be expected to contribute. The retail-minus or avoided costs approach does allow for such a contribution by the new entrant and it would be unfair to an incumbent universal service provider not to receive such contribution to the maintenance and renewal.

In any event, it would seem inconsistent, on the basis of the above objectives, for regulators to continue with the dual policies of encouraging cost-plus charges for downstream access to an incumbent's network whilst at the same time imposing or maintaining rigorous price controls in respect of the incumbents services to end users.

In our view, it is not appropriate to bring the grant of downstream network access, whether based on regulatory access obligations or on the non-discrimination principle (obliging the incumbent to grant the same discounts for pre-sorted bulk mail delivered by competitors or by customers) within the scope of the universal service obligation. In postal services as in other regulated, network-based utilities, the granting of network access as a means of facilitating upstream competition is a different activity from the provision of a universal service to end users. In particular, the granting of discounts, on a work-sharing basis, for pre-sorted mail should in our view be seen as a departure from the universal service obligation whereby such work-sharing on mutually acceptable terms is agreed between the universal service provider and the customer in place of the universal service provision. The scope of the universal service obligation should be confined to the provision of upstream collection and downstream delivery on a geographically uniform basis. Any different approach would in our view result in unacceptable and unnecessary complications and could unfairly inhibit the universal service provider from being able to safeguard its competitive position upstream whilst both granting access to its network on reasonable terms where required and providing the universal service (sometimes uneconomically for remote geographical areas) for individual end users.

In this connection, it is helpful to note that Postcomm, in its February 2005 decision document *Giving Customers Choice: A Fully Open Postal Services Market,* stated that it recognizes the link between market opening and the definition of the universal service and the impact that this has on the amount of pricing flexibility Royal Mail is subsequently allowed. Postcomm stated that it aims to achieve a balanced package that allows Royal Mail the appropriate degree of pricing flexibility, and that in a fully competitive market place, Royal Mail should have a higher degree of flexibility.

In the Netherlands, not only is the balance between market opening and universal service obligations taken into account but also the economic effects of liberalization. Although the Minister of Economic Affairs concludes in his 2004 policy note on the future development of the postal sector that full liberalization at the earliest possible date is in the best interest of consumers, consideration is also given to the position of TPG Post on an international level. Since full liberalization of the Dutch market means that postal incumbents from neighbouring countries (like Royal Mail and DPAG which have already entered the Dutch market) may compete freely with TPG Post on the Dutch market, it is considered important to establish a level-playing field by keeping the same pace of liberalization as in Germany and the UK.

For the EU member states, which have chosen a more cautious approach towards liberalization, the European Commission, meanwhile, continues to map out the path of liberalization. In its recent report on the application of the Postal Directive, the Commission advocates an in-depth debate on the future postal policy and, to support that process, has announced the launch of two studies on the development of competition and the evolution of a regulatory model for European postal services as well as, towards the end of 2005, a study on the impact on the universal service of the full accomplishment of the internal postal market.

Chapter 20

Benefit-Cost Regulation of Negotiated Service Agreements*

David M. Levy, Joy M. Leong, Lawrence G. Buc, and Michael K. Plunkett
Sidley Austin Brown & Wood LLP, SLS Consulting Inc., and United States Postal Service

1. INTRODUCTION AND SUMMARY

During the past 30 years, many regulatory commissions have abandoned their traditional hostility to customized rate and service contracts between regulated carriers or public utilities and individual customers. In 2002, the U. S. Postal Rate Commission ("PRC") joined this trend, announcing that the PRC would look favorably on Negotiated Service Agreements ("NSAs") between the United States Postal Service ("USPS") and individual mailers. To date, however, the NSA mechanism has failed to live up to its potential. In contrast to the flourishing of customized contracts in other industries, only four NSAs with USPS have received regulatory approval in the past three years.

We argue here that the dearth of postal NSAs stems from both the high transaction costs of the NSA process and the PRC's decision to limit the aggregate discounts available in all NSAs approved to date to the estimated cost savings generated by other provisions of the NSA. The latter policy stems from the PRC's fear that mailers might trick the USPS into giving

---

* Levy and Leong have represented Bank One and several other mailers in negotiating and litigating proposed NSAs. Buc has served as an expert for mailer proponents of NSAs. Plunkett has been the lead negotiator for the USPS in all NSAs proposed to date. The views expressed here do not necessarily represent those of the USPS, Sidley, SLS, Bank One, or any other client of Sidley or SLS.

discounts for mail volume that a mailer would have entered anyway, even without the discounts. The cap on total discounts imposed by the PRC as a safeguard, however, is likely to diminish the potential benefits of existing NSAs to USPS and mailers, by choking off the additional high-margin volume that the NSAs could otherwise encourage. In addition, because the level of the cap is based on the USPS cost savings, the cap makes NSAs cost-effective only for a few dozen of the largest mailers in the United States.

We propose that the PRC, rather than pursue the chimera of perfect certainty, adopt an alternative standard that emulates the conduct of unregulated firms to manage similar risks in their own buy-sell contracts. First, a competitive firm minimizes these risks by gathering information about its negotiating partner's costs, demand, and business plans before and during negotiation of the contract, and by incorporating risk-limiting mechanisms in the contract itself. Second, the firm balances irreducible risks and uncertainties of the contract against its potential benefits to the firm. If the anticipated benefits exceed the anticipated costs, the firm can prudently enter into the contract. The PRC should apply a similar test.

2. NSAS AND THEIR POTENTIAL BENEFITS

A Negotiated Service Agreement ("NSA") is a *customized* rate and service contract between the USPS and an individual mailer. An NSA "provides for customer-specific rates or fees and/or terms in accordance with the terms and conditions of the contract." 39 Code of Federal Regulations ("CFR") §3001.5(r). Unlike other services offered by the Domestic Mail Classification Schedule, the postal counterpart of the common carrier tariff, an NSA offers service only to the individual mailer that is a party to the NSA.

The terms of an NSA can involve both rates and conditions of service. In the NSAs adopted to date, mailers have committed to: (1) waive physical return of undeliverable First-Class Mail, (2) update their mailing lists more often, and (3) enter more First-Class Mail, whether newly generated or switched from less profitable Standard Mail. In exchange, the USPS has agreed to (1) waive its customary charges for electronic address correction information, and (2) offer discounts for the additional First-Class Mail entered by the mailer above a specified minimum volume threshold. The threshold is set at a level close to the volume that the mailer would be expected to send if no NSA discounts were given (so-called "Before Rates volume"). Domestic Mail Classification Schedule ("DMCS") § 610 (Capital One NSA); *id.*, § 611 (Discover NSA); *id.* § 612 (Bank One NSA); *id.* § 613

(HSBC NSA). The USPS expects to gain from these contracts by reducing its costs of service and gaining additional contribution from the added volume of First-Class Mail that the mailer enters in response to the discount incentives of the NSA. The NSA partner expects to gain by reducing its postage costs at the margin.

The NSA feature with perhaps the most widespread potential is the volume discount. The volume discounts offered in existing NSAs take the form of declining block rate schedules, with progressively deeper discounts offered for progressively larger increments of additional volume entered by the mailer during the NSA. The general benefits of declining block rates, a form of non-linear pricing or second-degree price discrimination, are generally recognized in the economic literature: compared with a uniform rate, a declining block rate schedule can enable the supplier to capture a greater share of the potential surplus between the customer's demand curve and the supplier's marginal cost curve. If the discounts and volume increments are tailored properly to the customer, a declining block rate schedule can make both the supplier and the customer better off (Varian (1988), pp. 611-617; Willig (1978); PRC (2003), ¶¶ 5008-5031)).

Volume discounts have gained particular importance with the recent rise of electronic bill presentation and payment ("EBPP"). As noted elsewhere, there is a growing consensus that EBPP is an increasingly attractive substitute in the United States for First-Class Mail, one of the highest-margin products offered by the USPS.[1] Volume discount NSAs, if designed properly, could slow the loss of First-Class Mail volume to the Internet, particularly by big national banks and other financial institutions. Volume discount NSAs could also allow the Postal Service to attract additional volume of saturation mail (*i.e.*, mail sent to nearly every residential address in a block or neighborhood), for which newspaper delivery systems and other non-postal carriers now compete with Standard Mail. In these and similar circumstances, customized rate discounts could benefit not only the network carrier and its contract partners, but also the rest of the rate paying community. The logic is the general logic of economic price discrimination in network industries with large fixed costs, multiple outputs, and considerable customer heterogeneity: if the contracts allow the carrier to increase its contribution to fixed costs, the burden borne by other ratepayers can be reduced (Baumol and Willig (1983)).

---

[1] A summary of some recent assessments appears in Levy (2005), pp. 278-280. The extent to which EBBP will displace First-Class Mail volume in the United States is still in question. Some recent studies indicate that the rate of substitution is lower than previously predicted. Flynn (2005); Tamayo *et al.* (2005).

Recognizing these benefits, regulators of other network industries in the United States—including common carrier railroads, energy pipelines and telephone companies—have allowed volume discounts on these grounds for decades (Levy (2005), pp. 281-82). Within the past 30 years, regulators have also overcome their traditional hostility to NSA-like contracts between regulated companies and individual ratepayers, and have allowed these contracts to embody volume discounts (Levy (2005), p. 283).

Internationally, postal regulators have also moved toward relatively light-handed oversight of NSA-like arrangements and volume discounts. In Canada, for example, non-generic postal rates are established through "negotiated, confidential agreements that are customized for individual, large-volume business customers," which do not require regulatory approval of the Canadian government ((United States General Accounting Office (1997), p. 49). The same is true of postal administrations in many other advanced Western economies (Motley (1996)).

The American railroad industry provides a dramatic illustration of the potential benefits of NSAs. Beginning in 1978, the Interstate Commerce Commission ("ICC") and several reviewing courts held that the traditional ratemaking provisions of the Interstate Commerce Act, which (like the Postal Reorganization Act) required that rates be just, reasonable, and not unduly discriminatory, gave the ICC discretion to give effect to customized rate and service contracts on a case-by-case basis.[2] In 1980, Congress codified these rulings into the Interstate Commerce Act itself (Pub. L. No. 96-448, Title II, § 208(a), 94 Stat. 1908).

The statutory language, which remains in effect today, sharply curtailed regulatory oversight of NSA-like contracts (49 U.S.C. § 10709). The ICC (and its successor, the Surface Transportation Board) were authorized to review the justness and reasonableness of a proposed contract only if a third party filed a complaint challenging the contract before it took effect. 49 U.S.C. §§ 10709(c) and (g). Most shippers not party to the contract could challenge it only on the grounds that it would unduly impair the ability of the rail carrier to meet its common carrier obligations to the complainant (*e.g.*, by tying up too large a share of the carrier's specialized rail cars). *Id.*, § 10709(g)(2)(A)(i). Contracts for the transportation of agricultural commodities (but no other commodities) could also be challenged on the grounds that (1) the railroad party to the contract had failed to offer a contract on similar terms to other, similarly situated shippers, or (2) the proposed contract would constitute a "destructive competitive practice." *Id.*,

[2] *Railroad Contract Rates: Policy Statement*, Ex Parte No. 358-F, 43 Fed. Reg. 58189 (1978) (Policy Statement I); *Burlington Northern R.R. Co. v. ICC*, 679 F.2d 934 (D.C. Cir. 1982); *Sea-Land Serv., Inc. v. ICC*, 738 F.2d 1311 (D.C. Cir. 1984).

§ 10709(g)(2)(B).[3] Significantly, the statute did not authorize challenges to a proposed contract on the theory that the discounts offered by the railroad were deeper than needed to get the business, or that the resulting rates were below contribution-maximizing levels.

The results of this new regulatory approach have been dramatic. Contract rates have replaced common carrier tariff rates as the dominant legal framework for service in those regulated industries. By 1982—just two years after the enactment of legislation expressly authorizing such contracts—some 2,000 individual railroad transportation contracts were on file with the ICC (*Railroad Transportation Contracts*, 367 I.C.C. 9, 32 (Oct. 8, 1982)). By 1997, approximately 82 percent of all railroad traffic was moving under contract rates and other non-tariff rates (United States General Accounting Office (1999), p. 23). The industry, teetering on the brink of financial collapse in 1980,[4] was reborn. Between 1981 and 2003, the average railroad rate declined by 60 percent in real dollars, while industry productivity more than doubled, traffic volume increased by 60 percent, and returns on net investment surged (Association of American Railroads (2005)). And when certain interest groups sought to re-regulate the industry, much of the shipping industry fought against a return to the *status quo ante*.

3. SLOW DEPLOYMENT OF NSAS BY THE USPS

The PRC did not expressly authorize the USPS to enter into NSAs until early 2002. In response to a query from a Congressional committee, the PRC announced that a postal rate contract with an individual mailer would be lawful if (1) the contract was subject to the usual review procedures of the Postal Reorganization Act for proposed rate and classification changes before the contract became effective, (2) the terms of the contract satisfied the general ratemaking standards of the Act and benefited mailers as a whole, and (3) the rates and services specified in the contract were offered "on the same terms to other potential users willing to meet the same conditions of service" (PRC (2002)).

In September 2002, the USPS filed a request with the PRC for approval of an NSA with Capital One Services, Inc., a major issuer of credit cards and

---

[3] Ports could also challenge contracts as unduly discriminatory. 49 U.S.C. § 10709(g)(2)(A)(ii).

[4] Penn Central (the largest railroad in the United States) and six other major railroads went bankrupt between 1967 and the early 1970s; two other large carriers went bankrupt in the late 1970s; and by 1980 several other carriers were near collapse. *See* S. Rep. No. 470, 96th Cong., 1st Sess. 3-4 (1979); H.R. Rep. No. 1035, 96th Cong., 2d Sess. 99 (1980). In 1980, Congress found that the industry would face a capital shortfall between $16 and $20 billion by 1985. Staggers Rail Act of 1980, Pub. L. No. 96-448, § 2.

one of the largest individual mailers of First-Class Mail in the United States. The proposed NSA required Capital One to (1) update the addresses in its mailing lists more often than required by USPS's existing address hygiene rules and (2) waive physical return of undeliverable-as-addressed ("UAA") First-Class solicitation mail. In exchange, USPS agreed to (1) waive its usual fee for providing electronic information on undeliverable mail, and (2) provide rate discounts, ranging from three to six cents per piece, for First-Class Mail entered by Capital One in excess of 1.225 billion pieces per year (approximately the annual volume Capital One was projected to mail without discounts) during any of the three years of the NSA. The PRC recommended implementation of the proposed NSA, with certain modifications, on May 15, 2003 (PRC (2003)). The Governors of USPS voted on June 2, 2003, to implement the NSA as recommended (Governors of the USPS (2003)).

The rapid deployment of NSAs experienced by railroads and other regulated network industries has not materialized in the USPS, however. The USPS has sought approval of only four other NSAs since 2003. Three of the four have been with large financial institutions—Discover Financial Services, Bank One (now J.P. Morgan Chase), and HSBC North America Holdings Inc.—and were proposed as similar ("functionally equivalent," in postal parlance) to the Capital One NSA. The Discover and Bank One NSAs were approved in 2004 (PRC (2004b and 2004c)). The HSBC NSA was approved in 2005 (PRC (2005c)).[5]

The limited number of NSA proposals stems in part from the transaction costs of obtaining them. Negotiating and obtaining PRC approval of an NSA requires a mailer to incur transaction costs—primarily attorney and consultant fees and the opportunity costs of the months of management time diverted to obtaining the NSA. These costs, once incurred, are sunk, and cannot be recovered should the mailer abandon the NSA proposal. These costs are also large, for the Commission's standards and procedures for approval of NSAs have departed little from the traditional model of monopoly rate regulation, which may include the full gamut of testimony, discovery, hearings, and briefs found in traditional adversarial litigation. The financial and other data that the proponents must submit in support of an NSA are comparable in detail to those required for a traditional rate or classification proposal, and NSA partners may be requested to provide data

[5] On July 14, 2005, the USPS jointly filed for approval of an NSA with Bookspan, the largest owner of book clubs in the United States (PRC Docket No. MC2005-3). The proposed Bookspan NSA differs from the previous NSAs in a number of respects. Most significantly, the proposed volume discounts are for Standard Mail, not First-Class Mail, and the proponents of the NSA do not claim that the NSA will generate any cost savings. The Bookspan NSA thus would be a pure volume incentive deal.

that they consider proprietary or competitively sensitive. 39 C.F.R. §§ 3001.193 *et seq*. Any third parties may intervene, challenge a proposed NSA, and embroil its proponents in a full-blown rate and classification case with little or no showing of probable cause to believe that the NSA provisions would violate the Postal Reorganization Act.[6]

However, the paucity of postal NSAs is also due in large part to the risk aversion of the PRC. The PRC has been unwilling to approve an NSA without a high level of assurance against the possibility that the USPS might be awarding the mailer discounts for volume that the mailer would have entered anyway, even without the discounts (so-called "Before Rates" volume). Concerned that mailers are poised to game the system by understating their projected Before Rates volume, and that USPS has failed to erect adequate safeguards against this "moral hazard," the PRC has arbitrarily limited the aggregate volume discounts paid over the life of each NSA to the total cost savings that the USPS is expected to receive from the changes in mailing practices that the NSA obligates the mailer to undertake.

The Commission's "cost savings" cap first emerged in the Capital One NSA case. Noting "the variability in the volume history of Capital One" and "the company's history of rapidly increasing First-Class Mail volume" (Governors of the USPS (2005), p. 11), the Commission found that Capital One's Before Rates volume estimates were "unreliable [and] that without a stop-loss provision there [wa]s no reasonable assurance that USPS w[ould] not lose money on the NSA" (*id.*). Accordingly, the PRC limited the aggregate discounts available to Capital One over the three year term of the NSA to $40.6 million, the total projected savings attributed by the Commission to the NSA for the same period (*id.*, p. 2).

The Commission has imposed cost savings caps in all three NSA cases decided since the Capital One case. Indeed, in the Bank One case, the PRC imposed a cost savings cap even though (1) the Bank One NSA had risk-limiting provisions lacking in the Capital One NSA,[7] (2) no participant sought such a cap, and (3) the proposed NSA was *supported* in a near-unanimous and unopposed settlement by all the participants, including the Office of Consumer Advocate (the arm of the Commission chartered with defending the interests of ordinary consumers) and a variety of sophisticated mailer and labor groups with an economic interest in avoiding the needless

[6] *Compare* Bank One Corporation (2004a); Bank One Corporation (2004b); *and* United States Postal Rate Commission (2004a), p. 5-6.

[7] These included an annual adjustment to the minimum volume threshold for discounts and a more elaborate mechanism for dealing with the volume effects of mergers and acquisitions. These detailed merger provisions protected against any volume changes that might have resulted from the merger of Bank One and JP Morgan Chase in 2004. Postal Rate Commission (2004c), pp. 70-71.

payment of discounts by USPS to large First-Class mailers (PRC (2004c), ¶¶ 2014). The Commission, defending its unilateral action, asserted that such a cap was necessary to "provide . . . adequate protection of mailers not party to the agreement"—in particular, protection against the "moral hazard" that Bank One might have understated its Before Rates volume (PRC (2005a), 70 Fed. Reg. 4802, n. 7).

In February 2005, the Governors of USPS took the unusual step of sending the Bank One case back to the PRC for reconsideration. The Governors asked the PRC to (1) clarify and elaborate on the evidentiary requirements necessary to support volume discounts, and its policy and standards for recommending NSAs in the future, (2) reevaluate the record evidence and determine if the $11.5 million cap should in fact be imposed or otherwise modified, and (3) explain what weight (if any) the Commission intended to give to unopposed settlement agreements in future NSA cases (Governors of the USPS (2004)). The Governors expressed concern that the Commission's restrictive approach had chilled prospects for future NSAs (*id.* at 9-10):

The fact is that, in the current environment, with three Commission NSA recommendations as a guide, we are informed by postal management that many firms with whom the Postal Service has been pursuing ideas for NSAs have either now lost interest, as a result of the artificial constraints the Commission has imposed, or have been deterred by the complications and expense that future NSA litigation promises, with little assurance of ultimate success.

As noted above, the Bookspan NSA, proposed by the USPS in July 2005, would be a pure volume discount arrangement, without any projected cost savings at all. Several competitors of the Postal Service have already intervened in opposition to the NSA. Between the reconsideration of the Bank One case and the more recent Bookspan proposal, the appropriateness of the cost savings cap remains very much a live issue before the Commission.

4. PROBLEMS WITH THE PRC'S RISK-AVERSE REGULATION OF NSAS

The PRC's concern over the possibility that mailers might have an incentive in some circumstances to game the USPS by understating their "before rates" mail volume is not irrational. A postal customer is likely to enter NSA negotiations knowing better than the USPS (or any other third party) what volumes the customer intends to mail at existing postal rates in future periods. At least in some circumstances, this information asymmetry might create an incentive for the customer to understate its Before-Rates volume in the hope of persuading the USPS to set the volume thresholds for rate discounts below the volume that the customer would enter anyway, and thus obtain discounts for this "anyhow" mail. If the customer actually pursued such a strategy, and it succeeded in fooling the USPS, the USPS would be giving away potential revenue needlessly.

The cost-savings cap on discounts, however, is a misguided response. First, the amount of the cap bears no logical relation to the magnitude of the risk it supposedly prevents. One can conceive of NSA rate discounts that are offered purely as incentives for additional volume (e.g., as in the Bookspan NSA); NSAs discounts offered purely to induce cost saving activity by the mailer, with no expectation of additional volume; and NSAs that are varying mixes of the two (i.e., the Capital One, Discover, Bank One and HSBC NSAs). Even assuming for the sake of argument that the possible underestimation of Before Rates volume is a serious concern, limiting discounts to cost savings is a crude, one-size-fits-all remedy.

Moreover, a cost savings cap almost certainly will give mailers the wrong incentives. If volume incentive discounts induce the mailer to enter more mail, and if the incremental cost of this increased volume is less than the incremental revenue, then the USPS is ahead. (The mailer presumably is ahead as well; otherwise it would not have entered the additional volume.) A cap on total discounts is likely to choke off at least some of this increase in volume, for the obvious reason that once the total discounts reach the cap, the mailer must pay the full undiscounted postage for each additional piece of mail. Moreover, for mailers with few cost-saving opportunities, a cost savings cap is likely to preclude the reaching of any NSA agreement in the first place. In this section, we offer a rough assessment of the magnitude of these costs.

4.1 Loss of Potential Benefits from NSAs That Take Effect

The most immediate outcome of a cap on total discounts is a reduction of the mailer's incentive to enter additional mail that would otherwise qualify for discounts in the absence of a cap—and a consequent loss of the contribution that this additional volume would have provided. If the Before-Rates and After-Rates volume projections of the NSA proponents are close to accurate, the resulting loss of contribution could run into tens of millions of dollars over the life of an NSA.

The evidence in the Bank One case indicates that Standard Mail and First-Class Mail are close enough substitutes for Bank One and similar financial institutions for delivery of solicitation mail that discounts of two to five cents per piece could stimulate massive increases in the volume of First-

Class solicitations. (The current price differential is about 10 cents. Because First-Class Mail is regarded as a higher quality service, all Standard Mail presumably would switch to First-Class Mail if the price differential between the classes were eliminated (*i.e.*, for a discount of 10 cents). Hence, it is unsurprising that massive amounts of mail will switch for discounts of between two and five cents.) Much of this new First-Class Mail volume represents a migration of mail from Standard Mail, which generates a much smaller per unit contribution margin to USPS (Rappaport (2004), p. 8). In the Bank One case, Buc performed a Monte Carlo analysis to estimate the magnitude of the additional contribution that a stop-loss cap would choke off. The analysis showed an 80 percent probability that a cap such as the one subsequently imposed by the Commission would cost USPS at least $6.1 million in annual contribution; a 50 percent probability that the cap would cost USPS at least $8.7 million in annual contribution; and a ten percent probability that the cap would cost USPS at least $11.4 million in annual contribution (Bank One Corporation (2004c), p. 50). Over the three-year term of the NSA, these results are equivalent to an 80 percent probability that the lost contribution would exceed $18.3 million, an even probability that the lost contribution would exceed $26.2 million, and a ten percent probability that the lost contribution would approach or exceed $34.5 million (*id.*). These are substantial losses in contribution for a business facing a competitive environment as daunting as the USPS.

4.2 Fewer Mailers Willing To Seek NSAs

The PRC's stop-loss cap is also likely to shrink the potential universe of mailers willing to pursue an NSA through negotiations with the USPS and the required rate and classification litigation before the PRC. As noted above, obtaining an NSA may require the mailer to incur substantial transaction costs. A mailer will rationally incur these costs only if they are less than the expected value of the NSA to the mailer. The expected value of the NSA depends on several factors, including the size of the individual mailer, which, in this context, can be thought of as total spending on mail.[8] Other relevant factors are the class and physical characteristics of the mail. For instance, mailers whose spending is concentrated in mail subclasses that already have many worksharing opportunities may be unable to offer any significant additional cost savings under an NSA, and would therefore view

[8] Though NSAs may directly affect only the price of postage, customers rationally will evaluate the effect of an NSA on total mail expenditures, which might include paper, printing equipment, addressing services and even capital investments.

their NSA options as limited. Stated otherwise, a cost-savings cap penalizes mailers whose mail already has below-average costs for USPS to handle.

The individual mailer's purpose for using postal services is perhaps the most important determinant of expected value. Because NSAs must result in a net gain in contribution for USPS, all agreements must, by definition, include some combination of cost savings or increased revenue, or both. Mailers whose use of the mail is discretionary and hence price-elastic (*e.g.* direct mail advertisers) would arguably have more options, *ceteris paribus*, than those mailers whose demand for service is relatively inelastic (*e.g.* mailers of utility bills). Similarly, those mailers using mail for customer acquisition can increase the total potential value of an NSA by using cost savings and incentives to increase the size of their businesses. Even if such gains are not shared directly with USPS, mailers that can derive value apart from postage savings are more likely to be able to fashion a feasible negotiating range. Thus, the expected value of an NSA is a function of a mailer's postage spending (P), class of mail and related elasticities of demand (C), and purpose in using postage (U): $EV_{nsa} = f(P, C, U)$.

It is assumed, for this paper, that all agreements must be litigated and that transaction costs that mailers incur are directly associated with this litigation. While large commercial customers have legal departments, financial analysts, and purchasing departments, these departments rarely have specialized expertise in postal ratemaking. Moreover, transaction costs are assumed to be positively correlated with the duration of litigation, because consultants and attorneys with specialized expertise in NSA litigation typically charge for their work by the hour. It is unsurprising then, that factors serving to lengthen litigation time tend to increase costs. Although an exhaustive treatment of these factors is beyond the scope of this paper, one could surmise that the factors affecting transactions costs include agreement complexity (X), novelty (N), and the class of mail (C). To a significant extent, these factors are beyond the control of the proponents of an agreement. For instance, the duration of litigation will be affected by the number of opponents of the NSA, and their vigor in opposing an agreement or some of its features. Experience has already shown that such opponents need not be direct competitors of the proponents; they may choose to oppose a specific NSA to call attention to issues that they would otherwise have to litigate in a more complex proceeding.

Empirical results to date, although limited, provide some guidance as to how financial eligibility (the condition where EV>EC) is defined. In the first thirteen months of the Cap One NSA, Capital One's total postage discount was $2.2 million—approximately one-half of one percent of the company's total spending of $407.6 million on First-Class Mail (USPS (2004)). Under the PRC-imposed cap, Capital One could earn as much as

$43 million in discounts over its three-year NSA period—an amount equivalent to slightly less than a three percentage average discount on the total spending on postage needed to qualify for the maximum aggregate discount. This could be considered an approximately maximal result for several reasons: First, Capital One is in the unusual position of being able to offer a large pool of cost savings (*id.*). Second, much of Capital One's First-Class Mail is used for advertising, and therefore is more price elastic. Third, First-Class Mail has higher average margins than most other postal services, and therefore allows more room for USPS to negotiate incentives.

With those qualifications, a ratio of 0.5 percent appears to be a more reasonable basis for establishing EV_{nsa}. At that rate, if one arbitrarily assumes transaction costs of $1,000,000, a customer would need to spend $200 million on postage in order that $EV_{nsa} = EC_{nsa}$. In 2004, approximately 69 Postal Service customers had postage spending greater than $50 million. The breakdown of these customers by product follows:

First-Class Mail	22
Standard Mail	35
All Other	12

The composition by product is unsurprising, for Standard and First-Class Mail account for most of USPS's revenues. Fairness dictates that a monopolist like USPS treat all similarly situated customers in a like manner. Generally, a customer's level of postage spending has not been a basis for discrimination by USPS. However, the transaction costs of obtaining NSAs effectively discriminate in essentially this fashion. The Commission's cost-savings cap essentially bars the NSA door to all but the largest mailers in the United States, for only those mailers have a large enough volume base to generate aggregate NSA discounts large enough to offset the transaction costs of obtaining the NSA. Moreover, to the extent that NSAs could otherwise produce net increases in postage spending from individual mailers, a cost-savings cap results in under-utilization of the postal network. Over the long term, this will inevitably require higher tariff prices to offset the foregone contribution.

5. AN ALTERNATIVE TO THE COST-SAVINGS CAP

The behavior of firms in unregulated competitive industries provides a more appropriate standard for dealing with uncertainties in Before Rates volume estimates. The risk that a customer might fool its supplier into offering needlessly deep discounts is hardly unique to postal NSAs. Asymmetric information and the risks it creates are pervasive in buy-sell transactions. Unless both parties engage in industrial espionage, each party to a potential deal normally will enter negotiations with more information about its actual costs, potential input substitutes, demand curves, and behavioral plans than the other party possesses (Williamson (1975), pp. 31-33). Yet rational competitive businesses do not throw up their hands and refuse to enter into business contracts whenever these information asymmetries are present, or limit price discounts to the value of the cost savings, if any, that the other party can offer.

Instead, a supplier in a competitive market normally takes a variety of steps to minimize the risk of being duped by a customer in price negotiations. First, the supplier obtains as much information as possible—not only from independent sources but also from the customer itself—about its demand and strategic plans. Second, the supplier negotiates structural safeguards in the contract terms to limit the ability of the customer to obtain discounts for volume that would have been entered in any event. Third, the supplier avoids needlessly long contract terms: as the industrial organization literature indicates, incentives to bluff a supplier or the other party are reduced when both parties expect that deal may be renewable for several terms (Dore (1996), pp. 359-382).

Finally, a rational supplier balances the potential costs of a proposed deal—including the residual risk that the customer, despite the supplier's best efforts, has managed to hoodwink the supplier into offering deeper discounts than necessary—against the expected benefits from the contract. If the expected benefits justify the likely costs, the supplier will rationally enter into the contract. By contrast, it is not rational for the firm to refuse to enter into a contract merely because some potentially costly uncertainty remains. Virtually every business or regulatory action involves some uncertainty about its costs. As (Lave (1981), p. 12) has noted, the zero-risk framework for regulation "is a straw man unworthy of serious consideration. Even the attempt to maintain the facade is increasingly recognized by the regulatory agencies to be impossible."

The PRC's review of volume discount terms in proposed NSAs should focus on similar issues.[9] Instead of the default approach of imposing a cost-savings cap on every NSA, the PRC should consider whether the USPS has made a diligent investigation of the mailer's actual costs, demand, and likely Before Rates volumes, and whether the USPS has a reasonable basis for

---

9 In general, the conduct and performance of competitive markets is often regarded as a useful benchmark for regulating the prices and service of monopoly network industries. Federal Communications Commission, (1996) at ¶¶ 635, 679, 683, 709, 717, 738, 740, 767, 1393.

concluding that the potential benefits of the NSA outweigh the potential costs.

The following are examples of the kinds of analysis and restrictions on the terms of an NSA that the PRC should look for the USPS to use in NSA negotiations:

1. Background research on the customer's industry, from competitors, securities analysts, and trade journals.
2. Analysis of historical data to determine the factors that have affected demand by the customer (and the customer's industry generally) for the classes of mail to be covered by the proposed NSA.
3. Analysis of current technological and competitive trends to identify developing changes in the market that may shift the mailer's demand curves from historical levels.
4. Analysis of the mailer's Before Rates volume projections for consistency with the mailer's actual mail volumes, currently and in the past.
5. Comparison of the mailer's Before Rates volume projections with the forward-looking projections about the mailer's business (a) provided in reports to shareholders and the Securities and Exchange Commission (e.g., annual reports and 10-K filings), and (b) used by its management in the ordinary course of business, including for internal business planning.
6. Comparison of the mailer's Before Rates volume projections with the industry projections available from competing firms, securities analysts, and other independent analysts.
7. Analysis of the likely responsiveness (price elasticity) of the mailer's volume through optimization models or other tools.
8. Testing of the actual preferences of the mailer through offers and counteroffers in negotiations.
9. Inclusion of NSA contract terms that appropriately limit the ability of the mailer to claim discounts for increases in Before Rates volume. (Terms of this kind include provisions requiring an upward adjustment of the volume thresholds if the scale of the mailer's underlying business grows through internal growth, mergers or acquisitions, or exogenous changes in the economy.)
10. Limits on the term of the NSA. (The NSAs approved to date all have a maximum life of three years. After that, they must be renegotiated and resubmitted to the PRC for review.)
11. Finally—and perhaps most importantly—the PRC should consider whether the likely benefits of the NSA to the USPS are large enough to justify the residual risks of the NSA, including the possibility that the

USPS may be inadvertently offering discounts for Before Rates volume.[10]

In applying these tests, the PRC should refrain from demanding an unrealistic level of certainty in the data and analyses. As noted above, uncertainty is a fact of life in estimates of a negotiating partner's demand, costs and alternatives. Prudent businesses do not demand perfect certainty before entering into deals with a high expected payoff. Neither should the PRC.

6. CONCLUSION

For the potential of NSAs to become a reality in the United States, the PRC needs to jettison arbitrary caps on discounts in favor of an approach to risk that emulates the benefit-cost analysis engaged by firms in competitive markets. The PRC, in reviewing a proposed NSA, should consider whether there is a reasonable basis for finding that: (1) the USPS has performed appropriate due diligence in scrutinizing the claims of the mailer about its anticipated Before-Rates volume; and (2) the potential financial benefits of the NSA appear likely to outweigh its expected costs, including the potential costs of needless discounting. If a proposed NSA satisfies these tests, the PRC should approve the NSA.

REFERENCES

Association of American Railroads, 2005. *The Impact of the Staggers Rail Act of 1980* (Feb. 2005) (available on line at http://www.aar.org/).

Bank One Corporation. 2004a. Docket No. MC2004-3, *Rate and Service Changes to Implement Functionally Equivalent Negotiated Service Agreement with Bank One Corporation*, Bank One Corporation Comments on Limitation of Issues and Response to Requests for Hearing (refiled Aug. 5, 2004).

Bank One Corporation. 2004b. Response of Bank One Corporation to August 5 Reply Comments Of OCA and Valpak in Docket No. MC2004-3, *Rate and Service Changes to Implement Functionally Equivalent Negotiated Service Agreement with Bank One Corporation* (filed Aug. 10, 2004).

Bank One Corporation. 2004c. Brief of Bank One Corporation in Docket No. MC2004-3, *Rate and Service Changes to Implement Functionally Equivalent Negotiated Service Agreement with Bank One Corporation* (Oct. 6, 2004).

---

[10] This paper does not discuss the separate question of what safeguards (if any) should be imposed by the PRC to protect against unreasonable injury to competitors of the mailer that would receive postage discounts under the NSA. Although the PRC has invited aggrieved challengers to raise such claims, none of the financial industry NSAs proposed to date have been challenged by any competitor of the mailer party to the NSA.

Baumol, W.J., and R.D. Willig. 1983. "Pricing issues in the Deregulation of Railroad Rates." In *Economic Analysis of Regulated Markets*, edited by J. Finsinger. Palgrave Macmillan.

Dore, R. 1996. "Goodwill and the Spirit of Market Capitalism." In *Firms, Organizations and Contracts: A Reader in Industrial Organization*, edited by P.J. Buckley and J. Michie. Oxford University Press.

Federal Communications Commission. 1996. *Implementation of the Local Competition Provisions in the Telecommunications Act of 1996*, 11 F.C.C.Rcd. 15499 (1996).

Flynn, S.P. 2005. *Bill Presentment & Payment: Electronic vs. Mail*, Pitney Bowes Background Paper No. 9 (July 13, 2005) (downloaded Aug. 16, 2005 from http://www.postinsight.pb.com/)

Governors of the United States Postal Service. 2003. Decision on the Opinion and Recommended Decision of the Postal Rate Commission Recommending Experimental Rate and Service Changes to Implement Negotiated Service Agreement with Capital One, Docket No. MC2002–2 (June 2, 2003).

Governors of the United States Postal Service. 2004. Notice of United States Postal Service of Decision of the Governors, Docket MC2004-3, *Rate and Service Changes to Implement Functionally Equivalent Negotiated Service Agreement with Bank One Corporation.*

Interstate Commerce Commission. 1978. *Railroad Contract Rates: Policy Statement*, Ex Parte No. 358-F, 43 Fed. Reg. 58189 (1978) (Policy Statement I).

Interstate Commerce Commission. 1982. *Railroad Transportation Contracts*, 367 I.C.C. 9 (Oct. 8, 1982).

Lave, L.B. 1981. *The Strategy of Social Regulation: Decision Frameworks for Policy.*

Levy, D.M. 2005. "Selective Rate Discounts to Preserve First-Class Mail Volume." In *Regulatory and Economic Challenges in the Postal and Delivery Sector*, edited by M.A. Crew and P.R. Kleindorfer. Boston: Kluwer Academic Publishers.

Motley, M.E. 1996. Statement before the U.S. Congress, Senate Subcomm. on Post Office & Civil Service, and the House Comm. on Government Reform & Oversight, U.S. GAO, *U.S. Postal Service: A Look at Other Countries' Postal Reform Efforts* (released Jan. 25, 1996).

Rappaport, B. 2004. Direct Testimony of Brad Rappaport on Behalf of Bank One Corporation in Docket No. MC2004-3, *Rate and Service Changes to Implement Functionally Equivalent Negotiated Service Agreement with Bank One Corporation.*

Tamayo, X., L. Jiminez, and S.P. Flynn. 2005. *Trends in Consumer Payments Systems*, Pitney Bowes Background Paper No. 8 (July 13, 2005) (downloaded Aug. 16, 2005 from http://www.postinsight.pb.com/)

Staggers Rail Act of 1980, Pub. L. No. 96-448, 94 Stat. 1908.

United States Congress. 1979. S. Rep. No. 470, 96th Cong., 1st Sess.

United States Congress. 1980. H.R. Rep. No. 1035, 96th Cong., 2d Sess.

United States Court of Appeals. 1982. *Burlington Northern R.R. Co. v. ICC*, 679 F.2d 934 (D.C. Cir. 1982);

United States Court of Appeals. 1984. *Sea-Land Service, Inc. v. ICC*, 738 F.2d 1311 (D.C. Cir. 1984)

United States General Accounting Office. 1997. *Postal Reform In Canada: Canada Post Corporation's Universal Service & Ratemaking* (March 1997).

United States General Accounting Office. 1999. *Railroad Regulation: Changes in Railroad Rates and Service Quality Since 1990* (April 1999).

United States Postal Rate Commission. 2002. *Report to Congress: Authority of the USPS to Introduce New Products and Services and to Enter into Rate and Service Agreements with Individualized Customers or Groups of Customers* (Feb. 11, 2002).

United States Postal Rate Commission. 2003. Docket No. MC2002-1, *Experimental Rate and Service Changes to Implement Negotiated Service Agreement with Capital One Services, Inc.*, Opinion and Recommended Decision (May 15, 2003).

United States Postal Rate Commission. 2004a. Docket No. MC2004-3, *Rate and Service Changes to Implement Functionally Equivalent Negotiated Service Agreement with Bank One Corporation*, Presiding Officer's Ruling No. MC2004-3/2 (Aug. 13, 2004).

United States Postal Rate Commission. 2004b. Docket No. MC2004-4, *Rate and Service Changes to Implement Functionally Equivalent Negotiated Service Agreement with Discover Financial Services*, Opinion and Recommended Decision (September 30, 2004).

United States Postal Rate Commission. 2004c. Docket No. MC2004-3, *Rate and Service Changes to Implement Functionally Equivalent Negotiated Service Agreement with Bank One Corporation*, Opinion and Recommended Decision (December 17, 2004).

United States Postal Rate Commission. 2005a. Docket No. RM2005-2, *Solicitation of Comments on First Use of Rules Applicable to Negotiated Service Agreements*, Order No. 1429, 70 Fed. Reg. 4802 (Jan. 31, 2005).

United States Postal Rate Commission. 2005b. Docket No. MC2004-3, *Rate And Service Changes to Implement Functionally Equivalent Negotiated Service Agreement with Bank One Corporation*, Notice of the USPS of Decision of Governors (February 22, 2005).

United States Postal Rate Commission. 2005c. Docket No. MC2005-2, *Rate and Service Changes to Implement Functionally Equivalent Negotiated Service Agreement with HSBC North America Holdings Inc.*, Opinion and Recommended Decision (May 20, 2005).

United States Postal Service. 2004. USPS Data Collection Report in Docket No. MC2002-2, for Sept. 1, 2003, to Sept. 30, 2004.

Varian, H.R. 1989. "Price Discrimination." In *Handbook of Industrial Organization*, edited by R. Schmalensee and R.D. Willig. Elsevier Science Publishers, B.V.

Williamson, O.E. 1975. *Markets and Hierarchies: Analysis and Antitrust Implications*. New York: Free Press.

Willig, R. 1978. "Pareto-superior nonlinear outlay schedules." *Bell Journal of Economics* 9: 56-69.

Wilson, R., and E. Crouch. 1982. *Risk-Benefit Analysis*. Harvard Center for Risk Analysis.

Chapter 21

The "Real" Graveyard Spiral

Experiences from the Liberalized Swedish Postal Market

Per Jonsson and Sten Selander
Swedish Post and Telecom Agency

1. INTRODUCTION

This paper contributes to the debate about the possible effects on postal markets of the introduction of competition. Crew and Kleindorfer's (2005) theory of the incumbent's graveyard spiral argues that liberalization of the postal market can put the universal service provider in a devastating financial spiral of increasing prices and continuing losses. The graveyard spiral is described as a dynamic process triggered by entrants' capture of the incumbent's most profitable business, as they will price below the incumbent in low-cost markets. The loss of profitable business forces the incumbent to raise prices for its remaining business activities, making previously unprofitable volumes profitable for entrants, who then capture more volume by pricing below the incumbent. Under appropriate conditions, the incumbent is put in a downward spiral of lost volume and continued financial losses, which, without direct subsidies, can eventually force the incumbent to end its services to a range of predominantly rural areas.

Our paper describes the developments of the liberalized Swedish postal market, with a key focus on five observations, which actually deviate from the effects described by the Crew and Kleindorfer theory. It is difficult to draw any conclusions of universal validity from these observations. Rather, our aim is to encourage further discussion on the subject of how to best take an old monopolistic postal market into the world of competition.

2. THE HISTORY OF SWEDISH POSTAL MARKET LIBERALIZATION

The letter mail monopoly of the incumbent Swedish postal operator and USP, Posten AB (hereinafter Sweden Post), was brought to an end by a 1992 parliamentary decision. The decision abolished a 1947 public notice, which conferred on the incumbent an exclusive right to collect and deliver all Swedish letter mail items. Since the parcel business sector had never been regulated, the parliamentary decision created the world's first completely free and liberalized postal market.

One important trigger for the liberalization had been the establishment of the entrant, CityMail, in 1991. Its business concept, largely unchanged over thirteen years, was basically to offer a less expensive distribution of pre-sorted bulk mail destined for the city of Stockholm and other large cities. CityMail encouraged mailers to have their computers sort outgoing bulk mail by postal code and rewarded them for this by offering reduced postage. Another ground for offering reduced postage was the new mail distribution model, in which delivery to each address takes place every third weekday. With this new delivery routine, each CityMail postman would cover three of the incumbent's separately manned routes, which were served on a five days a week basis.

In order to establish itself on the postal market, CityMail had to convince the incumbent's customers of the necessity to make changes in their outbound postal flow management. CityMail expended much effort in encouraging customers to try their new bulk mail solutions. The widespread reluctance to change among Sweden Post's customers was mainly due to three factors:

1. The incumbent's reputation as a reliable supplier.
2. Postage often being considered a low priority cost item.
3. The customer still found it necessary to turn to the incumbent for the major part of its outbound mail.

Having reached the conclusion that mail distribution is not a natural monopoly, the Swedish government's 1992 decision to terminate the legal monopoly was intended to pave the way for various benefits from competition. At Sweden Post, the very threat of competition triggered a large-scale program of improved productivity and an awareness that safeguarding a monopolistic position at continued high margins was no longer an option.

There were two main choices for the direction of the incumbent's strategic decision making:

1. Give up market share, but keep healthy margins.
2. Keep market share, but lose healthy margins.

In our view, Sweden Post clearly chose to defend its absolute market share, even at the cost of eroding margins. Its strategy in dealing with the threat from CityMail was to either eliminate the competitor or allow it to take on only a tiny portion of the market.

Following the introduction of competition, discrepancies from the predicted course of events as described by the theory of the graveyard spiral were observed.

One: The incumbent was able to defend its absolute market power by creative renegotiation of terms and conditions with its customers.

The first observation is that of an incumbent who responds to the challenge from new entrants by renegotiating customer terms of agreements. The incumbent took prompt and powerful strategic action upon the very threat of future competition. This initial strategy appears to have been an attempt to eliminate the competitor, CityMail, as loyalty premiums, year-end kickbacks and terms of supplier exclusivity appeared as common practice in Sweden Post's customer negotiations. After several legal interventions by the Swedish Competition Authority, these practices seem to have subsided around 1997.

Two: The incumbent was able to defend its absolute market power by offering price cuts in the competitive segment of the market.

The second observation describes the incumbent's response to competition as taking strategic action in its pricing operations. Sweden Post's loyalty programs appear to have been replaced later by policies of discounts offers. In 1996, the incumbent introduced geographical pricing, so developing a four-zone pricing model. The model, however, was rejected by the Competition Authority in the 1998 Swedish Market Court proceedings, stating, "Sweden Post has violated the prohibition against the abuse of a dominant position by announcing its intention to apply selective geographical pricing, which is not acceptable since it was not justified by costs." In its decision, the Market Court ruled that Sweden Post's application of the four-zone price list would, indeed, constitute abuse of its position.

Following the four-zone model, Sweden Post introduced a two-zone price list, with a general discount for mail destined to 19 city areas, not all served by CityMail. The Market Court approved the new model, with some hesitation, providing specific conditions for determination of the discount size. The general discount is still applied and has been fixed at 0.40 Swedish kronor since its introduction in 1999.

Due to its setbacks in the Market Court, Sweden Post abandoned much of its zonal pricing strategies. Instead, the incumbent's new strategy was to offer individual price discounts, as outlined below in Figure 1.

Figure 1: Postal developments in the liberalized Swedish letter mail market.

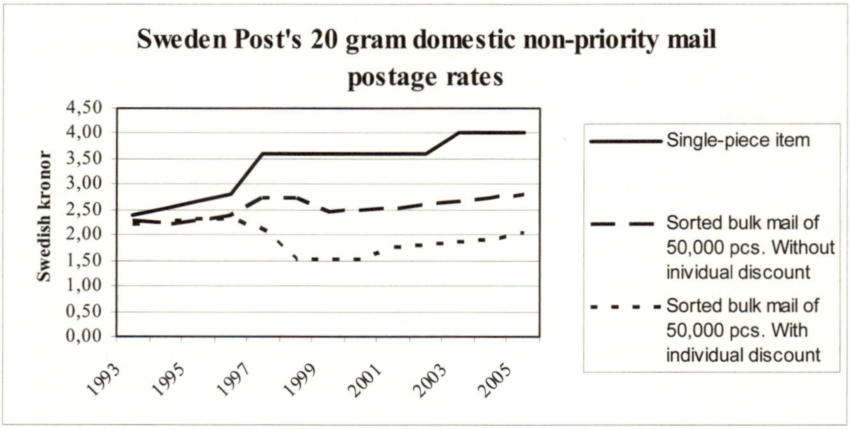

The lower dotted line represents the postage rates offered to one key customer (the Swedish tax authority). Note that the bulk rates with individual discounts are those of one key customer. Other key customers may have had lower rates, but it is more likely that the majority of key customers would have had higher rates. There are no individual discounts for single-piece items.

In 1993, the incumbent's offer was basically a flat rate for distribution of all letter mail items of a certain weight. Discounts for bulk mail exceeding 10,000 items had been introduced but were in the range of one eurocent per letter. The price developments in Figure 1 indicate that Sweden Post introduced offers of substantial individual discounts to its key customers on a broad front in 1997. These offers of large discounts, compared to the public price list, appear to have changed the incumbent's pricing significantly, and took place at a time when the competitor, CityMail, was in the process of expanding into new geographical areas.

Three: The incumbent was tempted to finance price cuts in the competitive area by increasing prices in the non-competitive area.

The Swedish regulator determined that mail distribution is not a natural monopoly. This view was supported in a recent study by the government agency, the Swedish Institute for Growth Policy Studies (ITPS). Its researchers concluded that the Swedish letter mail market only includes certain elements of a natural monopoly. According to the study, a natural monopoly does not exist for the separate production stages of the mail distribution process, but rather only for the specific market segment of nationwide overnight distribution of single-piece items. In our view, the nationwide overnight distribution, in its entirety, may be a natural monopoly, as Sweden is a large and sparsely populated country, with a population density of 22 inhabitants per sq km, compared with Denmark's 128, Germany's 236 and the Netherlands' 484.

Since the 1993 liberalization, the incumbent has pressed for higher prices in certain non-competitive areas of the postal market. A price cap was introduced in 1994 to protect households and non-key postal customers, i.e., unprofitable segments of the business, from rapid price increases. However, due to a number of circumstances, the price cap did not protect customers in the way intended. For instance, the price for domestic overnight 20 gram letters has risen by 90 percent over ten years. Taking into account the imposed 25 percent VAT, this price increase still substantially exceeds the accumulated national inflation rate of 14 percent.

In other segments of the market, where price caps and competition are absent, the price increases have been substantially greater. Postage for a 20 gram letter to the neighboring Nordic countries has increased by 129 percent, and postage for a domestic 20 kg parcel has increased by 189 percent.

According to Figure 1, the incumbent's pricing policy for large individual discounts is still in active use. Table 1 below shows one current key customer's discount rates compared to the generic price. Interestingly, the incumbent offers substantial discounts in areas lacking competition. For instance, non-sorted nationwide overnight bulk mail is offered a 22 percent discount, even though the competition does not offer either sorting services or nationwide overnight distribution. Perhaps the discount functions as an incentive for customers not to have their mail sorted and thereby not subject to competing offers from CityMail's competitors.

However, as the large majority of key customers have third parties processing their outbound mail, and these printing companies offer low cost sorting, the key customer demand for the lower-priced sorted price list item exceeds the demand for the more expensive non-sorted option.

Table 1: Government agency discounts with Sweden Post

2005 Product discounts compared to price list	**Discount (%)**
Single-piece 20 gram priority letter mail	0%
Single-piece 20 gram cross border priority letter mail	0%
Cross border parcel 20 kg	8%
Non-sorted domestic 20 gram bulk mail non competitive area	22%
Sorted domestic 20 gram bulk mail of 10000 non competitive area	23%
Sorted domestic 20 gram bulk mail of 10000 competitive area	27%
Domestic parcel 20 kg	65%

Four: Deliveries in rural areas have not proven more expensive than those in more urban areas.

One important assumption in the graveyard spiral theory is that deliveries in rural areas are more costly than those in city areas. In our view, this has not been sufficiently examined. Strong indications are that this is not the case for some city areas, in relation to the unit delivery cost. This would apply for city areas with the following characteristics:

1. Low post office box density;
2. Complex handling of keys and codes to the buildings;
3. High postmen staff turnover, high job vacancy rates, and high sick leave figures;
4. Difficult traffic and parking conditions;
5. Poor quality of addresses due to high resident mobility and predominantly secondary rental agreements.

The description above could, for instance, apply to an urban area with a university campus. The mail distribution to that area would most likely have higher operating costs than that in a more sparsely populated rural area, whose characteristics were:

1. Near non-existent postmen staff turnover, no vacancies, and low sick leave figures;
2. Excellent traffic and parking conditions;
3. Excellent address quality due to low resident mobility.

Five: Entrants lack the financial strength to carry them through the opening years' losses.

CityMail's bumpy road towards being established as the world's first entrant with a significant portion of a domestic letter mail market has included two bankruptcies and several changes in ownership: CityMail has been owned by Sweden Post, the Royal Mail and, presently, Norway Post. According to the findings of Cohen et al. (2004), CityMail would not have been able to attract investors had their original business plan been analyzed correctly, or, alternatively, had the counter strategy of the incumbent been reasonably anticipated.

Cohen et al. (2004) provide strong evidence that a venture capital market, such as Wall Street, would not be able to supply enough funds for an entrant's successful challenge to the incumbent. In order to challenge the incumbent, the entrant would have to look for funding from investors with a lot more patience for their returns than those found within the more traditional financing facilities.

3. NEW MEASURES TO INCREASE FUTURE COMPETITION

Finally, we will discuss some recent proposals from the Swedish Postal Market Committee to make the postal market more competitive.

Twelve years after the liberalization, the Committee faced a letter mail market strongly dominated by the incumbent, Sweden Post. Although Sweden Post's market share has steadily decreased, it still controls 92 percent of the total market.

Real competition can be seen in certain segments of the letter mail market. For instance, in the segment with the toughest competition, bulk mail suitable for sorting, the market share of the entrant, CityMail, is estimated to be around 25 percent. The overall market share for all entrants is 8 percent, while CityMail alone has 7.5 percent.

In its bid to increase competition, the Postal Market Committee recently presented a 400-page report containing a number of proposals for improving the efficiency of the postal market.

Perhaps the most interesting proposal, "Measures against unclear pricing and discrimination," sets out to further clarify and increase the requirements for non-discriminating terms and conditions offered by the incumbent. Implementation is proposed as a provision to the Postal Services Act, whereby the universal service provider will have to apply the principal of non-discrimination in connection with the use of special prices and other special conditions for certain customers.

According to one proposal from the committee, the Swedish National Post and Telecom Agency would be assigned to evaluate individual price levels offered by the incumbent. This would be done by comparing the individual prices with that of a standard single-piece service; consisting of collection, sorting, transport and delivery. Furthermore, the regulator would reinforce its efforts to ensure that the special prices and other conditions offered by the incumbent will be applied equally, for all customers as well as for other postal operators.

In our view, this proposed addition would enhance competition by making the incumbent's individual discounts and prices known to the public. An offer from the incumbent of extremely low prices to a single customer would be known to all customers and be attainable for other similar bulk mailings. The benefits of this transparency are likely to exceed the hardships of determining and estimating the cost of a standard single-piece item, against which all discounts should be measured. The proposed transparency of the incumbent's individual prices and discounts, together with the requirement that such prices and discounts be applied in a non-discriminatory manner, will support the supply side of the letter mail market, offering sustainable prices and discounts.

4. CONCLUSIONS

The five observations from the liberalized Swedish postal market, described above, reveal discrepancies from the possible outcome predicted by the Crew and Kleindorfer theory of the graveyard spiral. This does not imply, however, that the methods used by Sweden Post in order to meet competition will prove profitable in the long run. In order to be financially successful, the incumbent would need to eliminate the entrant in an early stage of the competition. A continuing struggle to defend market share at the expense of healthy margins could, in the long run, put the incumbent into a different kind of graveyard spiral than the one described by Crew and Kleindorfer.

REFERENCES

Crew, M.A. and P.R. Kleindorfer. 2005. "Competition, Universal Service and the Graveyard Spiral." In *Regulatory and Economic Challenges in the Postal and Delivery Sector*, edited by M.A. Crew and P.R. Kleindorfer. Boston: Kluwer Academic Publishers.

Cohen, R.H., M. Robinson, R. Sheely, J. Waller, and S. Xenakis. 2005. "Will Entrants into a Liberalized Delivery Market Attract Investors?" In *Regulatory and Economic Challenges in the Postal and Delivery Sector*, edited by M.A. Crew and P.R. Kleindorfer. Boston: Kluwer Academic Publishers.

Postal Reform in Japan

Chapter 22

Competition Structure and Future Postal Reform in Japan

*In Comparison with International Liberalization**

Shoji Maruyama
Japan Post

1. INTRODUCTION

The possibility that a former monopolistic postal operator could maintain a dominant market position even after market liberalization has been discussed repeatedly at the Conference on Postal and Delivery Economics (CPDE). The logic of this possibility is that private entry may not be sufficiently profitable, as an established postal operator has significant cost advantages derived from economies of scale. Japan's postal market is an interesting case in point. Japan Post Corporation (hereafter Japan Post), the incumbent universal service provider, faces competition from private parcel and mail delivery businesses. How this market will develop and what regulatory and legal framework will be applied are both topics of intense debate at present in Japan. A key concern is the financial sustainability of the postal business and the continuing stability of Japan Post to provide universal service throughout the country.

In this paper, I will investigate in detail Japan's postal market, and explain why previous international market liberalization outcomes cannot be applied readily to Japan. Presented first will be the point that private companies can exploit economies of scope between their parcel and mail businesses. Secondly, the focus will be Japan Post's obligations and

---

* The contents of this paper solely reflect the author's opinions and do not represent the official opinions of Japan Post.

restrictions as the sole universal service provider. Recent debates in the Diet[1] over the future privatization of Japan Post highlighted the problem of financial soundness in preserving a stable public service.

The paper proceeds as follows: Section 2 summarizes the current competition structure of Japan's parcel and mail market with reference to previous debate in articles and international discussion over the outcome of market liberalization. Section 3 investigates the characteristics of the incumbent and private companies, which have brought about the present state of competition in parcel and mail delivery, and briefly describes the deliberation of postal reform in the 2005 regular session of the Diet. Section 4 concludes the discussion.

2. COMPETITIVE STRUCTURE OF THE POSTAL MARKET

2.1 International Experiences of Liberalization

Feasibility of entry into postal markets was examined and simulated in many articles presented at previous Rutgers University conferences on postal and delivery economics. Analytical models, as well as the experiences of (partially or fully) liberalized postal markets in most European countries, indicate that an incumbent postal operator, formerly a monopolist with brand loyalty, can succeed in sustaining significant competitive advantage, while private operators have difficulty in entering. (For theoretical discussion, see Cohen et al. 2005 and Burns, Carslake, and Houpis 2002). Previous analysis implies that, especially for postal markets with large mail volumes, and whose postal operating cost structure is characterized by a low fixed-cost proportion, the impact of volume decline caused by market liberalization on postal management is not severe and that the 'graveyard spiral' is unlikely to occur (Crew and Kleindorfer 2005; Cohen et al. 2004).

In Sweden, where full entry was implemented under the license scheme in 1993, Posten AB has been recognized as the sole operator providing a full range of logistics solutions and, given its nationwide coverage and long history as a postal provider, does not need to spend much on campaigns to bolster its brand or market awareness. Even reducing delivery frequency to two or three days per week, did not allow competitors to challenge the nationwide delivery network. This made it difficult to gain customer loyalty from those not willing to split mail between different contractors (Jonsson

[1] The Diet is the Japanese equivalent of the U.S. Congress.

2004). In Germany, although approximately 1,600 private operators had been granted postal licenses until 2003, more than five hundred exited the market. Many licensees could not afford the large investment needed to retain their position and earn a profit, as some of that spending could become 'sunk costs' (Schwartz-Schilling 2002). In most EU countries, market openings were conducted stage by stage in compliance with Postal Directives (97/67/EC and 2002/39/EC) and, in 2006, the weight and postal rate threshold will be lowered from the combination of current one hundred grams and three times the standard postal rate, to fifty grams and two and a half times the standard postal rate.[2] Postal operators were given incentives to operate in an efficient and innovative manner during the time that a reserved area was guaranteed, until 2009, to prepare for the upcoming fully competitive market. As a result, a partially liberalized market enabled incumbents to preserve a *de facto* monopolistic position without inviting sufficient entry. According to WIK (2004), revenue share of postal operators in most European countries was still over 95% in 2003, e.g., in the UK (99.7%), Germany (96%), and the Netherlands (95%). Of particular note is the UK, where limited activities, such as bulk mail, integration, and niche service within the reserved area, were admitted to approximately ten private operators. The desirable consequences of competition did not develop, as the regulatory authority, Postcomm, had expected, due to barriers to entry into the postal market governed by the incumbent, Royal Mail.[3] This forced the announcement in February 2005 that full market opening would occur fifteen months ahead of schedule, in January 2006 (Moriarty and Smith 2005, Postcomm 2005).[4]

To summarize, the postal market liberalization of European countries with large mail volume has been difficult for entrants, because:

1. The incumbent has a cost advantage due to economies of scale.

---

[2] According to WIK (2004), which is based on information from postal operators and regulatory authorities, volume share of mail items over one hundred grams was 18%, while for those over fifty grams it was only 25%. Such a demand structure may have a significant impact on postal management at the third or last stage of liberalization (i.e., full competition).

[3] The McAfee et al. (2003) categories of barriers to entry are: (1) standalone barriers, which are barriers in and of themselves; and (2) ancillary barriers, which are barriers that reinforce other barriers. Cost advantages derived from economies of scale may be thought of as 'ancillary barriers,' since new entrants can also benefit from such economies after successfully entering the market.

[4] Postcomm has determined that, although private entry has been allowed in the restricted reserved area since 2003, negotiations over downstream access conditions between Royal Mail and UK mail in this period also caused the delay of sufficient entry in the short term (Postcomm 2004).

2. The incumbent has brand loyalty from providing universal service for hundreds of years.
3. The incumbent has 'special privileges,' such as a value-added tax exemption, and priority treatment in the case of road transport or international clearance.

With regard to economies of scale in postal service, numerous estimations showed significant overall scale effects, especially in delivery businesses (NERA 2004). These results imply that a larger incumbent, handling greater amounts of postal items, can achieve predominant power in the market through enormous economies of scale. Japan Post, however, is facing severe competitive pressure from private companies, despite several factors in its favor:

1. A relatively large market, handling twenty-six billion letter post annually (the second largest in the world after the United States Postal Services (USPS)) and earning an operating revenue of two trillion JPY
2. Earned brand loyalty from, not only delivery, but also financial services (such as savings and insurance)
3. A history of over one hundred years, much like major postal providers in European countries

The investigation of these market differences should also include the strategic advantages of new entrants. This has not been sufficiently applied to vigorous analysis in previous literature. In the next section, Japan's liberalized postal market will be the focus, as its outcomes have differed greatly from those of many other developed countries.

2.2 The Postal Market in Japan

Japan Post provides nationwide mail and parcel delivery in a manner 'fair' to all residents: easy to access at affordable rates. Its 130-year history began with the introduction of modern postal services in 1871, while postal savings was established in 1875, and insurance services in 1916. Japan Post was incorporated with the objective of operating more efficiently through the introduction of private-sector-style management by the former Postal Services Agency in 2003. The two categories of domestic postal products that Japan Post currently provides are: correspondence (a document which expresses the sender's will to a specific person or provides notification of a fact) and non-correspondence.[5] Non-correspondence products include

[5] The concept of 'correspondence' in Japan almost parallels 'letter' in most developed countries. The definition of direct mail (DM) in Japan, however, may cause some confusion. According to the guideline for correspondence stipulated by the regulatory authority, the Ministry of Internal Affairs and Communications (MIC), "DM is not correspondence if it contains only public and publishable facts, and...is delivered

envelopes containing leaflets, credit cards, and gift coupons; periodicals; and booklet and ordinary parcels. It must be stressed that currently there are no statutory reserved areas permitted in these categories for Japan Post, which means that postal products compete fully with private products, as shown in Figure 1. A detailed investigation of the competitive structure of the parcel, correspondence and non-correspondence market between postal and private operators follows.

Figure 1: Competitive products by postal and private operators

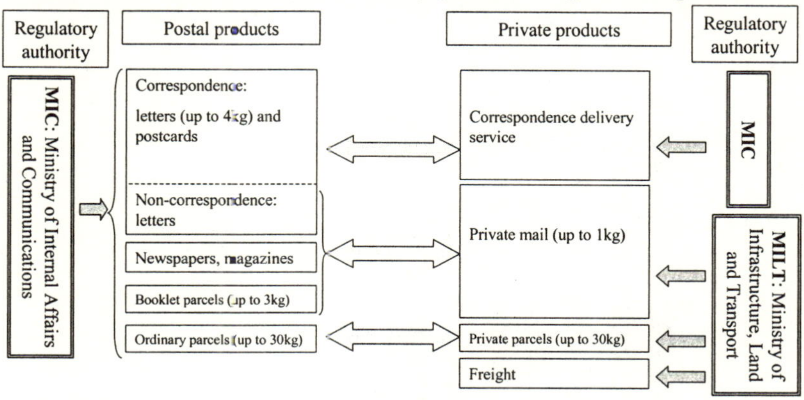

Japan's parcel market has been exposed to significant competition from private operators, similar to the United States postal market.[6] Until the 1970s the Japanese market was notably divided between the postal service and Japan National Railway. At that time a private delivery company began a parcel business that overlapped with postal parcel services. Figure 2 below shows that the market share for postal business significantly dropped from 70% in the 1970s to 10% in the 1990s, and then to 6% in 2003.[7] Private operators that successfully expanded their businesses could afford to invest

---

assuming it is distributed also in the store." It is not possible, however, to distinguish between 'correspondence-DM' and 'non-correspondence-DM' since it is illegal for mail to be opened by anyone other than its recipient.

6 The USPS' 60% share of package delivery in the 1970s has fallen to under 10% after United Parcel Service and other private companies successfully entered and penetrated the market. Private expansion was partly due to the Postal Restructuring Act (PRA), which no longer allowed the incumbent, the USPS, to operate on a loss basis and included competitors in the postal rate setting process (Robinson, Crowder, and Rawnsley, 2003).

7 According to the Ministry of Infrastructure, Land, and Transport (MILT), a private parcel is defined as "a package under the weight of thirty kilograms that is handled individually and is specially named for the product." Approximately thirty operators have entered into this market, handling a total of 3 billion items annually. Most small operators only handle Business-to-Business (B2B) parcels that are not competitive with Business-to-Customer (B2C) and Customer-to-Customer (C2C) postal parcel business.

their cash flow in the delivery network and information technology necessary for providing a variety of value-added delivery to improve quality of service. For example, track-and-trace service for several stages, from collection to delivery, is available by using the Internet or mobile phone Web sites, for no additional fees. Delivery is seven days per week, 365 days per year, with the guarantee of next-day delivery between major cities. Public and private operators have been competing in Japan for thirty years to provide such value-added parcel products.

Figure 2: Market share in Japan's parcel delivery

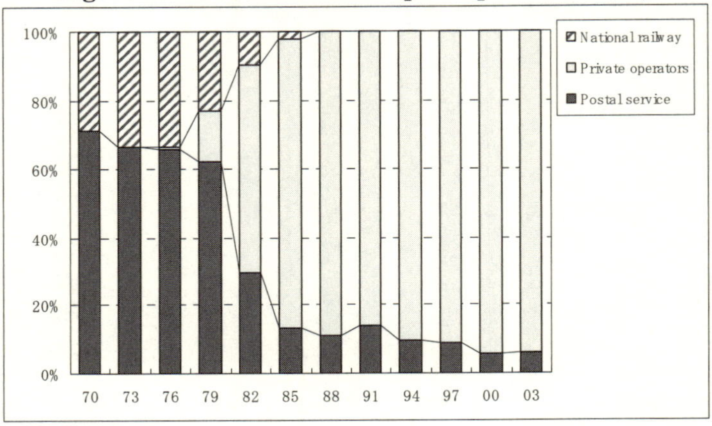

Source: MILT and Japan Post

Important to note is that the parcel business is completely differentiated from letter business on the basis of corporate accounting, and that 'customized rates' for selected senders, which are commonly applied by private delivery in Japan and foreign postal operators, such as the USPS and New Zealand Post, are not permitted for Japan Post. These restrictions help explain the insistence that the public operator not charge unreasonable parcel rates and that the operating profit for parcels is derived solely from continuous cost management and effective sales promotion.[8]

As noted above, the mail market can be categorized into two products: non-correspondence items and correspondence items. Private entry into the

---

[8] Private parcel giant Yamato Transport Co. filed a lawsuit against Japan Post in 2004 claiming that Japan Post started accepting postal parcels at convenience retail stores by offering a size-based rate lower than Yamato's rates. Japan Post insists that, while the postal rate certainly is lower than Yamato's, it is higher than that of other major private operators. Additionally, that special rate was designated for island areas (e.g., Okinawa) as part of the government's policy to promote local welfare, stemming from the era of (the now defunct) Ministry of Posts and Telecommunications.

non-correspondence category began in 1997, when a private company, Yamato Transport Co., started to deliver magazines throughout the country on consignment from the publisher. As of 2003, the total market volume handled by ten private operators has expanded to over 1.3 billion items. Items handled by Japan Post in the same year are estimated to be about 5.4 billion: thus, it is possible that private mail occupies 20% of the non-correspondence market share.[9] In 2003, Yamato lowered its minimum rate for items up to fifty grams to the same as the minimum standard rate for postal letters up to twenty-five grams (80JPY), and simplified its contracts with customers. These changes led to significant progress, especially in the past two years, as shown in Figure 3. The decline in the number of postal items for three consecutive years until 2004, despite a stable postal rate, can be attributed partly to the evolution of private mail business.[10]

Figure 3: Recent progress in private mail business

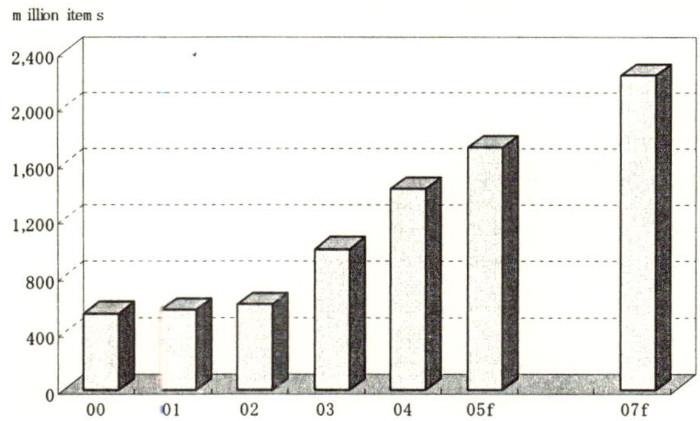

Private mail items handled by Yamato Transport Co. between 2000 and 2004. Bars for 05f and 07f indicate expectations by the company (no information published for the year 2006).

In addition to competition in non-correspondence products, "correspondence delivery" came into effect in 2003, which is handled by

---

9 Japan's postal statistics do not distinguish between the exact volumes of correspondence and non-correspondence mail, since the first-class category (letters) and the second-class category (postcards) includes both types of mail. The estimated number of postal non-correspondence mail as a competitive product of private mail was derived from the sum of advertisement mail (a subcategory of first- and second-class mail), third-class mail (mainly newspapers and periodicals), and booklet parcels.

10 Another major factor for the postal volume decline in recent years is the demand substitution effects of communications via the Internet and mobile phones (text messaging) as observed in most developed countries. For example, many telephone and credit card companies are eager to offer customers the choice of not being sent monthly statements by physical mail in exchange for allowing them to check their statements via a Web site.

licensed operators as stipulated by the law on correspondence operators. This law seeks to ensure fair and impartial delivery services and to increase the opportunities for customers to benefit from more diversified services by granting private operators a license to engage in correspondence delivery services (MIC 2003). According to the new permissions granted, private operators licensed by MIC may offer the following two types of delivery services:

1. Restricted correspondence delivery, whereby the handling of any (combination) of the following mail items is permitted:
   a. Items that are to be delivered within three hours from collection
   b. Items that cost a rate of 1,000JPY or more
   c. Items that have a dimension of more than ninety centimeters in length or four kilograms in weight
2. General correspondence delivery, whereby nationwide handling of correspondence items is permitted, and the installation of mailboxes is required, and delivery is provided at least six days a week, at a set uniform domestic rate (no greater than 80JPY for up to twenty-five grams)

Figure 4: Number of licensed correspondence operators

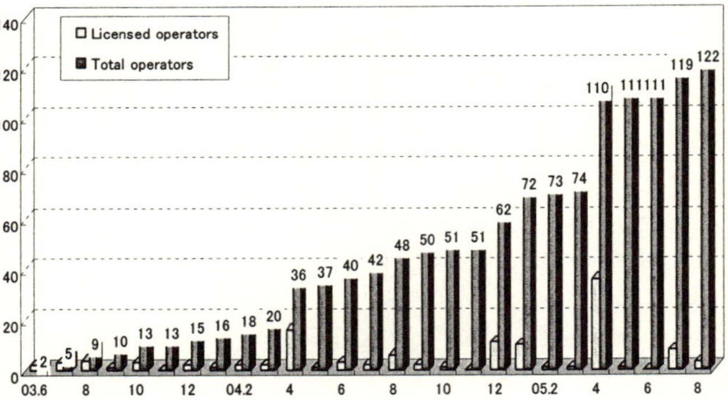

Source: MIC

As shown in Figure 4, the number of licensed operators has increased to 122 for 'restricted' correspondence delivery, but, as of the end of August 2005, no operators have applied for the 'general' category.[11] More than 80% of the delivery areas of licensed operators locate in cities, such as Tokyo,

[11] No entries for general correspondence delivery implies that the requirements concerning correspondence rates, frequency of collection and delivery, and installation of mailboxes may be regarded as high barriers to entry into the postal market. The necessity of these requirements for private operators given the current competitive market structure in Japan will be discussed below.

Yokohama, and Osaka. This entry structure implies that these operators may skim a large amount of postal demand. Notably, downstream access, which is quite prevalent in most liberalized European markets, is not permitted for any correspondence delivery. A private operator who applies for correspondence handling must submit a business plan, which includes a delivery guarantee: delivery of correspondence by either itself or by working in cooperation with other private contractors.[12] These unique restrictions for private correspondence operators may be necessary in Japan's postal market, as the incumbent is granted no reserve areas. Promoting competition by removing these restrictions is unlikely to be appropriate when the number of constraints on Japan Post is also considered, as explained below.

3. CHARACTERISTICS OF JAPAN'S POSTAL MARKET

3.1 Entry by Private Operators

This section investigates postal market structures in Japan that have led to significant competitive pressure on Japan Post. The focus is mainly on the reasons private entry into the parcel and mail market could be viable in Japan, even though in many developed international markets the postal incumbent was able to attain a *de facto* monopoly after partial or full liberalization. This discussion is divided into two distinct sections: private-operator-related factors and postal-operator-related factors.

First, it should be noted that all major private mail operators also provide parcel and freight business to nationwide consumers as 'special integration and transport operators,' which are defined as operators that collect a mixture of freights from mainly business customers, and sort and transport them between sorting centers on a regular basis. Their parcel and mail business is based upon a nationwide freight network.[13] Currently, some private parcel products have national brand recognition and are considered trustworthy after thirty years of competition in B-to-C and C-to-C delivery. Literature about private operators in foreign countries revealed that such operators usually had to depend on downstream access provided by a postal

---

12 Correspondence delivery operators are required to receive permission from the MIC if they intend to consign a part of their business to other operators or make any contracts with other correspondence operators.

13 Some parts of the private parcel supply chain (e.g., transportation between sorting centers and delivery in rural areas) are completed in cooperation with affiliates or contractors.

operator and had have little brand loyalty.[14] In Japan's parcel market, however, top private operators are recognized as providing more reliable quality of service than Japan Post does, although the latter has been in business for one hundred years. According to JD Power's 2004 customer satisfaction survey, which targeted individual package users, the postal service ranks fourth in sending, and third in collecting (JD Power 2004). The two characteristics of a nationwide delivery network and high brand loyalty has enabled private operators to accept more handling of items destined for anywhere including rural areas, enabling an accumulation of retained earnings, which are then invested in other businesses, such as mail activities.

Another reason private operators were able to effectively enter into the mail market is the utilization of 'economies of scope' between their parcel and mail businesses. Private operators could only establish efficient delivery networks for their parcel business when a postal operator's network was restricted through the simultaneous targeting of quality mail delivery. Private companies were also able to transfer their efficient parcel network to mail business, which is characterized as an advantage to the new entrants.

Figure 5: Operational structure of private mail

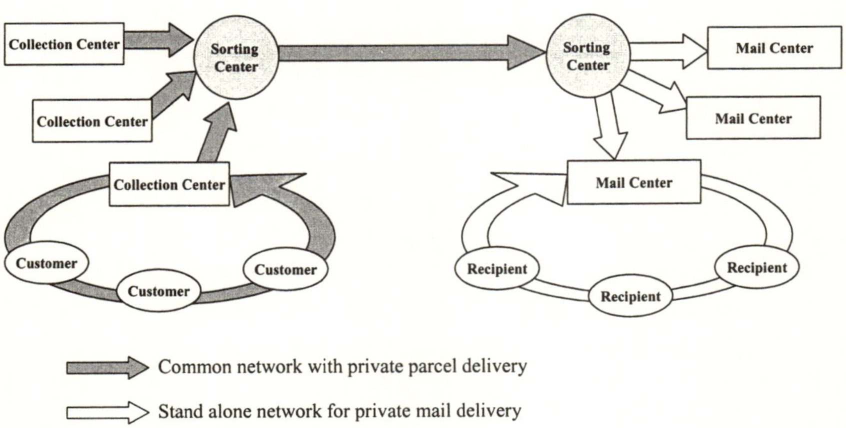

Source: Nomura Securities Co.

Figure 5 summarizes a typical operational flow for private mail businesses, demonstrating that most activities for mail are shared with those for parcels. Private mail accepted at collection centers will be sent to the originating sorting centers and distributed according to destination areas.

---

[14] CityMail, a Swedish private mail operator and a rival to Posten AB, only covers 60–65% of all addresses in Sweden (Jonsson 2005). Most licensed operators in the UK are involved in integration activities, whereby delivery to each address ("the final mile") is completely dependent on the downstream access or delivery network of Royal Mail.

The sorting process is usually based on a 'postal zip code' printed by senders and fed through the same machines used for parcel sorting, especially in rural areas, since larger cities have installed mail-specific sorting machines.[15] Private mail is also transported between sorting centers by the same vehicles used for parcels, which contributes to improved load efficiency since the weight of each mail item is less than one kilogram on average. Only for delivery are the activities handled separately. For supply chains of private mail business, most production factors such as workforce, transportation system, and sorting equipment can be commonly utilized with the parcel business. Thus, like postal operators, private operators are able to achieve economies of scope between mail and parcel businesses.

To summarize, private mail market entry was effectively conducted after a delivery network was established to handle the relatively higher-rate parcels (approximately 600-700 JPY per item compared to 70 JPY for private mail), and after brand loyalty was acquired nationwide. Establishing a national and reliable mail network without handling a large amount of parcels, as postal industry literature indicates, was certainly to be a complex and time-consuming process for private companies. However, major freight operators in Japan could effectively exploit economies of scope between their parcel and mail businesses. Additionally, both efficient entry into the postal market and continuous expansion of their mail business would be impossible if the incumbent could react hostilely to private entry. In reality, such strategic responses by Japan Post were constrained by regulation. The next section will examine the restrictions and obligations imposed on Japan Post.

3.2 Restrictions on Japan Post

Japan Post, as a sole universal service provider, has been given the role of providing postal service "at the lowest possible rates on a nationwide scale and in a manner fairly to all" (Article 1 of the Postal Law). The concept and definition of universal service in Japan is quite concise in this short stipulation of the law, contrary to most European countries, where the scope of universal service is defined in detail according to the product

---

15 Private operators adopt a seven-digit postal zip code for sorting their packages, but do not compensate the postal institution. Mailboxes installed at each doorstep are also accessible, free of charge, to any operators. This is in contrast to the United States postal market, whereby only the USPS has access rights to mailboxes. In this sense, postal infrastructure such as zip codes and mailboxes are regarded as public goods rather than as an 'essential facility' for mail delivery provision in Japan.

category, the weight and the quality of service standards.[16] Japan's simple definition, however, does not necessarily translate into fewer universal service obligation (USO) burdens when compared with other foreign operators. The first noteworthy obligation is to provide several postal products at no charge or at preferentially lower rates, as stipulated by the law. Japan Post, therefore, must provide mail delivery to the blind, free of charge, as is the case in many developed countries, and, moreover, mail from or to devastated areas after earthquakes or other natural disasters, also free of charge. Along with newspapers and magazines, periodicals published by organizations for the handicapped are also provided at lower rates than ordinary products. Additionally, postal service must support elderly customers through the daily delivery of necessities in 210 rural areas of the nation's three thousand municipalities. Since 1997, this program, in cooperation with municipal authorities, allows the elderly to register at the local post office and then give postmen their requests on postcards. The delivery of necessities incurs no additional fees other than the postal rate, and Japan Post receives no funding from other entities, such as central or local government offices. The cost of these policies is funded by cross subsidization of non-monopoly products, as Japan Post is not guaranteed any reserve areas (as noted in previous sections).

Some of the restrictions on the postal operator are unique to Japan. Firstly, Japan Post is not allowed to acquire or invest in any companies unless the target business is related to either information processing of transportation systems or the compounding and sending of mail items. If, for example, Japan Post intended to provide logistics solutions for customers in order to optimize their distribution costs, it would have to depend on a contract partner for most of the supply chain, such as inventory management, distribution modifications, and checking and labeling. These restrictions place Japan Post in a disadvantageous position compared with a private 'one-stop' logistics provider. The same story can be told for the fast growing international express delivery sector. Cross-border mail products accepted at Japan's post offices are completely dependent upon transportation and delivery networks of other postal operators overseas under the framework determined by the Universal Postal Union (UPU). Japanese operators cannot compete, in terms of service quality, with international operators, who commit to door-to-door delivery by utilizing their own aircraft and vehicles

---

[16] The EU Directive (97/67/EC) stipulates that universal service products are postal items up to two kilograms, postal packages up to ten kilograms, and items registered and insured. Most EU member countries adopt the standard of twenty kilograms rather than ten kilograms for parcels. Japan Post handles mail up to four kilograms, and packages up to thirty kilograms, appealing to customer demand, although the law does not stipulate these specific standards.

within subsidized overseas companies. Furthermore, the law does not permit Japan Post to establish subsidized or partnership companies overseas.

Further legal restrictions include the scope of retail counter activities. Other than the three original businesses (postal service, savings, and insurance), only the sale of fiscal stamps, consigned by the Ministry of Finance, and the collection of fees for local telephone or public broadcasting services, consigned by the companies and institutions of NTT (telephone) and NHK (broadcasting) can be contracted out.[17] These restrictions on transaction business have been deregulated to a certain extent after the establishment of a public corporation in 2003, which allowed for leasing specific areas within post offices to private retailers such as flower shops or convenience stores. By June 2005, however, the number of such contracts remained at twelve cases around the country; therefore, it is expected to take sufficient time for retail activity to become major component of revenue.

In summary, the current Japanese postal market can be characterized as having relatively low barriers to entry for private operators; but for Japan Post, high barriers into the logistics, international and retailing business. This market structure can be represented as having 'asymmetric barriers to entry' for both parties. This likely reflects the mindset in Japan that public business should simply complement private business, and that the invasion of the public sector into private business areas should be prevented, if possible. This assertion, however, is not justified, as the public service has been obliged to provide loss-making business inherited from the former Ministry of Posts and Telecommunications, and because government or other third-party institutions are not permitted to fund the cost of public service.

3.3 Postal Regulatory Reform

Although Japan Post is operating in the middle of a midterm management plan set by the MIC until March 2007, the privatization bills of Japan Post were vigorously debated at the 2005 regular session of the Diet, and finally rejected at the House of Councilors (Upper House) in August 2005. The fundamental framework for privatizing Japan's postal services, decided by the cabinet in September 2004, proposed that Japan Post would be privatized by being transformed into a wholly government-owned company in April

[17] In post offices in major European postal networks, stationery goods, prepaid cards and a variety of tickets are handled for sale, and some consigned activities related to various licenses are also permitted. Deutsche Post, for example, acquired a stationery company 'McPaper' in the late 1990s, which indicates that the expansion of retail business is in part related to acquiring other businesses, an activity that is severely restricted for Japan Post.

2007,[18] and initially the parent company would hold all stocks of the four subsidiaries: postal service, savings, insurance, and network business. The former three correspond with the ongoing main businesses within the current public corporation, whereas the latter would be newly established to manage nationwide post offices expected to receive transaction fees from the other three. Also, by utilizing the network, operating revenue through expanding retail sales would be ensured. All stocks of the savings and insurance units held by the parent company would be required to be sold in the public market by 2017,[19] whereas at least one-third of the parent company's stock, comprising all postal and network units, would be held by the government. Thus, these two businesses would still be considered public services even after privatization. Almost the same USO would be imposed on newly-establishing postal companies except for parcel service, which may be excluded due to current highly competitive market conditions. Regarding the compensation for postal burden, the debate over the 'contribution fund for local and social programs' was proposed for ensuring certain activities, such as free or lower-rate products and the social welfare program for elderly customers (as shown in Section 3.2). This new fund, whose aim was to maintain the current post office network and financial services, especially in rural areas, would also cover payments for social activities, based upon the business plans submitted by postal and network companies. Apparently, the government or other entities would fund partially the provision of universal service and the social welfare program. The source of the funding, however, would not be rate revenue from postal users nor tax revenue from general customers, but mainly issuing revenues from the two financial companies' stocks that would be published gradually after the 2007 privatization.

For future possible postal reform in Japan, the following two points should be considered: Firstly, private operators already have the capacity to expand their postal business, especially in non-correspondence areas such as catalogue and magazine delivery. Deregulating the restrictions for correspondence service should not yet be discussed, as more entry into the postal market could seriously damage the financial stability of the postal incumbent, which is already facing continuously decreasing mail demand and postal revenues. Secondly, current restrictions preventing the expansion of business for Japan Post could also lead to the deterioration of its

---

[18] One possible reason for the 2007 target date is that this coincides with the end of the four-year midterm management period. Japan Post is required to achieve management goals concerning retained earnings, cost ratio, and quality of delivery service.

[19] The privatized postal and network company might be permitted to hold some portion of the two financial companies' stocks after public offerings. This case is similar to Deutsche Post's, which acquired financial unit (Postbank) stocks until 1999's full subsidization, and currently owns a 50% share.

capability to provide public service throughout the country. The postal operator should be able to diversify its business into logistics, international and retail activities, by such means as merger, acquisition and capital alliance to pursue revenue and profits in the same way as major European postal companies are doing so on a worldwide basis. Earlier and more reasonable decisions on these issues, even before the possible privatization of Japan Post, would enable the stabilization of efficient and sound management of the public corporation, which would also ensure stable universal service provision for customers.

4. CONCLUSIONS

Market liberalization processes in most industrialized countries indicate that barriers to entry are significantly high for private operators, resulting in the lack of successful entry. Japan Post, which handles a significantly large number of mail items, (only second to the USPS in the world), however, faces serious erosions from private competitors, and its market share, both in postal parcel and mail delivery, is continuously declining. This paper showed that both the cost structure of private operators and the regulatory framework for a postal incumbent have brought about the current situation in Japan. One of the reasons that private companies have successfully entered the mail market after establishing nationwide parcel business was their effective utilization of economies of scope by transferring their parcel delivery network, including staff and infrastructure, to the mail business. Another important factor was the restrictions imposed on the postal operator, including the prohibition of unlimited acquisitions and the requirement of funding and providing free, low-rate and social welfare services. Japan's postal market is thus characterized as having a high barrier for the postal operator to enter into other business areas, such as logistics and the international market, while barriers for nationally-operated private companies entering into the postal market are low.

The proposal to privatize Japan Post and to establish postal, financial, and network companies in 2007 was rejected in the 2005 regular session of the Diet. However, for ensuring a reliable postal market in the future, no matter what the management structure of Japan Post, the restrictions imposed for private correspondence delivery should remain unchanged to prevent additional entry into the postal market. Simultaneously, measures should be taken to ensure that Japan Post could expand revenue via new business activities in order to maintain the financial sustainability of postal operations and thereby to provide stable universal service throughout Japan.

REFERENCES

Burns, P., I. Carslake, and G. Houpis. 2002. "Brand Loyalty and Limited Entry in Postal Markets." In *Postal and Delivery Services Delivering on Competition*, edited by M.A. Crew and P.R. Kleindorfer. Boston: Kluwer Academic Publishers.

Cohen, R., C. Pace, M. Robinson, G. Scarfiglieri, R. Scocchera, V. Visco Comandini, J. Waller, and S. Xenakis. 2002. "A Comparison of the Burden of Universal Service in Italy and the United States." In *Postal and Delivery Services: Pricing, Productivity, Regulation and Strategy*, edited by M.A. Crew and P.R. Kleindorfer. Boston: Kluwer Academic Publishers.

Cohen, R., M. Robinson, R. Sheehy, J. Waller, and S. Xenakis. 2005. "Will Entrants into a Liberalized Delivery Market Attract Investors?" In *Regulatory and Economic Challenges in the Postal and Delivery Sector*, edited by M.A. Crew and P.R. Kleindorfer. Boston: Kluwer Academic Publishers.

Crew, M.A., and P.R. Kleindorfer. 2005. "Competition, Universal Service and the Graveyard Spiral." In *Regulatory and Economic Challenges in the Postal and Delivery Sector*, edited by M.A. Crew and P.R. Kleindorfer. Boston: Kluwer Academic Publishers.

Jonsson, P. 2004. "Regulatory Challenges in the Liberalised Swedish Postal Market." Paper presented at CRRI – Rutgers University's 12th Conference on Postal and Delivery Economics, June 2004, in Cork, Ireland.

Maruyama, S., and T. Nakajima. 2002. "The Productivity Analysis of Postal Services: A Global Comparison of Technical Efficiency and Total Factor Productivity." In *Postal and Delivery Services: Delivering on Competition*, edited by M.A. Crew and P.R. Kleindorfer, Boston: Kluwer Academic Publishers.

McAfee. R.P., H.M. Mialon, and M.A. Williams. 2003. "What is a Barrier to Entry?" mimeo.

Moriarty, R., and P. Smith. 2005. "Barriers to Entry in Post and Regulatory Responses." In *Regulatory and Economic Challenges in the Postal and Delivery Sector*, edited by M.A. Crew and P.R. Kleindorfer. Boston: Kluwer Academic Publishers.

Robinson, A., A. Crowder, D. Rawnsley. 2003. "Competition in Parcel and Mail Delivery or The Challenge of Maintaining Dominance." Paper presented at CRRI – Rutgers University's 11th Conference on Postal and Delivery Economics, June 2003, in Toledo, Spain.

Schwarz-Schilling, C. 2002. "Market Results of Postal Reform in Germany." In *Postal and Delivery Services Delivering on Competition*, edited by M.A. Crew and P.R. Kleindorfer. Boston: Kluwer Academic Publishers.

Japan Post. 2004. *Postal Service in Japan 2004.* Annual report.

JD Power. 2004. *The Results of Customer Satisfaction Survey Concerning B-to-C Delivery in Japan.*

Ministry of Internal Affairs and Communications (MIC). 2003. *Overview of the Law Concerning Correspondence Delivery Provided by Private-Sector Operators (Abstracts).*

NERA. 2004. *Economics of Postal Services: Final Report.* The European Commission.

Postcomm. 2004. *Postcomm Annual Report.*

Postcomm 2005. *Giving Customers Choice: A Fully Open Postal Services Markett*. 18 February.

WIK. 2004. *Main Developments in the European Postal Sector.* The European Commission.

Chapter 23

The Privatization of Japan Post

Ensuring both a Viable Post and a Level Playing Field

Amelia Porges and Joy M. Leong
Sidley Austin Brown & Wood LLP

1. INTRODUCTION

In the last year, postal reform in Japan has emerged from the shadows to become the single policy issue that could remake Japanese politics. After his legislative package for postal privatization was blocked by opposition from his own party, Prime Minister Junichiro Koizumi has dissolved the lower house of the Diet and made the election into a referendum on postal reform. Appealing to urban voters with an attack on entrenched interests, he won a landslide victory. His legislative package will be resubmitted soon to the Diet and is predicted to pass easily, ushering in a new political era.

In contrast to Europe, the driving force behind postal reform in Japan is not competition in postal delivery, but unlocking the immense financial assets of the postal system. Japan's postal system now includes not just postal delivery, but also huge postal bank and postal life insurance operations. The postal bank is the world's largest bank, with total assets of ¥227 trillion (US$2.07 trillion)[1] in individual accounts – 30% of household savings in Japan and over twice the asset size of Mizuho Financial or Citigroup, the two next largest banking groups in the world. The postal life insurance scheme, with ¥122 trillion (US$1.11 trillion) in policies, has 40% of Japanese households' life-insurance assets and is larger than its four largest private competitors combined. Postal savings and postal life

---

[1] Exchange rates used are the yen-dollar rate for specific dates, or otherwise the yen-dollar rate (¥109.6/US$1) as of August 15, 2005.

insurance together hold a quarter of Japan's personal financial assets. (Economist, 2004). Postal privatization will make it possible to remobilize these assets, and remove distortions to competition in the banking and insurance sectors. Yet postal savings and postal life insurance are now provided only by the postal network of close to 25,000 post offices, which also provides postal collection and delivery. This means that while Koizumi's reform program may be driven by public finance concerns, it will necessarily entail fundamental changes in the postal delivery sector – creating opportunities in delivery and logistics services for Japan Post and perhaps for its competitors. This paper presents a political perspective on the evolution of postal reform in Japan, an account of the Koizumi proposals, and an evaluation of them in the context of legal and economic principles of postal reform.

Japan's policymakers face the dual dilemmas of postal reform: In privatizing Japan Post, they must structure four viable entities – a privatized bank, insurance company, postal network, and postal delivery company – and at the same time ensure a level playing field for competition in these markets. The concern expressed by many observers is that policymakers will create either a strong post that enjoys so much preferential treatment and so many subsidies that it can overpower its competitors and threaten competition in the industry, or a weak post that will struggle to meet its universal service obligations and its deferred liabilities and ultimately need a government bail-out. This paper examines some of the challenges and pitfalls in structuring a privatization scheme that walks a line between these two extremes and attempts to ensure both a viable post and a strong competitive market.

2. BACKGROUND

The official provider of postal services in Japan is Japan Post (Nihon Yūsei Kōsha), a public corporation established under the Japan Post Law of 2002 as the inheritor of the people, assets and organization of the former Postal Services Agency (Yūseichō), including 271,000 employees and close to 25,000 post offices. In fiscal 2003-04, Japan Post delivered 25.6 billion items, down 2.3% from the year before. Per capita mail volume in Japan (202 items) was slightly over half the European level and less than 30% of the level in the United States. Sealed mail (designated First Class) and postcard mail (designated Second Class) together accounted for approximately 90% of mail items. Parcels delivered by Japan Post accounted for only 698 million items. (Japan Post, 2004).

Japan Post has less than a 10% share of the parcel market, compared to the market leader, Yamato Transport, which has over 30%. Yamato

Transport gained its market position through its "black cat" *takkyūbin* parcel pickup and delivery service, and other value-added product innovations. Direct mail advertising constitutes a relatively small sector in Japan; the number of persons in Japan receiving direct mail is one seventh of the number in the United States and one half of that in Europe. (Yamato, 2004).

For Japanese public policy as a whole, the most important aspect of the postal complex has been its connection to postal savings and postal insurance. After launching a national post office in 1871, Meiji period modernizers established a postal savings scheme in 1875. The postal savings scheme offered small savers a government-guaranteed place to put their money, and starting in 1916, the post office also sold life insurance. The postal savings scheme has been exempt from banking regulation: it does not pay any deposit insurance premiums or taxes, and the interest rate was historically set higher than bank interest rates. The most popular postal savings product is the *teigaku chokin*, a high-interest ten-year time deposit account with no early withdrawal penalty after six months. The postal life insurance scheme is similarly exempt from taxes and insurance regulations applicable to other insurance providers. Both postal savings accounts and postal life insurance policies are still guaranteed by the state.

Historically, postal savings and life insurance monies were placed with the Ministry of Finance Trust Fund Bureau, which then provided the funds to the Fiscal Investment and Loan Program (FILP). FILP provided money to public corporations, local government and other government entities, for public works projects, housing, small business assistance and policy finance. As of March 2001, FILP involved ¥418 trillion (US$3.3 trillion), equal to 82% of GDP, and FILP's uses of funds statement totaled more than the GDP. In the 1990s, FILP began to come under increasing criticism as a source of wasteful spending.

Prime Minister Hashimoto then took up the cause of administrative reform in the late 1990s. The Administrative Reform Council (*Gyosei Kaikaku Kaigi*) issued a draft plan in August 1997 to reorganize the government, privatize postal insurance, and consider privatization of postal savings. After lobbying by special postmasters and their political allies in the ruling Liberal Democratic Party (LDP), the Council's December 1997 final report called for the combined postal delivery, savings and insurance business to be shifted to a single independent public corporation. The report urged follow-up consideration of breaking the link between postal savings funds and the FILP, and of allowing private sector entry into postal delivery. (Kawabata, 2004)

The legislation to carry out these recommendations became one of Prime Minister Koizumi's major agenda items when he took office in April 2001. His ascent in 2001 reflected widespread public desire for fundamental change to pull Japan out of the economic doldrums and to build a better future. Koizumi immediately chartered a commission to study the future of the three postal businesses and moved forward on the first round of postal reform legislation. After difficult negotiations within the LDP, he finally sent his package of four bills to the Diet without prior LDP approval, and it was enacted in July 2002 after debate and amendment. (Kawabata, 2004).

The 2002 package established Japan Post as a public corporation staffed by civil servants and supervised by the Ministry of Internal Affairs and Communications (MIC). It also authorized limited competition for some types of mail delivery. Postal account monies were no longer sent to the Finance Ministry, but were to be invested in Japanese Government Bonds (JGBs), or bonds issued by FILP on capital markets. (Japan Post owns about one quarter of the outstanding stock of JGBs today.) Koizumi did not stop there; in 2003 he was re-elected as head of the LDP promising postal privatization, and postal privatization by April 2007 was part of his platform for the 2003 Diet election (Kawauchi, 2005).

Koizumi then gave the job of developing a plan for postal privatization to his chief policymaking group, the Council on Economic and Fiscal Priorities (CEFP), led by the economist Heizo Takenaka, Koizumi's Minister for Economic Reform.[2] On April 26, 2004, the CEFP issued an interim report proposing to split Japan Post into four units, to have the four businesses compete in the marketplace, and to liberalize their management. The cabinet then established an advisory committee on postal privatization, with a preparatory secretariat staffed by almost a hundred experts from government and business, to plan the details and draft legislation. The planning process and its related political discussions involved a dialogue of interests. On the one side were Japan Post president Masaharu Ikuta, MIC Minister Taro Aso, and LDP Dietmen aligned with the postal lobby, seeking to maximize the postal network and maximize the post's ability to enter new areas; on the other side were Takenaka, Koizumi and competing private businesses, pushing for smaller government and for placing the system's financial assets in private hands.

The plan finally came together with the CEFP's Outline of Basic Privatization Policy announced on August 6, 2004. After difficult political discussions, the Cabinet adopted a Basic Policy on Privatization of Japan Post on September 10, 2004. Takenaka, tapped as the Minister for Postal

---

2 The eleven-member Council, chaired by Prime Minister Koizumi and includes five key Cabinet members (Takenaka, Minister for Internal Affairs and Communications Taro Aso, Minister of Finance Sadakazu Tanigaki, Minister of Economy, Trade and Industry Shoichi Nakagawa, Chief Cabinet Secretary Hiroyuki Hosoda) plus five private sector members (Bank of Japan Gov. Toshihiko Fukui, Toyota Motor Corp. Chairman Hiroshi Okuda, Ushio Inc. Chief Executive Officer Jiro Ushio, Prof. Masaaki Honma of Osaka University, Prof. Hiroshi Yoshikawa of Tokyo University).

Privatization, then moved forward on planning with the privatization secretariat, consulting with an advisory committee, with a new cabinet-level Postal Privatization Headquarters chaired by Koizumi, and with Japan Post, Diet members, and stakeholders.[3]

2.1 The Basic Policy on Privatization

The policy announced in September 2004 promised a reform of historic dimensions. It envisioned three phases: preparation, a ten-year transition starting on the privatization date of April 1, 2007, and a final post-privatization configuration of companies. After April 1, 2017, operations would be split into six more or less privatized entities: (1) a privately-owned bank; (2) a privately-owned insurance company; (3) a majority-private holding company which would wholly own (4) a postal delivery company and (5) a postal network company; and (6) an entity to hold pre-privatization bank and insurance assets.

During the fall of 2004, work proceeded on fleshing out the business and legal details of privatization, and on drafting the legislation. The privatization headquarters prepared a management simulation for the four operational companies, predicting that all four could show after-tax profits in FY 2008. (Yuseimineika Junbishitsu, 2004; Ikuta, 2004) LDP resisters continued to seek a broad USO including financial services and parcel delivery, tax concessions for the privatized postal units, and measures to maintain post-office employment by prolonging the linkage and cross-subsidy between the banking and insurance units and the postal units. Banking and insurance interests weighed in as well.

In January 2005, Koizumi announced that postal privatization would be his number one legislative priority for the New Year, and he and Takenaka pursued negotiations. While many LDP members supported economic reform unconditionally, and some opposed any privatization, others were willing to consider privatization if the four businesses were under integrated management. Koizumi's negotiators tried to win over this middle group without losing too much of their original objective to remobilize the assets of the postal bank and insurance system.

During the early months of 2005, more details fell into place. Japan Post released accounts for individual post offices showing that the great majority run a deficit on their mail operations. The negotiators agreed to provide tax breaks to the privatized companies, and to require network offices throughout Japan assisted by a USO fund of ¥1 trillion (US$9.35 billion). On February 24, the government released a scenario projecting profits of ¥1

---

3 The documents from this process, and summaries of meetings, are all available at the official postal privatization webpage, http://www.yuseimineika.go.jp/index.html.

trillion in 2016, premised on successful entry of the privatized units into new lines of business: the postal delivery business would enter international distribution and logistics, the postal bank would enter securitization and lending, the insurance company would issue large-value policies and health insurance, and all of these activities would yield enhanced commissions for the postal network. Attempts by the LDP to block foreign ownership of the privatized bank and insurance companies were rebuffed, as the government concluded that such action would violate Japan's commitments under the WTO General Agreement on Trade in Services.

On April 27 the Koizumi Cabinet transmitted to the Diet its package of six privatization bills. After much discussion and minor amendments, the legislation ultimately passed the lower house by 233 to 228, but on August 8 failed in the upper house by 125 to 108. Koizumi had consistently threatened to call a snap election if the bills did not go through. He then delivered on his promise. On August 8, by Cabinet resolution, the Emperor dissolved the lower house of the Diet.

Koizumi then did everything he could to focus election on postal privatization as the turning point for shrinking government and pursuing economic and political reform. He blocked LDP endorsement of Dietmembers who had voted against the postal bills, and ran competing LDP-endorsed "assassin" candidates against them. After the short campaign, Japan gave a landslide victory to Koizumi on September 11. The LDP won 296 seats, and with the 31 seats of Kōmeitō, its coalition partner, gained a majority sufficient to override the upper house. Upper house Dietmembers who voted against the postal legislation announced they would support it in the next Diet session; newspapers predicted easy passage of the bills within a few weeks.

2.2 The Legislative Package

Like the September 2004 proposal, Koizumi's postal privatization bills called for activity in three periods: a preparation period through March 31, 2007, a transition period from April 1, 2007 through March 31, 2017, and the period from April 1, 2017 onward. On September 16, Koizumi's team announced that his resubmitted legislation will be revised to postpone the target date for privatization to October 1, 2007, retain the ten-year transition period, and incorporate changes agreed to in earlier Diet deliberations; they stated that there will be no other substantive changes. The discussion below is based on these assumptions.

The legislation provides for establishment of a new government company, the Japan Postal Services Corporation (JPSC), to be set up within six months of enactment. The legislation also establishes a Cabinet-level

Postal Privatization Headquarters, advised by a five-person Postal Privatization Commission (PPC), both of which will cease to exist on October 1, 2017. The Prime Minister and MIC Minister, through the Headquarters, are to develop a succession plan, and JPSC is to produce an implementation plan subject to approval by the Prime Minister and MIC with input from the Commission The succession plan will resolve key issues such as how the assets, liabilities and employees of Japan Post will be divided between the successor companies.

The legislation authorizes Japan Post to enter or invest in international freight transportation and related domestic delivery services before 2007, if approved by MIC after receiving the views of the PPC. The bills call for MIC to consider potential damage to the interests of competing private sector businesses, when it decides whether to permit Japan Post to enter or invest in competitive areas. Japan Post had reportedly been negotiating with TPG and other international distribution firms, with plans to invest ¥10-20 billion (US$93.5-187 million) over the two years from fiscal 2006, but the upper house's rejection of the bills put these talks on hold. (Nikkei, 2005)

On October 1, 2007, Japan Post is to be dissolved and its functions inherited by new companies established for four business areas: government-chartered companies for postal delivery and the postal network (counter services), and private companies carrying on the postal bank and postal life insurance businesses. JPSC will initially hold all the stock in these four companies. In addition, a government corporation will be established to hold pre-privatization savings and insurance accounts of Japan Post. Present Japan Post employees will become employees of JPSC or one of the new companies. The four companies will be taxable, but will receive special tax benefits. The postal bank and insurance companies will pay into depositor or policyholder security funds, and the government will not guarantee bank accounts and insurance policies opened after October 1, 2007.

During the period between October 1, 2007, and September 30, 2017, JPSC will be required to progressively sell off all of the shares in the postal bank and the postal life insurance business, and the government will sell almost 2/3 of JPSC's shares. The Minister of Finance has stated that the proceeds will be used to reduce Japan's national debt. The four companies will be able to expand into new areas with the approval of the Prime Minister and/or MIC (not the Ministry of Land Transport, which regulates freight companies).

As of October 1, 2017, the postal bank and postal life insurance company will be privately held, and subject to the same regulation as private banks and insurance companies. Both the Postal Privatization Headquarters and the PPC will cease to exist on October 1, 2017. JPSC will continue in operation as a holding company for the postal delivery and postal network companies.

Much political attention has gone into the continuing relationship between the financial units and the network company. As Takenaka pointed out in August 2004, 60 to 70 percent of current postal operations are supported by financial operations. (Kyodo, 2005) The privatization package envisions that the network company will provide counter services for the other ex-postal units, private companies and local government, and receive fees in return. This separation will make visible any cross-subsidization by postal financial services units. Resisters from the LDP and the opposition Democratic Party (DPJ) sought to prevent any post-office closures and maintain postal jobs, attempting to build in cross-holding of stock between the four ex-postal enterprises and to prevent full privatization of the postal bank. Koizumi and Takenaka agreed only that after JPSC sells all of the bank and insurance company shares, it will not be prevented from buying the shares back. During Diet deliberations on June 30, Koizumi clarified that if these two units have become a normal bank and insurance company, the shares can be held by the postal network company. It is also clear that the postal bank and insurance company will be *de facto* compelled to enter into long-term agency contracts with the postal network.

The legislation required JPSC to set up a ¥1 trillion (US$9.1 billion) fund, to be financed by share sales. JPSC will make grants from this fund to the postal delivery and postal network companies for the costs of socially mandated free and reduced-rate mail, and other USO-related functions in local areas. In June, Koizumi agreed that JPSC will be able to retain up to ¥2 trillion (US$18.2 billion) in the fund; the purpose of increasing the fund is to ensure that universal service includes not just mail delivery but also financial services.

3. ANALYSIS

As regulators throughout the world have struggled with adjusting the monopoly aspects of postal delivery to today's competitive markets, they have confronted a similar set of problems, much discussed in the postal economics literature. In Japan, however, we are presented with a situation that confounds some of our standard approaches. The government has proposed a privatization scheme for postal services to move the huge financial assets now tied up in postal savings into investments to create jobs and growth in the Japanese economy. The benefits of postal competition may only be an afterthought. In fact, concerns running in the other direction, as the LDP pushes for maximum retention of the existing postal network, may lead to cross-subsidization of postal services, competitive distortions in financial services, and sub-optimal solutions that reduce the value of the assets to be privatized. Moreover, the postal system presently in place in

Japan has unique characteristics. For example, there is no "sanctity of the mailbox" in Japan, the "last mile" of postal delivery has not been accepted to be a natural monopoly (Maruyama, 2005), and "special postmasters" have been a potent political force.[4] (MacLachlan, 2004).

As Koizumi's policymakers implement the postal reform package, they will face the dual dilemma of postal reform: they must structure the privatized post so that the post has a fair chance of increasing mail volume, offering stable rates, maintaining service standards, and, most importantly, meeting its universal service obligation. At the same time, they cannot create such overwhelming advantages for the privatized entities of Japan Post that competitors are discriminated against and competition is discouraged. The playing field must be level – not tilted in favor of Japan Post or its successors, nor tilted in favor of competitors. We examine below the specific decisions facing policymakers and how each may be resolved to favor either the post or competitors or to balance the interests of both.

As has been demonstrated in other countries, one of the basic problems of introducing competition into postal services is the vertical integration of a natural monopoly component (local delivery of letter mail to mailboxes) with potentially competitive activities (e.g., sorting or transportation). The service provider that controls the monopoly component can use its control to block access to this component, to cross-subsidize activities in the competitive domain, and to thus frustrate competition. To address these problems, policymakers may use such mechanisms as opening access to the monopoly component, requiring structural separation between the monopoly and non-monopoly businesses (and corresponding accounting transparency), allowing limited competition through worksharing, and regulating the ability of the monopoly service provider to compete in non-monopoly businesses. Or the regulator can create a legally reserved area as a *quid pro quo* for the post's universal service obligation.

Prime Minister Koizumi and his postal policymakers have chosen neither the path of worksharing, as in the United States, nor the path of liberalization based upon the weight of the mail piece, as in the EU. Instead, driven by the problem of financial and fiscal reform, they have chosen the more radical

---

4 Of Japan's 24,715 post offices as of March 31, 2004, 77 percent were special post offices, each headed by a special postmaster; 81 percent of the special post offices do not pick up or deliver to individual delivery points. (Japan Post, 2004). Until Koizumi split from the special postmasters over privatization, they were a major element in mobilizing rural voters for the LDP. Special postmasters are selected by regional postal bureau officials from local notables. Reportedly one quarter to one third of them inherit their jobs, and they often own the space leased for special post offices. (MacLachlan, 2004). The September 2005 Koizumi landslide left them, and the postal unions, shaken. (Yomiuri Shimbun, 2005).

solution of privatization to unwind the financial (banking and insurance) and postal (network and delivery) activities.

3.1 Concerns of the Post

Universal Service Obligation (USO): One of the primary missions of a post is to fulfill its universal service obligation. The new legislation obligates the postal delivery company to provide ubiquitous six-day delivery at a regulated price, and requires the postal network company to provide offices throughout Japan. The USO debate has focused on whether postal network offices must offer savings and insurance services in addition to classic postal services. Japan Post, MIC and postal-lobby Diet members have argued that the private sector will not meet the demand for financial services in rural areas, and that the privatized postal bank and postal insurance companies should have a USO so that they do not leave rural areas unserved. Takenaka and others have argued that extending the USO this way would impair competitive conditions for regional banks and other financial services companies, and ultimately increase government burdens. The legislation would not formally extend the USO to cover financial services, but during previous Diet debate it was amended to provide explicitly that post offices' business activities will include banking and insurance, and the final legislation will include that change.

Reserved Area: The mainstay of support for the USO for postal delivery is revenue from the reserved area. Although competitors can use household mailboxes, Article 5 of the Postal Law forbids anyone other than Japan Post or its subcontractors to engage in postal business, or to engage as a business in delivery of "correspondence," defined as "a document expressing the intentions of the sender or communicating facts to a specific recipient." The law specifically forbids transportation businesses from delivering correspondence. The reserved area does not include parcel delivery, and companies such as Yamato Transport have successfully competed with Japan Post in the parcel market by establishing nationwide collection, sorting, and distribution networks. These competitors have used their economies of scope to deliver not only parcels, but also magazines, catalogues, and form letters to household mailboxes all over Japan. (Maruyama, 2005).

The Correspondence Delivery Law, enacted as part of the 2002 postal reform package, created an exception to the reserved area – if MIC grants a license to a private operator for either "special correspondence delivery" or "general correspondence delivery." The law and its regulations define "special correspondence delivery" as delivery of correspondence items whose combined length, width and thickness exceed 90 cm, or which weigh over 4 kg, or which are delivered within three hours, or for which the delivery fee exceeds ¥1000 (US$9.12). If the licensee is engaging only in *special* correspondence delivery, it need only show that it is fit to carry out this business, and that its business plan is appropriate and is adapted to protecting the confidentiality of correspondence. Over a hundred firms have obtained such licenses. However, entry into *general* correspondence delivery is subject to much more stringent rules, designed to avoid cream-skimming. A provider of general correspondence delivery may handle all types of correspondence, but must deliver throughout Japan at least six days per week, must set up approximately 100,000 of its own collection boxes (distinct from Japan Post boxes) throughout Japan, must meet service standards set by MIC order, and must charge MIC-regulated uniform rates. Upon passage of the 2002 law, Yamato Transport, the firm considered most likely to enter the general correspondence delivery business, issued a statement stating that the conditions were impossible to meet. (Yamato, 2002)

The spring 2005 legislative package did not alter the existing provisions of the Postal Law on "correspondence" or on entry by general or special correspondence providers. Thus, after privatization, the postal delivery entity's *de facto* monopoly of general correspondence delivery will not change. The question is whether revenues from that business alone will be sufficient to sustain the postal delivery company.

New opportunities: Most commentators believe that Japan Post's postal operations have been subsidized by the more profitable banking and insurance branches. When the banking and insurance operations are separated from the postal operations, cross-subsidies will end. The postal delivery company will also be required to pay the postal network company for counter services and other services the postal network supplies. The USO fund is intended to provide some support for the postal delivery company's universal service obligations, but the prerequisites for tapping into the fund are as yet unclear. The postal delivery company will have an incentive to take dramatic steps to compensate for the loss of subsidies by entering new lines of business, increasing its mail volumes, and cutting costs. One such step, already articulated by Japan Post, would be to enter the logistics industry. This is a growing but complex industry, one which may require the Post to partner with an established logistics provider at the outset.

Throughout the political process described previously, the Post has consistently advocated maximum freedom for its privatized companies to enter new business areas. Business studies carried out by the postal privatization policy team in February 2005 projected that the new entities would reap increased profits if allowed to enter new businesses such as international logistics, securitization, consumer lending, and health insurance, with increased commissions paid to the postal network. (Yūseimineika Junbishitsu, 2004).

Another step for the Post to take would be to develop a strategy to increase mail volume, an action that other posts have focused on in order to sustain the USO and fend off a graveyard spiral.[5] A fruitful avenue for Japan Post may be to encourage addressed solicitation mail, which would fall within the general correspondence monopoly. Whereas, for example, the average household in the UK receives 157 items of direct mail per year, and in the US 356 items per year, the average Japanese household receives only 44 items per year. UPU statistics for 2003 show 32 addressed advertising items per capita for Japan compared to 246 in the US. In the United States, the growth of solicitation mail has had a major positive impact on the postal industry. There is thus much potential for growth in direct mail for Japan Post.

The survival of Japan Post's delivery unit may be of great concern to Japan's policymakers as they structure the privatized Post. They may want to equip the postal delivery entity with the ability to enter new businesses, maintain or increase mail volume, control its costs, and meet its USO. On the other side of the equation from the Post's survival, however, stands the need to encourage competition in competitive services, not allowing the Post so many advantages that it can squeeze out its competition.

3.2 Concerns of competitors

Encouraging competition in postal services is based on sound economic principles which provide that increased competition generally results in greater efficiency and lower costs and/or better service to the consumer. To ensure viable competition in special services, Japan's policymakers must not give preferential treatment to the Post or allow cross-subsidies from its monopoly services to its competitive services – even as they attempt to equip the Post for survival.

Preferential treatment: To the extent the privatized postal delivery business receives preferential treatment that discriminates against its competitors, the playing field will be tilted toward the Post, with negative effects on competition. For example, if the Post does not pay taxes, parking tickets, or other government fees that its competitors must pay, the Post receives an unfair advantage. If the Post enjoys priority treatment in customs processing, it receives preferential treatment that allows it to outpace its competitors – not based on its own efficiency but based on the government's regulatory scheme. If the Post has sole access to key facilities

5 For an example of an approach to maintaining and/or increasing mail volume, *see* Levy, Leong, Buc, and Plunkett (2005).

(such as post offices) or pays less than its competitors to rent those facilities, it again receives preferential treatment. The regulator for Japan Post and its postal successor entities is MIC, not the Ministry of Land, Infrastructure and Transport, which regulates its competitors in the package and express industry. Moreover, the LDP has reportedly agreed to reduce by half the fixed asset tax payable to municipalities on postal buildings and other assets. Japan Post has also sought exemption from the consumption tax for fees and commissions received by the postal network from the other ex-postal companies. Adoption of these proposals could grant Japan Post preferential treatment and place its competitors at an unfair competitive disadvantage.

Cross-subsidies: The design for privatization in the legislation represents an attempt to achieve structural separation between the postal delivery and network businesses and the Post's financial services businesses. The final privatization of the bank and insurance company will complete that process, but only after a ten-year transition. As long as the banking and insurance businesses are tied to the network and/or delivery companies by equity or contract relationships, the pressures for cross-subsidies will continue. If the postal banking and insurance entities are compelled to subsidize the postal network, and indirectly the postal delivery entity, the cross-subsidies will not only prevent a level playing field, but will also reduce the value of the banking and insurance assets to be sold in the privatization process, lower the expected reduction of Japan's national debt and reduce the benefit to Japan's fiscal position.

Furthermore, even assuming that the postal delivery entity no longer receives subsidies from the banking or insurance operations, unfair cross-subsidization may arise if the postal delivery entity uses funds from its monopoly services to cross-subsidize its competitive services. Oversight by an independent regulator together with accounting transparency by the Post in the allocation of costs and revenues may be a critical factor in preventing cross-subsidies.

Independent Regulator: Postal reform experience in other countries has shown that the role of an independent regulator is critical in striking a fair balance between the interest of the Post, the competitors, the consumers, and the public. The Koizumi reform package requires MIC approval for major decisions of the successor companies; key decisions concerning the postal bank and insurance company must be made jointly by the Prime Minister and the Minister of Internal Affairs and Communications. As noted above, the legislation also establishes the cabinet-level Postal Privatization Headquarters led by the Prime Minister, and within it the Postal Privatization Commission (PPC), a body of five persons of "superlative judgment," appointed by the Prime Minister for renewable three-year terms. The PPC, which will have its own staff, will carry out reviews each three years and must be consulted about many decisions in the course of postal reform. The Headquarters and the PPC will exist only through the end of March 2017, and will be abolished thereafter.

The PPC will have an important, but limited role in ensuring fair and efficient advancement of privatization. For instance, MIC must obtain the PPC's opinion about any authorization for Japan Post to enter or invest in international freight transportation, or for the postal delivery company to enter new business areas. The PPC will also have the authority to obtain accounts and information from the ex-postal companies, like the subpoena powers of postal rate regulators in other countries. This is a step toward greater transparency to detect unfair cross-subsidies or preferential treatment. The leadership of the present and future Prime Ministers and Ministers of Internal Affairs and Communications, and the expertise and independence of future Commissioners, will be critical in ensuring successful privatization with equitable results.

However, proposed provisions on postal ratemaking, in amendments to the Postal Law that are part of the Koizumi package, appear to give the postal delivery company increased ability to set rates with reduced regulatory supervision. While Japan Post now must obtain MIC approval for postal rates, under the revised Postal Law the postal delivery company would set postal rates and simply notify MIC. MIC approval would only be required for discounted third and fourth class mail, and there would be no role at all for the PPC or private parties in postal ratemaking.

Allocation of Assets: Many crucial issues remain to be resolved. One of the most important from a business standpoint is the allocation of assets to each of the successor companies. Under the Koizumi plan, when Japan Post is dissolved on April 1, 2007, its remaining employees, assets, and liabilities will be divided among the successor entities; obviously, this division will be key to each company's future. In the case of mail delivery, the physical plant must be divided between the network and delivery entities, perhaps allocating all counter service facilities to the postal network company, and allocating trucks and sorting facilities to the postal delivery company. These allocation decisions will affect the playing field – making it level or tilted – and transparency in accounting will again be a key factor in whether the regulator will be able to accurately allocate assets and liabilities.

Capitalization: It is not clear how Japan Post's net capital position will be treated. As of March 31, 2004, Japan Post's postal delivery business had ¥2.2 trillion (US$20.8 billion) in assets and ¥2.7 trillion (US$25.6 billion) in liabilities, for a negative net worth of -¥0.5 trillion (US$-4.8 billion). Observers, including President Ikuta of Japan Post, have argued that the postal delivery business will need additional capital of ¥1.4 trillion (US$12.8 billion) to ¥1.8 trillion (US$16.8 billion) in order to be a viable competitor.

Recapitalizing Japan Post through a cash infusion from the government would be contrary to Koizumi's liberalization and privatization agenda. Observers have suggested that this capital could also come from private sector investment. (Feldman, 2004).

3.3 Business Opportunities

Banking reform, enhanced financial sector regulation and remobilization of assets have been the key to pulling the Japanese economy out of stagnation under Koizumi's plan. As the September 2004 Basic Policy promised, postal privatization, if done right, can yield "enormous value for the Japanese people." It can unlock the value of the assets tied up in postal savings and insurance, use the proceeds to reduce public debt overhang, and remobilize those assets in private hands. In the process, opportunities will be created for collaborators, investors, or competitors in Japan's delivery, insurance and banking industries. A decision to invest in these opportunities, however, will turn upon the result of the September Diet elections and the legislation enacted thereafter.

New business opportunities will include competing with the newly formed entities, which will no longer have a strangle-hold on their respective markets. Other opportunities capitalize on partnering with the new postal entities. For example, mutual funds, other funds management companies, and a range of service companies could develop new opportunities to market to Japanese consumers through the postal bank or the postal network company. The postal bank and insurance company may seek to invest their assets more effectively through improved money management or through securitizations offered by other companies. The postal delivery company could utilize the freedom provided by the legislation and enter into arrangements with international partners, such as logistics services or services using the postal network as an agent to collect mail. The bank and insurance company may choose to collaborate with partners in offering new banking or insurance products. The legislation appears to leave all of these opportunities open. Again, a strong independent regulator will be critical as each of the entities enters new lines of business during the transition period.

4. CONCLUSION

In crafting the final design for privatization of Japan Post, Japan's policymakers must structure four viable entities: a privatized bank, insurance company, postal network, and postal delivery company. The electorate has overwhelmingly endorsed Koizumi's vision of postal privatization, but many details remain to be decided as the plan is implemented. Will Japan's policymakers create a strong post with so much preferential treatment and so many subsidies that it will overpower its competitors and threaten competition in the industry, or a weak post that will struggle to meet its universal service obligations and its deferred liabilities and ultimately need a government bail-out? Koizumi's team and the Diet have a challenging, but not impossible, task before them: to create a postal privatization scheme that walks a line between these two extremes and results in both a viable post and a flourishing competitive market.

REFERENCES

Economist. 2004. "Ready, steady, go – Japan Post." *The Economist* (Sept. 4, 2004).

Feldman, R. "Japan: Postal Privatization? Political Drama, Economic Revolution." Morgan Stanley Global Economic Forum, Oct. 8, 2004, posted at http://www.morganstanley.com/GEFdata/digests/20041008-fri.html#anchor5

Ikuta, M. 2004. "Kokkaku keiei shisan ni taisuru iken" (Views on the skeleton management estimate), Nov. 22, 2004, posted at http://www.yuseimineika.go.jp/iken/041124iken.html

Japan Post. 2004. "Postal Services in Japan 2004: Annual Report," at http://www.japanpost.jp/top/disclosure/e2004/index.html

Kawabata, E. 2004. "Dual Governance: The Contemporary Politics of Posts and Telecommunications in Japan." *Social Science Japan Journal* 7:21-39.

Kawauchi, A. 2005. "Yūsei kaikaku no dōkō" (Trends in Postal Reform), National Diet Library Issue Brief No. 469, Feb. 23, 2005.

Koizumi, J. 2004. Koizumi Cabinet E-mail Magazine No. 160, "Lion Heart – Message from Prime Minister Junichiro Koizumi." Oct. 21, 2004.

Kyodo. 2005. "Ministers criticize DPJ plan on postal savings, fiscal reforms." Kyodo News, Aug. 15, 2005.

MacLachlan, P. 2004. "Post Office Politics in Modern Japan: The Postmasters, Iron Triangles, and the Limits of Reform." *Journal of Japanese Studies* 30:281-313.

Maruyama, S. 2005. "Competition Structure and Future Postal Reform in Japan," Presented at CRRI – Rutgers University's 13th Conference on Postal and Delivery Economics, June 1-3.

Nikkei. 2005. "Japan Post to Mothball International Ambitions." Nikkei Report, Aug. 11, 2005.

Yamato. 2002. "'Shinshō ni gaitō suru bunshō ni kansuru hōshin' ni kansuru tōsha no iken" (Company views regarding the "Guidelines on documents constituting correspondence"), Nov. 8, 2002, posted at http://www.kuronekoyamato.co.jp/news/141108_1news.html

Yamato. 2004. Annual Report 2004, Yamato Transport Co., Ltd., at http://www.kuronekoyamato.co.jp/english/investors/annual2004/annual_report_2004.pdf

Yomiuri Shimbun, 2005. "Poll puts postal lobbyists' backs to wall." Yomiuri Shimbun (English ed.), Sept. 13, 2005.

Yūseimineika Junbishitsu. 2004. "Juyō kentō kōmoku ni tsuite (Sono 2-2)," (Major issues for consideration: 2 – 2), Nov. 17, 2004, posted at http://www.yuseimineika.go.jp/dai18/18siryou.pdf